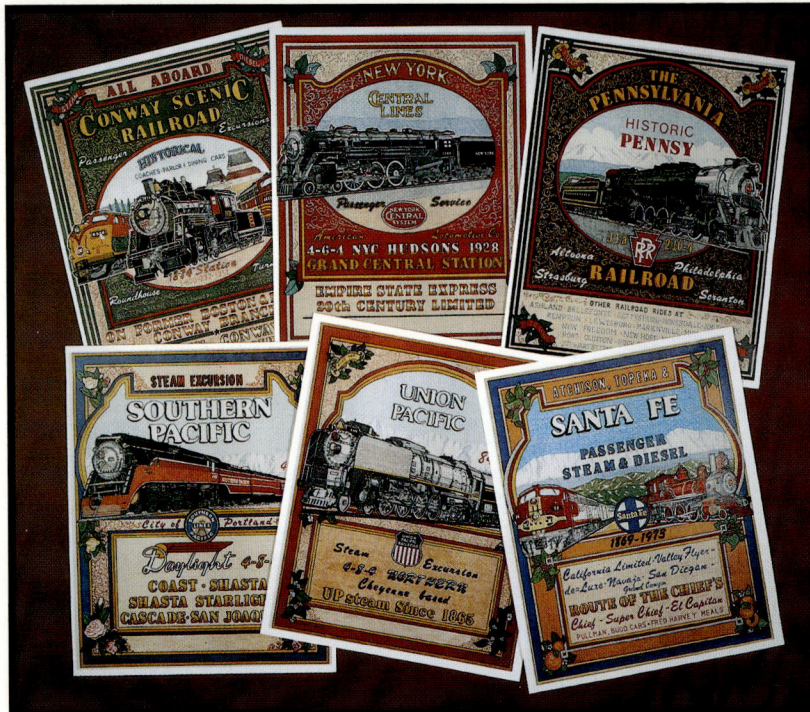

RAILROAD ARTWORK

Color prints of WaterColor and Ink originals by Harvey Hoover, Railroad and Museum Artist. The style is the 1930's and 1940's orange crate label in bright colors and includes an information box for the important railroad information. Available in 36 Railroad theme designs. Limited number of originals available. Full Color Brochure $3.00 ppd.

PRINT SIZING PRICES

6" by 8" print with 8" by 10" Mat	$15 ppd	. . . . . .	Oak Framed $30 S&H $9.95
10" by 12" print with 14" by 16" Mat	$20 ppd	. . . . .	Oak Framed $40 S&H $9.95
12" by 14" print with 16" by 18" Mat	$25 ppd	. . . . .	Oak Framed $50 S&H $9.95
18" by 22" print with 22" by 26" Mat	$30 ppd	. . . . .	Oak Framed $60 S&H $9.95
20" by 24" print with 24" by 28" Mat	$35 ppd	. . . . .	Oak Framed $70 S&H $9.95

New Product Alert!

Same beautiful artwork comes to life on a mirrored background. 12 X 14 printed mirror in rich oak frame. 10 most popular Railroad themes. $65.95 plus $7.95 S&H

DEALER INQUIRIES WELCOME!

Ask about our risk-free merchandising program.

CHECKS-MONEY ORDERS-VISA-MASTERCARD-AMERICAN EXPRESS-DISCOVER

CHUGGA-CHUGGA

Phone 970-282-7007 • Fax 970-377-3665
PO Box 270730 • Fort Collins, CO 80527

www.chugga-chugga.com • Email: info@chugga-chugga.com

Empire State Railway Museum's 36ᵗʰ Annual

Guide to
Tourist Railroads
and Museums
2 0 0 1

KALMBACH
BOOKS

Front cover: Durango & Silverton Narrow Gauge Railroad, Mike Danneman photo
Back cover: Collis P. Huntington Railroad Historical Society, Jean Chapman photo

Cover Design: Kristi Ludwig   ISSN: 0081-542X

To the Museums and Tourist Railroads

Listings: We would like to consider for inclusion every tourist railroad, trolley operation, railroad museum, live-steam railroad, and toy train exhibit in the United States and
Canada that is open to the public and has regular hours and about which reliable information is available.

2002 Directory: To be published in February 2002. A packet that includes all pertinent
information needed for inclusion in the 2002 Guide will be mailed to all organizations
listed in this book. New listings are welcomed. For information, please write to:

> Editor—Guide to Tourist Railroads and Museums
> Books Division
> Kalmbach Publishing Co.
> P.O. Box 1612
> Waukesha, WI 53187–1612

On the web go to www.kalmbach.com/books/touristguide.html

Advertising: Advertising space for the 2002 Guide must be reserved by November 16,
2001. Please contact Mike Yuhas at 1-888-558-1544, extension 625, or Lori Schneider
at 1-888-558-1544, extension 654.

Publisher's Cataloging in Publication
(Prepared by Quality Books, Inc.)

Empire State Railway Museum's 36th annual guide to
   tourist railroads and museums — 2001 ed.
      p. cm
      Includes index.
      ISBN: 0-89024-425-1

      1. Railroad museums—United States—
Directories. 2. Railroad museums—Canada—
Directories.   I. Empire State Railway Museum.
II. Title: Guide to tourist railroads and museums

TF6.U5S75 2001   385'.22'02573
                                   QBI99-1882

Contents

Advertising Contents

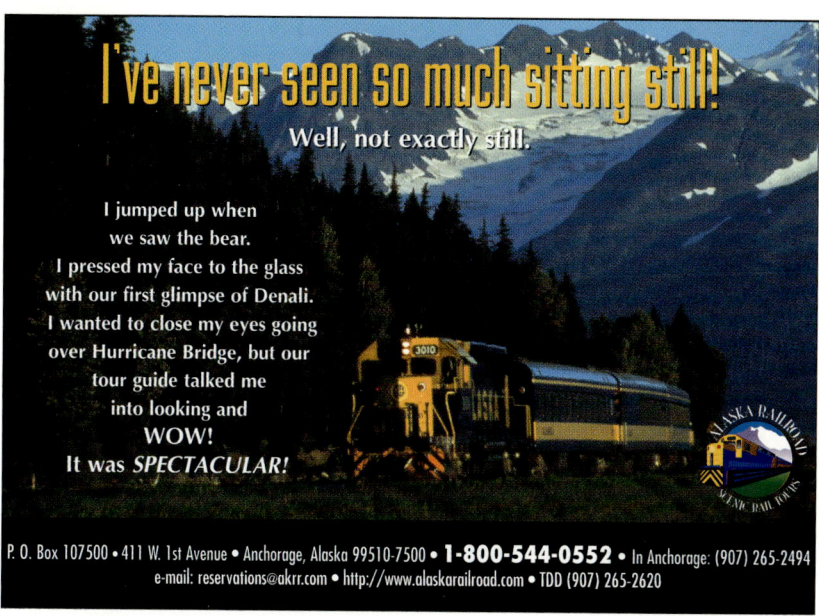
A-4

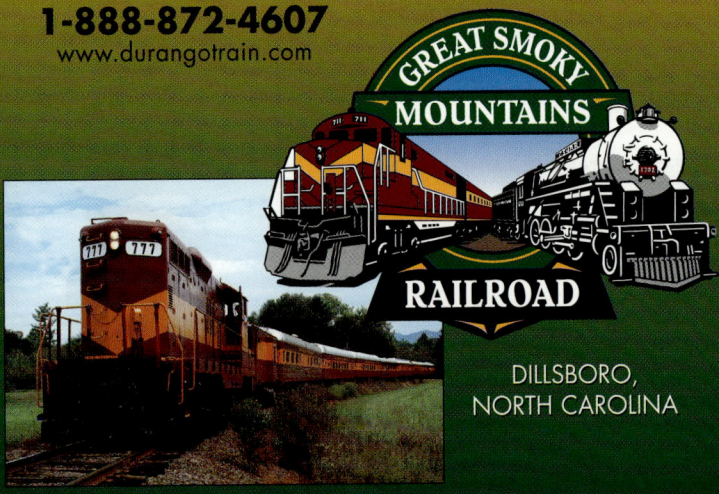

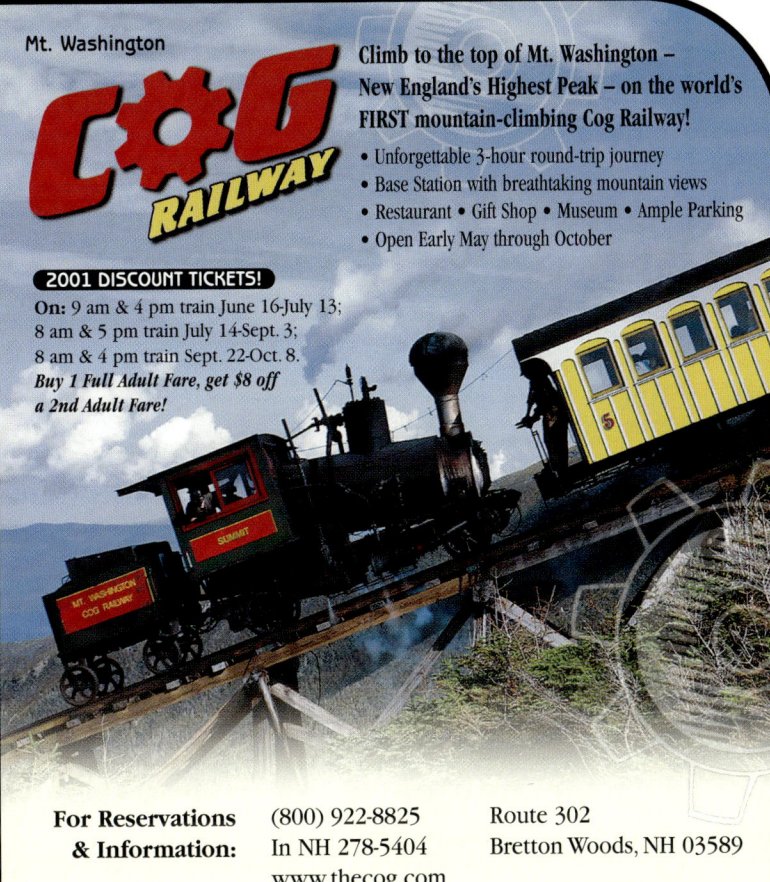

Mt. Washington

COG RAILWAY

Climb to the top of Mt. Washington –
New England's Highest Peak – on the world's
FIRST mountain-climbing Cog Railway!

- Unforgettable 3-hour round-trip journey
- Base Station with breathtaking mountain views
- Restaurant • Gift Shop • Museum • Ample Parking
- Open Early May through October

2001 DISCOUNT TICKETS!

On: 9 am & 4 pm train June 16-July 13;
8 am & 5 pm train July 14-Sept. 3;
8 am & 4 pm train Sept. 22-Oct. 8.
*Buy 1 Full Adult Fare, get $8 off
a 2nd Adult Fare!*

**For Reservations
& Information:**

(800) 922-8825
In NH 278-5404
www.thecog.com

Route 302
Bretton Woods, NH 03589

Don't Miss These 2001 Special Events at The Cog Railway:

May 13 - Mother's Day: Moms Ride Free with the purchase
of a full-fare adult or child ticket!

June 17 - Father's Day: Dads Ride Free witht the purchase of
a full-fare adult or child ticket!

July 8 - Family Day: A full day of railroad fun for all ages,
with guided tours, storytelling, clowns and more!

October 13-14 - Railfan's Weekend: Special activities for the
railfan including special runs, photo opportunites, equipment
demos, plus museum and shop tours!

The Roundhouse Railroad Museum

Georgia's State Railroad Museum -- The oldest and most complete Antebellum railroad manufacturing and repair facility still in existence in the U.S. Collection highlights southern industrial technology. Included are the massive Roundhouse, Operating Turntable, and the 125-foot Smokestack. Also, an HO scale layout of Savannah, shaft and belt driven machinery exhibit, and the oldest portable steam engine in the U.S.

Open daily from 9 am - 4 pm.

For information on tours and private parties:

601 West Harris Street	**Phone: (912) 651-6823**
Savannah, GA 31401	**Fax: (912) 651-3691**

www.chs.org

THE *New* 20ᵀᴴ CENTURY LIMITED

NEW YORK - *16 hours* - CHICAGO

NEW YORK CENTRAL SYSTEM

AMERICA'S FAMILY ALBUM

Inside the Altoona Railroaders Memorial Museum, you will be taken to a community where 17,000 people worked for the same company. You will experience Altoona and the Pennsylvania Railroad at the height of industrial America. The Altoona Railroaders Memorial Museum holds lessons for every member of your family - lessons of human spirit, business, achievement, creativity, bravery and hardship. Through many interactive experiences, your family will meet the families of Altoona, Pennsylvania.

McCLOUD RAILWAY OPEN-AIR TRAIN RIDES

Bring the whole family for a delightful, inexpensive, excursion trip featuring either diesel locomotives or historic steam locomotive No. 25. Try our new "double deck" car for incomparable views of unspoiled northern California.

Hear the "clickety clack" as your trains winds its way around the base of Mt. Shasta. Open Air Excursion Trains depart McCloud, California, May through September 30th, with trips Thursday through Saturday in mid-summer. Call for schedule details.

ALL ABOARD! SHASTA SUNSET DINNER TRAIN

A nostalgic train ride through spectacular scenery in the shadow of Mt. Shasta featuring elegant four-course dining aboard restored vintage rail cars. A memorable evening riding the rails into yesterday!

Experience true luxury in our 1916-vintage rail cars amid surroundings of mahogany and brass. Shasta Sunset Dinner Train departs McCloud, California, weekends year round, Thursday through Saturday June through September. Reservations are required.

To reach McCloud from I-5, take the McCloud/Reno exit and travel ten miles east turning left on Columbero Drive. Follow Columbero into town turning right after the railroad tracks.

For schedules & reservations call the

Shasta Sunset Excursions
P.O. Box 1199 McCloud, CA 96057
(800) 733-2141 (530) 964-2142

LSB4000™

LOCOMOTIVE STEAM BOILER WATER TREATMENT

TERLYN INDUSTRIES utilized an advanced chemical technology to develop a revolutionary high performance locomotive steam boiler water treatment. LSB4000 offers unprecedented performance, simplicity and savings over traditional boiler water treatments with greatly reduced maintenance and lower fuel costs.

The outstanding performance of LSB4000 has been proven worldwide on hundreds of saturated and superheated steam engines using both softened and raw water make-up.

- An advanced technology single feed treatment
- Exceptional scale & corrosion control, tender to exhaust
- No hazardous phosphates, nitrites, caustics or sulfites
- Extends boiler tube life & reduces fuel consumption
- No foaming or carryover to damage superheaters
- Works with both softened & unsoftened water
- Removes exisiting scale without acid cleaning
- Prevents oxygen pitting & crevice corrosion

Engine house foremen, state and federal inspectors continue to report locomotives on the *TERLYN* LSB program to have the cleanest boilers and tenders they have ever seen. Engine crews and roundhouse staffs agree the engines run better, are more reliable, and are easier to maintain. Owners report savings at several times the cost of the *TERLYN* LSB program. Now is the time to bring your steam locomotive in line with the 21st Century.

IRON HORSE W A T E R

Lakewood, Colorado
(303) 378-2460
www.ironhorsewater.com

TERLYN INDUSTRIES *Incorporated*

Kalamazoo, Michigan
(616) 383-8242
www.terlyn.com

The Kenosha Transit Electric Streetcar Circulator Project

The "Cincinnati"

Harvey H. Stone, P.E.
President

How exciting it is to watch someone's dream come true! That is exactly what happened on June 17, 2000 when Joe McCarthy, director of Transportation for the City of Kenosha, watched the first run in revenue service of his newly refurbished PCC streetcars.

Stone Consulting & Design is proud to have been chosen by Stanley Consultants, Inc. and the City of Kenosha to provide the preliminary and final design for the trackage, overhead wire, auxiliary power supply and the rectifier package for this two-mile intermodal urban connector.

The 2-mile historic trolley system connects Harborpark into the existing central city area, the METRA commuter rail station and the city bus transfer station. This $4 million project is public transportation as it should be!

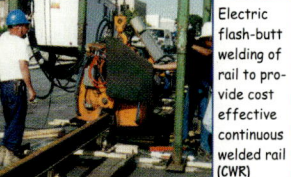

Electric flash-butt welding of rail to provide cost effective continuous welded rail (CWR)

The Kenosha Streetcar Circulator Project incorporates a typical embedded track design with a new "turf" track design developed by Stone Consulting & Design, Inc. that hides the track in grass-seeded areas on median strips & throughout the landscaped areas of Harborpark.

Facing west toward downtown, the new "turf" track construction.

Turf track construction consists of new continuous welded rail fastened to concrete ties, laying on a compacted crushed concrete subgrade section, secured with typical railroad ballast between and on the ends of the ties. The track section is surrounded by geotextile filter fabric and has a layer of topsoil over the ties and up to the rail to facilitate vegetation growth.

Stringing wire—April 2000

Stone Consulting & Design, Inc.
324 Pennsylvania Avenue West
P. O. Box 306, Warren PA 16365
Phone: 814.726.9870   Fax: 814.726.9855
Email: scdemail@stoneconsulting.com
Visit our Web Site at www.stoneconsulting.com

All of us at Stone Consulting & Design mourn the loss of Joe McCarthy who passed away August 19, 2000

A-13

A-15

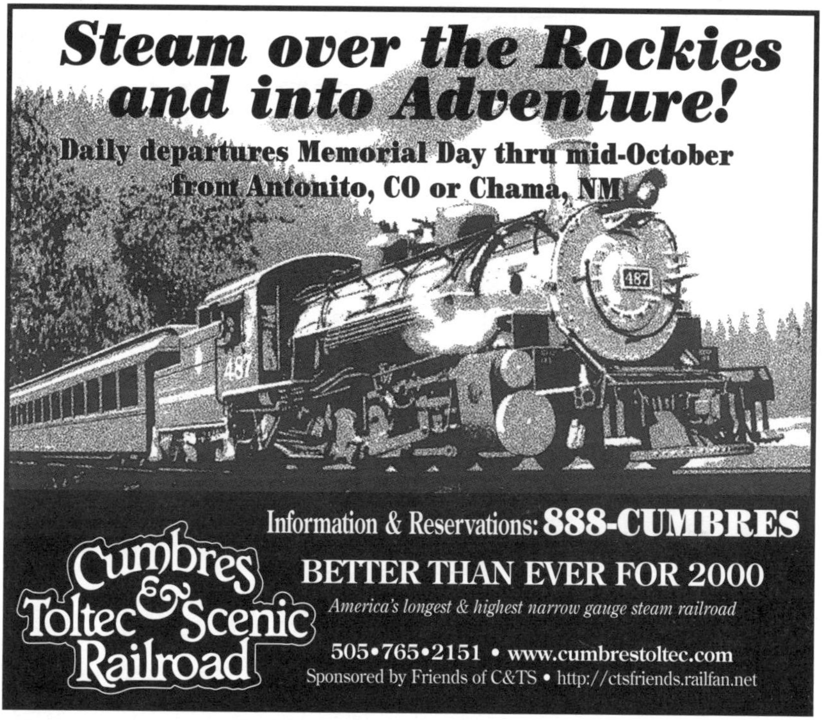

Steam over the Rockies and into Adventure!
Daily departures Memorial Day thru mid-October from Antonito, CO or Chama, NM
487
Information & Reservations: 888-CUMBRES
Cumbres & Toltec Scenic Railroad
BETTER THAN EVER FOR 2000
America's longest & highest narrow gauge steam railroad
505•765•2151 • www.cumbrestoltec.com
Sponsored by Friends of C&TS • http://ctsfriends.railfan.net

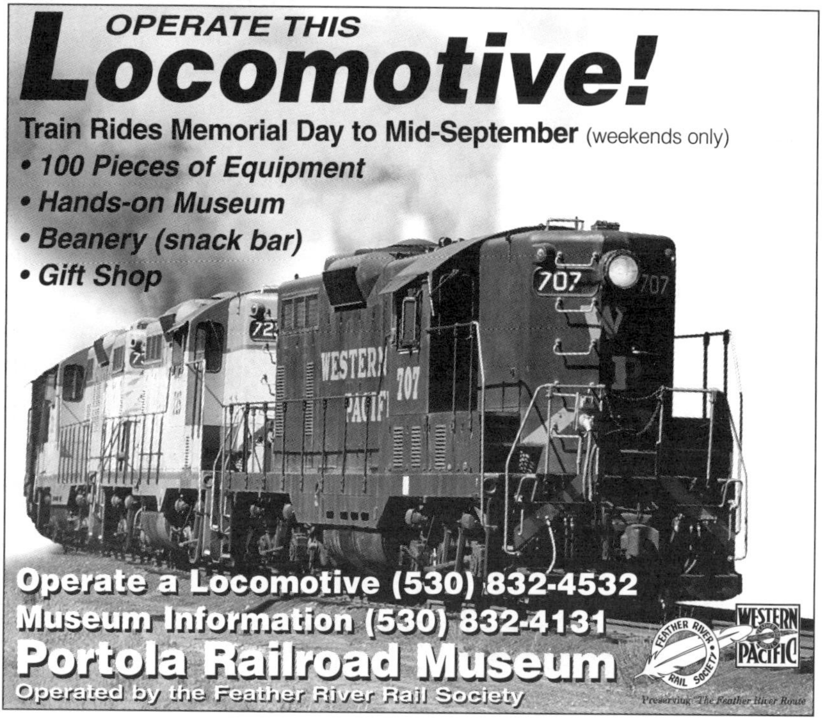

OPERATE THIS Locomotive!
Train Rides Memorial Day to Mid-September (weekends only)
• 100 Pieces of Equipment
• Hands-on Museum
• Beanery (snack bar)
• Gift Shop
707
WESTERN PACIFIC
Operate a Locomotive (530) 832-4532
Museum Information (530) 832-4131
Portola Railroad Museum
Operated by the Feather River Rail Society
FEATHER RIVER RAIL SOCIETY
WESTERN PACIFIC
Preserving The Feather River Route

A-18

^{17th}_{Year} 2001 RAILROAD TOURS

**CHINA STEAM SPECTACULAR - March 10-25 - Mainline and industrial steam.

**TIJUANA & TECATE RAIL ADVENTURE - March 24 - Charter Tijuana to Campo.

**MEXICAN RAIL ADVENTURE - March 31-April 8 - Charter on Ferromex Los Mochis-Guadalajara-Manzanillo-Aguacalientes-Chihuahua-Los Mochis.

**SAN DIEGO & ARIZONA EASTERN RAILFAN DAY - Apr. 21 - Charter steam/diesel Tijuana to Miller Creek with passenger & freight consists.

**CARIBOO STEAM SPECIAL - May 26-28 - Charter steam Vancouver to Kelly Lake on the BCR with photo run-bys. 386 miles behind No. 3716, a 2-8-0.

**GREAT CANADIAN RAIL ADVENTURE - May 19-31 - 11 train rides Vancouver-Jasper-Banff-Cariboo-Vancouver Island, including the Canadian and Rocky Mountaineer.

**NORTHERN CHILE RAILFAN ADVENTURE - June 16-24 - 9 Northern Chile railroads.

**GREAT PERUVIAN RAIL ADVENTURE - August 5-18 - 12 charters in the high Andes of Peru with steam-diesel-railcars plus steamship on Lake Titicaca.

**FALL NORTHERN WILDERNESS - Sept. 10-18 - RDC Budd charter over the BCR.

**WHITE PASS STEAM SPECTACULAR - Sept. 15-18 - Steam to Carcross & doubleheader.

**NORTHERN WILDERNESS & WHITE PASS - Sept. 10-18 - RDC Budd car & White Pass.

**NEW ENGLAND FALL COLORS RAIL ADVENTURE - Sept. 22-29 - Mass. & New Hampshire.

**RIO GRANDE SPECTACULAR - Sept. 27-28 - Cumbres steam photo freight.

**WISCONSIN FALL COLORS RAIL CRUISE - Oct. 6-8 - Charter across Wisconsin.

**COPPER CANYON RAIL ADVENTURE - Dec. 3-9 - Charter USA border to the canyon.

**RUSSIAN & TRANS-SIBERIAN CHARTERS - 10 departures in 2001.

Please call for our 2001 all-color brochure
1-800-359-4870 USA   1-800-752-1836 Canada   (530) 836-1745   Fax (530) 836-1748

TRAINS UNLIMITED, TOURS ▬ P.O. Box 1997 • Portola, California 96122 USA
Visit our website
http://www.trainsunltdtours.com

Leadership in Creative Railroading

TRAIN, Inc., the Tourist Railway Association, Inc. was formed in 1972 to foster the development and operation of tourist railways and museums. Membership is open to all railway museums, tourist railroads, excursion operators, private car owners, railroad publishers, industry suppliers and other interested persons and organizations. **TRAIN, Inc.** is the only trade association created to represent the broad spectrum of what is called "creative railroading".

Our members included in the Guide to Tourist Railroads and Museums may be identified by the **TRAIN** logo on their listing page. Members receive our bi-monthly magazine, **TrainLine**, which contains articles on creative railroading and railroad preservation. Our annual convention provides educational seminars, speakers of national import, updates on federal regulations along with product and supplier displays.

TRAIN, Inc. is a leader on issues such as insurance, safety and legislation affecting the operation and display of vintage and historic railway equipment. **TRAIN, Inc.** serves as a voice for the total industry and keeps members informed on laws , regulations and actions that affect us all.

For More Information Contact:

Tourist Railway Association, INc.
P.O. Box 1511
Felton, CA 95018-1511
1-800-67TRAIN
(831) 335-4366
FAX (831) 335-5758
Email address: calshay@aol.com
Visit our website at *http://www.train.org*

Subscribe to TrainLine, the bi-monthly magazine of railroad preservation and tourist railroads. Send $18 and your address to the above address.

Take a trip back in time...

Take a seven-mile, 50-minute round trip on a former Chicago & North Western branch line built in 1903, and experience small town America in simpler times.

Depart from a restored 1894 C&NW depot. Then visit the museum with its nationally acclaimed, restored, turn-of-the century wooden passenger and freight cars. North Freedom is near Baraboo and Wisconsin Dells, in the heart of one of America's favorite tourist destination areas.

There are special event trains and dinner trains with first-class service.

Call 608-522-4261, email midcon@baraboo.com or write P.O. Box 358, North Freedom, WI 53951, for brochure and schedule materials or member and volunteer information.

MidContinent Railway

www.midcontinent.org

Guide to
Tourist Railroads
and Museums

To the Reader

In 1966, railroad enthusiasts Marvin Cohen and Steve Bogen produced, and the Empire State Railway Museum published, the first *Steam Passenger Service Directory* (now titled *Empire State Railway Museum's Guide to Tourist Railroads and Museums*). At that time, tourist railroading was in its infancy, and the book featured 62 tourist railroads and steam excursion operations. Four years later, in 1970, the Museum and *Directory* sponsored a tourist railroad conference, and the Tourist Railroad Association, Inc. (TRAIN), was founded.

The tourist railroad industry has flourished over the past three decades, with local groups of rail enthusiasts and preservationists banding together to return to service locomotives and rolling stock that have sat dormant and neglected for too many years. The mission of these organizations includes educating and entertaining the general public. That's where the Empire State Railway Museum and this book fit in. Through the foresight and perseverance of the Museum, this book continues to be published so that rail enthusiasts, as well as those who are only casually interested in trains, can become aware of the hundreds of wonderful tourist railroads and railroad attractions available for them to enjoy and learn from. Kalmbach Publishing Co. is pleased and proud to be able to produce this book on behalf of the Empire State Railway Museum.

Guest Coupons: The reduced-rate coupons provided by many operations in this edition of the *Guide to Tourist Railroads and Museums* will be honored by the museums. Be sure to present them when purchasing tickets.

Brochures: Many operations offer brochures and/or timetables. Please see the symbol sections in the listings for those operations that provide brochures.

Every effort has been made to ensure the accuracy of the contents. However, we depend on the information supplied by each operation. Internet addresses, business office locations, and phone and Fax numbers are subject to change. We cannot assume responsibility for errors, omissions, or fare and schedule changes. Be sure to write or phone ahead to confirm hours and prices.

Finally, if you don't see a full listing in the book for a railroad or museum you know exists, check the abbreviated listings at the back of this book. These are organizations that did not respond to our mailings, but which we felt would be of interest to our customers. Again, in all cases, be sure to write or phone ahead.

If you know of an operation that is not included in the book, please send information to the publisher. See page ii.

Symbols

 Handicapped accessible

 Parking

 Bus/RV parking

 Gift, book, or museum shop

 Refreshments

 Restaurant

 Dinner train/dining car

 Guided tours

 Picnic area

 Excursions

 Arts and crafts

 National Register of Historic Places

 Brochure available; send SASE

M Memberships available

 Association of Railway Museums, member

 Tourist Railway Association, Inc., member

 Amtrak service to nearby city

VIA VIA service to nearby city

 Credit cards accepted

Alabama, Calera

HEART OF DIXIE
RAILROAD MUSEUM
Train ride, museum
Standard gauge

NEIL SMART, JR.

Description: The museum, located in a 100-year-old Southern Railway depot, displays various railroad memorabilia. An 8-mile (round trip), 45-minute train ride uses equipment built between 1910 and 1951.

Schedule: Museum: Monday through Saturday, 10 a.m. to 4 p.m., year round, and Sundays, 1 p.m. to 4 p.m. April 1 through December 16, except major holidays. Train rides: first and third Saturdays, April 7 to December 15, or on specially requested dates.

Admission/Fare: Museum: admission free. Donations appreciated. Train rides: adults, $6; children, $4.

Locomotives/Rolling Stock: Two 1951 EMD SW-8 locomotives; one 1953 Fairbanks Morse H12-44 locomotive; one Whitcomb 25-tonner; and four steamers from 0-4-0 to 2-8-0; 15 passenger cars; more.

Special Events: Halloween Nightmare Special, October 26-27. Polar Express, Nov. 30, Dec. 1, 7, 8, 14, 15. Santa Claus Express, December 1, 2, 8, 9, 15, 16.

Nearby Attractions/Accommodations: American Village, Oak Mountain State Park; Birmingham, 30 miles, has numerous museums, parks, historic sites.

Location/Directions: Take exit 228 off I-65, go ⁹⁄₁₀ mile on State Route 25 south, turn left on Ninth St., drive to the museum.

Radio frequency: 151, 515, 154.54

Site Address: 1919 Ninth St., Calera, AL
Mailing Address: PO Box 727, Calera, AL 35040
Telephone: (205) 668-3435 and (800) 943-4490
Fax: (205) 663-9370
Internet: www.heartofdixierrmuseum.org

2

Description: The depot is one of the nation's oldest remaining railroad structures. A tour includes a one-hour guided experience of the three-story building, including a glimpse into the depot's Civil War era.

Schedule: Monday through Saturday, 9 a.m. to 5 p.m. Closed Thanksgiving, Christmas, and New Year's Day.

Admission/Fare: Depot–adults, $6; seniors, $5; children, 4-17, $3.50. Age 3 and under free.

Nearby Attractions/Accommodations: The depot is part of the EarlyWorks History Complex, which includes the Alabama Constitution Village and a large hands-on history museum.

Location/Directions: I-565 east, exit 19-C. The depot is directly on your right.

        arm TRAIN

Site Address: 320 Church St., Huntsville, AL
Mailing Address: 404 Madison St., Huntsville, AL 35801
Telephone: (256) 564-8100 and (800) 678-1819
Fax: (256) 564-8151
Internet: www.earlyworks.com

**NORTH ALABAMA
RAILROAD MUSEUM, INC.**
Train ride, museum, display
Standard gauge

HUGH DUDLEY

Description: The Chase Depot offers exhibits, a display passenger train, and a self-guided walking tour. A guided tour, "All Aboard Railroading," is available. Ride on a 10-mile round trip excursion on the museum's Mercury and Chase Railroad.

Schedule: Museum–April through October: Wednesdays and Saturdays; call for hours. Train–Usually third Saturday of the month; contact for information.

Admission/Fare: Museum, parking, and self-guided walking tour–free. Guided tour–adults, $4; children 6-11, $2. Train–adults, $10; children under 12, $5.

Locomotives/Rolling Stock: Excursion train–Alco S-2 no. 484; coach no. 6082; baggage no. 139; and dining car no. 1000. Display train–Boxcab no. 11; refrigerator car; RPO car; coach; 6-10 Pullman sleeper; more.

Special Events: North Alabama Railroad History Festival; Goblin Train; Santa Train; call for dates.

Nearby Attractions/Accommodations: Alabama Space and Rocket Center (home of Space Camp), Huntsville Depot Museum, Museum of Art, Botanical Garden, Dogwood Manor Bed & Breakfast.

Location/Directions: From east end of I-565 in Huntsville, continue east on U.S. 72 for 2 miles, take left on Moores Mill Rd. for 1 mile, cross second railroad track, left on Chase Rd. for ½ mile to museum on left.

P   TRAIN M

Radio frequency: 452.325 & 457.325

Site Address: 694 Chase Rd., Huntsville, AL
Mailing Address: PO Box 4163, Huntsville, AL 35815-4163
Telephone: (256) 851-6276 (voice Wed. and Sat., 8 to 2, otherwise recording)
E-mail: fredrrman@aol.com
Internet: www.suncompsvc.com/narm/

WHITE PASS & YUKON ROUTE
Train ride
36" gauge

DEDMAN'S PHOTO

Description: Built in 1898, the White Pass Railroad is one of the most spectacular mountain railroads in the world. The WP&YR offers round trip excursions from Skagway to the White Pass Summit, Lake Bennett, Carcross, and through rail/bus connections to Whitehorse, Yukon.

Schedule: May through September: daily. Summit Excursion–depart Skagway 8:30 a.m. and 1 p.m., 3-hour round trip and Lake Bennett Adventure 8 a.m. (8-hour round trip). Through service northbound–depart Skagway 8 a.m. (train); arr. Fraser, B.C., 10 a.m. (change to bus); arr. Whitehorse, Yukon, 1 p.m. Through service southbound–depart Whitehorse, Yukon, 1:30 p.m. (bus); arr. Fraser, B.C., 2:30 p.m. (change to train); arr. Skagway, Alaska, 4:30 p.m. Steam Train–June through August: every Saturday, departs at 8 a.m.

Admission/Fare: Summit Excursion–adults, $82; children, $41. Through service–adults, $95; children, $47.50. Bennett steam train–adults, $156; children, $78. Bennett diesel train–adults, $128; children, $64. Reservations recommended.

Locomotives/Rolling Stock: 1947 Baldwin no. 73 2-8-2; 1920 Baldwin no. 40, 7-101 Alco; 10 GE diesels; 55 train cars.

Special Events: Private rail charters to/from Carcross now available.

Nearby Attractions/Accommodations: Klondike Gold Rush National Park.

Radio frequency: 160.325

Site Address: Second and Spring Streets, Skagway, AK
Mailing Address: PO Box 435, Skagway, AK 99840
Telephone: (907) 983-2217 and (800) 343-7373
Fax: (907) 983-2734
E-mail: info@whitepass.net
Internet: www.whitepassrailroad.com

5

MUSEUM OF ALASKA
TRANSPORTATION & INDUSTRY
Museum
Standard gauge

PATRICK DURAND

Description: See Alaska Railroad locomotives and 26 items of rolling stock; also, aircraft, boats, automobiles, heavy equipment, and other varieties of transport important in Alaska's history.

Schedule: Museum–May 1 through September 30: open daily, 9 a.m. to 6 p.m.; October 1 through April 30: Saturday, 9 a.m. to 5 p.m.

Admission/Fare: Adults, $5; seniors and students, $4; children under age 8 are free; family rate, $12.

Locomotives/Rolling Stock: Alaska Railroad RS-1 no. 1000; Chitina auto trailer; EMD F7A no. 1500; USAF Baldwins nos. 1841 and 1842; GM Center Cab Diesel, Pullman McCord, U.S. Bureau of Mines Safety Car.

Special Events: Blast from the Past, July. Great Alaska Antique Power Show, August.

Nearby Attractions/Accommodations: Alaska Live Steamers 1½" scale railroad is next door. Train ride, $2 each, operates the third Saturday of the month May through September; also holiday and other weekends.

Location/Directions: Follow signs at mile 47 of Parks Highway, north of Wasilla. Museum is ¾ mile west of highway, next to airport.

Site Address: 3800 W. Neuser Dr. off Mile 47, Parks Highway, Wasilla, AK
Mailing Address: PO Box 870646, Wasilla, AK 99687
Telephone: (907) 376-1211
Fax: (907) 376-3082
E-mail: mati@mtaonline.net
Internet: www.alaska.net/~rmorris/mati1.htm

VERDE CANYON RAILROAD, LC
Train ride, museum
Standard gauge

Description: The Verde Canyon Railroad is Arizona's longest-running nature show. See Sinagua Indian ruins, eagles, wildlife and a 680-foot man-made tunnel on this four-hour scenic excursion First-class or coach seating is available and both have access to open-air viewing cars.

Schedule: Year round; train schedules vary with the seasons. Depot open daily 8 a.m. to 5 p.m.

Admission/Fare: First-class, $54.95. Adult coach, $35.95. Senior coach (65+), $32.95. Child coach (2-12), $20.95

Locomotives/Rolling Stock: Two FP7 series engines built by General Motors in 1953; passenger cars, either Pullman Standard, built in 1946-47, originally used in a commuter capacity along the eastern seaboard, or Budd Stainless Steel cars, built in the late '30s to '40s, part of the Sanat Fe's "El Capitan" route between Chicago and Los Angeles.

Special Events: Starlight Trains, May through October.

Nearby Attractions/Accommodations: Blazin' M Ranch, Cottonwood, Tuzigoot and Montezuma Castle National Monument, Historic Jerome, Red Rocks of Sedona, Cliff Castle Casino, Fort Verde State Historic Park, Slide Rock, Red Rock, and Dead Horse Ranch State Parks, more.

Location/Directions: I-17 exit 260 to Cottonwood, 89A to Clarkdale.

Site Address: 300 N. Broadway, Clarkdale, AZ
Mailing Address: 300 N. Broadway, Clarkdale, AZ 86324
Telephone: (520) 639-0010
Fax: (520) 639-1653
E-mail: info@verdecanyonrr.com
Internet: www.verdecanyonrr.com

Description: The Arizona Train Depot is a model railroad retail store.

Schedule: Year round: Mondays, Tuesdays, Thursdays, Fridays, and Saturdays, 9 a.m. to 6 p.m.; Wednesdays, 9 a.m. to 9 p.m.; Closed Sundays.

Admission/Fare: None.

Locomotives/Rolling Stock: N, HO, O and G models only.

Special Events: Summer sale each August.

Location/Directions: Highway 202 to McKellips exit, east about 2 miles to Horne, southwest corner of McKellips and Horne.

Site Address: 755 E. McKellips Rd. (southwest corner), Mesa, AR
Mailing Address: 755 E. McKellips Rd., Mesa, AR 85203
Telephone: (480) 833-9486 and (888) 207-3564
Fax: (480) 834-4644

MC CORMICK-STILLMAN
RAILROAD PARK
Train ride, museum,
15" gauge

Description: A 30-acre theme park offering train rides, carousel rides, railroad museum, retail shops, picnic area, two playgrounds, snack stop, Hartley's General Store, and model railroad displays.

Schedule: Year round, seven days a week: daily 10 a.m. to sunset. Call for summer hours.

Admission/Fare: Train or carousel ride–$1 per person for anyone 3 or older. Museum–$1 for anyone 13 and older.

Locomotives/Rolling Stock: 5-inch scale locomotives. Steam–2-8-2, 4-6-0, 2-6-2. Diesel–GP7, SW1; 20 various cars.

Special Events: Railfair, October 14-15. Holiday Lights, December 15-30 (no December 24, 25, 31). Exclusively Little, March 4. Free summer concerts, May 14 through July 16.

Nearby Attractions/Accommodations: Shopping, resorts, restaurants, casino.

Location/Directions: Southeast corner of Scottsdale Rd. and Indian Bend Rd.

Site Address: 7301 E. Indian Bend Rd., Scottsdale, AZ
Mailing Address: 7301 E. Indian Bend Rd., Scottsdale, AZ 85250
Telephone: (480) 312-2312
Fax: (480) 312-7001
Internet: www.ci.scottsdale.az.us/mccormick

OLD PUEBLO TROLLEY
Trolley ride
Standard gauge

STEVE RENZI

Description: One mile of trolley track through historic business and residential areas.

Schedule: Year round: Fridays, 6 to 10 p.m.; Saturdays, noon to midnight; Sundays, noon to 6 p.m.

Admission/Fare: Adults $1 one way; children 7-11, half fare; children 6 and under, free.

Locomotives/Rolling Stock: Historic trolleys from the United States, Canada, Japan, and Europe.

Special Events: Family Days with reduced fares on Sundays; charters available at any time and for any purpose.

Nearby Attractions/Accommodations: Route through historic business district with specialty stores and 20 restaurants of all types within 100 feet of car stops.

Location/Directions: Take I-10 to St. Mary's Rd. exit, go 2 miles east on Sixth St. to Fourth Ave., turn south to Eighth St. Car barn at Fourth Ave. and Eighth St.

Site Address: 360 E. Eighth St., Tucson, AZ
Mailing Address: PO Box 1373, Tucson, AZ 85702
Telephone: (520) 791-1802 and (520) 791-0225
Fax: (520) 791-4964
E-mail: opt@worldnet.att.net
Internet: www.oldpueblotrolley.org

Description: Relive the excitement of the Old West aboard a historic train to America's national treasure, the Grand Canyon. After a 2¼-hour journey, passengers have 3¼ hours to explore the canyon before the train returns to Williams. Many passengers spend the night inside Grand Canyon National Park.

Schedule: Year round: daily except Dec. 24-25. Williams departure–10 a.m., arrives Grand Canyon National Park 12:15 p.m., departs Grand Canyon 3:30 p.m., returning to Williams at 5:45 p.m.

Admission/Fare: Adults, $54.95; children age 16 and under, $24.95. Additional park entrance fee and tax. Upgrades available.

Locomotives/Rolling Stock: Steam: no. 18, 1910 Alco SC-4 2-8-0; no. 29, 1906 Alco SC-3 2-8-0; no. 4960, 1923 Baldwin O1A 2-8-2 Mikado type; Diesel: no. 2134 GP7 Electro-Motive Division of GM Corporation, more. Many historic coach and other passenger cars.

Special Events: Memorial Day: Steam engine returns to service

Nearby Attractions/Accommodations: Fray Marcos Hotel and Max & Thelma's Restaurant. Historic downtown Williams and Route 66. Golf. Amtrak now stops in Williams for an all-rail trip to the Grand Canyon.

Location/Directions: I-40 exit 163 (Williams), Grand Canyon Blvd. ½ mile south to Williams depot.

Site Address: 235 N. Grand Canyon Blvd., Williams, AZ
Mailing Address: 1201 W. Route 66, Ste. 200, Flagstaff, AZ 86601
Telephone: (800) THE TRAIN (843-8724)
Fax: (520) 773-1610
E-mail: info@thetrain.com
Internet: www.thetrain.com

Description: A 34-mile, 3-4 hour round trip alongside the Colorado River. Enjoy the native wildlife and agriculture as you journey through the desert in 1922, 1923, or 1950 Pullman coaches pulled by either a 1952 Davenport-Beshler or 1957 G.E. diesel-electric.

Schedule: October: Saturday, 10 a.m.; November through March: Saturday and Sunday, 1 p.m.; April and May: Sunday 1 p.m.; June through September: by appointment only.

Admission/Fare: Adults, $11; seniors (55+), $10; children (4-16), $6.

Locomotives/Rolling Stock: 1952 Davenport-Beshler (former U.S. Army); 1957 G.E. Centercab (former USMC); 1922 Pullman chair car (former Apache Railway); 1923 Pullman Club Car (former U.S. Army ambulance car); 1950 Pullman Chair Car (former Rhode Island Railroad). Also, in retirement, a 1941 Whitcombe diesel chain-drive 30-ton Minig engine (former Apache R.W.)

Special Events: Yuma Crossing Day, last weekend of February.

Nearby Attractions/Accommodations: See web sites of Yuma Chamber of Commerce and local paper for up-to-date information.

Location/Directions: I-8 to Fourth Ave. exit. Next to Yuma Crossing Park.

*Coupon available, see coupon section.

 M

Site Address: 100 N. Second Ave., Yuma, AZ
Mailing Address: PO Box 10305, Yuma, AZ 85366-8305
Telephone: (520) 782-1583

**EUREKA SPRINGS &
NORTH ARKANSAS RAILWAY**
Train ride
Standard gauge

Description: Five-mile round-trip excursion trains; also, diesel-pulled dining cars.

Schedule: Excursions, 10 a.m. to 4 p.m. Dining trains, 12 and 5 p.m. daily. Closed Sundays, except Memorial Day, July 4th, and Labor Day weekends.

Admission/Fare: Excursion: adults, $8; children ages 4-10, $4. Lunch: $14.95; dinner: $23.95. All plus tax.

Locomotives/Rolling Stock: No. 1, 1906 Baldwin 2-6-0, former W.T. Carter; no. 201, 1906 Alco 2-6-0, former Moscow, Camden & San Augustine; no. 226, 1927 Baldwin 2-8-2, former Dierks For. & Coal; six commuter cars, former Rock Island; no. 4742, 1942 EMD SW1.

Nearby Attractions/Accommodations: Tourist town with many opportunities.

Location/Directions: Eureka Springs is 45 miles northeast of Fayetteville, 9 miles south of the Missouri state line. Take Highway 23 north to the city limits.

Site Address: 299 N. Main, Eureka Springs, AR
Mailing Address: PO Box 310, Eureka Springs, AR 72632
Telephone: (501) 253-9623
Fax: (501) 253-6406
E-mail: depot@esnarailway.com
Internet: www.esnarailway.com

FORT SMITH TROLLEY MUSEUM
Trolley ride, museum
Standard gauge

Description: Ride a restored Fort Smith Light & Traction Birney Safety Car over ½ mile of track in the downtown area.

Schedule: May through October: Mondays through Saturdays, 10 a.m. to 5 p.m.; Sundays, 1 to 5 p.m. November through April: Saturdays, 10 a.m. to 5 p.m.; Sundays, 1 to 5 p.m. Tours by appointment.

Admission/Fare: Trolley ride: Adults, $1; children, $ .50. Museum is free.

Locomotives/Rolling Stock: Fort Smith Light & Traction nos. 205, 224, 10; locomotives Frisco no. 4003 (steam); USAF no. 1246; August Railroad no. 6; ARR no. 7; diner MKT no. 100162; troop sleeper (power car) MKT no. 100186; three cabooses, more.

Nearby Attractions/Accommodations: Fort Smith Historic Site, Fort Smith Museum of History, Civic Center, Fort Smith National Cemetery

Location/Directions: From west Highway 64 to Garrison Ave., Garrison to S. Fourth St., south four blocks. From east I-54 to Rogers exit, west on Rogers to S. Fourth St., south three blocks to museum.

arm M

Site Address: 100 S. Fourth St., Fort Smith, AR
Mailing Address: 100 S. Fourth St., Fort Smith, AR 72901
Telephone: (501) 783-0205 and (501) 783-1237
Fax: (501) 782-9289
E-mail: info@fstm.org
Internet: www.fstm.org

Description: Self-guided or interpretive tours upon request. Beautifully restored Victorian depot built in 1885/1886. Operated by the Frisco Railroad 1901 to 1968. Nine exhibits depicting 13 lifesize figures, dressed in historical costumes each with their own audio unit telling their story. Two videos are shown about history of the railroad in Mammoth Spring and life in Mammoth Spring in the 1900s.

Schedule: Year round: Tuesdays through Sundays, 8 a.m. to 5 p.m. Closed Mondays except Monday holidays.

Admission/Fare: Adults, $2.25; children, $1.25; age 5 and under are free; special rates for groups of 15 or more with 2 weeks notice; season passes.

Locomotives/Rolling Stock: Wooden Frisco caboose SL-SF no. 1176.

Special Events: Mammoth Spring Park offers events and programs March through October and by request. Call for information.

Nearby Attractions/Accommodations: Mammoth Spring State Park, Mammoth Spring Federal Fish Hatchery, camping, canoeing, trout fishing on Spring River, museums, antique stores.

Location/Directions: Located in Mammoth Spring State Park on Highway 63. Twenty-seven miles south of West Plains, Missouri, and 16 miles north of Hardy, Arkansas.

Radio frequency: 160.35000

Site Address: U.S. Highway 63, Mammoth Spring, AR
Mailing Address: PO Box 36, Mammoth Spring, AR 72554
Telephone: (870) 625-7364
Fax: (870) 625-3255
E-mail: mammothsprg@arkansas.com
Internet: www.arkansasstateparks.com

BARRY ROBINSON

Description: Located in the 1.5-acre former Cotton Belt erecting and machine shop. It contains the last two SSW steam locomotives and other railroad equipment and artifacts.

Schedule: Year round: Mondays through Saturdays, 9 a.m. to 3 p.m. Closed during periods of extremely cold weather. Call before your visit during hottest summer weather.

Admission/Fare: Free; donations appreciated.

Locomotives/Rolling Stock: SSW 4-8-4 no. 819; SSW 2-6-0 no. 336; GP 30; SSW relief crane and outfit train; cabooses; passenger cars; snowplow.

Special Events: Annual Model Train Show and Sale, April. Mainline steam excursions with SSW 819.

Nearby Attractions/Accommodations: Jefferson County Museum in Old Union Station; Band Museum; Arkansas Entertainment Hall of Fame.

Location/Directions: Highway 65, Port Rd. exit.

        M

Site Address: 1700 Port Rd., Pine Bluff, AR
Mailing Address: PO Box 2044, Pine Bluff, AR 71613
Telephone: (870) 535-8819

CHARLES HOOT DESIGN

Description: Reader Railroad, the oldest all-steam standard gauge carrier to operate in the United States, offers a 7-mile, one-hour round trip. Open-platform wooden coaches are drawn by veteran logging engines, operations reminiscent of the railroad's earliest days.

Schedule: Write or call for information.

Admission/Fare: Adults, $6; children 4-11, $3.60; children under 4 ride free with parent. Group rates available. Fares may be slightly higher for special events.

Locomotives/Rolling Stock: Locomotive: no. 7, 1907 Baldwin 2-6-2, former Victoria, Fisher & Western. Rolling stock: open-platform wooden coaches; open-air car; caboose.

Location/Directions: Off State Route 24 between Camden and Prescott on Highway 368.

Site Address: Highway 368, off State Route 24 between Camden and Prescott
Mailing Address: PO Box 507, Hot Springs, AR 71902
Telephone: (501) 624-6881
internet: www.movietrains.com

ARKANSAS & MISSOURI RAILROAD
Train ride
Standard gauge

Description: A vintage excursion train will take you on a breathtaking ride through the beautiful Boston Mountains over towering trestles and through a remarkable manmade tunnel.

Schedule: April through September, Wednesdays and Saturdays. October through November: Wednesdays, Fridays, and Saturdays. There are other special excursion dates available.

Admission/Fare: Call or write for information

Locomotives/Rolling Stock: Six T-6s, nos. 12, 14, 15, 17, 18; two RS-1s, nos. 20, 22; one RF-32, no. 42; 12 C-420s; one C-630, no. 4500; all Alco.

Special Events: Mardi Gras, March; Springfest and Feather fest, April; Rodeo of the Ozarks, July 4th weekend; Frisco festival, August; Autumn Fest, October; fall foliage run, October; Christmas Train, December.

Nearby Attractions/Accommodations: Shiloh Museum, Walton Art Center, AQ Chicken, Daisey Museum, Prairie Grove Battlefield State Park, University of Arkansas, Pea Ridge National Military park, Devil's Den State Park. Beaver Lake.

Location/Directions: On our website at arkansasmissouri-rr.com

Site Address: 306 E. Emma St., Springdale, AR
Mailing Address: 306 E. Emma St., Springdale, AR 72764
Telephone: (501) 751-8600
Fax: (501) 751-2225
E-mail: Brendab@arkansasmissourirr.com
Internet: www.arkansasmissouri-rr.com

DESCANSO, ALPINE & PACIFIC RAILWAY

Train ride
24" gauge

GRANT KERN

Description: Passengers ride an industrial 2-foot-gauge railway to yesteryear among 100-year-old Engelman oaks in San Diego County's foothills. The train leaves Shade Depot and makes a ½-mile round trip, climbing the 6½-percent grade to High Pass/Lookout and crossing a spectacular 112-foot-long wooden trestle, giving passengers magnificent views of the surrounding area. At Shade Depot and Freight Shed is a display of railroad artifacts, including those of the DA&P. Mail service with mailer's postmark permit canceling is available.

Schedule: June through August: Sundays, 1 to 3 p.m., every half hour. September through May: intermittent Sunday operation. Rides and tours may be scheduled at other times with advance notice; please call to arrange.

Admission/Fare: Free.

Locomotives/Rolling Stock: No. 2, 1935 2½-ton Brookville, SN 2003, powered by original McCormick-Deering 22½-horsepower P-12 gasoline engine, former Carthage (Missouri) Crushed Limestone Company.

Location/Directions: Thirty miles east of San Diego. I-8 exit Tavern Rd., travel south on Tavern 1.9 miles, turn right on South Grade Rd. and travel .6 mile, turn left onto Alpine Heights Rd.; the DA&P is the fifth driveway on the right.

Site Address: 1266 Alpine Heights Rd., Alpine, CA
Mailing Address: 1266 Alpine Heights Rd., Alpine, CA 91901
Telephone: (619) 445-4781
E-mail: dapry@juno.com

Description: Twenty-minute train ride that circles the perimeter of Disneyland and makes four stops. Also takes guest through major Grand Canyon Diorama and Primeval World, featuring lifelike dinosaurs. Steam trains pull open-air cars.

Schedule: Daily, according to Disneyland Park hours.

Admission/Fare: Included with admission to Disneyland.

Locomotives/Rolling Stock: Locomotives: C.K. Holliday, 4-4-0, 1995 Disney; E.P. Ripley, 4-4-0, 1955 Disney; Fred G. Gurley, 2-4-4, 1894 Baldwin; Ernest S. Marsh, 2-4-0, 1925 Baldwin. Various open-air cars used to transport guests.

Nearby Attractions/Accommodations: Located within Disneyland Park. Disneyland is located in Anaheim, which offers many restaurants, hotels, Anaheim Angels baseball, Mighty Ducks ice hockey, and shopping.

Location/Directions: Disneyland is located about 35 miles east of downtown Los Angeles. Take the 5 freeway south, exit at Harbor Blvd. in Anaheim, and turn right to the Disneyland entrance.

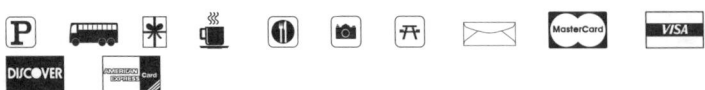

Site Address: 1313 Harbor Blvd., Anaheim, CA
Mailing Address: Guest Communications, Disneyland, 1313 Harbor Blvd., Anaheim, CA 92803
Telephone: (714) 781-4565
Internet: www.disneyland.com

GOLDEN GATE LIVE STEAMERS, INC.

Layout
2½", 3¼", 4¾", 7½" gauges

JIM LOWE

Description: We are a club of some 200+ members. Our purpose is to build and operate live steam engines. We offer a 10-minute ride over ½ mile of 7½" gauge track.

Schedule: Sundays 12-3 p.m., weather permitting and depending on availability of club engine.

Admission/Fare: Donations appreciated.

Locomotives/Rolling Stock: Two club engines, a Pacific and an Atlantic, plus various club members' engines and cars.

Special Events: Spring Meet, June 2-3. Fall Meet, October 13-14.

Nearby Attractions/Accommodations: Redwood Valley Railway 15" gauge.

Location/Directions: In the Berkeley Hills of Route 24 use Fish Ranch Rd. exit, one mile to Grizzly Peak Blvd., right one mile to Lomas Contatas.

Site Address: 2501 Grizzly Peak Blvd., Berkeley, CA
Mailing Address: 130 Pereira Ave., Tracy, CA 95376
Telephone: (209) 835-0263

California, Berkeley　　　　**REDWOOD VALLEY RAILWAY CORP.**

Train ride
15" gauge

Description: A 1¼-mile ride in the East Bay Hills through Redwood groves. Authentic scale narrow gauge steam equipment and trackwork.

Schedule: Year round: weekends and holidays, 11 a.m. to 6 p.m., weather permitting. Summer weekdays, mid-June through Labor Day, 12 to 5 p.m.

Admission/Fare: Single-ride ticket, $1.75, five-ride family ticket, $7, under age 2 ride free.

Locomotives/Rolling Stock: No. 4, 1875 2-4-2 "Laurel"; no. 5, 1890 4-4-0 "Fern"; no. 11, 4-6-0 "Sequoia"; no. 2, 0-4-0 gas/hydraulic switcher "Juniper." (Current project, no. 7, 1930 2-6-2 "Oak.") Wood bodies, truss rods, archbar trucks; D&RGW-style caboose, 4-wheel work "Jimmies," and special purpose work cars.

Nearby Attractions/Accommodations: Tilden Regional Park with antique merry-go-round (with food service), 18-hole golf course, Botanical Gardens, pony rides, Little Farm, Environmental Education Center, hiking trails, picnic areas.

Location/Directions: Tilden Regional Park in Berkeley Hills. Grizzly Peak Blvd. at Lomas Cantadas. Off Highway 24 at Fish Ranch Rd.

Site Address: Grizzly Peak Blvd. at Lomas Cantadas, Berkeley, CA
Mailing Address: 2950 Magnolia St., Berkeley, CA 94705
Telephone: (510) 548-6100
Fax: (510) 841-3609
Internet: www.hometown.aol.com/rvrytrain

BOB HAYDEN

Description: Original 1883 depot and agent's house, including over 20 other historic buildings with exhibits, and 11 acres of mining, farming, and railroad equipment. Located on the original location of the Carson-Colorado and later the Southern Pacific site.

Schedule: Year round: daily, 10 a.m. to 4 p.m. except Thanksgiving and Christmas.

Admission/Fare: New Year's Day, Easter, suggested $2 donation per person.

Locomotives/Rolling Stock: 1909 Baldwin 4-6-0, former Southern Pacific; Brill motor car, 1927; 12 boxcars; one A frame gondola; one stock car; one combination caboose; postal caboose.

Nearby Attractions/Accommodations: Fishing, skiing, hunting, camping.

Location/Directions: From Bishop follow Highway 6 north 5 miles, then turn right on Silver Canyon Rd.

        M

Site Address: Silver Canyon Rd., Bishop, CA
Mailing Address: Box 363, Bishop, CA 93515
Telephone: (760) 873-5950
Internet: www.the sierraweb.com/bishop/laws

Description: The Ghost Town & Calico Railway (GT&C) is America's only narrow-gauge passenger train operating on a daily, year-round basis. America's first theme park and the newest member of the Cedar Fair family of amusement parks and resorts nationwide, Knott's Berry Farm is 165 wild rides, live shows, and attractions designed for real family fun and adventure.

Schedule: Open daily except Christmas. Please call (714) 220-5200 or click on www.knotts.com for operating hours.

Admission/Fare: Adults, $40; seniors (60+) and kids 3-11, $30. Southern California residents (zip codes 90000-93599): adults, $30; kids 3-11, $15.

Locomotives/Rolling Stock: No. 41 "Red Cliff" Rio Grande Southern; no. 40 "Green River" Denver & Rio Grande and Denver & Rio Grande Western; railway coaches; special cars; Galloping Goose gasoline-driven railway car former Rio Grande Southern; more.

Nearby Attractions/Accommodations: Knott's is 10 minutes from Disneyland Park. The Radisson Resort Knott's Berry Farm is adjacent.

Location/Directions: Please call (714) 220-5200 or click on www.knotts.com for directions.

Site Address: 8039 Beach Blvd., Buena Park, CA
Mailing Address: 8039 Beach Blvd., Buena Park, CA 90620
Telephone: (714) 220-5200
Fax: (714) 220-5124
E-mail: pr@knotts.com
Internet: www.knotts.com

Description: Over 800 feet of G gauge model railroad winding past all dining tables. A railroad museum, all major Kalmbach magazines, fun for all ages!

Schedule: Monday through Saturday, 11 a.m. to 8 p.m. Closed all Sundays and major holidays.

Admission/Fare: Free. Parties with children under 12 must buy food or pay a cover of $9.50 per family.

Special Events: Model railroad club (G gauge) meets every Thursday night after closing. Admission free to all. Must be 18 years old.

Nearby Attractions/Accommodations: Only 15 minutes from Roaring Camp Railroad in Felton. Just 10 minutes from the Santa Cruz Boardwalk. Just 2 minutes from the beach!

Location/Directions: Exit California Highway 1 on 41st Ave., west one mile, turn left into parking lot at Capitola Station.

*Coupon available, see coupon section.

Site Address: 1820-F 41st Ave., Capitola, CA
Mailing Address: 1820-F 41st Ave., Capitola, CA 95010
Telephone: (831) 438-1226
Fax: (831) 438-3426
Internet: www.thetrainplace.com

**CLOVIS TOURIST INFORMATION &
VISITOR CENTER AT TARPEY DEPOT**

Description: A restored, century-old train depot, which currently serves as an information and visitor center.

Schedule: May 1 through October 30: Tuesdays through Fridays, 2 to 6 p.m. November 1 through April 30: 10 a.m. to 2 p.m. Saturdays and Sundays. 10 a.m. to 2 p.m. year-round. Closed Mondays and all major holidays.

Admission/Fare: Free.

Special Events: Big Hat Days: first weekend of April. Clovis Rodeo: last weekend of April. Farmers Market: May through September, Fridays 5 to 9 p.m. National Olympic Pole Vault tryouts: first weekend of August.

Nearby Attractions/Accommodations: Yosemite National Park, 90 minutes. Kings Canyon National Park, 60 minutes. Sequoia National Park, 60 minutes. Wild Water Adventures water park, 10 minutes.

Location/Directions: U.S. Highway 99 to Freeway 41 north, onto 180 east, then onto 168 east. Take the Bullard off ramp, go east ½ mile, then north on Clovis Ave., and one block to Fourth St., where the visitor center is located.

Site Address: 399 Clovis Ave., Clovis, CA
Mailing Address: 399 Clovis Ave., Clovis, CA 93612
Telephone: (559) 297-2696 and (877) 7CLOVIS
Fax: (559) 297-5826
E-mail: tarpeydepot@ci.clovis.ca.us
Internet: www.ci.clovis.ca.us

RAILROAD PARK RESORT
Dinner train, display
Standard gauge

C. MURPHY

Description: A 28-room caboose motel and restaurant, dinner house in refurbished train cars. RV park and campground on premises.

Schedule: Year round.

Admission/Fare: Room–$70 to $75 per night. Dinner average $15 per person.

Locomotives/Rolling Stock: Willamette Shay; snowplow, flanger; cabooses; speeders.

Nearby Attractions/Accommodations: Golfing, skiing, camping, hiking, lakes, fishing, boating, and state park.

Location/Directions: I-5, Railroad Park exit. Forty miles north of Redding, just south of city of Dunsmuir.

Site Address: 100 Railroad Park Rd., Dunsmuir, CA
Mailing Address: 100 Railroad Park Rd., Dunsmuir, CA 96025
Telephone: (530) 235-4440
Fax: (530) 235-4470
E-mail: rrp@rrpark.com
Internet: www.rrpark.com

MICHAEL KELLOGG

Description: Fort Humbolt State Historic Park includes a logging museum. The exhibit emphasizes historic steam logging equipment used in redwood logging. Several artifacts have been restored to operating condition and are demonstrated on occasion by the Northern Counties Logging Interpretive Association. Two small steam locomotives provide short rides once a month during the summer. Cab rides for members.

Schedule: The museum is open daily, 9 a.m. to 5 p.m. Steam trains and equipment operate April 28-29 (Donkey Days), May 19, June 16, July 21, August 18, and September 15, 11 a.m. to 4 p.m.

Admission/Fare: Museum and displays–free. Train rides–adults, $1; children, $.50.

Locomotives/Rolling Stock: Bear Harbor Lumber Co., Marshutz & Cantrell, 1892, 12-ton 0-4-0, no. 1 "Gypsy"; Elk River Mill and Lumber Co., Marshutz & Cantrell, 1884, 9-ton 0-4-0, no. 1 "Falk"; more.

Special Events: Dolbeer Steam Donkey Days, April 28-29.

Nearby Attractions/Accommodations: Historic military fort adjacent; national and state redwood parks in the area.

Location/Directions: Off Highway 101 at the southern end of Eureka, opposite Bayshore Mall.

      M

Site Address: 3431 Fort Ave., Eureka, CA
Mailing Address: 3431 Fort Ave., Eureka, CA 95503
Telephone: (707) 445-6567

**ROARING CAMP &
BIG TREES RAILROAD**
Train ride
Narrow gauge

Description: Antique steam locomotives taking passengers on a 6.5-mile round trip through the redwoods of Santa Cruz County. Situated in the re-created townsite of an old-time logging camp complete with 1880s general store, operating sawmill and chuckwagon barbecue.

Schedule: April through October, daily with additional departures during the summer. November through March, weekends.

Admission/Fare: Adults, $14.75; children 3-12, $9.75. Parking, $5.

Locomotives/Rolling Stock: No. 1 1912 Lima 2-truck Shay, former Coal Processing Corp; no. 2 1899 2-truck Heisler, former West Side Lumber; more.

Special Events: Civil War Re-enactment, Memorial weekend. Frog Jump and Race, July. Labor Day Roundup. October Harvest Fare. Thanksgiving Mountain Man Rendezvous.

Nearby Attractions/Accommodations: Winchester Mystery House, Mystery Spot, Marine World, Monterey Bay Aquarium, Santa Cruz Beach and Boardwalk, Paramount's Great America, Red and White Fleet, Pier 39.

Location/Directions: Off State Route 17/880 to Santa Cruz, Mt. Hermon exit, 3.5 miles to left on Graham Hill Rd., ½ mile to Roaring Camp.

Site Address: Graham Hill Rd. and Roaring Camp Rd., Felton, CA
Mailing Address: PO Box G-1, Felton, CA 95018
Telephone: (831) 335-4484
Fax: (831) 335-3509
E-mail: RCamp448@aol.com
Internet: www.roaringcamprr.com

SANTA CRUZ, BIG TREES & PACIFIC RAILWAY
Train ride
Standard gauge

Description: Our Santa Cruz, Big Trees & Pacific Railway carries passengers from Roaring Camp, through Henry Cowell Redwood State Park, then proceeds down the spectacular San Lorenzo River Canyon. After leaving the forest, this turn-of-the-century passenger train rolls sedately through a beautiful "gingerbread" residential section of downtown Santa Cruz. The train then stops in front of the Carousel at the Beach/Boardwalk in Santa Cruz.

Schedule: Call or write for information.

Admission/Fare: Call or write for information.

Locomotives/Rolling Stock: Nos. 2600 & 2641, CF7 1500-horsepower diesels, former Santa Fe; no. 20, 50-ton center-cab Whitcomb; three 1900-era wooden passenger coaches; two 1920s-era steel coaches; seven open-air cars; restored 1895 caboose, former Lake Superior & Ishpeming.

Special Events: Railroad Olympics and motorcar rallies, July.

Location/Directions: Six miles inland from Santa Cruz on Graham Hill Rd.

Site Address: Graham Hill Rd., Felton, CA
Mailing Address: PO Box G-1, Felton, CA 95018
Telephone: (831) 335-4484
Fax: (831) 335-3509
Internet: www.roaringcamp.com

FILLMORE & WESTERN RAILWAY
Train ride, dinner train
Standard gauge

Description: Day and evening diner car service, 2½- to 3½-hour rides; Murder Mystery dinners on Saturday evenings; barbecue; school field trips; Pumpkinliner; Christmas Tree excursion trains; dance car (with dinner) wine train.

Schedule: Year round; weekends. Group excursions by prior arrangement.

Admission/Fare: Day excursions: adults, $16; seniors (62+), $14; children, $8; infant-3 years, $5.

Locomotives/Rolling Stock: 1906 Baldwin steam locomotive no. 51; 1891 0-4-0 Porter no. 1 Sespe; 1949 F7 engines nos. 100 and 101; more.

Special Events: Railroad Days Festival, March (Fillmore town festival); Fourth of July (festival, arts and crafts, chili cook-off, etc.); Pumpkinliner, October; Christmas Tree Trains, December.

Nearby Attractions/Accommodations: Six Flags; Magic Mountain; Ventura County Beaches; Santa Barbara. All major hotels in Santa Clarita, Ventura, Oxnord, Camarillo and Santa Barbara.

Location/Directions: I-5 to Highway 126 (Ventura County, California) and Central Ave. in Fillmore. Two blocks north to Main St.

Site Address: 351 Santa Clara Ave., Fillmore, CA
Mailing Address: PO Box 960, Fillmore, CA 93016
Telephone: (805) 524-2546 and (800) 773 TRAIN (773-8724)
Fax: (805) 524-1838
E-mail: fwry@earthlink.net
Internet: www.fwry.com

YOSEMITE MOUNTAIN-
SUGAR PINE RAILROAD

Train ride
36" gauge

Description: The YMSP operates a one-hour narrated steam-powered excursion over a restored section of the Madera Sugar Pine Lumber Co. The 4-mile trip runs through the scenic Sierra Nevada at an elevation of 5000 feet, winds down a 4 percent grade into Lewis Creek Canyon, passes Horseshoe Curve, Cold Spring Crossing, and stops at Lewis Creek Loop. Ex-Westside Lumber Co. Shays provide the motive power for the train. Converted logging cars using sectioned logs are used for passenger cars.

Schedule: Railcars: April through October: daily. Steam train: May through September: daily. April and October: weekends.

Admission/Fare: Railcars: adults, $8; children 3-12, $4. Steam train: adults, $12; children 3-12, $6.

Locomotives/Rolling Stock: 1928 Lima 3-truck Shay, no. 10; 1913 Lima 3-truck Shay, no. 15; Vulcan 1935 10-ton switcher; four model A powered railcars; logging cars; covered and open converted flatcars, more.

Special Events: Moonlight Special with steak barbecue and music every Saturday and Wednesday night in summer; reservations advised. Gold panning, group tours, theme events, and private charters.

Nearby Attractions/Accommodations: Operating in the Sierra National Forest, 4 miles south of Yosemite National Park on Highway 41. Narrow Gauge Inn next door.

Site Address: 56001 Yosemite Highway 41, Fish Camp, CA
Mailing Address: 56001 Yosemite Highway 41, Fish Camp, CA 93623
Telephone: (559) 683-7273
Internet: www.ymsprr.com

California, Folsom
(Folsom City Zoo)

FOLSOM VALLEY RAILWAY
Train ride
12" narrow gauge

TERRY GOLD

Description: A ¾-mile ride through a 50-acre city park features vintage wooden freight cars drawn by a ⅕-scale coal-burning locomotive representative of late 19th-century steam motive power.

Schedule: February through November: Tuesdays through Fridays, 11 a.m. to 2 p.m.; weekends and holidays, 11 a.m. to 5 p.m. December through January: weekends and school holidays., 11 a.m. to 4 p.m. All are weather permitting.

Admission/Fare: $1.25 per person.

Locomotives/Rolling Stock: 1950 Ottaway old-time wooder; truss rod-style freight cars; cattle car; hopper car; five open gondola cars; bobber caboose.

Special Events: Train will operate all day until 10 p.m., week of July 4.

Nearby Attractions/Accommodations: Folsom City Zoo.

Location/Directions: Folsom is 25 miles east of Sacramento off U.S. 50.

Site Address: 50 Natoma St., Folsom, CA
Mailing Address: 121 Dunstable Way, Folsom, CA 95630
Telephone: (916) 983-1873
Fax: (916) 983-1873 (Call first.)
E-mail: goldtown@jps.net or goldtown@juno.com

CALIFORNIA WESTERN RAILROAD
THE SKUNK TRAIN
Train ride
Standard gauge

GARY RICHARDS

Description: Located on the Pacific Ocean in Fort Bragg. Come ride the Skunk Train where the redwoods meet the river. We offer 2- to 3½-hour excursions from either Willits or Fort Bragg; also, one full day 8-hour excursion from either Willits or Fort Bragg

Schedule: Daily, 8 a.m. to 5 p.m.

Admission/Fare: Call or write for information.

Locomotives/Rolling Stock: 1924 Baldwin 2-8-2 no. 45; 1924 Baldwin 2-6-2 no. 14; 1955 EMD GP9 nos. 64, 65, 66.

Nearby Attractions/Accommodations: Historic logging museum and railroad equipment, Fort Bragg, lodging, dining.

Location/Directions: Highway 1 and Laurel St. in Fort Bragg or Highway 101 and Commercial St. in Willits.

Radio frequency: 160.650

Site Address: Fort Bragg and Willits, CA
Mailing Address: PO Box 907, Fort Bragg, CA 95437
Telephone: (800) 77-SKUNK and (707) 964-6371
Fax: (707) 964-6754
E-mail: skunk@mcn.org
Internet: www.skunktrain.com

California, Fremont

SOCIETY FOR THE PRESERVATION OF CARTER RAILROAD RESOURCES

Train ride
36" gauge

RICH HILL

Description: This group is dedicated to acquiring and restoring railroad cars constructed by Carter Brothers of Newark, California, in the late 1800s. The society currently has seven Carter cars and three other cars. The cars are restored using appropriate hand tools, following the techniques used in the original construction. The 1½-mile ride is powered by a draft horse, making this the only regularly scheduled horse-drawn railroad in the U.S.

Schedule: Call or write for information.

Admission/Fare: Call or write for information.

Locomotives/Rolling Stock: "Tucker" and "Jiggs" 1989 Belgians, 0-2-2-0T hay burners; 1940 Whitcomb no. 2 14-ton, former ASARCO; 1922 Plymouth DL 7-ton, former Old Mission Cement Company.

Nearby Attractions/Accommodations: The museum is located in the Ardenwood Historic Farm, which demonstrates life on a farm at the turn of the century. It consists of a historic farmhouse, blacksmith shop, farmyard, and operating Best steam tractor.

Location/Directions: Fifteen miles south of Oakland at the intersection of I-880 and Highway 84.

          arm

Site Address: 34600 Ardenwood Blvd., Fremont, CA
Mailing Address: SPCRR, PO Box 783, Newark, CA 94560
Telephone: (408) 370-3555
E-mail: rkhill@worldnet.att.net

35

California, Goleta

SOUTH COAST RAILROAD MUSEUM
Museum
Standard gauge

Description: The centerpiece is the historic Goleta Depot, a Victorian-styled Southern Pacific country station. The museum features refurnished rooms and station grounds, and a variety of informative displays, including a 300-square-foot HO scale model railroad exhibit. Other attractions include miniature train and handcar rides, Gandy Dancer Theater, picnic grounds, and a museum store and gift shop.

Schedule: Museum–Wednesdays through Sundays, 1 to 4 p.m. Miniature train–Wednesdays and Fridays, 2 to 3:40 p.m.; weekends, 1 to 3:45 p.m. Handcar–third Saturday of each month, 1 to 3:45 p.m.

Admission/Fare: Museum–donations appreciated. Handcar–free. Miniature train–$1.

Locomotives/Rolling Stock: 1960s Southern Pacific bay window caboose no. 4023.

Special Events: Depot Day, September 30, 11 a.m. to 4 p.m.

Location/Directions: Goleta is seven miles west of Santa Barbara, U.S. 101 north exit Los Carneros Rd.

Site Address: 300 N. Los Carneros Rd., Goleta, CA
Mailing Address: 300 N. Los Carneros Rd., Goleta, CA 93117-1502
Telephone: (805) 964-3540
Fax: (805) 964-3549
E-mail: museum@goletadepot.org
Internet: www.goletadepot.org

RAILTOWN 1897
SIERRA RAILWAY COMPANY
Train ride, museum
Standard gauge

Description: Operated by the California State Railroad Museum; one of Hollywood's most popular filming locations. The Historic Sierra Railroad Shops and Roundhouse at Railtown 1897 have been in continuous operation as a steam locomotive maintenance facility for over a century. Six-mile, 40-minute round trip route passing through Gold Country.

Schedule: Open daily 9:30 a.m. to 4:30 p.m., except Thanksgiving, Christmas, and New Year's. Steam trains operate weekends April to October (Saturdays only in November), departing hourly 11 a.m. to 3 p.m. Guided roundhouse tours available daily.

Admission/Fare: Roundhouse tours: adults, $2; children (6-12), $1. Train rides: adults, $6; children (6-12), $3; 5 and under are free.

Locomotives/Rolling Stock: Sierra Railroad 2-8-0 no. 28; 4-6-0 no. 3; combine no. 5; coach no. 6; former Feather River Shay no. 2; former Southern Pacific commuter coaches; more.

Nearby Attractions/Accommodations: Jamestown, "Gateway to the Mother Lode," Sonora, "Queen of the Southern Mines," preserved Gold Rush town of Columbia (State Historical Park), Yosemite National Park.

Location/Directions: Located 3 blocks east of downtown Jamestown on Highways 49/107 just west of the Highway 120 junction.

*Coupon available, see coupon section.

Site Address: Fifth Ave. and Reservoir Rd., Jamestown, CA
Mailing Address: PO Box 1250, Jamestown, CA 95327
Telephone: (209) 984-3953
Fax: (209) 984-4936
E-mail: railtown@mlode.com
Internet: www.csrmf.org

California, Lomita

Description: A replica of the Boston & Maine station at Wakefield, Massachusetts. On display are lanterns of the steam era, chinaware, and silverware of the period, scale model live steam engines, spikes, tie date nails, insulators, prints, photographs, postcards, clocks, and a wooden water tower 35 feet high and 14 feet in diameter next to the engine.

Schedule: Year round. Wednesday through Sunday, 10 a.m. to 5 p.m. Closed Thanksgiving and Christmas.

Admission/Fare: Adults, $2; children under age 12, $1.

Locomotives/Rolling Stock: 1902 Baldwin 2-6-0 (Mogul) no. 1765 with a whale-back tender, former Southern Pacific. 1910 yellow caboose, UP OWR&N; 1913 UP boxcar; 1923 oil tank car, Union Oil Co.; Santa Fe red caboose no. 531.

Special Events: Golden Spike Day, call or write for details.

Nearby Attractions/Accommodations: South Coast Botanical Gardens, Torrance Cabrillo Museum, San Pedro, Banning House and Drum Barracks, Wilmington.

Location/Directions: 110 (Harbor Freeway) south to Pacific Coast Highway off ramp. Right (west) to Narbonne Ave. Right to second signal. Right (east) one block. Parking on 250th St.

*Coupon available, see coupon section.

          M

Site Address: 250th St. and Woodward Ave., Lomita, CA
Mailing Address: 2137 W. 250th St., Lomita, CA 90717
Telephone: (310) 326-6255

California, Los Angeles

CRYSTAL SPRINGS & CAHUENGA VALLEY RAILROAD
Train ride
Standard gauge

CHARLES FORSHER

Description: The first section of a planned demonstration railroad through Griffith Park. A diesel locomotive pulls caboose train on available track at the Travel Town Museum.

Schedule: First weekend of every month, 10 a.m. to 4 p.m.

Admission/Fare: Donations appreciated.

Locomotives/Rolling Stock: EMD model 40, CS&CV no. 1; California Western Railroad RS12; AT&SF caboose no. 999110; SP caboose no. 4049.

Nearby Attractions/Accommodations: Griffith Park, Griffith Observatory, Los Angeles Zoo, Autry Museum of Western Heritage, Universal, Warner Brothers, and NBC studios.

Location/Directions: Ventura Freeway exit 134 (Forest Lawn Dr.) located at Griffith Park and Zoo Dr. in the Travel Town Museum.

       M TRAIN

Site Address: 5200 Zoo Dr., Los Angeles, CA
Mailing Address: 3900 W. Chevy Chase Dr., Los Angeles, CA 90039
Telephone: (323) 662-5874 and (213) 485-5520
Fax: (818) 243-0041
Internet: www.cityofla.org/rap/grifmet/tt/index.htm.

Description: One of the oldest displays of pre-World War II passenger cars and steam locomotives in the United States, concentrating on railroads in the west, specifically California.

Schedule: Year round: weekdays 10 a.m. to 4 p.m., weekends 10 a.m. to 5 p.m.

Admission/Fare: Museum–free. Scale train ride–adults, $2; children age 12 and under, $1.50.

Locomotives/Rolling Stock: No. 1, 1864 Norris-Lancaster 4-4-0, former Stockton Terminal & Eastern; no. 664, 1899 Baldwin 2-8-0, former Santa Fe; no. 3025, 1904 Alco 4-4-2, former Southern Pacific; no. 1544, 1902 steeple-cab electric, former Pacific Electric; 1955 Baldwin RS-12, former McCloud River no. 33, later California Western no. 56; "The Little Nugget," 1937 club-dorm no. 701 from the Union Pacific Streamliner *City of Los Angeles,* and sleeping cars "Rose Bowl" (1937) and "Hunters Points" (1940), both originally on *City of San Francisco;* others.

Special Events: Pullman car tours, third weekend of every month.

Nearby Attractions/Accommodations: Griffith Park, Griffith Observatory, Los Angeles Zoo, Autry Museum of Western Heritage, Universal, Warner Brothers, and NBC studios.

Location/Directions: Ventura Freeway exit 134 (Forest Lawn Dr.), located at Griffith Park and Zoo Drives.

Site Address: 5200 Zoo Dr., Los Angeles, CA
Mailing Address: 3900 W. Chevy Chase Dr., Los Angeles, CA 90039
Telephone: (323) 662-5874 and (213) 485-5520
Fax: (818) 243-0041
Internet: www.cityofla.org/rap/grifmet/tt/index.htm.

NAPA VALLEY WINE TRAIN
Train ride, dinner train
Standard gauge

Description: Year round gourmet dining excursions for brunch, lunch or dinner, 3-hour, 36-mile round trip. Three different restaurant options, special events regularly.

Schedule: Year round, daily, 8 a.m. to 10 p.m.

Admission/Fare: $29.50-$110 per person

Locomotives/Rolling Stock: Four Alco FPA-44 diesels, nos. 70, 71, 72, and 73; seven Pullman dining and lounge cars, circa 1915-1917; one 1952 Pullman Vista Dome car; one Pullman coach converted to professional viewing kitchen.

Special Events: Monthly murder mystery dinner theatre, monthly family fun dinners.

Nearby Attractions/Accommodations: Over 200 wineries, 30 parks, 24 museums, 30 galleries, 180 hotels/inns/bed & breakfasts.

Location/Directions: One hour north of San Francisco in downtown Napa off Soscol Ave. and First St.

*Coupon available, see coupon section.

Site Address: 1275 McKinstry St., Napa, CA
Mailing Address: 1275 McKinstry St., Napa, CA 94559
Telephone: (707) 253-2111 and (800) 427-4124
Fax: (707) 253-9264
E-mail: www.winetrain.com
Internet: www.winetrain.com

NATIONAL CITY DEPOT
Museum, display
Full gauge

Description: One- and 3-mile rides on the Coronado Belt Line. The museum depicts the Santa Fe and San Diego Electric Railway Company.

Schedule: Saturday and Sunday, 12 to 4 p.m.

Admission/Fare: Adults, $5/10; Children, $3/7. Museum: Adults, $3; Children, $1.

Locomotives/Rolling Stock: Santa Maria Railbus; various LRV/Speeders.

Nearby Attractions/Accommodations: National City and Otay (NC&O) no. 1 Car Plaza across the street; Sea World; world-famous San Diego Zoo; Tijuana, Mexico.

Location/Directions: Five miles south of San Diego. Take I-5 south to Bay Marina Dr. exit in National City and turn right. Go west two blocks and the museum is on the right.

Site Address: 922 W. 23rd St., National City, CA
Mailing Address: 1240 E. Plaza Blvd. #604-132, National City, CA 91950
Telephone: (619) 474-4400
Fax: (619) 474-4400
E-mail: ncd@trainweb.com
Internet: www.trainweb.com/sandiegorail/sdera

NEVADA COUNTY TRACTION COMPANY
Train ride
24" and 36" gauge

Description: Take a 3-mile round-trip, 1½-hour train ride. View rolling stock dated from 1888 to early 1900s. Visit a 1850s Chinese cemetery.

Schedule: Summer hours, May through September: daily, 10 a.m. to 2 p.m. and 4 p.m. October: Halloween all month, with same time schedule (and Friday and Saturday night Haunted Forest of Terror at 7 p.m. and 8 p.m.

Admission/Fare: Daily rides: adults, $8; children, $5. In October, daily rides: adults, $9; children, $6. Haunted Forest, $10.

Locomotives/Rolling Stock: Argent no. 5 former Stone Machine Co.; Daisy Tenn. 2-6-2, 26-ton Lima Operational West Side Lumber Co.; railbus, 1939 0-4-0 Henschel 14-ton electric speeder; 1959 0-4-0 Plymouth 12-ton 1985 street trolley.

Special Events: October, Haunted Forest of Terror.

Nearby Attractions/Accommodations: Empire Mine State Park, Malahoff Digging State Park, Historical Nevada City (Independent Trail is wheelchair accessible), Sacramento Railroad Museum.

Location/Directions: On Highway 49 and 20, 55 miles northeast of Sacramento. Take Sacramento St. exit, right on Railroad Ave., ⅛ mile on right. Located at Northern Queen Inn upper parking lot.

*Coupon available, see coupon section.

Site Address: 402 Railroad Ave., Nevada City, CA
Mailing Address: 402 Railroad Ave., Nevada City, CA 95959
Telephone: (530) 265-0896
Fax: (530) 265-0869
E-mail: depot.people@onemain.com

HERITAGE JUNCTION HISTORIC PARK
Museum, display

Description: We offer a collection of historic structures, including 1886 Southern Pacific train station.

Schedule: Saturdays and Sundays, 1 to 4 p.m.

Admission/Fare: Free. Donations appreciated.

Locomotives/Rolling Stock: All railroad cars–1629 steam engine, tank car, caboose–are undergoing restoration.

Special Events: Christmas Open House, always second Sunday in December. Cowboy Poetry and Music Festival, March 30-April 1, 2001.

Nearby Attractions/Accommodations: Historic Old Town Newhall; ten minutes from Six Flags California, amusement park; five minutes from Placerital Canyon State County Park (site of California's first gold discovery in 1842).

Location/Directions: In the heart of downtown Newhall historic district; part of William S. Hart County Park; off State Highway 14 at San Fernando Rd.

         M

Site Address: 24141 San Fernando Rd., Santa Clarita, CA
Mailing Address: PO Box 221925, Newhall, CA 91322-1925
Telephone: (661) 254-1275
Fax: (661) 298-5594
Internet: www.scvhs.org

California, Oakdale　　　　　　**SIERRA RAILROAD GOLDEN**
SUNSET GOURMET DINNER TRAIN
Dinner train

Description: The "Golden Sunset" dinner train takes passengers on a 38-mile long trip through the countryside to the Sierra foothills. Along the way, the passengers enjoy fine dining and our lounge car.

Schedule: Trips every Saturday and Sunday, as well as numerous other special trips.

Admission/Fare: $59 per person for brunch and $69 per person for dinner. Children 7 and under are approximately half off.

Locomotives/Rolling Stock: GP9 Sera 46, Baldwin S-12s, nos. 40, 42, 44; GP-7 no. 47; GP-20s, nos. 48 and 50; dining cars, lounge car, cabooses.

Special Events: Oakdale Chocolate Festival, May; Oakdale Rodeo, second weekend in April; Antique Festival, third weekend in June.

Nearby Attractions/Accommodations: Yosemite National Park; fishing; wine and cheese festival; Hershey's Chocolate plant; River Journeys; Oakdale Cheese Factory; Civil War living history reenactment.

Location/Directions: From San Francisco, take 580 and 120 east to Oakdale. From Sacramento, take Highway 99 south and 120 east 70 miles. From Los Angeles, take Highway 99 and J14 north 300 miles to Oakdale.

Site Address: 220 S. Sierra Ave., Oakdale, CA
Mailing Address: 220 S. Sierra Ave., Oakdale, CA 95361
Telephone: (209) 848-2100 or (800) 866-1690
Fax: (209) 848-8595
E-mail: sierrarail@aol.com
Internet: www.sierrarailroad.com

California, Orange

IRVINE PARK RAILROAD
Train ride
24" gauge

JOHN FORD

Description: Irvine Park Railroad is located on 500 acres in Irvine Regional Park, the oldest county park in the state of California. The train departs from an old-fashioned depot, where railroad folk songs fill the air. The locomotive will make a scenic one-mile journey around the park during which riders can view two lakes complete with waterfalls and fountains, a grove of oak trees, and the Orange County Zoo. The ride is narrated by the engineer and lasts approximately 12 minutes.

Schedule: Winter–daily, 10 a.m. to 4 p.m. Summer–daily, 10 a.m. to 4:30 p.m. Closed Thanksgiving and Christmas.

Admission/Fare: $3; children under age 1 are free. School group rates are available.

Locomotives/Rolling Stock: A ⅓ scale replica of the 1863 C.P. Huntington; four coaches.

Special Events: Christmas train two weeks prior to Christmas. Call for times.

Nearby Attractions/Accommodations: Bicycle and paddleboat rentals, Orange County Zoo, food concessions, pony rides.

Location/Directions: From State Highway 55 take the Chapman Ave. exit and drive east to Jamboree Rd. Turn left into the park entrance.

Site Address: 1 Irvine Park Rd., Orange, CA
Mailing Address: 1 Irvine Park Rd., Orange, CA 92669
Telephone: (714) 997-3968
Fax: (714) 997-0459
Internet: www.irvineparkrr.com

ORLAND, NEWVILLE & PACIFIC RAILROAD
Train ride
15" gauge

Description: The ON&P is an all-volunteer railroad operating in the Glenn County Fairgrounds. A 1-mile ride takes visitors past the original Orland Southern Pacific depot, the picnic site, and the demonstration orchard, then through a tunnel and along Heritage Trail. The train is normally pulled by a magnificent 5/12-scale live-steam model of the North Pacific Coast's 1875 Baldwin narrow-gauge locomotive "Sonoma." The picnic grounds at Deadowl Station are open whenever the train is running. Former Orland Southern Pacific depot, 1918 Southern Pacific 2-8-0 no. 2852, caboose, schoolhouse, blacksmith shop, print shop, 1920s gas station, miscellaneous steam machinery, old farm equipment. Livestock is also exhibited at fair time, during May and October.

Schedule: 12 noon to 5 p.m. Saturday and Sunday; Spring: April 7-8 through May 26-28; Fall: Sept. 1-3 through October 20-21.

Admission/Fare: $1.

Locomotives/Rolling Stock: No. 12 replica of 1876 Baldwin 4-4-0; no. 2 4-4-0 amusement park type; Davenport switch engine; four open gondolas; covered car.

Special Events: Glenn County Fair, May 16-20. Harvest Festival, October 20-21. Spook Train, October 31.

Location/Directions: Glenn County Fairgrounds.

Site Address: 221 E. Yolo St., Orland, CA
Mailing Address: PO Box 667, Orland, CA 95963
Telephone: (530) 865-1168 and (530) 865-9747
Fax: (530) 865-1197

ORANGE EMPIRE RAILWAY MUSEUM
Train ride, museum
Standard and narrow gauge

JIM WALKER, JR.

Description: Trains run on 1.5-mile right-of-way, streetcars on 0.7-mile loop within the museum's property.

Schedule: Demonstration railroad–year round: weekends and some holidays, 11 a.m. to 5 p.m. Museum grounds–daily: 9 a.m. to 5 p.m. Closed Thanksgiving and Christmas.

Admission/Fare: Free admission. All day ride pass–adults, $7; children 5-11, $5; under age 5 are free. Special events have additional fees.

Locomotives/Rolling Stock: VC Railway 2 Prairie; GF 2 Mogul; UP 2564 Mikado; SP 1474 S4; SP 3100 U25B; UP 942 E8A; and more.

Special Events: Rail Festivals in April; Railroadiana Swap Meets in March and October; Pumpkin Train in October; Santa Train in December; trips to March Field Air Museum in May and November.

Nearby Attractions/Accommodations: Perris Valley Skydiving Center; Perris Auto Speedway; Lake Perris Recreation Area; March Field Air Museum; Temecula Wineries; Best Western Perris Inn; Mission Inn in Riverside.

Location/Directions: I-215, exit west onto Fourth St./Route 74, left on "A" St. to museum.

Site Address: 2201 S. "A" St., Perris, CA
Mailing Address: PO Box 548, Perris, CA 92572-0548
Telephone: (909) 657-2605 and (909) 653-3020
Fax: (909) 943-2676
E-mail: oerm@juno.com
Internet: www.oerm.mus.ca.us

**GOLDEN STATE MODEL RAILROAD
MUSEUM**
Museum, display, layout

GEORGE HALL

Description: Three layouts and fixed displays occupying 10,000 square feet.

Schedule: May through October, Sundays 1 to 5 p.m.

Admission/Fare: Adults, $2; children under 14 and seniors, $1; family, $5.

Special Events: Holiday Shows: Sunday after Thanksgiving, Sundays on either side of Christmas.

Nearby Attractions/Accommodations: Miller-Knox Regional Park (we are in it), picnics, views of San Francisco, ATSF Railroad Ferry Pier (former), ASTF Richmond yard, USS Red Oak Victory (tours).

Location/Directions: Exit I-580 in Richmond at Canal Blvd. from either direction. Turn at signal to Garrard Blvd. (a right from the East Bay, or a left when coming from the San Rafael Bridge). Turn left at the stop sign onto Garrard Blvd. Proceed straight past two stop signs, and the natatorium, and into Ferry Point Tunnel. Dornan Drive is on the other side of the tunnel. We are located about ½ mile past the tunnel on the left across from Miller-Knox Regional Shoreline Park.

Site Address: 900-A Dornan Dr., Point Richmond, CA
Mailing Address: PO Box 1243, El Cerrito, CA 94530
Telephone: (510) 234-4884
Internet: www.gsmrm.org

**RAILWAY & LOCOMOTIVE
HISTORICAL SOCIETY**
Museum
Standard and narrow gauge

Description: Former ATSF Arcadia Depot (1895) houses exhibits and a gift shop. There is an outside display of locomotives and rolling stock, including motor cars; ice refrigerator car; caboose; berth and galley section of business car; horse car showing stable section.

Schedule: Open the second Saturday and Sunday of every month, 9 a.m. to 4 p.m. When Easter or Mother's Day falls on the second Sunday, the museum will open on the preceeding weekend, same hours. Daily during the Los Angeles County Fair in September. Other times by request.

Admission/Fare: No charge, except during the County Fair which requires a general fair admission.

Locomotives/Rolling Stock: Union Pacific/Alco 4-8-8-4 Big Boy, no. 4014 (1941); Atchison Topeka and Santa Fe/Baldwin 4-5-4 Hudson, no. 3450 (1927); more.

Special Events: Meetings are held in the basement meeting room of the California Federal Bank building, 401 N. Brand Blvd., Glendale, on the first Tuesday of every month (September-June) at 7:30 p.m.

Nearby Attractions/Accommodations: Fairplex R.V. Park; Sheraton Suites Fairplex; NHRA Pomona Drag Strip; NHRA Museum.

Location/Directions: Enter the Fairplex at Gate 1, or Main Gate, off Fairplex Dr.

Site Address: Los Angeles County Fairplex, Pomona, CA
Mailing Address: PO Box 2250, Pomona, CA 91769
Telephone: (909) 623-0190
Internet: www.trainweb.org/rlhs

PORTOLA RAILROAD MUSEUM
Museum
Standard gauge

NORMAN HOLMES

Description: A one-mile ride around a balloon turning track through pine forest. On display are more than 70 freight cars representing nearly every car type of the Western Pacific Railroad; several passenger cars; other rolling stock; railroad artifacts in the diesel shop building.

Schedule: Museum–March through mid-December 10 a.m. to 5 p.m. Train–Memorial Day through Sunday after Labor Day: weekends, 11 a.m. to 4 p.m. Grounds open in winter weather permitting.

Admission/Fare: Call or write for information.

Locomotives/Rolling Stock: Two steam, 1 electric and 32 diesels of all types including 13 former Western Pacific, 6 former Southern Pacific and 3 former Union Pacific. Manufacturers represented: Alco, Baldwin, Electro-Motive, Fairbanks-Morse, General Electric, Ingersol-Rand, and Plymouth. Steam locomotives are former UP 737, an 1887 4-4-0 and former SP 1215, a 1913 0-6-0.

Special Events: Feather River Railroad Days, August 18-19. Railfan Photographers Day, September 15.

Location/Directions: From State Route 70, travel one mile south on County Road A-15 (Gulling) across the river and through town. Follow signs to the museum.

Site Address: 700 Western Pacific Way, Portola, CA
Mailing Address: PO Box 608, Portola, CA 96122-0608
Telephone: (530) 832-4131
Fax: (530) 832-1854
E-mail: 76043.741@compuserve.com
Internet: www.wprrhs.org/ or www.oz.net/~samh/frrs/

RIVERSIDE LIVE STEAMERS
Train ride, layout
7½" gauge

Description: One-eighth size trains, all steam, on a 6,800-foot track in Hunter Park.

Schedule: Second and fourth Sundays, 10 a.m. to 3 p.m.

Admission/Fare: Donation only.

Special Events: Spring Meet, April 21-22. Fall Meet, October 27-28.

Location/Directions: Corner of Columbia and Iowa, approximately one mile northeast of the junction of California 60/91 and I-215.

   M

Site Address: 1496 Columbia Ave., Riverside, CA
Mailing Address: PO Box 5512, Riverside, CA 92517
Telephone: (909) 779-9024

CALIFORNIA STATE RAILROAD MUSEUM
Museum
Standard and 36" gauge

Description: One of the finest interpretive railroad museums in North America, CSRM's 11-acre facilities in Old Sacramento include the 100,000-square-foot museum of railroad history, a reconstructed 1870s Central Pacific passenger station, and an extensive library and archive.

Schedule: Year round: daily, 10 a.m to 5 p.m. Closed Thanksgiving, Christmas, New Year's Day.

Admission/Fare: Adults, $3; youth and children ages 16 and under, free.

Locomotives/Rolling Stock: More than 30 meticulously restored locomotives and cars on display dating from the 1860s to present. Favorites are Pullman-style sleeper, streamlined dining car, 1870s Victorian coaches, and a railway post office.

Special Events: CSRM 20th Anniversary, May; Sacramento Jazz Jubilee, Memorial Day weekend; Gold Rush Days, Labor Day weekend; Scarecrow Festival/Goosebump Express, October; Train Time for Santa, Thanksgiving weekend and weekend before Christmas.

Nearby Attractions/Accommodations: Old Sacramento (California's largest concentration of restored 19th century commercial structures), state capitol, Sutter's Fort, Crocker Art Museum, dining, shopping, and lodging.

Location/Directions: In Old Sacramento, adjacent to I-5 exit "J" St.

      M

      Radio frequencies: 160.335 and 160.440

Site Address: Corner of Second and "I" Streets, Old Sacramento, CA
Mailing Address: 111 "I" St., Sacramento, CA 95814
Telephone: (916) 445-6645
Fax: (916) 327-5655
E-mail: csrmf@csrmf.org (general) and csrmlibrary@csrmf.org (library/archives)
Internet: www.csrmf.org

California, Sacramento   **CALIFORNIA STATE RAILROAD MUSEUM**
SACRAMENTO SOUTHERN RAILROAD
Train ride
Standard gauge

Description: Sacramento Southern is the excursion railroad of the California State Railroad Museum. Built as a subsidiary of the Southern Pacific at the turn of the century, the museum trains have been in regular service since 1984. A 6-mile, 40-minute round trip takes passengers along the Sacramento River on vintage 1920s coaches and open-air excursion cars.

Schedule: Steam–April through September: weekends, 11 a.m. to 5 p.m., departing hourly behind steam locomotives. Trains also operate selected fall weekends, during special events

Admission/Fare: Adults, $6; youth 6-12, $3; children under age 6, free.

Locomotives/Rolling Stock: No. 10 1942 Porter 0-6-0T, former Granite Rock Company; no. 4466, 1920 Lima 0-6-0, former Union Pacific; more.

Special Events: CSRM 20th Anniversary, May; Sacramento Jazz Jubilee, Memorial Day weekend; Gold Rush Days, Labor Day weekend; Scarecrow Festival/Goosebump Express, October; Train Time for Santa, Thanksgiving weekend and weekend before Christmas.

Nearby Attractions/Accommodations: Old Sacramento (California's largest concentration of restored 19th century commercial structures), state capitol, Sutter's Fort, Crocker Art Museum, dining, shopping, and lodging.

Location/Directions: Northern terminus is the reconstructed Central Pacific Railroad Freight Depot at Front and "K" Streets in Old Sacramento.

Radio frequencies: 160.335 and 160.440

Site Address: Front and "K" Streets, Sacramento, CA
Mailing Address: 111 "I" St., Sacramento, CA 95814
Telephone: (916) 445-6645
Fax: (916) 327-5655
E-mail: csrmf@csrmf.org
Internet: www.csrmf.org

Description: Over 80 pieces of rail equipment on display and regularly scheduled train trips, featuring trips to Mexico.

Schedule: Year round: weekends and some holidays.

Admission/Fare: Adults, $12; children 6-12, $3; ages 5 and under are free.

Locomotive/Rolling Stock: No. 2353 4-6-0 Baldwin steam; 1950s vintage diesels; variety of cars.

Special Events: Ticket to Tecate rail trips, Starlight Express, Dinner Train, Wine Train.

Nearby Attractions/Accommodations: Viejas Indian Casinos. Old Stone Store Museum.

Location/Directions: Highway 94 to Campo in east San Diego County. Or I-8 east to rest stop, south on Buckman Springs Rd.

Site Address: Highway 94 and Campo, San Diego, CA
Mailing Address: 1050 Kettner Blvd., San Diego, CA 92101
Telephone: (619) 478-9937
Fax: (619) 595-3034
Internet: www.sdrm.com

California, San Francisco

GOLDEN GATE RAILROAD MUSEUM

Railway museum
Standard gauge

Description: The museum is dedicated to the preservation of vintage steam and diesel locomotives and passenger equipment. It owns and operates many locomotives related to the Bay Area railroads.

Schedule: Year round: weekends, 10 a.m. to 4 p.m. Call to confirm.

Admission/Fare: Adults, $3; Children, $2.

Locomotive/Rolling Stock: SP Baldwin P8 4-6-2 no. 2472; SF Belt Railway Alcos nos. 25 and 49; SF Belt Railway no. 4 0-6-0; SP nos. 3194 and 4450; assorted suburban commuter coaches; daylight cars, other passenger equipment.

Special Events: Railroad Retirees Reunion, last weekend in June. Garlic Train to Gilroy Garlic Festival, last weekend in July. Rent-a-Locomotive Program (learn to run steam and diesel locomotives), by appointment. Excursions, other special events as announced.

Nearby Attractions/Accommodations: San Francisco Zoo with restored steam train, cable cars, many parks and other attractions.

Location/Directions: Highway 101 to Cesar Chavez St. (Army St.) to Evans Ave. to Hunters Point Shipyard, Building 809. Need vehicle registration, proof of insurance, and picture ID for admission to shipyard.

Site Address: Bldg. 809, Hunter's Point Naval Shipyard, San Francisco, CA
Mailing Address: PO Box 881686, San Francisco, CA 94188-1686
Telephone: (415) 822-8728
Fax: (415) 822-8739
E-mail: info@ggrm.org
Internet: www.ggrm.org

**CALIFORNIA TROLLEY AND
RAILROAD CORPORATION**
Display
Standard gauge

KEN MIDDLEBROOK

Description: The non-profit CTRC is developing a railroad museum that will include several relocated railroad structures. Visitors can watch the extensive restoration of steam locomotive no. 2479. A nearby bay window caboose displays the organization's activities and current museum development. The CTRC, in partnership with the History Museums of San Jose, also operates the Trolley Barn in Kelley Park.

Schedule: Year round: Saturdays 9 a.m. to 4 p.m. and by appointment.

Admission/Fare: Donations appreciated.

Locomotives/Rolling Stock: 1923 Baldwin 4-6-2; Southern Pacific no. 2479; 1941 65-ton diesel; Kaiser cement no. 0002; two passenger cars; two cabooses.

Nearby Attractions/Accommodations: Kelley Park, Children's Discovery Museum, Tech Museum.

Location/Directions: Santa Clara County Fairgrounds, Tully Rd., two miles west of U.S. Highway 101.

Site Address: 344 Tully Rd., San Jose, CA
Mailing Address: PO Box 403, Campbell, CA 95009
Telephone: (408) 985-2479
Internet: www.ctrc.org

California, San Jose

Museum, layout, trolley car ride
Standard gauge

Description: The trolley car operates for rides on ½ mile of track.

Schedule: Year round, Saturdays and Sundays. Closed holidays.

Admission/Fare: Adults, $6; seniors, $5; youth, $4; under age 5 are free.

Locomotives/Rolling Stock: Trolley car no. 124 ex-San Jose; no. 143 Birney; 168 ex-Porto; horse car no. 7 ex-San Francisco.

Nearby Attractions/Accommodations: Many attractions within a radius of 40 miles.

Location/Directions: Located in Kelley Park, which is a short distance from Highways 280, 680, and 101. Take the no. 73 bus from downtown San Jose.

Site Address: 1650 Senter Rd., San Jose, CA
Mailing Address: 1650 Senter Rd., San Jose, CA 95112
Telephone: (408) 293-2276
Fax: (408) 287-2291

Description: Train Town is a 10-acre railroad park filled with thousands of trees, animals, lakes, bridges, tunnels, waterfalls, and historic replica structures. Fifteen-inch-gauge live-steam locomotives and diesel replicas pull long passenger trains through the park. Railroad shops and a complete miniature town, built to the same ¼ scale as the railroad. Full-sized rail equipment includes Santa Fe caboose no. 999648; Union Pacific caboose no. 25155; and Southern Pacific's first steel caboose, no. 11.

Schedule: June 1 through September 30: daily. Year round: Fridays through Sundays. Closed Christmas and Thanksgiving. Call or write for hours.

Admission/Fare: Adults, $3.75; seniors and children 15 months to 15, $2.75.

Locomotives/Rolling Stock: Replica of no. 5212, 1937 Alco J-1a 4-6-4, former New York Central; no. 1, 1960 Winton Engineering 2-6-0; SW 1200, 1992 custom locomotive; no. 401, 1975 gas-electric motor car.

Location/Directions: Sonoma is in wine country, less than an hour north of San Francisco. Train Town is on Broadway (Highway 12), one mile south of the Sonoma Town Square.

Site Address: 20264 Broadway, Highway 12, Sonoma, CA
Mailing Address: PO Box 656, Sonoma, CA 95476
Telephone: (707) 996-2559
Fax: (707) 966-6344
Internet: www.traintown.com

California, Suisun City

WESTERN RAILWAY MUSEUM
Museum
Standard gauge

BART NADEAU

Description: A 9.5-mile interurban round trip over re-electrified Sacramento Northern Railway interurban in rural Solano County. Additional electrification is in progress, planned to open in 2000 and 2001.

Schedule: Year round: weekends 11 a.m. to 5 p.m. July 4 through Labor Day: Wednesdays through Sundays 11 a.m. to 5 p.m.

Admission/Fare: Adults, $7; seniors (65 and over), $6; children age 14 and under, $4.

Locomotives/Rolling Stock: Wood interurbans: Peninsular Railway no. 52; Petaluma & Santa Rosa no. 63; Sacramento Northern no. 1005. Steel interurbans: Napa Valley no. 63; key units 182 and 187. Crandic III steel locomotives: CCT no. 7; SN nos. 652, 654; many streetcars; more.

Special Events: Special Montezuma Hills Trains in April, Pumpkin Patch Trains in October, Santa Trains in December.

Nearby Attractions/Accommodations: Marine World, Africa USA.

Location/Directions: On Highway 12. I-80, 12 miles from the Suisun/Rio Vista exit; or I-5, 23 miles from the Rio Vista/Fairfield exit.

     M arm TRAIN

Site Address: 5848 State Highway 12, Suisun City, CA
Mailing Address: 5848 State Highway 12, Suisun City, CA 94585
Telephone: (707) 374-2978
Fax: (707) 374-6742
Internet: www.wrm.org

ALAN FRANK

Description: A 13-mile round trip over the route of the original transcontinental railroad through the scenic canyon along Alameda Creek.

Schedule: Call or write for information.

Admission/Fare: Everyone over the age of 3, $7.

Locomotives/Rolling Stock: Ten steam locomotives; eight diesel locomotives; vintage rolling stock.

Special Events: Wildflower trains, April; Polar Express Christmas trains; call for information.

Nearby Attractions/Accommodations: Marine World, Six Flags Vallejo, Marriot's Great America Santa Clara, many parks and hiking trails.

Location/Directions: One mile west of I-680 between Pleasanton and Freemont, in southern Alameda County, California.

        arm

M   Radio frequency: 160.695

Site Address: Depot at Kilkare and Main St., Sunol, CA
Mailing Address: PO Box 2247, Niles Station, Fremont, CA 94536-0247
Telephone: (925) 862-9063
E-mail: jswofford@home.com or pla_ncry@ncry.org
Interenet: www.ncry.org

California, Woodland

RICHARD JONES

Description: A 28-mile, two-hour round trip between Woodland and West Sacramento over former Sacramento Northern Interurban track. Crosses 8,000-foot Fremont Trestle and offers views of the Sacramento River and scenic Yolo County farmlands and wetlands. The railroad also offers specials to Clarksburg.

Schedule: Spring Specials: March 18 and 25 and April 22 and 29. Regular season, May through Ocotber: weekends and major holidays. Charters are available year round.

Admission/Fare: Adults, $14; seniors, $12; children, $9; family $37; family pizza fare, $52; diesel cab ride, add $10; steam cab ride, add $25.

Locomotives/Rolling Stock: No. 1233, former Southern Pacific 0-6-0 switcher; nos. 131, 132, 133 GP-9 EMD diesels, former Southern Pacific.

Special Events: Great Train Robberies, Lunch Cruises, Pizza Trains; steam engine runs third weekend every month.

Nearby Attractions/Accommodations: Hayes Truck and Tractor Museum, Southern Pacific Depot (under restoration), Woodland Opera House.

Location/Directions: I-5 or Highway 113, Main St. exit, one mile west to E. Main and Thomas Streets. Twenty minutes north of Sacramento.

Radio Frequency: 160.260

Site Address: E. Main and Thomas, Woodland, CA
Mailing Address: 341 Industrial Way, Woodland, CA 95776
Telephone: (530) 666-9698
Fax: (530) 666-2919
E-mail: jasdavis@pacbell.net
Internet: www.ysrr.com

Colorado, Canon City

ROYAL GORGE ROUTE RAILROAD
Train ride
Standard gauge

RON HILL

Description: Experience the grandeur of traveling by train through the spectacular Royal Gorge on the Royal Gorge route. The train operates alongside the Arkansas River from Canon City, traveling over the famous "Hanging Bridge" where the canyon rim towers 1,000 feet above. This is a 24-mile, two-hour round trip ride.

Schedule: Mid-May through mid-October: three departures daily. Mid-October through mid-May: every Saturday and Sunday (except Christmas) at 12:30 p.m.

Admission/Fare: Round trip: adults, $26.95; children (3-12), $16.50; age 2 and under no charge if carried on lap.

Locomotives/Rolling Stock: FC&NW EMD F7A nos. 402, 403; VIA Rail CC&F passenger car nos. 3225, 5497, 5541, 5562, 5580, 5586, club car 650.

Nearby Attractions/Accommodations: Royal Gorge Bridge, rafting, horseback riding, fishing, camping.

Location/Directions: Located at the Santa Fe Depot, 401 Water St. (one block south on Third St. off Highway 50). Canon City is 45 miles southwest of Colorado Springs.

Site Address: 401 Water St., Canon City, Co 81212
Mailing Address: PO Box 859, Georgetown, CO 80444
Telephone: (303) 569-2403 and (888) RAILS-4-U
Fax: (303) 569-2894
E-mail: mark@royalgorgeroute.com
Internet: www.royalgorgeroute.com

DENVER & RIO GRANDE
U.S. NATIONAL PARK SERVICE
Display
36" gauge

NPS PHOTO BY LISA LYNCH

Description: At Cimarron, 20 miles east of Montrose, a historic narrow gauge railroad exhibit with engine no. 278, its coal tender, a boxcar, and a caboose sit on a stone and steel trestle one mile into the Cimarron River Canyon. At the Cimarron Visitor Center, a cattle car, sheep car, outfit car, hoist car, livestock corral, and interpretive panels illustrate early mountain railroad operations of the Denver & Rio Grande.

Schedule: Year round.

Admission/Fare: Free.

Locomotives/Rolling Stock: Locomotive no. 278, C-16 280, 1882/Baldwin Locomotive Work, Philadelphia, Pennsylvania; tender and D&RGW 0577 caboose.

Nearby Attractions/Accommodations: Black Canyon of the Gunnison National Park; Curecanti National Recreation area.

Location/Directions: Cimarron is 20 miles east of Montrose on U.S. Highway 50. The exhibit can be seen from the highway. Follow Curecanti National Recreation Area signs.

Site Address: U.S. Highway 59, Cimarron, CO
Mailing Address: Curecanti NRA, 102 Elk Creek, Gunnison, CO 81230
Telephone: (970) 249-1914 ext. 23 and (970) 641-2337 ext. 205
Fax: (970) 641-3127
E-mail: cure_vis_mail@nps.gov
Internet: www.nps.gov/cure

Colorado, Colorado Springs

PIKE'S PEAK HISTORICAL STREET RAILWAY FOUNDATION, INC.

Ride, museum, display
Standard gauge

Description: This interpretive center displays street railway history with a strong emphasis on Colorado Springs street railway history. We also offer a lecture on history and the return of streetcars to Colorado Springs. There are several trips over a 500-foot test track. The operation and history of the car are explained during the ride. You can visit a working car house (former Rock Island Engine House) built in 1888, see cars under restoration, and take a guided tour of the cars on hand and the shop area.

Schedule: Year round: Saturdays, 10 a.m. to 4 p.m., closed Thanksgiving, Christmas, and New Year's week. Other times please write or call. Group tours, please call ahead for special showing.

Admission/Fare: Adults, $2; children 12 and under, $1.

Locomotives/Rolling Stock: Nine Southeastern Pennsylvania Transportation Authority PCCs (Philadelphia) 1947; Los Angeles Railways PCC 1943; Colorado Springs double truck, 1901 Laclede Car Co.; Ft. Collins Municipal Railway, single truck, 1919 Birney, American Car Co.; Colorado Springs Double Truck, 1901 J. G. Brill Car Co.

Location/Directions: I-25, exit Fillmore St. east, south on Tremont St., west on Polk St. When forced to turn south, you will automatically be on Steel Dr. The site is located at the end of Steel Dr.

       arm M

Site Address: 2333 Steel Dr., Colorado Springs, CO
Mailing Address: PO Box 544, Colorado Springs, CO 80901
Telephone: (719) 475-9508 and (719) 471-2619
Fax: (719) 475-2814
Internet: www.colospringtrolleys.home.att.net.

Colorado, Cripple Creek

CRIPPLE CREEK AND VICTOR NARROW GAUGE RAILROAD

Train ride
Narrow gauge

Description: A 4-mile, 45-minute round trip over a portion of the old Midland Terminal Railroad. The train runs south out of Cripple Creek past the old MT wye, over a reconstructed trestle and past many historic mines to the deserted mining town of Anaconda.

Schedule: Mid-May through mid-October: daily, 9:30 a.m. to 5:30 p.m., departing every 45 minutes.

Admission/Fare: Adults, $9; seniors, $8; children 3-12, $5; under age 3 are free.

Locomotives/Rolling Stock: No. 1 1902 Orenstein & Koppel 0-4-4-0; no. 2 1936 Henschel 0-4-0; no. 3 1927 Porter 0-4-0T; no. 13 1946 Bagnall 0-4-0T.

Nearby Attractions: Cripple Creek District Museum, Mueller State Park, restaurants, lodging.

Location/Directions: From Colorado Springs west on Highway 24 to Highway 67 south to Cripple Creek. Trains leave from former Midland Terminal Railroad Bull Hill Depot.

Site Address: 520 E. Carr, Cripple Creek, CO
Mailing Address: PO Box 459, Cripple Creek, CO 80813
Telephone: (719) 689-2640
Fax: (719) 689-3256
Internet: ccvngrailroad@webjump.com

PLATTE VALLEY TROLLEY
Train ride
Standard gauge

WALTER WEART

Description: A 25-minute, 2½-mile round trip along the west bank of the South Platte River across from downtown Denver. One-hour Route 84 excursions are made to Lakewood at scheduled times.

Schedule: April, May, and September through November: weekdays, 11 a.m. to 3 p.m.; weekends, 11 a.m. to 4 p.m., every half hour. June through August: daily, 11 a.m. to 4 p.m., every half hour. Route 84 excursion: April through October: weekdays, 12 noon; weekends, 2 p.m.

Admission/Fare: Adults, $2; senior citizens and children, $1. Route 84 excursion: adults, $4; senior citizens, $3; children, $2. Group and charter rates available.

Locomotives/Rolling Stock: Trolleys: No. 1977, built 1986 by Gomaco Trolley Co., reproduction of open-air car built by J.G. Brill Company; no. 04, last Denver Tramway car to operate in revenue service, built by Woeber Carriage Works in 1911 as Denver & Intermountain 11, awaiting restoration. Santa Fe Caboose 999010 on display.

Nearby Attractions/Accommodations: Children's Museum, Denver Union Station, restored historic downtown Denver.

Location/Directions: West of downtown Denver with stops at 15th St., Fishback Park, and Children's Museum. Map available on website.

    M TRAIN

Site Address: Front entrance of Children's Museum just off I-25 exit 211
Mailing Address: PO Box 481211, Denver, CO 80248
Telephone: (303) 458-6255
E-mail: mail@denvertrolley.org
Internet: www.denvertrolley.org

Colorado, Denver

THE SKI TRAIN
Train ride
Standard gauge

Description: A 130-mile round trip on the historic Moffat Line between Denver and Winter Park Resort.

Schedule: Weekends, December through April. Saturdays only, June through August.

Admission/Fare: $40

Locomotives/Rolling Stock: Varies.

Location/Directions: Train departs from Denver Union Station.

Site Address: Denver Union Station, Denver, CO
Mailing Address: 555 17th St., Ste. 2400, Denver, CO 80202
Telephone: (303) 296-4754
Fax: (303) 298-8881
Internet: www.skitrain.com

GALLOPING GOOSE HISTORICAL SOCIETY OF DOLORES, INC.

Train ride, museum
36" gauge

Description: Train ride, operating in spring on the C&TS, in fall on the D&SNGRR.

Schedule: Tuesday through Saturday, 8:30 a.m. to 4:30 p.m.

Admission/Fare: Museum is free. Donations appreciated for Goose runs at museum.

Locomotives/Rolling Stock: Narrow gauge motor car built in 1933, fully restored in 1998 to railworthy standards.

Special Events: Escalante Days, hosted railroad runs on the C&TS and the D&SNGRR.

Nearby Attractions/Accommodations: Mesa Verde, McPhee Lake, Historic Rio Grande Southern B&B, numerous campgrounds located near museum, Anasazi Heritage Center, Ponderosa restaurant, Dolores Mountain Inn, Outpost Motel and RV Park, Cozy Comfort RV Park, Dolores River RV Park, Dolores River block away.

Location/Directions: In the town of Dolores, in Montezuma County, in southwest Colorado.

      M arm

Site Address: 421 Railroad Ave., Dolores, CO
Mailing Address: PO Box 297, Dolores, CO 81323
Telephone: (970) 882-7082
Fax: (970) 882-2224
Internet: doloresgallopinggoose5.org

Colorado, Durango

DURANGO & SILVERTON
NARROW GAUGE RAILROAD
Train ride, museum
Narrow gauge

ROBERT ROYEM

Description: Steam-powered narrow gauge railroad through the scenic San Juan mountains of Colorado. The 90-mile round trip begins in Durango and takes about 9 hours, with a 2¼-hour layover in Silverton for lunch.

Schedule: Silverton–May 5 through October 27: daily 8:15 a.m. Additional trains operate at 7:30, 9, and 9:45 a.m. later in the summer. Cascade Canyon Winter Trains–November 22 through May 4: 10 a.m. Closed Christmas. Call for information.

Admission/Fare: Silverton round trip–adults, $55-$60; children ages 5-11, $27-$30; parlor car (over 21), $100. Winter Cascade Canyon–adults, $42; children, $22; parlor car (over 21), $75. All tickets include admission to the D&SNGRR Museum. (fares subject to change)

Locomotives/Rolling Stock: Locomotives nos. 473, 476, 478, 480, 481, 482, 486, 493, 498, 42; B-2 Cinco Animas, B-3 Nomad, more.

Special Events: May 4, Narrow Gauge Days; May 26, Iron Horse Bicycle Classic; August 23-26, 3rd Annual Railfest; September 22, Photo Special; December Holiday Trains; Moonlight Trains.

Nearby Attractions/Accommodations: Many attractions, sports, lodging.

Location/Directions: At the intersection of U.S. Highways 550 and 160 in southwest Colorado. Depot is at the far south end of Main Ave.

Site Address: 479 Main Ave., Durango, CO
Mailing Address: 479 Main Ave., Durango, CO 81301
Telephone: (970) 247-2733
Fax: (970) 259-9349
Internet: www.durangotrain.com

FORT COLLINS
MUNICIPAL RAILWAY
Train ride
Standard gauge

Description: Trolley ride; 3-mile round trip through a residential section of Fort Collins.

Schedule: Weekends and holidays, May through September, noon to 5 p.m.

Admission/Fare: Adults, $1; seniors, $.75; children under 12, $.50.

Locomotives/Rolling Stock: 1919 Birney single-track streetcar, Ft. Collins car no. 21.

Location/Directions: From I-25: west on Mulberry St. (exit 269A-B) to Shields St.; right on Shields to Mountain; left on Mountain to Roosevelt; left on Roosevelt one block to loading platform.

 M

Site Address: Roosevelt, Fort Collins, CO
Mailing Address: PO Box 635, Fort Collins, CO 80522

GEORGETOWN LOOP RAILROAD

Train ride
Narrow gauge

RON RUHOFF

Description: A 6.5-mile, 70-minute round trip over the right-of-way of the former Colorado & Southern. The train travels through scenic, mountainous terrain and over the reconstructed Devil's Gate Viaduct, a spectacular 96-foot high curved trestle. The Georgetown Loop Railroad is a project of the Colorado Historical Society.

Schedule: Memorial Day weekend through first weekend in October: daily. Silver Plume (exit 226)–9:20 and 10:40 a.m., 12, 1:20, 2:40, and 4 p.m. Devil's Gate (exit 228)–10 and 11:20 a.m., 12:40, 2:00, and 3:20 p.m.

Admission/Fare: Adults, $14.50; children (5-15), $9.50. Mine tour–adults, $5; children, $3. Charters and groups rates available. Tickets must be purchased at Old Georgetown Station, 1106 Rose, Georgetown.

Locomotives/Rolling Stock: 1920 Baldwin 2-8-0 no. 44, 1921 Baldwin 2-8-0, both former International Railways of Central America; Lima 3-truck Shay, nos. 8, 12, 14; more.

Nearby Attractions/Accommodations: Old Georgetown Station, Historic Georgetown & Silver Plume

Location/Directions: I-70 exit 228 for Devil's Gate or exit 226 for Silver Plume. Tickets must be purchased at Old Georgetown Station, 1106 Rose, Georgetown.

Radio frequency: 161.115

Site Address: 1106 Rose St., Georgetown, CO
Mailing Address: PO Box 217, Georgetown, CO 80444
Telephone: (303) 569-2403 and (800) 691-4FUN
Fax: (303) 569-2873
E-mail: markg@gtownloop.com
Internet: www.georgetownloop.com

Colorado, Golden

BOB JENSEN

Description: An extensive collection of Colorado railroad memorabilia and over 70 historic cars and locomotives, both standard and narrow gauge. It is the home of the Denver HO Model Railroad Club and the Denver Garden Railway Society. "Galloping Goose" motorcars operate on selected weekends.

Schedule: Museum–June through August, daily, 9 a.m. to 6 p.m.; September through May, 9 a.m. to 5 p.m. Train–call, fax, or write for schedule. HO model railroad–first Thursday of every month, 7:30 to 9:30 p.m. Richardson Railroad Research Library–Tuesdays through Saturdays, 11 a.m. to 4 p.m.; Thursdays to 9 p.m.

Admission/Fare: Adults, $6; seniors, $5; children under age 16, $3; families (parents and children under age 16), $14.50.

Locomotives/Rolling Stock: Three RGS "Galloping Geese" motorcars; D&RGW Baldwin 1890 2-8-0 no. 683; Rio Grande Zephyr EMD F9s 5771 and 5762; Chicago Burlington & Quincy 4-8-4 no. 5629; Santa Fe Super Chief 1937 observation car Navajo; more.

Nearby Attractions/Accommodations: Coors Brewery, Buffalo Bill Museum, Blackhawk and Central City casinos.

Location/Directions: Twelve miles west of downtown Denver. I-70 westbound exit 265 or eastbound exit 266 to W. 44th Ave.

Site Address: 17155 W. 44th Ave., Golden, CO
Mailing Address: PO Box 10, Golden, CO 80402
Telephone: (303) 279-4591 and (800) 365-6263
Fax: (303) 279-4229
E-mail: mail@crrm.org
Internet: www.crrm.org

LEADVILLE, COLORADO & SOUTHERN RAILROAD

Train ride
Standard gauge

BARBARA MALLETTE, THE LEADVILLE PICTURE COMPANY

Description: The 22.5-mile, 2.5-hour train trip follows the headwaters of the Arkansas River to an elevation of 11,120 feet, over an old narrow-gauge roadbed converted to standard gauge in the 1940s. The train leaves from the restored 1894 railroad depot (formerly Colorado & Southern, built originally for the Denver, South Park & Pacific) in Leadville, the highest incorporated city in the United States. We offer enclosed, open, and sun cars along with snacks, souvenirs, and restrooms in the boxcars.

Schedule: May 26 through June 10, 1 p.m. June 11 through September 3, 10 a.m. and 2 p.m. September 4 through September 30, 1 p.m.

Admission/Fare: Adults, $22.50; children 4-12, $12.50; age 3 and under are free. Group rates available for 20 or more.

Locomotives/Rolling Stock: 1955 EMD GP9 no. 1714, former Burlington Northern; EMD GP-9 no. 1918.

Nearby Attractions/Accommodations: National Mining Museum, Matchless Mine, Leadville's historic mining district, Tabor Opera House, San Isabel National Forest.

Location/Directions: Located 25 miles south of I-70 on Highway 91, Copper Mountain exit. Travel south to Leadville, turn east on E. Seventh St. to depot.

Site Address: 327 E. Seventh St., Leadville, CO
Mailing Address: Box 916, Leadville, CO 80461
Telephone: (719) 486-3936
Fax: (719) 486-0671
E-mail: info@leadville.train
Internet: www.leadville-train.com

MANITOU & PIKE'S PEAK RAILWAY
Train ride
Standard gauge (cog)

Description: The M&PP, the highest cog railway in the world, was established in 1889 and has been operating continuously since 1891; it celebrated its centennial of passenger operations in June 1991. A 3¼-hour round trip takes passengers to the summit of Pike's Peak (elevation 14,110 feet) from Manitou Springs (elevation 6,575 feet) and includes a 40-minute stop at the summit.

Schedule: Daily; May through mid-June, September and October, 9:20 a.m. and 1:20 p.m.; mid-June through August, every 80 minutes, 8:00 a.m. to 5:20 p.m.

Admission/Fare: Adults, $23.50; children 5-11, $11; July through August 15: adults, $24.50; children, $12.50. Children under 3 free if held on lap. One-way tickets sold on space-available basis.

Locomotives/Rolling Stock: Twin-unit diesel hydraulic railcars and single-unit diesel electric railcars.

Special Events: Occasional steam-up of former M&PP steam locomotive no. 4, built by Baldwin in 1896.

Location/Directions: Six miles west of Colorado Springs.

Radio frequency: 161.55 and 160.23

Site Address: 515 Ruxton Ave., Manitou Springs, CO
Mailing Address: PO Box 351, Manitou Springs, CO 80829
Telephone: (719) 685-5401
Fax: (719) 685-9033
E-mail: cogtrain@iex.net
Internet: www.cograilway.com

Colorado, Morrison

TINY TOWN RAILROAD
Train ride
15" gauge

Description: Tiny Town Railroad, a ¼-scale live steam railroad, takes passengers from its full-sized station on a one-mile loop around Tiny Town. Started in 1915, Tiny Town is the oldest miniature town in the United States. It features more than 100 handcrafted, ⅙-sized structures laid out in the configuration of a real town, rural and mountain area.

Schedule: Memorial Day through Labor Day: daily. May, September, and October: weekends. 10 a.m. to 5 p.m. Train runs continuously.

Admission/Fare: Display–adults, $3; children 3-12, $2; children under age three are free. Train–$1.

Locomotives/Rolling Stock: 1970 standard-gauge 4-6-2 "Occasional Rose" propane-fired; 1970 narrow-gauge 2-6-0 "Cinderbell" coal-fired; 1954 F-unit "Molly," gas-powered; 1952 A- and B-unit "Betsy" gas-powered. Open amusement-park-style cars, propane tank car and caboose.

Nearby Attractions/Accommodations: Red Rocks Park and Dinosaur Ridge.

Location/Directions: Approximately 30 minutes southwest of Denver, off Highway 285.

Site Address: 6249 S. Turkey Creek Rd., Morrison, CO
Mailing Address: 6249 S. Turkey Creek Rd., Morrison, CO 80465
Telephone: (303) 697-6829

PUEBLO LOCOMOTIVE & RAIL HISTORICAL SOCIETY INC., PUEBLO RAILWAY MUSEUM

Museum

Standard and narrow gauge

RICHARD M. HOLMES

Description: Static displays, museum car, and gift shop. Take a motor car or hi-rail ride on the old Pueblo Union Depot passenger tracks on selected weekends. Restoration work is ongoing on former ATSF steam locomotive no. 2912. There is fantastic trainwatching on the BNSF and UP main, adjacent to the museum.

Schedule: Museum–Memorial Day through mid-October: weekends or by appointment. Static Displays–year round: daily. Hours are 9:30 a.m. to 4 p.m.

Admission/Fare: Free, donations appreciated.

Locomotives/Rolling Stock: ATSF Baldwin 4-8-4 Northern no. 2912; Colorado Fuel and Iron, GE 25-ton diesel no. 11; Colorado & Southern caboose no. 10538; Colorado & Wyoming locomotive simulator training car no. 100; Denver & Rio Grande Western caboose no. 01432; Southern Pacific bay window caboose nos. 4773, 4707; more.

Special Events: Open House, weekend following Memorial Day. Pueblo Railfest, October 6-7.

Nearby Attractions/Accommodations: Lake Pueblo State Park, Pueblo Weisbrod Aircraft Museum, Union Ave. Historic District.

Location/Directions: I-25, exit First St. West to Union Ave., south to "B" St., right turn on "B." Museum is located behind and to the west of the depot. Parking available behind the depot.

Site Address: 200 W. "B" St., Pueblo, CO
Mailing Address: PO Box 322, Pueblo, CO 81002
Telephone: (719) 250-0381
Fax: (719) 564-3460
E-mail: valleystation@aol.com
Internet: www.pueblorail.com

Connecticut, Danbury

DANBURY RAILWAY MUSEUM
Train ride, museum, displays
Standard gauge

RON FREITAG

Description: Museum with over 40 pieces of equipment representing ten different railroads. We offer vintage train rides in the yard to the only operable turntable in Connecticut. There is a gift shop, library (by appointment), and displays in the restored 1903 train station seen in Alfred Hitchcock's film "Strangers on a Train."

Schedule: Train rides, weekends April 21 through November 4. Museum open January through March, Wednesday through Saturday 10 a.m. to 4 p.m., Sunday 12 noon to 4 p.m. April through December, 10 a.m. to 5 p.m., Sunday 12 noon to 5 p.m.

Admission/Fare: Adults, $4; children 5-15, $2.

Locomotives/Rolling Stock: NH 0673 Alco RS-1; B&M 1455 Alco 2-6-0; NYC 4096 EMD E9; NYC 1390 Alco FPA; LIRR 617 (NH 0428) Alco FA; NH 32 Budd RDC-1; GCT-1 dual-ended crane; caboose NH C-627 & PC 23662; many freight and passenger cars.

Special Events: Easter Bunny Trains, April 7, 8, 13, and 14; Railfair, May 6-7; Haunted Railyard, Oct. 26-28; Holiday Express to New York City, December 8; Santa Trains, December 15, 16, 22, and 23.

Nearby Attractions/Accommodations: Railroad Museum of New England, Valley Railroad, Military Museum, many restaurants.

Location/Directions: I-84 exit 5, right on Main St., left on White St.

Site Address: 120 White St., Danbury, CT
Mailing Address: PO Box 90, Danbury, CT 06813-0090
Telephone: (203) 778-8337
Fax: (203) 778-1836
Internet: www.danbury.org/drm

SHORE LINE TROLLEY MUSEUM
Museum
Standard gauge

G. BOUCHER

Description: The Shore Line Trolley Museum operates the sole remaining segment of the historic 100-year-old Branford Electric Railway. The 3-mile round trip passes woods, salt marshes, and meadows along the scenic Connecticut shore.

Schedule: Memorial Day through Labor Day: daily. May, September, and October: weekends and holidays. April and November: Sundays. Hours 10:30 a.m. to 4:30 p.m. Cars depart every 30 minutes.

Admission/Fare: Unlimited rides and guided tours–adults, $5; seniors, $4; children 2-11, $2; under age 2 are free.

Locomotives/Rolling Stock: Connecticut Co. suburban no. 775; Montreal no. 2001; Johnstown no. 357; Brooklyn (New York) convertible no. 4573; Third Avenue no. 629.

Special Events: Santa Days, Thanksgiving to Christmas on weekends.

Nearby Attractions/Accommodations: Holiday Inn Express, East Haven. Yale University. Foxwoods Casino.

Location/Directions: I-95 exits 51 north or 52 south and follow signs.

*Coupon available, see coupon section.

Site Address: 17 River St., East Haven, CT
Mailing Address: 17 River St., East Haven, CT 06512-2519
Telephone: (203) 467-6927 and (203) 467-7635 group sales
Fax: (203) 467-7635
E-mail: BERASLTM@aol.com
Internet: www.bera.org

CONNECTICUT TROLLEY MUSEUM
Museum
Standard gauge

SCOTT R. BECKER

Description: A 1.5-mile trolley ride through the countryside.

Schedule: April through Memorial Day: Saturday, 10 a.m. to 5 p.m. and Sunday, 12 noon to 5 p.m. Memorial Day through Labor Day: Wednesday through Saturday, 10 a.m. to 5 p.m.; Labor Day through December: Saturday, 10 a.m. to 5 p.m., and Sunday, 12 noon to 5 p.m. Closed Thanksgiving, Christmas Eve, and Christmas Day.

Admission/Fare: Adults, $6; seniors (62+), $5; children ages 5-12, $3; under age 5 are free. Group rates are available.

Trolleys: Nos. 65, 355, 840, and 1326, former Connecticut Co.; nos. 4, 2056, and 2600, former Montreal Trainways; no. 1850, former Rio de Janeiro; more.

Special Events: Halloween program: Little Pumpkin Patch. Trolley rides, games, each child receives a pumpkin. Last three weekends in October. Winterfest: 1.5-mile trolley ride through tunnel of lights. Day after Thanksgiving through December, 6 to 9 p.m.

Location/Directions: Between Hartford, Connecticut, and Springfield, Massachusetts. I-91, exit 45, ¾ mile east on Route 140.

*Coupon available, see coupon section.

Site Address: 58 North Rd. (Rt. 140), East Windsor, CT
Mailing Address: PO Box 360, East Windsor, CT 06088-0360
Telephone: (860) 627-6540
Fax: (860) 627-6510
Internet: www.ceraonline.org

ESSEX STEAM TRAIN AND RIVERBOAT RIDE
Train ride, display
Standard gauge

Description: A 1.5-hour excursion through the scenic Connecticut River valley with views of the river and wetlands. The passenger trains consist of restored 1920s-era coaches.

Schedule: Mid-June through Labor Day, daily. May through mid-June, September, and October: Wednesday through Sunday.

Admission/Fare: Train and boat: adults, $16.50; children 3-11, $8.50. Train only: adults, $10.50; children 3-11, $5.50; under age 3 free. Parlor car: extra fare. Open car and caboose (when available): extra fare. Senior discounts. Group rates available. All tickets sold at Essex station only. Essex Clipper Dinner Train: $49.95 per person, gratuity and beverages extra.

Special Events: "A Day Out With Thomas," Easter Eggspress, North Pole Express, Eagle Festival Special, Caboose weekends, Your Hand on the Throttle, Hot Steamed Music Festival, Tuba Concern, and more.

Locomotives/Rolling Stock: No. 40, Alco 2-8-2, No. 97, Alco 2-8-0; more.

Nearby Attractions/Accommodations: Connecticut River Museum, Mystic Seaport, Mystic Aquarium, casinos.

Location/Directions: From New York and Boston, take I-95 to exit 69 and go north on State Route 9 to exit 3. From Hartford, take I-91 south to exit 22S and go south on State Route 9 to exit 3. Follow signs to Essex Steam Train.

Site Address: Near junction of State Routes 9 (exit 3) and 154 in Essex, CT
Mailing Address: PO Box 452, Essex, CT 06426
Telephone: (860) 767-0103
Fax: (860) 767-0104
Internet: www.valleyrr.com

**CONNECTICUT ANTIQUE
MACHINERY ASSOCIATION, INC.**
Museum
36" gauge

Description: Exhibits show the development of the country's agricultural and industrial technology from the mid-1800s to the present, including a collection of large stationary steam engines in the Industrial Hall; a display of large gas engines; a tractor and farm-implement display in the large tractor barn; and the reconstructed Cream Hill Agricultural School buildings. New this year is the mining museum.

Schedule: Memorial Day through Labor Day: weekends and by appointment.

Admission/Fare: Adults, $4; children 5-12, $2; under age 5 are free.

Locomotives/Rolling Stock: No. 4 1908 Porter 2-8-0, former Argent Lumber Co.; no. 16 1921 Plymouth D1, former Hutton Brick Co.; no. 18 1917 Vulcan limited Clearance 0-4-0t, former American Steel & Wire Co.; no. 5 Baldwin 2-4-2, former Hawaii Railway Co.; no. 111 caboose, former Tionesta Valley Railway; no. 6 coach, former Waynesburg & Washington.

Special Events: Spring Gas Up, May 5, 2001. Fall Festival, September 29-30, 2001.

Nearby Attractions/Accommodations: Sloane-Stanley Museum.

Location/Directions: One mile north of village on Route 7 adjacent to Sloane-Stanley Museum, Housatonic Railroad.

          M

Site Address: Kent, CT
Mailing Address: PO Box 1467, New Milford, CT 06776
Telephone: (860) 927-0050
Internet: www.ctamachinery.com

HOWARD PINCUS

Description: A 17.5-mile round trip over a former New Haven Railroad line, from the 1881 Thomaston Station along the scenic Naugatuck River and past 100-year old New England brass mills, on to the face of the Thomaston Dam. The original Naugatuck Railroad opened this route in 1849. The Naugatuck Railroad is operated by the not-for-profit Railroad Museum of New England.

Schedule: Starting May 26, weekends, 1 and 3 p.m. Earlier in May, operation for groups of 45 or more. During the fall: 11 a.m., 1 and 3 p.m.

Admission/Fare: Adults, $9.95; seniors, $8.95; children 3-12, $6.95. Group rates and charters available.

Locomotives/Rolling Stock: New Haven RS-3 no. 529; New Haven U25B no. 2525; Naugatuck GP-9 no. 1732; Canadian National open window heavyweight coaches from 1920s.

Special Events: Occasional excursions over entire 19.6-mile route between Waterbury and Torrington. Also, engineer-for-an-hour program.

Nearby Attractions/Accommodations: Amusement parks, vineyards, state parks.

Location/Directions: I-84, exit 20 to north on Route 8, exit 38 Thomaston.

Site Address: E. Main St., Thomaston, CT
Mailing Address: PO Box 400, Thomaston, CT 06787-0400
Telephone: (860) 283-RAIL
Fax: (203) 269-3364
E-mail: rrexc@snet.net
Internet: www.rmne.org

**CONNECTICUT EASTERN
RAILROAD MUSEUM**
Museum, display
Standard gauge

ROBERT A. LA MAY

Description: The museum is gradually restoring trackage (approximately 1.2 miles) and a small yard on the New Haven Railroad (Air Line). Columbia Junction six-stall roundhouse and turntable are being restored, complete with wye track. Smaller buildings and rolling stock are also being restored.

Schedule: May through October: Saturdays only 9 a.m. to 2 p.m.; other days by appointment only.

Admission/Fare: $3; seniors, $2; children 12 and under are free.

Locomotives/Rolling Stock: Alco S-4 K&L no. 1, former CV no. 8081; GE 44-ton Valley Railroad no. 0800, former LIRR; GE 25-ton Northeast Utilities; Alco RS-11 Lamoille Valley no. 3608, former CV no. 3608. New Haven coaches nos. 8673 and 8695; NH wooden boxcar no. 171568; other freight and passenger cars.

Special Events: April and September: train shows with open house at the museum.

Nearby Attractions/Accommodations: Windham Textile and History Museum, Jillson House Museum, bed and breakfasts.

Location/Directions: Follow Main St. (Route 66) in Willimantic to Bridge St. (Route 32 south). Cross railroad tracks, turn right at museum sign and continue to museum.

Site Address: 55 Bridge St. (Rt. 32), Willimantic, CT
Mailing Address: PO Box 665, Willimantic, CT 06226
Telephone: (860) 228-9671
E-mail: ctrailroad@iname.com
Internet: http://users.downcity.net/tomc

SMITHSONIAN INSTITUTION
NATIONAL MUSEUM OF AMERICAN HISTORY
Museum, display

Description: The Smithsonian's Railroad Hall symbolizes the achievements of railroads and rail transit in the United States from the 1820s to about 1965. On display are original pieces of the "Stourbridge Lion" and the "DeWitt Clinton," a complete Winton 201-A engine from the *Pioneer Zephyr,* a series of ½-inch-scale models showing locomotive development from the earliest steam engine to present-day diesels, and many other exhibits. Information leaflet no. 455, available on request, describes the railroad exhibits. (Extensive research inquiries cannot be answered.)

Schedule: Year round: daily, 10 a.m. to 5:30 p.m. Closed Christmas and New Year's.

Admission/Fare: Free.

Locomotives/Rolling Stock: No. 1401, 1926 Alco 4-6-2, former Southern Railway; "John Bull" 1831 Stephenson 4-2-0, former Camden & Amboy Railroad. "No. 3" 1836 coach, former Camden & Amboy Railroad; "Jupiter," 1876 Baldwin narrow gauge 4-4-0.

   arm

Site Address: 12th St. and Constitution Ave., Washington, D.C.
Mailing Address: National Museum of American History, Washington, D.C. 20560

Delaware, Wilmington

WILMINGTON & WESTERN RAILROAD
Train ride, dinner train
Standard gauge

MIKE CIOSEK

Description: A ten-mile, 1¼-hour round trip over a portion of former Baltimore & Ohio Landenberg Branch from Greenbank Station to Mt. Cuba. Occasional trips to Yorklyn and Hockessin are also offered.

Schedule: April through December: Saturdays and/or Sundays, one- and two-hour excursions along the Red Clay Valley. Call or write for timetable.

Admission/Fare: Varies, please call or write for information. Caboose rentals, group rates, and private charters are available.

Locomotives/Rolling Stock: Two SW-1 EMD switchers; 1909 Alco steam 4-4-0; 1907 Baldwin 0-6-0; 1910 Canadian Locomotive Co. 2-6-0; 1929 PRR railcar.

Special Events: Easter Bunny Special, Santa Claus Express, Dinner and/or Murder Mystery Trains, Civil War Weekend.

Nearby Attractions/Accommodations: Longwood Gardens, Hagley Museum, Kalmar Nyckel, Winterthur Museum.

Location/Directions: I-95, exit 5, follow Route 141 north to Route 2 west, then follow Route 41 north. Greenbank Station is on Route 41 just north of Route 2, 4 miles southwest of Wilmington

*Coupon available, see coupon section.

Radio frequency: 160.755

Site Address: 2201 Newport-Gap Pike, Route 41, Wilmington, DE
Mailing Address: PO Box 5787, Wilmington, DE 19808
Telephone: (302) 998-1930
Fax: (302) 998-7408
E-mail: schedule@wwrr.com
Internet: www.wwrr.com

FORT MYERS HISTORICAL MUSEUM
Museum

Description: A historical museum outlining the history of the Fort Myers area from prehistoric times to the present day. It is housed in an original ACL passenger depot with a 1929 private Pullman car as an outside exhibit.

Schedule: Year round: Tuesdays through Saturdays, 9 a.m. to 4 p.m.

Admission/Fare: Adults, $6; seniors, $5.50; children age 12 and under, $3.

Locomotives/Rolling Stock: Pullman Standard Car & Manufacturing Co. 1929/30 "Esperanza" no. 6242

Nearby Attractions/Accommodations: Thomas A. Edison winter home, baseball spring training site for Boston Red Sox and Minnesota Twins, Sanibel Island, beaches.

Location/Directions: I-75, exit 23, drive 5 miles west to downtown Ft. Myers. Peck St. is one block south of Dr. Martin Luther King Jr. Blvd.

Site Address: 2300 Peck St., Ft. Myers, FL 33901
Mailing Address: 2300 Peck St., Ft. Myers, FL 33901
Telephone: (941) 332-5955
Fax: (941) 332-6637

**RAILROAD MUSEUM'S
TRAIN VILLAGE**
*Train ride
7½" gauge*

JEANNE HICKAM

Description: A 15-minute, 1⅛-mile ride in county park with tunnel, bridges, gardens, and miniature villages along the right-of-way.

Schedule: Year round: daily, Mondays through Fridays, 10 a.m. to 2 p.m. Saturdays and holidays, 10 a.m. to 4 p.m. Sundays, 12 to 4 p.m. Weekends only August and September. Closed Christmas.

Admission/Fare: $2.50; children under age 5, $.50. Park charges for parking–$.75 per hour with $3 maximum.

Locomotives/Rolling Stock: FP7A diesels nos. 1994, 1996; 7½" gauge 0-6-0 no. 143 gasoline with steam sound; GP50 diesel with three to five riding cars; 1905 Baldwin 0-6-0 no. 143, former Atlantic Coast Line display (awaiting restoration).

Special Events: Easter Bunny Express–Good Friday, Saturday, Easter Sunday. Halloween Express and Holiday Express with night rides (extra fare). Call or write for information.

Nearby Attractions/Accommodations: Shell Factory, Edison and Ford winter estates, many motels, hotels, and campgrounds.

Location/Directions: Located in Lakes Park/Lee County Park, which is ⅛ mile west of route 41 (Cleveland Ave.) at the south end of Fort Myers.

*Coupon available, see coupon section.

       M

Site Address: 7330 Gladiolus Dr., Fort Myers, FL
Mailing Address: PO Box 7372, Fort Myers, FL 33911-7372
Telephone: (941) 481-7565 or (941) 574-4574

SEMINOLE GULF RAILWAY
Train ride, dinner train
Standard gauge

Description: A working railroad with daytime excursion trains, which can be boarded at Colonial Station for a 1½-hour round trip or for trips that include the scenic Caloosahatchee River bridge crossing. Dinner theater trains depart for a 3½-hour round trip from Colonial Station in Fort Myers. They stop on the Caloosahatchee Bridge for the scenic view before continuing the ride north. Special holiday trains include the Rail/Boat Christmas train to Punta Gorda featuring a tour by boat, viewing decorated homes and boats along the canals of Punta Gorda Isles.

Schedule: Excursion trains–year round: Wednesdays and weekends. Dinner train theater–Wednesday through Saturday, 6:30 p.m.; Sunday, 5:30 p.m. with choice of two Murder Mystery Shows, five-course dinner prepared on board.

Admission/Fare: Excursion train–adults, $7 and up; children 3-12, $4 and up. Dinner train theater, $44.98 and up.

Locomotives/Rolling Stock: Eight GP9s; three RDCs; four dining cars; Sanibel and Captiva, former CN, Marco, and Gasparillo; kitchen; more.

Special Events: Easter, Mother's Day, Father's Day, Thanksgiving, Christmas rail/boat dinner trains in December and New Year's Eve party dinner trip.

Location/Directions: Excursion and dinner trains depart from Colonial Station near the Colonial Blvd. (State Route 884) and Metro Parkway intersection in Fort Myers, 3 miles west of I-75 exit 22.

Site Address: Fort Myers, FL
Mailing Address: 4410 Centerpointe Dr., Ste. 207, Fort Myers, FL 33916
Telephone: (941) 275-8487, (800) SEM-GULF, and (800) 736-4853
Fax: (941) 275-0581
E-mail: appelberg@semgulf.com
Internet: www.semgulf.com

Florida, Miami　　　　　　**GOLD COAST RAILROAD MUSEUM**
Train ride, museum, display, layout
24" gauge

Description: The museum has over 30 pieces of rolling stock on display and hundreds of items of railroad memorabilia. Self-guided tours are available. On weekends we offer a 24" gauge train ride lasting about 20 minutes.

Schedule: Year round: Monday through Friday 11 a.m. to 3 p.m., weekends 11 a.m. to 4 p.m. Train ride: 1 to 3 p.m.

Admission/Fare: Adults, $5; children (3-12), $3; under 3 free.
Train ride: $2 each person

Locomotives/Rolling Stock: Nos. 113 and 153 Florida East Coast steam engines; "Ferdinand Magellan," also known as U.S. Presidential Car no. 1, the only Pullman car ever custom-built for the president of the U.S.; the "Silver Crescent," built in 1948 for the *California Zephyr*.

Nearby Attractions: Miami-Dade Metro Zoo; Penny Thompson Campgrounds (on same property); Weeks Air Museum; Coral Castle; Monkey Jungle; Everglades National Park; Deering Estate, etc., within 15 miles; restaurants, hotels, etc.

Location/Directions: Florida Turnpike to SW 152nd St. exit, follow the signs to Metro Zoo. U.S. Route 1 to SW 152nd St., take a right turn and follow the signs to Metro Zoo.

Site Address: 12450 SW 152nd St., Miami, FL
Mailing Address: 12450 SW 152nd St., Miami, FL 33177
Telephone: (305) 253-0063, (888) 60-TRAIN
Fax: (305) 233-4641
E-mail: lclltd@gate.net
Internet: www.goldcoast-railroad.org

MOUNT DORA, TAVARES & EUSTIS RAILROAD
Train ride
Standard gauge

Description: One-hour train ride on 1920s style "Doodlebug" motor car. As of July 2000, 90-minute ride on 1913 Baldwin 2-6-2 steam train with two coaches, combine, and open-air gondola car "Mount Dora Cannonball."

Schedule: June through October, trains run Thursday through Sunday; November through May, seven days a week. First train, 11 a.m.; last train, 3:30 p.m.

Admission/Fare: Doodlebug–adults, $8.50; seniors, $7.50; children (under 12), $5.50. Steam–adults, $16; seniors, $15; children (under 12), $8.

Locomotives/Rolling Stock: 1926 Edwards Railway Motor Car Company "Doodlebug" (steam operation planned for the future).

Special Events: Art fair, mid-November. Craft fair, antique car show, antique boat show.

Nearby Attractions/Accommodations: Antique shopping, restaurants, open-air cafes, Disney World, Universal Studios.

Location/Directions: Located 30 minutes north of Orlando, Highway 441 north, left on Donnell St., on the corner of Alexander St. and Third Ave.

Site Address: 150 W. Third Ave., Mount Dora, FL
Mailing Address: PO Box 641, Mount Dora, FL 32756
Telephone: (352) 383-4368 and (800) 625-4307
Fax: (352) 383-9360
Internet: www.doradoodlebug.com

Florida, Palm Beach
THE FLAGLER MUSEUM
Museum

© FLAGLER MUSEUM

Description: Whitehall, a 55-room Gilded Age estate and National Historical Landmark, was the winter home of Henry M. Flagler, developer of the Florida East Coast Railway that linked the east coast of Florida. Experience life during America's Gilded Age through the eyes of one of its most important citizens, Henry Flagler. Flagler, with partners John D. Rockefeller and Samuel Andrews, founded Standard Oil. Displays and exhibits focus on the contributions Flagler made to the state of Florida by building the Florida East Coast Railway and developing tourism and agriculture as the state's major industries.

Schedule: Year round: Tuesdays through Saturdays, 10 a.m. to 5 p.m. Sundays, noon to 5 p.m. Closed Thanksgiving, Christmas Day, and New Year's Day.

Admission/Fare: Adults, $8; children 6-12, $3. Free on Founders Day.

Locomotives/Rolling Stock: FEC Car no. 91, Henry Flagler's private railcar, built in 1886.

Special Events: Whitehall Lecture Series, February. Founders Day, June 5. Holiday tours, December.

Nearby Attractions/Accommodations: Museums, zoo, Atlantic Ocean.

Location/Directions: I-95 to exit 52 (Okeechobee Blvd.). Travel 3 miles across Intracoastal Waterway, left on Cocoanut Row. Museum is ¾ mile on left.

Site Address: One Whitehall Way, Palm Beach, FL
Mailing Address: PO Box 969, Palm Beach, FL 33480
Telephone: (561) 655-2833
Fax: (561) 655-2826
E-mail: flagler@emi.net
Internet: www.flagler.org

**FLORIDA GULF COAST
RAILROAD MUSEUM, INC.**
Train ride
Standard gauge

GLENN MILEY

Description: A 1½-hour train ride with some museum displays of railroad artifacts.

Schedule: Year round, Saturdays and Sundays, rain or shine. January through April: Saturdays, 11 a.m., 1 and 3 p.m. and Sundays, 1 and 3 p.m. May through December: Saturdays, 11 a.m. and 1 p.m. and Sundays, 1 and 3 p.m.

Admission/Fare: Adults, $10; children ages 3-11, $6; under 3 are free. Cab rides: adults, $20; children, $16.

Locomotives/Rolling Stock: GP7 no. 1835; RS3 No. 1633; GE 44-ton no. 100; more.

Special Events: Civil War weekends, Hole-in-the-Head Gang train robberies at various times of the year (usually fall and winter), caboose charters available for birthday parties.

Nearby Attractions/Accommodations: J.P. Igloos, Pizza & Pipes, Little Manatee River State Recreational area, Gamble Mansion, Tampa Union Station (Amtrak).

Location/Directions: I-75 exit 45, east 5 miles to U.S. 301, south ¼ mile to 83rd St. E., left into parking.

*Coupon available, see coupon section.

        Tampa

Site Address: 12210 83 St. E., Parrish, FL
Mailing Address: PO Box 355, Parrish, FL 34219
Telephone: (941) 365-5738 and (877) 869-0800
Fax: (941) 917-0081
E-mail: FGCRRM@aol.com
Internet: www.fgcrrm.org

Description: The world's foremost tropical showplace includes Cypress Junction, where ten high-speed model trains tour tiny replicas of U.S. landmarks–Miami, New Orleans, Mt. Rushmore–on 1,100 feet of track. An outdoor garden railway spanning 5,000 square feet at Cypress Gardens is included.

Schedule: Year round: daily, 10:30 a.m. to 5 p.m. Extended hours during special seasons.

Admission/Fare: Entrance price to theme park: adults, $31.95 plus tax; children (6-12), $14.95 plus tax; kids free. Each single-day ticket purchaser may bring in one child free.

Locomotives/Rolling Stock: Santa Fe no. 3571; B&O or Chessie System BTO no. 3597; Seaboard System no. 6378; Lehigh Valley no. 211; Atlantic Coast Line C-O no. 47124.

Nearby Attractions/Accommodations: Bok Tower, Fantasy of Flight, and all Orlando attractions.

Location/Directions: I-4 to U.S. 27 south to 540 west. Located in central Florida.

Site Address: 2641 S. Lake Summit, Winter Haven, FL
Mailing Address: PO Box 1, Cypress Gardens, FL 33884
Telephone: (863) 324-2111 and (800) 282-2123
Fax: (863) 324-7946
E-mail: rderidder@cypressgardens.com
Internet: www.cypressgardens.com

DICK HILLMAN

Description: A 3-hour round trip (includes layover) along the Toccoa River to McCaysville, Georgia, on the old L&N Hook and Eye Division. There is a large gift shop and tourist information area.

Schedule: April through mid-December: Friday, Saturday, and Sunday departures.

Admission/Fare: Adults, $26; children, $15.

Locomotives/Rolling Stock: Various diesel locomotives available to us through our parent company, Georgia Northeastern Railroad. GP7 no. 2097; GP9 no. 6576; GP10 no. 7529; GP10 no. 7562; GP18 no. 8704; GP18 no. 8705; GP20 no. 316; GP20 no. 4125; SW1 no. 77 1947; NW1 no. 81 1948.

Nearby Attractions/Accommodations: Amicalola Falls State Park; Helen, Georgia (alpine village), surrounded by national forests, hiking and biking trails; Ocoee Whitewater Center.

Location/Directions: Ninety miles north of Atlanta, Georgia and 85 miles southeast of Chattanooga, Tennessee.

Site Address: 241 Depot St., Blue Ridge, GA
Mailing Address: 241 Depot St., Blue Ridge, GA, 30513
Telephone: (706) 632-9833
Fax: (706) 258-2756
Internet: www.brscenic.com

SOUTHEASTERN RAILWAY MUSEUM
Train ride, display
Standard gauge

Description: Visitors meet rail history "hands on" through the display of over 90 pieces of retired railway rolling stock, including a World War II troop kitchen, railway post office, the 1911 Pullman "Superb" used by President Warren Harding, a modern office car, vintage steam locomotives, restored wooden cabooses. Short on-site train ride aboard vintage cabooses.

Schedule: April through November: Saturdays 9 a.m. to 5 p.m. Sundays, on third full weekend, 12 to 5 p.m. Train rides included with admission. Exhibits only–December through March: Saturdays, 9 a.m. to 5 p.m.

Admission/Fare: Adults, $6; seniors and children 2-12, $4; under age 2 are free.

Locomotives/Rolling Stock: 1950 and 1941 HRT GE 44-ton nos. 2 and 5; 1943 Georgia Power Porter 0-6-0T no. 97; 1954 CRR caboose no. 1064; SOU caboose XC7871; SCL caboose no. 01077.

Location/Directions: I-85 NW of Atlanta to west on exit 40 (Pleasant Hill Rd.) for 3.5 miles to U.S. 23 (Buford Highway). North ¼ mile to Peachtree Rd., turn west to museum entrance.

Site Address: 3595 Peachtree Rd., Duluth, GA
Mailing Address: PO Box 1267, Duluth, GA 30096
Telephone: (770) 476-2013
Fax: (770) 908-8322
E-mail: admin@srmduluth.org
Internet: www.srmduluth.org

Description: The Andrews Raid and the Great Locomotive Chase, one of the unusual episodes of the Civil War, has been much publicized over the years. The "General," now one of the most famous locomotives in American history, is enshrined in a museum within 100 yards of the spot where it was stolen on April 12, 1862. The old engine, still operable, last ran in 1962. The Kennesaw Civil War Museum was officially opened on April 12, 1972, 110 years after the historic seizure of the "General."

Schedule: April through September: Mondays through Saturdays, 9:30 a.m. to 5:30 p.m. and Sundays, 12 to 5:30 p.m. October through March: Monday through Saturdays, 10 a.m. to 4 p.m. and Sundays, 12 to 4 p.m.

Admission/Fare: Adults, $3; seniors, $2.50; children 7-15, $1.50; age 6 and under are free.

Locomotives/Rolling Stock: Rodgers Ketchum & Grosvenor 4-4-0 no. 3; Western & Atlantic "General."

Special Events: Big Shanty Festival, April. Kennesaw Antiques Fair.

Nearby Attractions/Accommodations: Kennesaw Mountain Park; more.

Location/Directions: I-75 north (from Atlanta) exit 273 (Wade Green Rd.), west 2.3 miles. Museum is on right.

*Coupon available, see coupon section.

      M

Site Address: 2829 Cherokee St., Kennesaw, GA
Mailing Address: 2829 Cherokee St., Kennesaw, GA 30144
Telephone: (770) 427-2117 and (800) 742-6897
Fax: (770) 429-4538
E-mail: kcwm@juno.com
Internet: www.thegeneral.org

Georgia, Savannah

ROUNDHOUSE RAILROAD
MUSEUM
Museum

PAINTING BY T.J. SCYPINSKI

Description: Antebellum five-acre site with 11 buildings, operational turntable, model railroad, 125-foot smokestack, and the oldest portable steam engine in the U.S.

Schedule: Seven days a week, 10 a.m. to 4 p.m. Closed Thanksgiving, Christmas, and New Year's Day.

Admission/Fare: Adults, $3.25; seniors (55), students, and military, $2.50; children 5 and under are free

Locomotives/rolling stock: GP35 no. 2715; Baldwin no. 15; Baldwin no. 8 "Maude"; Baldwin no. 223; Vulcan, Porter, Columbus office car, two Savannah Birney safety cars; Central of Georgia caboose no. X91

Special Events: Night in Old Savannah Blues and Barbecue, April, annual fundraiser.

Nearby Attractions/Accommodations: Eighth Air Force Museum, Ships of the Sea Museum, Girl Scout National Center, Savannah History Museum.

Location/Directions: Two blocks south of the visitor information center.

*Coupon available, see coupon section.

Site Address: 601 W. Harris St., Savannah, GA
Mailing Address: 601 W. Harris St., Savannah, GA 31401
Telephone: (912) 651-6823
Fax: (921) 651-3691
E-mail: hrs@chsgeorgia.org
Internet: www.chsgeorgia.org

HAWAIIAN RAILWAY SOCIETY
Train ride, museum, display
36" gauge

MARK D. BRUESHABER

Description: A 6½-mile, 90-minute ride along OR&L track from Ewa to Kahe Point where passengers can witness the surf crashing against the rocks. The train passes Barbers Point Naval Air Station, Ko'Olina Golf Course, and more. Fully narrated trip provides railroading history of the area.

Schedule: Sunday, 12:30 and 2:30 p.m. (weather permitting). Call for information.

Admission/Fare: Adults, $8; seniors and children ages 2-12, $5; under age 2 are free.

Locomotives/Rolling Stock: Two Whitcomb diesel-electrics, nos. 302 and 423; converted U.S. Army flatcars, parlor car no. 64.

Special Events: Halloween rides. Call or write for information.

Nearby Attractions/Accommodations: Ihilani Resort; Ko'Olina Golf Course; Paradise Cover Luau.

Location/Directions: Freeway H-1, exit 5A, continue on 76 (Fort Weaver Rd.) south to Renton Rd., take a right on Renton Rd., and left on Fleming Rd.

Site Address: 91-1001 Renton Rd., Ewa Town, HI
Mailing Address: PO Box 60369, Ewa Station, Ewa, HI 96706
Telephone: (808) 681-5461
Fax: (808) 681-4860
E-mail: hirailway@aol.com
Internet: http://members.aol.com/hawaiianrr/index.html

LAHAINA, KAANAPALI & PACIFIC RAILROAD
Train ride
36" gauge

Description: The "Sugar Cane Train" chugs its way through the colorful history and breath-taking scenes of Maui by bringing back memories, sounds, and experiences of turn-of-the-century sugar plantation life. The sugar trains of the past were used to transport sugar cane from the fields to the mills and were a popular means of transportation for sugar workers in the early 1900s. Passengers are taken on an entertaining and historical tour by one of our singing conductors. The train stations are designed to resemble turn-of-the-century boarding platforms and are a delightful glimpse at Hawaii's historical and cultural past.

Schedule: Year round: Call or write for information.

Admission/Fare: Call or write for information.

Locomotives/Rolling Stock: No. 1, "Anaka," 1943 Porter 2-4-0 and no. 3, "Myrtle," 1943 Porter 2-4-0, both former Carbon Limestone Co.; no. 45, "Oahu," 1959 Plymouth diesel, former Oahu Railway; nine 19th century King Kalakaua replica nostalgic coaches; two non-operational displays of Oahu 5 and Oahu 86 from Oahu Railway; more.

Nearby Attractions/Accommodations: Historic town of Lahaina, Maui and resort area of Kaanapali.

Location/Directions: Lahaina Station located near Pioneer Mill, turn off Highway 30 at Hinau St., turn right at Limahana St.

Site Address: 975 Limahana Pl., Ste. 203, Lahaina, Maui, HI
Mailing Address: 975 Limahana Pl., Ste. 203, Lahaina, Maui, HI 96761
Telephone: (800) 499-2307, (888) LKP-MAUI, and (808) 661-0089 (recording)
Fax: (808) 661-8389

Idaho, Horseshoe Bend

THUNDER MOUNTAIN LINE RAILROAD
Train ride
Standard gauge

Description: Two-and-a-half-hour, 34-mile round trip follows the Payette River through the mountains. It goes through the shortest solid rock railroad tunnel in the world. A variety of wildlife may be visible: elk, deer, fox, coyote, beaver, river otter, porcupine, bald eagles, osprey, sandhill cranes, blue heron, hawks, ducks, geese.

Schedule: Weekends, year-round; daily, summer months. Call for schedule.

Admission/Fare: Adults, $24 plus tax; seniors (65 and over), $22 plus tax; 12 and under, $14.

Locomotives/Rolling Stock: F10 diesel electric or EMD diesel electric; former Long Island coach INP no. 2969; former Great Northern dining car no. 1120; former UP dining car; former ATSF lounge car no. 3241; former Southern Pacific baggage car no. 6741; former Cotton Belt passenger coach no. 2636; open-air car.

Special Events: Pumpkin Liner, Thanksgiving, Christmas (Santa Train), New Year's Eve, Thunder Mountain Days, dinner trains, and train robberies.

Nearby Attractions/Accommodations: International Indian Powwow; Payette Whitewater Rodeo; Cascade Raft and Kayak outfitters and guides; Lake Cascade to the north.

Location/Directions: 25 miles north of Boise on Highway 55.

Site Address: Horseshoe Bend, ID
Mailing Address: PO Box 1335, Meridian, ID 83680
Telephone: toll free (877)-432-7245 (IDA-RAIL)
E-mail: rpo@thundermountainline.com
Internet: www.thundermountainline.com

Idaho, Lewiston

**LEWISTON EXCURSION
DINNER TRAIN**
Dinner train
Standard gauge

GEO. BROCKMAN

Description: Fabulous scenic five-hour dinner train on the famous and historic Camas Prairie Railroad along the Clearwater River out of Lewiston, Idaho, featuring cars from the American Freedom Train.

Schedule: Operating 52 weeks per year. Call 1-888-RR-DINER for information and reservations.

Admission/Fare: $75 per person.

Locomotives/Rolling Stock: American Freedom Train cars; using Camas Prairie Road locomotives for motive power; locomotives are GE B-23-7.

Special Events: Anniversaries, birthdays, class and family reunions, office parties and seminars, weddings, community celebrations and events, as well as holiday events and special trains.

Nearby Attractions/Accommodations: Lewiston, Idaho, and the surrounding region is a year-round recreational paradise with a variety of fine lodging facilities.

Location/Directions: Located on U.S. Highway 12, known as the official Lewis and Clark Bicentennial Trail Highway system. Lewiston, Idaho, is directly south of Spokane, Washington, traveling on Highway 95. Contact the Lewiston, Idaho, Chamber of Commerce (208) 743-3531.

Site Address: Fifth and Railroad (across from Buick Auto dealership), Lewiston, ID
Mailing Address: 610½ Main St., Lewiston, ID 83501
Telephone: (208) 743-2233 and (888) RR-DINER
Fax: (208) 746-8306 (auto)
Internet: www.rrdiner.org

**NORTHERN PACIFIC DEPOT
RAILROAD MUSEUM**
Museum

Description: The museum offers pictorial exhibits and railroad artifacts.

Schedule: April, 9 a.m. to 5 p.m. Monday through Saturday; May, 9 a.m. to 5 p.m. daily; June through August, 9 a.m. to 7 p.m. daily; September, 9 a.m. to 5 p.m. daily; October, 9 a.m. to 3 p.m. Closed October 15 for season.

Admission/Fare: Adults, $2; seniors, $1.50; children 6-16, $1; under 6 are free; family, $6. For tour information, please call.

Special Events: Annual Depot Day, Saturday before Mother's Day; car show, arts and crafts booths, food booth, family activities.

Nearby Attractions/Accommodations: Town of Wallace is on historical register, Silver Mine Tour, Hiawatha bike trail, museums, ski resorts, Glacier Park.

Location/Directions: I-90, exit 61 or 62, Wallace, Idaho.

*Coupon available, see coupon section.

Site Address: 219 Sixth St., Wallace, ID
Mailing Address: PO Box 469, Wallace, ID 83873
Telephone: (208) 752-0111

HISTORIC PULLMAN FOUNDATION
Museum

Description: The historic Pullman Foundation operates the Pullman Visitor Center and Hotel Florence Museum, which give an overview of the Pullman factory, and George Pullman's town, which still exits.

Schedule: Monday through Friday, 11 a.m. to 2 p.m.; Saturday, 10 a.m. to 2 p.m.; Sunday, 10 a.m. to 3 p.m.

Admission/Fare: Adults, $3; students, $2; group tours available.

Special Events: Annual Pullman House Tour, second weekend in October, 11 a.m. to 5 p.m. First Sunday guided walking tours, 12:30 and 1:30 p.m., May through October.

Nearby Attractions/Accommodations: Museum of Science and Industry, Downtown Chicago, riverboat casinos, Sandridge Nature Center, South Suburban Geneology Society, Ridge Historic District.

Location/Directions: I-94 to 117th St. (exit 66A), travel west four blocks. Metra Electric stops at 11th St. or 115th St.

*Coupon available, see coupon section.

Site Address: 11111 S. Forrestville Ave., Chicago, IL
Mailing Address: 11111 S. Forrestville Ave., Chicago, IL 60628-4649
Telephone: (773) 785-3828 (touring information)
Fax: (773) 785-8182
E-mail: PullmanHPF@aol.com
Internet: www.pullmanil.org

MUSEUM OF SCIENCE AND INDUSTRY
Display, layout

ALEX TREML

Description: The Museum of Science and Industry is one of the nation's preeminent centers for informal science and technology education. The model railroad exhibit was originally installed in 1941. The layout is approximately 3,000 square feet. Features include an O gauge track that is ¼₈ the actual size, totaling 1,200 feet, in addition to 10,000 feet of switchboard wire, 350 relays, 5,500 trees, 150 telegraph poles, as well as a host of freight cars.

Schedule: Labor Day through Memorial Day: weekdays, 9:30 a.m. to 4 p.m.; weekends and holidays, till 5:30 p.m. Memorial Day through Labor Day: daily, 9:30 a.m. to 5:30 p.m. Closed Christmas.

Admission/Fare: Adults, $7; seniors, $6; children 3-11, $3.50; under age 3 are free. Free on Thursdays.

Locomotives/Rolling Stock: Engine 999 was the first vehicle to go over 100 mph. The *Pioneer Zephyr* was the first streamlined diesel-electric train.

Nearby Attractions/Accommodations: Hyde Park, University of Chicago, Shedd Aquarium, Field Museum, Planetarium, Art Institute, Navy Pier.

Location/Directions: Lake Shore Dr. south to 57th St.

Site Address: 57th St. and Lake Shore Dr., Chicago, IL
Mailing Address: 57th St. and Lake Shore Dr., Chicago, IL 60637
Telephone: (773) 684-1414
Fax: (773) 684-2907
Internet: www.msichicago.org

**AMERICAN ORIENT EXPRESS
RAIL EXPEDITIONS**
Train ride
Standard gauge

RUSSELL INGRAHM

Description: Luxury rail vacations across the U.S. and Canada by vintage streamliner train. Seven- to ten-day programs.

Schedule: Operating season, February through November.

Admission/Fare: Prices based on tour and accommodations. Fares start at $3,190 per person. Vintage Pullman based on double occupancy.

Nearby Attractions/Accommodations: Tours include Antebellum South; Transcontinental Journey; Pacific Coast Explorer; Great Trans-Canada; Rail Journey; Rockies and Yellowstone; Great Northwest and Glacier; National Parks of the West.

Site Address: Varies.
Mailing Address: 5100 Main St., Suite 300, Downers Grove, IL 60515
Telephone: (800) 320-4206 or (630) 663-4550
Fax: (630) 663-1595
Internet: www.americanorientexpress.com

ELIZABETH DEPOT MUSEUM
Museum

Description: Depot museum displaying artifacts of the Chicago Great Western Railroad. This depot serviced the nearby Winston Tunnel, the longest railroad tunnel in Illinois. The museum features a model of the tunnel.

Schedule: May through October: weekends 1 to 4 p.m.

Admission/Fare: Free

Special Events: Great Western Days, first weekend in May, features additional displays relating to the railroad.

Nearby Attractions/Accommodations: Apple River Fort, also in downtown Elizabeth; Mississippi Palisades State Park, Apple Canyon State Park.

Location/Directions: Three miles east of the Great River Road on U.S. Highway 20; turn right on Myrtle St. at the Veterans' Monument in downtown Elizabeth.

      M

Site Address: Myrtle St., Elizabeth, IL
Mailing Address: PO Box 353, Elizabeth, IL 61028-0353
Telephone: (815) 858-2098

Illinois, Freeport   **SILVER CREEK & STEPHENSON RAILROAD**
Train ride, display
Standard gauge

STEVE SNYDER

Description: The turn-of-the-century Silver Creek Depot is a tribute to an important part of our country's transportation history. On display are lanterns, locks and keys, whistles, sounders, tickets, couplers, and more, representing railroads from across the country. The 4-mile train trip travels through Illinois farmland and stands of virgin timber known as "Indian Gardens," crossing Yellow Creek on a 30-foot-high cement and stone pier bridge.

Schedule: May 27 and 28; June 16 and 17; July 4, 27, 28, and 29; Sept. 3, 22, and 23; Oct. 6, 7, 20, and 21: 11 a.m. to 4 p.m.

Admission/Fare: Adults, $4; children (under 12), $2.

Locomotives/Rolling Stock: 1912, 36-ton Heisler; 1941 bay-window caboose, former Chicago, Milwaukee, St. Paul & Pacific; 1889 wooden caboose with cupola, former Hannibal & St. Joseph, reported to be the oldest running caboose in Illinois; 1948 caboose, former Illinois Central Gulf; covered flatcar; 14-ton Brookville switch engine; 12-ton Plymouth switch engine; and work cars.

Location/Directions: Intersection of Walnut and Lamm Roads, ½ mile south of Stephenson County Fairgrounds.

        M

Site Address: 2954 W. Walnut Rd., Freeport, IL
Mailing Address: PO Box 255, Freeport, IL 61032
Telephone: (800) 369-2955 and (815) 232-2306

ALICE ZEMAN

Description: The restored 1940s station features an operating HO layout replica of downtown Mendota in the 1940s during its heyday as a railroad center with the Milwaukee, Illinois Central, and Burlington Railroads. Also see the old time telegraphy office, railroad memorabilia, and more.

Schedule: June through August: daily except Mondays and Tuesdays, 12 to 5 p.m. September through May: Saturdays and Sundays, 12 to 5 p.m.

Admission/Fare: $2; children under age 12, $1; members are free. Tours available.

Locomotives/Rolling Stock: Burlington O-1A Mikado-type locomotive 2-8-2 no. 4978; tender; Burlington waycar no. 14451; Milwaukee Road combine car no. 2713.

Special Events: June 16 and 17, third weekend of June, Railroad Crossing Days. Mendota Sweet Corn Festival, second weekend of August.

Nearby Attractions/Accommodations: Hume-Carnegie Historical Museum, Breaking the Prairie Agricultural Museum, restaurants, lodging, campgrounds.

Location/Directions: I-39/51 and Route 34, approximately 100 miles west of Chicago and 50 miles south of Rockford.

      M

Site Address: 783 Main St., Mendota, IL
Mailing Address: PO Box 433, Mendota, IL 61342
Telephone: (815) 538-3800

MONTICELLO RAILWAY MUSEUM
Train ride, museum
Standard gauge

Description: A 7-mile round trip on former Illinois Central and Illinois Terminal trackage. Passengers board at either the Illinois Central depot at the museum or the 1899 Wabash depot downtown Monticello. Visitors view displays located both inside and outside railcars.

Schedule: May through October: weekends and holidays. Museum site departures: Saturdays, 11 a.m., 12:30, 2, and 3:30 p.m.; Sundays, 12:30, 2, and 3:30 p.m. Wabash depot departures: Saturdays, 11:30 a.m., 1 and 2:30 p.m.; Sundays, 1 and 2:30 p.m. Charters, private cars, on request.

Admission/Fare: Call or write for information.

Locomotives/Rolling Stock: 1907 Southern Railway Baldwin 2-8-0 no. 401; 1916 Mississippi Eastern Baldwin 4-6-0 no. 303; 1953 Wabash EMD F-7A no. 1189; 1959 CN MLW FPA-4 no. 6789; 1955 LIRR Alco RS-3 no. 301; more.

Special Events: Throttle Times; Caboose Days, August. Railroad Days, September. Ghost Train, October. Lunch with Santa, December.

Nearby Attractions/Accommodations: Rayville Railroad Museum, Allerton Park, nearby Amish and Lincoln sites, Best Western, Fosters Plaza and Inn.

Location/Directions: I-72 exit 166, Market St. Turn onto Iron Horse Pl. at traffic light, go past Best Western to museum.

*Coupon available, see coupon section.

    M arm

 Radio frequency: 160.635

Site Address: 993 Iron Horse Pl., Monticello, IL
Mailing Address: PO Box 401, Monticello, IL 61856-0401
Telephone: (217) 762-9011 (weekends)
E-mail: mrm@prairienet.org
Internet: www.prairienet.org/mrm

Illinois, Monticello

RAYVILLE RAILROAD MUSEUM
(PIATT COUNTY MUSEUM)
Museum, display, layout
Z, N, S, O, and Standard gauge

Description: A working 10 x 36-foot HO layout, plus standard, O gauge and S gauge trains running.

Schedule: Open Saturday and Sunday, May through October, or by appointment on other days. Also open on days of special events in Monticello, Illinois.

Admission/Fare: Adults, $2; children, $1.

Special Events: Open on Monticello Western Days (last Friday and Saturday in June) from 10 a.m. until 4 p.m.

Nearby Attractions/Accommodations: Monticello Railway Museum, Allerton Park, State St. historic homes, downtown Main St. historic shops and restaurants. Best Western Monticello, Gateway Inn.

Location/Directions: Off I-72 onto Route 105 through Monticello. Museum is a half block west of the courthouse on the corner of Route 105 and Washington St.

Site Address: 217 W. Washington, Monticello, IL
Mailing Address: Curator, 801 Tyler Ct., Monticello, IL 61856-2246
Telephone: (217) 762-2303

Illinois, Peoria (Dunlap) **WHEELS O' TIME MUSEUM**
Museum

Description: Steam locomotive with combo car, caboose, and switcher. Antique autos, fire trucks, clocks, tools, toys, farm equipment, and more.

Schedule: May through October: Wednesdays through Sundays and holidays, 12 to 5 p.m. and other times by appointment. Group tours available.

Admission/Fare: Adults, $4; children, $1.50. Group rates available.

Locomotives/Rolling Stock: Rock Island Pacific no. 886; Milwaukee Road combine no. 2716; TP&W caboose no. 508; Plymouth switcher.

Nearby Attractions/Accommodations: Wildlife Prairie Park, Lakeview Museum.

Location/Directions: On Route 40, north of Peoria, two miles north of the Route 6 intersection.

      M

Site Address: 11923 N. Knoxville, Dunlap, IL
Mailing Address: PO Box 9636, Peoria, IL 61612-9636
Telephone: (309) 243-9020 and (309) 243-5616
E-mail: wotmuseum@aol.com
Internet: wheelsotime.org

Description: Rochelle provides an area for train watching for everyone. Two busy mainline railroads (UP & BNSF) cross on the diamonds, averaging 80 to 90 trains in a 24-hour period. Gift shop and heated restrooms are available for all your needs.

Schedule: Park open 365 days a year. Gift shop open every day, except Tuesdays, year round.

Admission/Fare: Free.

Locomotives/Rolling Stock: Whitcomb locomotive on display for the children's enjoyment.

Nearby Attractions/Accommodations: Motels and restaurants nearby with Magic Waters only ½-hour drive away in Rockford, Illinois.

Location/Directions: From north and south, take I-39 to Illinois 38 exit west. From east and west, take I-88 to Illinois 251 north.

Site Address: 124 N. Ninth St., Rochelle, IL
Mailing Address: 124 N. Ninth St., Rochelle, IL 61068
Telephone: (815) 562-8107
E-mail: atsf525@aol.com
Internet: www.foxdir.net/rrpark

Description: Forty-five-minute trolley ride with historic narrative.

Schedule: June through August: Tuesdays and Thursdays, 11 a.m. to 3 p.m.; weekends, noon to 3 p.m.

Admission/Fare: Adults, $3.50; youth 5-17, $3; 4 and under free; resident discount of 50 cents per rider.

Locomotives/Rolling Stock: Trolley car no. 36

Nearby Attractions/Accommodations: Forest City Queen riverboat rides, Riverview Ice House.

Location/Directions: I-90 to East State St. exit. East on State St. to Madison St. Turn north onto Madison St. The trolley station is on the west side of the street.

Site Address: 324 N. Madison St., Rockford, IL
Mailing Address: 324 N. Madison St., Rockford, IL 61107
Telephone: (815) 987-8894; TTY (815) 963-DEAF
Fax: (815) 987-1597

RICHARD M. SCHROEDER

Description: Displays show the history of the former Chicago & Eastern Illinois and other area railroads. The Baggage Room contains an HO model railroad. The Depot Museum preserves the railroads' history in east Central Illinois and western Indiana in a former C&EI Railroad Depot.

Schedule: Memorial Day weekend through last Sunday in September: weekends, noon to 4 p.m. and by appointment.

Admission/Fare: Free. Donations are appreciated.

Nearby Attractions/Accommodations: Rossville Historical Society Museum, Mann's Chapel, Vermilion County Museum, 15 antique shops in downtown area.

Location/Directions: In Rossville, one block north on Illinois Route 1 to Benton St., east three blocks to CSX transportation tracks.

Site Address: E. Benton St., Rossville, IL
Mailing Address: PO Box 1013, Danville, IL 61834-1013
Telephone: (217) 748-6615
E-mail: djcnrhs@prairienet.org or rickshro@aol.com
Internet: http://www.prairienet.org/djc-nrhs/

FOX RIVER TROLLEY MUSEUM
Train ride, museum
Standard gauge

FRED LONNES

Description: Ride the historic 105-year-old remnant of an interurban rail-road aboard Chicago-area interurban and "el" equipment. Includes the oldest surviving American interurban: Chicago, Aurora & Elgin no. 20 (shown above).

Schedule: Sundays and holidays (Memorial Day, July 4, and Labor Day), May 13 through November 1. Saturdays, July 7 through Labor Day and October 20 and 27. Hours: 11 a.m. to 5 p.m.

Locomotives/Rolling Stock: Historic Chicago interurban and "el" equipment including CA&E no. 20; North Shore nos. 715 and 756; CTA nos. 40, 43, 4451, and L202; CRT 5001.

Special Events: Mother's Day; Spring Caboose Day, June 3; Father's Day; Red, White, Blue Day, July 4; Trolley Fest and Riverfest, August 18-19; Fall Foliage/Caboose Days October 7 and 14; Pumpkin Trolley, October 20, 21, and 27; Haunted Trolley, October 28.

Nearby Attractions/Accommodations: Grand Victoria Casino, Elgin Area Museum, Elgin, Batavia Depot Museum (CB&Q), Blackhawk Forest Preserve, South Elgin; historic towns of St. Charles, Geneva, and Batavia. Major motel/hotel accommodations available in the area.

Location/Directions: Illinois 31 south from I-90 or U.S. 20, or north from I-88. Site is three blocks south of State St. stoplight in South Elgin.

Site Address: 365 S. LaFox St. (Illinois 31), South Elgin, IL
Mailing Address: PO Box 315, South Elgin, IL 60177-0315
Telephone: (847) 697-4676
E-mail: info@foxtrolley.org
Internet: www.foxtrolley.org

ILLINOIS RAILWAY MUSEUM
Museum
Standard gauge

Description: The largest railroad museum in North America, having the most comprehensive collection found in any museum. A collection of over 300 pieces of equipment includes steam, diesel, and electric locomotives; electric interurbans, elevated cars and streetcars; trolley buses and motor buses, as well as passenger and freight equipment; a C&NW depot built in 1851, a signal tower, and a restored Chicago "el" station. A 5-mile, 25-minute round trip over the reconstructed right-of-way of the former Elgin & Belvedere featuring steam and/or diesel trains and electric interurbans on weekends and streetcars on weekdays.

Schedule: Daily, Memorial Day through Labor Day. Weekends, April, May, September, and October.

Admission/Fare: Weekends: adults, $8; children 5-11/seniors +62, $6. Weekdays: adults, $6; children 5-11/seniors +62, $4. Maximum family admission, $35. Higher fares for some special events.

Locomotives/Rolling Stock: No. 2903 Santa Fe 4-8-4; no. 2050 N&W 2-8-8-2; no. 9911A CB&Q EMC E5; no. 6930 UP DDA 40X; Electroliner; many more.

Special Events: Thomas the Tank Engine will be visiting the museum during 2001, so call for details.

Location/Directions: One mile east of Union off U.S. Route 20.

*Coupon available, see coupon section.

Site Address: 7000 Olson Rd., Union, IL
Mailing Address: PO Box 427, Union, IL 60180
Telephone: (815) 923-4391 or (815) 923-4000 recorded message
Fax: (815) 923-2006
Internet: www.irm.org

VALLEY VIEW
MODEL RAILROAD
Layout
HO gauge

Description: This display is modeled after the Chicago & North Western's Northwest line, with accurate track layouts of some of the towns modeled. Three to four trains operate simultaneously over the railroad, which has eight scale miles of track, 16 ever-changing trains, 250 buildings, 64 turnouts, 250 vehicles, 450 people, 84 operating signal lights, 250 pieces of rolling stock, and operating grade crossings with flashers and gates. Extra equipment is on static display in the gift shop.

Schedule: Memorial Day through Labor Day: Wednesdays, Saturdays, and Sundays.

Admission/Fare: Adults, $5; seniors, $4; children, $2.50; age 5 and under are free.

Nearby Attractions/Accommodations: Illinois Railway Museum, Wild West Town, McHenry County Museum.

Location/Directions: Travel north ¾ mile on Olson Rd. to Highbridge.

Site Address: 17108 Highbridge Rd., Union, IL
Mailing Address: 17108 Highbridge Rd., Union, IL 60180
Telephone: (815) 923-4135

WATERMAN & WESTERN RAILROAD
Train ride
15" gauge

Description: One-mile ride around a city park. Private train rides are available, upon request. Call office at (815) 264-7753.

Schedule: Memorial Day to Labor Day: Sundays 1 to 4 p.m. Special runs are available.

Admission/Fare: $1.

Locomotives/Rolling Stock: 15" gauge F3; Casey Jones railbus; assorted passenger cars.

Special Events: Haunted Pumpkin Train, weekends and Fridays in October; Holiday Lights Train, Thursday through Sunday, Thanksgiving to New Years: 100,000 lights and free admission

Location/Directions: U.S. Route 30 one mile west of State Route 23, Waterman, Illinois.

Site Address: Lions Park, Birch St., Waterman, IL
Mailing Address: PO Box 217, Waterman, IL 60556
Telephone: (815) 264-7753
Fax: (815) 264-3230
E-mail: wwrr@screwballexpress.com
Internet: www.screwballexpress.com

WHITEWATER VALLEY RAILROAD
Train ride
Standard gauge

JOHN R. HILLMAN

Description: This line offers a 32-mile, five-hour round trip to Metamora, Indiana, a restored canal town with 100 shops and a working grist mill. A two-hour stopover at Metamora gives passengers a chance to tour the town.

Schedule: May through October: weekends and holidays, 12:01 p.m. May: Wednesday through Friday, 10 a.m.; October: Thursday and Friday, 10 a.m.

Admission/Fare: Adults, $14; children 2-12, $7; under age 2 are free. One-way and group rates available.

Locomotives/Rolling Stock: No. 6, 1907 Baldwin 0-6-0, former East Broad Top; no. 8, 1946 General Electric, former Muncie & Western; no. 11, 1924 Vulcan 0-4-0T; no. 100, 1919 Baldwin 2-6-2; no. 25, 1951 Lima SW7.5; no. 210, 1946 General Electric 70-ton; no. 709, 1950 Lima SW10; no. 2561, 1931 Plymouth 32-ton gas engine; no. 9339, 1948 Alco S1; no. 9376, 1950 Lima SW12, former Baltimore & Ohio; more.

Special Events: Metamora Canal Days, first weekend in October; Christmas Trains, November and December. Train-to-Dinner, first and third Fridays of each month May through October.

Nearby Attractions/Accommodations: Whitewater State Park, Brookville Lake, Mary Gray Bird Sanctuary.

Location/Directions: Corner of Fifth and Grand in downtown Connersville (Market St.).

Radio Frequency: 160.650

Site Address: 455 Market St., Connersville, IN
Mailing Address: PO Box 406, Connersville, IN 47331
Telephone: (765) 825-2054
Fax: (765) 825-4550
Internet: www.whitewatervalleyrr.org

CORYDON SCENIC RAILROAD
Train ride
Standard gauge

RICHARD PEARSON

Description: A 16-mile train ride through Southern Indiana Hills on air-conditioned Silverliner cars; live entertainment and guide.

Schedule: May through October; schedule varies.

Admission/Fare: Adults, $9; children, $5.

Nearby Attractions/Accommodations: First state capitol building.

Location/Directions: I-64, exit 105 to train station in downtown Corydon.

*Coupon available, see coupon section.

Site Address: 210 W. Walnut St., Corydon, IN
Mailing Address: PO Box 10, Corydon, IN 47112
Telephone: (812) 738-8000
Fax: (812) 738-3101

**NATIONAL NEW YORK CENTRAL
RAILROAD MUSEUM**
Museum

TAIGMARTIN INC.

Description: The museum traces the rich history of the New York Central and its impact on Elkhart and the nation. Extensive hands-on exhibits bring railroading alive.

Schedule: Year round: Tuesdays through Fridays, 10 a.m. to 2 p.m.; Saturdays 10 a.m. to 4 p.m.; Sundays 12 to 4 p.m. Closed Mondays and major holidays.

Admission/Fare: Adults, $2; seniors (62+) and students 6-12, $1; children age 5 and under are free.

Locomotives/Rolling Stock: NYC 3001 L3a Mohawk Alco 1940; NYC 4085 E8 EMD 1951; PRR 4882 GG1; six passenger cars; seven freight cars, seven cabooses; six non-revenue.

Nearby Attractions/Accommodations: Northern Indiana Amish Country, Midwest Museum of American Art, Time Was Museum, S. Ray Miller Auto Museum, Woodlawn, Ruthmere, RV/MH Museum, Elkhart County Historical Museum.

Location/Directions: Indiana Toll Road exit 92. Main St. in downtown Elkhart. The museum is in the historic freighthouses next to the Norfolk Southern main line.

 Elkhart

Site Address: 721 S. Main St., Elkhart, IN
Mailing Address: PO Box 1708, Elkhart, IN 46515
Telephone: (219) 294-3001
Fax: (219) 295-9434
E-mail: artscul@michiana.org
Internet: nycrrmuseum.railfan.net

**FORT WAYNE RAILROAD
HISTORICAL SOCIETY**
Train ride, museum
Standard gauge

TOM NITZA

Description: The Fort Wayne Railroad Historical Society is home to steam
locomotive 765, which has operated excursions throughout the
Midwest. The society also has other historic railroad equipment. You
can tour the facility, talk to the people who maintain and operate this
historic rail equipment, sit in the engineer's seat of a 400-ton iron horse
and get a conductor's eye view from a 100-year old caboose. For the
ultimate railfan experience, the society offers an Engineer for an Hour
program on our diesel locomotive. Several times each year, the society
has operating days when you can see railroad equipment in action and
ride a vintage caboose.

Schedule: Call for a recorded message or write for information.

Admission/Fare: No admission charge for museum/self-guided tour.

Locomotives/Rolling Stock: NKP 2-8-4 Berkshire steam locomotive no.
765; Lake Erie & Fort Wayne 0-6-0 no. 1; NKP wooden caboose no. 141;
Wabash wooden caboose no. 2543; N&W wrecker no. 540019; 44-ton
Davenport diesel no. 1231; NKP wooden boxcar no. 83047.

Special Events: Caboose rides, tours, and annual open house in August;
write for details.

Location/Directions: From New Haven take Dawkins Rd. east to Ryan Rd.,
left to Edgerton Rd., turn right and site is 1.5 miles on the right.

Site Address: 15808 Edgerton Rd., New Haven, IN
Mailing Address: PO Box 11017, Fort Wayne, IN 46855
Telephone: (219) 493-0765
E-mail: info@765.org
Internet: www.765.org

FRENCH LICK, WEST BADEN & SOUTHERN RAILWAY

Train ride
Standard gauge

ALAN BARNETT

Description: A round trip between the resort town of French Lick and Cuzco, site of Patoka Lake. The train traverses wooded Indiana limestone country and passes through one of the state's longest railroad tunnels.

Schedule: April through October: weekends and May 29 and September 4: 10 a.m., 1 and 4 p.m. November: 1 p.m. June through October: Tuesdays, 1 p.m.

Admission/Fare: Adults, $8; children 3-11, $4; under 3 ride free.

Locomotives/Rolling Stock: 1947 General Electric 80-ton diesel no. 3; 1947 Alco RS-1 no. 4; open-window Rock Island coaches.

Special Events: Wild West holdups are scheduled for many holiday weekends. Call or write for dates and times.

Nearby Attractions/Accommodations: French Lick Springs Resort.

Location/Directions: Trains depart the old Monon Passenger Depot on Highway 56 in French Lick.

Site Address: 1 Monon St., French Lick, IN
Mailing Address: 1 Monon St., French Lick, IN 47432
Telephone: (812) 936-2405 and (800) 74-TRAIN
Fax: (812) 936-2904

HESSTON STEAM MUSEUM
Train ride, museum
Various gauges

RON STAHOUIAK

Description: Train rides from full scale to amusement-park size to hobby scale. Each railroad has 2 to 2.5 miles of mainline trackage, all live steam operation. Also see steam sawmill, steam light plant, 92-ton steam railroad crane, and more. All are operational.

Schedule: Memorial Day weekend through Labor Day: Saturdays and Sundays. September through October: Sundays. Noon to 5 p.m.

Admission/Fare: Free admission except Labor Day weekend. Train rides, adults, $3; children, $2.

Locomotives/Rolling Stock: Darjeeling & Himalayan built by Atlas Works; New Mexico Lumber Shay built by Lima Locomotive; Orenstein and Koppel no. 080, German-built in 1938; Koblen Danake Werke no. 040, built in Czechoslovakia 1939.

Special Events: Whistle-Stop Days, Memorial Day weekend; Whistle Fest, July 4; Annual Steam Show, Labor Day weekend.

Nearby Attractions/Accommodations: Lighthouse Mall, Dunes National Lakeshore, Washington Park Beach/Zoo, Blue Chip Casino, charter boat fishing, Door Prairie Auto Museum, motels.

Location/Directions: South of Indiana-Michigan state line. Four miles east of State Road 39 north of LaPorte or south of New Buffalo to 1000 North, turn east, traveling for about 3 miles.

      M

Site Address: LaPorte County Rd. 1000 North
Mailing Address: 2946 Mt. Clair Way, Michigan City, IN 46360
Telephone: (219) 872-5055
Fax: (219) 874-8239
Internet: www.hesston.org

CARTHAGE, KNIGHTSTOWN & SHIRLEY RAILROAD
Train ride
Standard gauge

Description: A 10-mile, one-hour round trip from Knightstown to Carthage, Indiana.

Schedule: May through October: weekends and holidays, 11 a.m., 1 and 3 p.m. Fridays, 11 a.m.

Admission/Fare: Adults, $6; children 3-11, $4; under age 3 ride free. Group rates available.

Locomotives/Rolling Stock: No. 215 44-ton GE, miscellaneous coaches and cabooses.

Location/Directions: Thirty miles east of Indianapolis on U.S. 40; three miles out of I-70 on State Route 109.

Site Address: 112 W. Carey St., Knightstown, IN
Mailing Address: 112 W. Carey St., Knightstown, IN 46148
Telephone: (765) 345-5561 or 800-345-2704 (Indiana only)

LINDEN RAILROAD MUSEUM
Museum

Description: Operated by the Linden-Madison Township Historical Society, this museum is housed in the former Linden depot built by the Chicago, Indianapolis & Louisville Railway and the Toledo, St. Louis & Western Railroad in 1908. Restored to its 1950s appearance, the depot houses a collection of railroadiana from the Nickel Plate and Monon railroads. An HO model railroad club operates a 1950s depiction of Linden in the Monon baggage room. Both O and N gauge layouts are featured in the NKP baggage room.

Schedule: May through September: Friday through Sunday, 1 to 5 p.m. Group tours by appointment.

Admission/Fare: Adults, $2; teens 13-17, $1; children 6-12, $.50; under age 6 are free.

Locomotives/Rolling Stock: Former Nickel Plate caboose no. 497; Fairmont A-3 motor car; Monon boxcar no. 1620; Monon caboose no. 283.

Special Events: Fifth Annual Civil War Weekend, August 11-12.

Nearby Attractions/Accommodations: Old jail museum, Crawfordsville, Indiana.

Location/Directions: South of Lafayette on U.S. 231 and 7.9 miles north of the Crawfordsville exit off I-74. The depot museum is across from Jane Stoddard Park in Linden.

*Coupon available, see coupon section.

        M

Site Address: 520 N. Main St., Linden, IN
Mailing Address: PO Box 154, Linden, IN 47955
Telephone: (765) 339-7245 or (800) 866-3973
E-mail: weaver@tctc.com
Internet: http://www.tctc.com/~weaver/depot.htm

Indiana, Madison   **JEFFERSON COUNTY HISTORICAL SOCIETY**
MUSEUM AND RAILROAD
Museum

Madison Railroad Station
Built 1895

© Jefferson County Historical Society 1992

Description: Restored 1895 Pennsylvania Railroad station known for its 2½-story octagon waiting room topped by stained glass windows. View other local railroad memorabilia, civil war and steam boat displays.

Schedule: May 1 through October 31: Mondays through Saturdays 10 a.m. to 4:30 p.m., Sundays 1 to 4 p.m. November through April, weekdays only.

Admission/Fare: $3; youth 16 and under are free.

Locomotives/Rolling Stock: 1920 L&N caboose.

Special Events: Madison in Bloom, last weekend in April and first weekend in May.

Nearby Attractions/Accommodations: Clifty Falls State Park, Lanier Mansion, antique shops, wineries, bed and breakfast, Ohio River.

Location/Directions: Highways 56 and 421, located in downtown historic Madison.

        M

Site Address: 615 W. First St., Madison, IN
Mailing Address: 615 W. First St., Madison, IN 47250
Telephone: (812) 265-2335
Fax: (812) 273-5023
E-mail: jchs@seidata.com
Internet: www.seidata.com/~jchs

INDIANA TRANSPORTATION MUSEUM
Train ride, display
Standard gauge

JIM VAWTER

Description: Memorial Day through October, weekends: two-hour train ride. Alternate Fridays: dinner train. Special excursions and events.

Schedule: Call or write for information.

Admission/Fare: Call or write for information.

Locomotives/Rolling Stock: Mikado no. 587, former NKP; F7 no. 83, former Monon; F7 no. 96, former Monon; private car no. 90, former FEC; Budd stainless-steel coaches; Indianapolis mule car no. 69; diner "Cross Keys," former L&N.

Nearby Attractions/Accommodations: Conner Prairie Museum in Fishers, Children's Museum in Indianapolis, Hamilton County Convention and Visitors Bureau.

Location/Directions: Located 20 miles north of Indianapolis in Forest Park/Noblesville, about 20 miles northeast of Indianapolis; between U.S. 31 and I-69, north of State Route 32, on State Route 19.

Site Address: 325 Cicero Rd., Noblesville, IN
Mailing Address: PO Box 83, Noblesville, IN 46061-0083
Telephone: (317) 773-6000 recording
E-mail: itm@indy.net
Internet: www.itm.org

Indiana, North Judson

HOOSIER VALLEY RAILROAD MUSEUM, INC.
Train ride, museum
Standard gauge

M.W. KNEBEL

Description: Established in North Judson since 1988, the organization has been in the process of building the physical plant for a working railroad museum. The collection today consists of 30 pieces of railroad rolling stock. This includes the former 2-8-4 Chesapeake & Ohio steam locomotive no. 2789, which is under roof. We offer short caboose rides spring through fall.

Schedule: Year round: Saturdays, 8 a.m. to 5 p.m.

Admission/Fare: No admission fee.

Locomotives/Rolling Stock: C&O 1947 Alco K-4 2-8-4 no. 2789; Erie 1947 Alco S-1 switcher no. 310; EL caboose no. C345; 30 pieces rolling stock.

Nearby Attractions/Accommodations: Tippecanoe River State Park, Bass Lake State Beach, Kersting's Cycle Center & Museum, Oak View Motel.

Location/Directions: Seventy miles southeast of downtown Chicago, Indiana 10 and 39.

Site Address: 507 Mulberry St., North Judson, IN
Mailing Address: PO Box 75, North Judson, IN 46366
Telephone: (219) 223-3834 (treas.), (219) 946-6499 (sec.), (219) 896-3950 (museum)
E-mail: hurm@yahoo.com
Internet: http://hurm.railfan.net

OLD WAKARUSA RAILROAD
Train ride, museum
15" gauge

Description: One-and-a-half-mile ride over trestles and through tunnel to petting zoo.

Schedule: April through October, 11 a.m. to dark.

Admission/Fare: Adults, $4; children 1-3 years are free.

Locomotives/Rolling Stock: Sandley Steamer 1957, no. 98; Merrick Diesel no. 90866.

Special Events: Pumpkin Harvest every October.

Nearby Attractions/Accommodations: Amish community.

Location/Directions: Highway 19, between Nappanee and Elkhart, Indiana.

Site Address: 66402 S.R. 19, Wakarusa, IN
Mailing Address: PO Box 591, Wakarusa, IN 46573
Telephone: (219) 862-2714
Fax: (219) 862-4677

BOONE & SCENIC VALLEY RAILROAD
IOWA RAILROAD HISTORICAL SOCIETY

Train ride, dinner train, museum
Standard gauge

Description: Fifteen- and 22-mile round-trip train rides.

Schedule: Saturdays in May; Memorial Day weekend through October, daily. Call for times.

Admission/Fare: Weekdays: Adults $10, $5 children 3-12. Weekends: Adults, $12; children 3-12, under 3 in arms, free. Dinner and Dessert Trains, call our toll-free number for prices and reservations.

Locomotives/Rolling Stock: JS419 Steam; BSV 1003 diesel; UP 1098 diesel; BSV 1058 diesel; BSV 2254 diesel, CCW 50 Electric, Chicago South Shore 38 and 39; Erie Lackawanna passenger 9101, 3218, 3213, 3238, and 3207; CNW caboose 11136; Rock Island Caboose 17051; Southern Pacific 9044.

Special Events: Pufferbilly Days, second weekend in September.

Nearby Attractions/Accommodations: Mamie Eisenhower's birthplace, Boone Cultural Center, Ledges State Park, accommodations call 1-800-266-6312 Boone CVB.

Location/Directions: West from I-35 at Ames, Iowa, on Highway 30 to Boone. Turn north at stop sign, go to 11th St., turn left and go six blocks.

Radio frequency: 463.800

Site Address: 225 10th St., Boone, IA
Mailing Address: PO Box 603, Boone, IA 50036
Telephone: (515) 432-4249, (800) 626-0319
Fax: (515) 432-4253
E-mail: b&svrr@tdsi.net
Internet: www.scenic-valleyrr.com

Iowa, Council Bluffs

RAILSWEST RAILROAD MUSEUM
Museum, display, layout
HO, O

ROBERT HASTINGS

Description: The RailsWest Railroad Museum and HO model railroad are housed in an 1899 former Rock Island depot. The museum contains displays of historic photos, dining car memorabilia, uniforms, and many other interesting items used during the steam era. The 22 x 33-foot model railroad depicts scenery of the Council Bluffs/Omaha area, featuring train lines that served the heartland: Union Pacific; Chicago & Northwestern; Wabash; Chicago Great Western; Wabash, Rock Island; Milwaukee Road; Chicago, Burlington & Quincy.

Schedule: May: weekends, 1 to 5 p.m. Memorial Day through Labor Day: Tuesdays through Saturdays, 10 a.m. to 4 p.m. and Sundays, 1 to 5 p.m. December: weekends, 1 to 5 p.m. Closed major holidays.

Locomotives/Rolling Stock: UP steam locomotive no. 814; CB&Q steam engine no. 915; CB&Q waycar no. 13855; CB&Q Omaha club car; Budd RPO former UP no. 5908; 1967 Rock Island caboose 17130; UP boxcar no. 462536.

Special Events: Depot Days, last weekend in September. Christmas at the Depot, weekends in December

Location/Directions: I-80 exit 3, travel north one mile or I-29 exit Lake Manawa.

*Coupon available, see coupon section.

Site Address: 1512 S. Main St., Council Bluffs, IA
Mailing Address: PO Box 2, Council Bluffs, IA 51502
Telephone: (712) 323-5182

DELMAR DEPOT MUSEUM
Museum
Standard gauge

Description: Railroad and community museum.

Schedule: Friday, Saturday, Sunday, 1 to 4 p.m., or by appointment.

Admission/Fare: Free. Donations graciously accepted.

Locomotives/Rolling Stock: Caboose CC no. 199506, Illinois Central (Iowa Division).

Special Events: Labor Day Celebration: car show, softball and volleyball tournament, art show, and railroad displays. Festival of Lights, first Sunday in December: horse-drawn wagon rides to view Christmas lights, games, and Santa.

Nearby Attractions/Accommodations: LeeAr's Victorian Retreat, Old Railroad Calaboose, Quad Cities (Bettendorf and Davenport, Iowa, and Moline and Rock Island, Illinois), and Dubuque are all within 40 miles, Maquoketa Caves State Park, Maquoketa lime kilns. Food: Mary's Cafe, Interludes, and BamBam's, all in Delmar.

Location/Directions: Thirty miles north of Quad Cities or 40 miles south of Dubuque on Hwy. 61, then three miles east on Hwy. 136.

Site Address: 414 Lincoln Ave., Delmar, IA
Mailing Address: PO Box 239, Delmar, IA 52037
Telephone: (319) 574-4256
Fax: (319) 574-4262
E-mail: sjebsen@netins.net

FORT MADISON, FARMINGTON & WESTERN RAILROAD

Train ride, museum
Standard gauge

Description: An authentic re-creation of a pre-World War II branchline terminus. A country village, roundhouse with displays, an extensive collection of hand and motor cars, and the yard are on display. A wye is demonstrated and there are many restored pieces of rolling stock. The ride is two miles through woods, up grade, and over a trestle.

Schedule: September 22-23, Railroad Days, 8 a.m. to 8 p.m. December 8-9, 15-16, Santa Train, 12 to 5 p.m. Trains depart hourly on the half hour.

Admission/Fare: Adults, $5; students, $4; under age 5 are free. Price includes admission and ride. Santa Train higher.

Locomotives/Rolling Stock: Plymouth 35-ton; 8-ton Vulcan no. 1; 1913 Baldwin no. 4; Edwards Doodlebug no. 507; 30-ton steam crane no. 3; more.

Special Events: Railroad Days, September 22-23. Santa Train, December 8-9, 15-16.

Nearby Attractions/Accommodations: Old Fort Madison, Midwest Old Threshers Heritage Museums.

Location/Directions: Off Highway 2 between Fort Madison and Donnellson in southeast Iowa.

Radio frequency: 464.9750

Site Address: 2208 220th St., Donnellson, IA
Mailing Address: 2208 220th St., Donnellson, IA 52625
Telephone: (319) 837-6689
Fax: (319) 837-6080
E-mail: dminer@minermfgco.com
Internet: www.minermfgco.com/Minerville/Railroad.htm

SANTA FE DEPOT MUSEUM & HISTORIC CENTER
Museum, display, layout

DAVE SALLEN

Description: The former Santa Fe depot in Fort Madison, a building in the mission revival style, is the nucleus of Fort Madison's historic district. It is a museum of railroad history, firefighting equipment, and fountain pens, reflecting Fort Madison's industrial history. Recently added to the museum is a section on the great floods of 1993. Outside is a Santa Fe caboose, which is open to view.

Schedule: Memorial Day through Labor Day: Wednesdays, Thursdays, Fridays, Saturdays 12:30 to 4:30 p.m.

Admission/Fare: Adults, $2; children under age 12, $.50. Group rates available.

Special Events: Annual North Lee County Historical Society Open Antique Car Show, third Sunday in May.

Location/Directions: The historic district is at the foot of Tenth St. Fort Madison is in the southeast corner of Iowa near Illinois and Missouri on U.S. Route 61 and Iowa Highway 2.

*Coupon available, see coupon section.

      M

Site Address: 814 Tenth St., Fort Madison, IA
Mailing Address: PO Box 285, Fort Madison, IA 52627
Telephone: (319) 372-7661
Fax: (319) 372-7363
E-mail: dssallen@notmail.com

MIDWEST CENTRAL RAILROAD
Train ride
36" gauge

SCOTT A. WILEY

Description: A one-mile steam train ride encircling the grounds of the Midwest Old Threshers grounds, with two trains and three section cars.

Schedule: June 8, 9, 10. August 30 to September 3, 9 a.m. to 10 p.m.; October 13 and 20, 6 to 10 p.m.

Admission/Fare: Adults, $2; children, $1. Reunion–one day, $7; five days, $15.

Locomotives/Rolling Stock: 1891 Baldwin 2-6-0 Surrey, Sussex & Southhampton Railway no. 6; 1923 Lima three-truck Shay, West Side Lumber no. 9; 1951 Henschel 0-4-0T no. 16; 1935 Vulcan gas mechanical switcher; three vintage speeders; five wooden coaches; wooden caboose; White Pass & Yukon steel caboose no. 903.

Special Events: Red Power Roundup. Midwest Old Thresher's Reunion, August 30 through September 3. Halloween Ghost Train, October 13 and 20.

Location/Directions: From intersection of U.S. 34 and 218 proceed west to first traffic light (Walnut St.), then south five blocks to McMillan Park.

Site Address: McMillan Park, Mt. Pleasant, IA
Mailing Address: Box 102, Mt. Pleasant, IA 52641
Telephone: (319) 385-2912
Internet: www.mcrr.org

ABILENE & SMOKY VALLEY RAILROAD
Train ride
Standard gauge

Description: A 1½-hour, 10-mile round trip through the Smoky Hill River Valley from historic Abilene to Enterprise, Kansas. The track crosses the Smoky Hill River on a high steel span bridge.

Schedule: Memorial Day through Labor Day: Tuesdays through Sundays. May, September through October: weekends. Dinner train specials. Call or write for more information.

Admission/Fare: Adults, $8.50; children 3-11, $5.50. Dinner train prices vary. All prices subject to change without notice.

Locomotives/Rolling Stock: 1945 Alco S1; 1945 GE 44-ton; 1945 Whitcomb 45-ton side-rod; more.

Special Events: Abilene–Chisholm Trail Day, Saturday of first full weekend in October. Easter Bunny Train. Santa Claus Train. Call or write for details.

Nearby Attractions/Accommodations: Eisenhower Center, Dickinson County Heritage Center, C.W. Parker Carousel, Greyhound Hall of Fame, Great Plains Theater Festival, Abilene Community Theater.

Location/Directions: I-70 exit 275, south 2 miles on K-15 (Buckeye St.). Park in lot west of Eisenhower Center (shared lot with Greyhound Hall of Fame).

Site Address: 417 S. Buckeye, Abilene, KS
Mailing Address: PO Box 744, Abilene, KS 67410
Telephone: (785) 263-1077, (888) 426-6687 and (888) 426-6689 (reservations)
Fax: (785) 263-1066
Internet: www.asvrr.org

MIDLAND RAILWAY
Train ride
Standard gauge

E.N. GRIFFIN

Description: This line was constructed in 1867 as the Leavenworth, Lawrence & Galveston, the first railroad south of the Kansas River. The Midland Railway is a volunteer-operated intrastate common-carrier passenger railroad. Trains operate to the former town site of Norwood for an 11-mile round trip through scenic eastern Kansas farmland and woods.

Schedule: Memorial Day weekend through October: trains depart at 11:30 a.m., 1:30 and 3:30 p.m.

Fare/Admission: Adults, $8; children ages 4-12, $4; under age 4 ride free. All-day fare (all ages), $15. Discounts for groups of 25 or more.

Locomotive/Rolling Stock: No. 524, 1946 EMD NW2, former Chicago, Burlington & Quincy; no. 142 RS-3M, former Missouri-Kansas-Texas; no. 652 E8, former CRI&P, 8255 RS-3, former NYC-630 CRIP E6.

Special Events: Maple Leaf Festival, third weekend in October; Halloween Trains, last weekend in October. Railfans Weekend, date to be announced (call for information).

Location/Directions: About 30 miles southwest of Kansas City on U.S. 56 at the 1906 former AT&SF depot, seven blocks west of downtown.

 Lawrence

Radio Frequency: 161.055

Site Address: 1515 High St., Baldwin City, Kansas
Mailing Address: PO Box 412, Baldwin City, KS 66006
Telephone: (785) 594-6982 and (800) 651-0388
Fax: (816) 873-3387
Internet: www.midland-ry.org

GREAT PLAINS TRANSPORTATION MUSEUM, INC.
Museum
Standard

J. HARVEY KUEHN

Description: Museum with indoor and outdoor displays of steam, electric, and diesel locomotives and cars.

Admission/Fare: Adults, $3.50; children 3-12, $2.50.

Locomotives/Rolling Stock: ATSF no. 3768; BNSF no. 93; BN no. 421; Whitcomb GM-2; Frisco caboose 876; Central Kansas Railroad caboose 1959; CB&Q caboose 13519; ATSF coach, baggage, caboose 2312; MOP caboose 13495; RI caboose 2A538; ATSF baggage 190006.

Nearby Attractions/Accommodations: In the heart of historic Old Town.

Location/Directions: Across from Wichita Union Station.

*Coupon available, see coupon section.

Site Address: 700 E. Douglas Ave., Wichita, KS
Mailing Address: 700 E. Douglas Ave., Wichita, KS 67202
Telephone: (316) 263-0944

MY OLD KENTUCKY DINNER TRAIN
Dinner train

Description: Thirty-five-mile round trip through the Kentucky countryside. Fine dining and whisper-perfect service aboard vintage 1940s dinner train.

Schedule: Lunch on Saturdays, 12 noon; dinner, Tuesday through Saturday, 5 p.m.; year-round operation. Schedule subject to change.

Admission/Fare: Lunch, $36.95 plus tax, per person; dinner, $59.95 plus tax, per person.

Locomotives/Rolling Stock: Two FP7A units nos. 1940 and 1941; Budd diner 1940 era, nos. 011 (Eisenhower's family funeral car), 007, 777 and 021.

Special Events: Bourbon Festival, September. Murder Mysteries, fall and spring.

Nearby Attractions/Accommodations: Bardstown is a major historical site with many attractions; most major chain hotels; home to "My Old Kentucky Home."

Location/Directions: Forty-five minutes south of Louisville, Kentucky, on Highway 31E.

Site Address: 602 N. Third St., Bardstown, KY
Mailing Address: PO Box 279, Bardstown, KY 40004
Telephone: (502) 348-7300
Fax: (502) 348-7780
Internet: www.kydinnertrain.com

RAILWAY MUSEUM OF GREATER CINCINNATI
Museum, display
Standard gauge

Description: Museum with static displays. We offer guided tours through the interiors during the season.

Schedule: Guided tours: Sundays, May through October, 12:30 to 4:30 p.m. Free exterior visits every Wednesday and Saturday, 9:30 a.m. to 4 p.m. Closed holidays and holiday weekends.

Admission/Fare: Guided tour admission: adults, $4; children, $2.

Locomotives/Rolling Stock: Over 80 pieces of rolling stock, including Pullman heavyweight train set and PRR streamlined train set. Operable Brookeville, Plymouth, and Baldwin V-1000 locomotives.

Nearby Attractions/Accommodations: Near Cincinnati, Ohio, Reds baseball, Bengals football, Paramount Kings Island Amusement Park, Museum Center at Union Terminal.

Location/Directions: From I-275 in Kentucky, exit Route 17. Turn right at Latonia Ave., left to Southern Ave., ends at museum entrance.

Site Address: 315 W. Southern Ave., Covington, KY
Mailing Address: PO Box 15065, Covington, KY 41015
Telephone: (859) 491-7245
Internet: www.recoman63@fuse.net

HARDIN SOUTHERN RAILROAD
Train ride, display
Standard gauge

Description: This line is a working common-carrier railroad offering seasonal Nostalgia Train passenger service for a two-hour, 18-mile journey to the past. Built in 1890, the railroad was once a portion of the Nashville, Chattanooga & St. Louis Railway's Paducah main line through the Jackson Purchase in western Kentucky. The railroad is a designated Kentucky State Landmark. Today's trip features the rural farms and lush forests of the Clarks River Valley.

Schedule: May 25 through October 31: weekends, mid-day and late afternoon.

Admission/Fare: Adults, $9.75; children 3-12, $6. Tour, group, and charter rates available.

Locomotives/Rolling Stock: No. 863, 1940 Electro-Motive Corporation SW1, former Milwaukee Road; no. 4 Baldwin 1914 2-6-2 steam locomotive; air-conditioned coaches.

Special Events: Easter, Mother's Day, Halloween, Christmas.

Nearby Attractions/Accommodations: Land Between the Lakes National Recreation Area. Hardin's Railroad Restaurant.

Location/Directions: In western Kentucky, southeast of Paducah via I-24 and State Route 641; 6 miles from the Tennessee Valley Authority's Land Between the Lakes National Recreation Area. Hardin is located at junction of Routes 641/80. Depot is on Route 80 in the center of town.

         M

Site Address: Hardin, KY
Mailing Address: PO Box 20, Hardin, KY 42048
Telephone: (270) 437-4555
Fax: (270) 753-7006
E-mail: office@hsrr.com
Internet: www.hsrr.com

KENTUCKY RAILWAY MUSEUM
Train ride, dinner train, museum, display, layout
Standard gauge

ELMER KAPPELL

Description: Twenty-two-mile round trip through Rolling Fork River valley.

Schedule: March through May, weekends; June through September, Tuesday through Sunday; October through December, weekends. Call for trip times.

Admission/Fare: Adults and teens, $12.50; children 3-12, $8; under 3, free; cab rides, $25. Steam weekends, adults and teens, $15; children 3-12, $8; under 3, free; cab rides, $35.

Locomotives/Rolling Stock: L&N 4-6-2 no. 152; Monon BL-2 no. 32; SF CF-7 no. 2546; USA F-M H-12-44 no. 1846; L&N 2554; L&N 2572; SAL 821; MKT 884; TC 8038 (diner); other locomotives and rolling stock on display.

Nearby Attractions/Accommodations: My Old Kentucky Home State Park, Historic Bardstown, Mammoth Cave National Park, Lincoln birthplace (national historic site), Lincoln boyhood home, Maker's Mark Distillery (national landmark), Bernheim Forest.

Location/Directions: Three-and-one-half miles east of I-65 at exit 105 (Boston exit); 12 miles south of Bluegrass Parkway at exit 21 (New Haven exit).

*Coupon available, see coupon section.

 Radio Frequency: 160.545

Site Address: 136 S. Main St., New Haven, KY
Mailing Address: PO Box 240, New Haven, KY 40051
Telephone: (502) 549-5470 and (800) 272-0152
Fax: (502) 549-5472
E-mail: kyrail@bardstown.com
Internet: www.kyrail.org

KENTUCKY CENTRAL RAILWAY
Museum
Standard gauge

RUTH ANN COMBS

Description: Excursions pending reinstatement.

Schedule: By appointment.

Admission/Fare: Free.

Locomotives/Rolling Stock: 1925 Baldwin 2-6-2, former Reader no. 11; no. 9, VO, 1000 Baldwin diesel, former LaSalle & Bureau County Railroad; three coaches, former Erie Lackawanna; KCR no. 1, former Southern Railway concession/observation car; bay-window caboose no. 225, former Southern Railway; caboose no. 904055, former Baltimore & Ohio.

Location/Directions: U.S. 460 E (North Middletown Rd.).

Site Address: U.S. 460 East, Paris, KY
Mailing Address: 1749 Bahama Rd., Lexington, KY 40509
Telephone: (859) 293-0807

BIG SOUTH FORK SCENIC RAILWAY
Train ride
Standard gauge

Description: Three- and four-hour trips into the remote beautiful Big South Fork National Park. Each trip includes stopovers at restored Blue Heron and Barthell Mining Camps. Included in the ticket price is admission to the McCreary County Museum.

Schedule: May 1 through September 30: Wednesday through Saturday, 10 a.m.; Wednesday through Sunday and Memorial Day and Labor Day, 11 a.m.; weekends, 2:30 p.m. October 1 through October 31: Tuesday through Saturday, 10 a.m.; Tuesday through Sunday, 11 a.m.; weekends, 2:30 p.m.

Admission/Fare: Adults, $15; seniors, $14; children, $7.50. Group rates available.

Locomotives/Rolling Stock: Nos. 102 and 105, 1942 Alcos; open cars; caboose.

Special Events: Haunted Halloween Train, last three Fridays in October. Cumberland Heritage Day, middle of October (call).

Nearby Attractions/Accommodations: Cumberland Falls State Park, Big South Fork National River and Recreation Area.

Location/Directions: Kentucky 92, one mile west of U.S. 27 on State Route 92 and 33 miles south of Somerset, Kentucky.

Site Address: 21 Main St., Stearns, KY
Mailing Address: Box 368, Stearns, KY 42647
Telephone: (800) GO-ALONG
Fax: (606) 376-5332
Internet: www.bsfsry.com

BLUEGRASS RAILROAD MUSEUM
Train ride
Standard gauge

Description: The Bluegrass Railroad Museum offers a 1½-hour, 11½-mile round trip train ride through horse, cattle, and tobacco farms, over an ex-Southern Railway branch line that was built by the Louisville Southern Railroad in 1889. At the end of the line, passengers detrain to view the Kentucky River Palisades and the 1,659-foot-long and 281-foot-high Young's High Bridge, which was built by the Louisville Southern Railroad and completed in 1889. The bridge is named for Confederate Civil War hero and Louisville Southern president Bennett H. Young. Displays of railroad artifacts are housed in special cars.

Schedule: Mother's Day through End of October, open weekends only. Saturdays, 10 a.m. to 4 p.m.; Sundays, 12 noon to 4 p.m.

Admission/Fare: Call for current information

Locomotives/Rolling Stock: Alco MRS1s nos. 2043 and 2086; Fairbanks Morse H12-44 1849, former U.S Army; L&N caboose no. 1086; Southern caboose X471.

Special Events: Mother's Day, Book Bandits Robbery, Father's Day, Wild West Train Robbery, Civil War Train Robbery, Buckley Wildlife Trains, Clown Days, Halloween Trains, Santa Claus Special

Location/Directions: Woodford County Park off U.S. 62 (Tyrone Pike).

Radio frequency: 160.275, 161.160, 160.500, 161.190

Site Address: Versailles, Kentucky
Mailing Address: PO Box 27, Versailles, KY 40383-0027
Telephone: (859) 873-2476 or (800) 755-2476
Internet: www.bgrm.org

BIG EASY STEAM TRAIN
Train ride
Standard gauge

Description: Two-hour excursion featuring live Dixieland Jazz.

Schedule: Wednesdays through Sundays, 10:30 a.m., 2:30 and 6:30 p.m.

Admission/Fare: Adults, $32; children, $16.

Locomotives/Rolling Stock: 1901 Baldwin former Southern Pacific; NOGC 2013; NOGC 2014; NOGC 1106 F-unit.

Special Events: Many special events; call for information.

Nearby Attractions/Accommodations: Fifteen minutes from New Orleans, French Quarter, Casinos Convention Center, downtown hotels and Bayou Segnette/Jean Lafitte Parks.

Location/Directions: U.S. 90 over Mississippi River onto elevated expressway to Lafayette St. exit. Turn on Lafayette St. away from river. Proceed through tunnel into Belle Chasse.

Site Address: 9413 Highway 23 S., Belle Chasse, LA
Mailing Address: 9413 Highway 23 S., Belle Chasse, LA 70053
Telephone: (877) 431-1744 or (504) 393-8400
Fax: (877) 404-1788
E-mail: kcamardelle@BigEasySteamTrain.com
Internet: www.bigeasysteamtrain.com

DEQUINCY RAILROAD MUSEUM
Museum

Description: Nestled among tall pines at the beginning of Louisiana's foothills in north Calcasieu County, the city of DeQuincy was at the intersection of two major railroads in 1895. Its turn-of-the-century beginnings have been preserved, including two major historical land-marks–the All Saints Episcopal Church and the Kansas City Southern Railroad Depot. Both structures are on the National Register of Historic Places, and the depot now houses the railroad museum. There are a vintage caboose, a passenger coach, and a host of railroad artifacts.

Schedule: Mondays through Fridays, 9 a.m. to 4 p.m. and weekends, 12:00 to 4 p.m.

Admission/Fare: Free, donations appreciated.

Locomotives/Rolling Stock: No. 124 0-6-0 steam engine, built 1913 by America Locomotive Co.; Pullman railcar no. 4472, 85 feet in length; caboose no. 3487, built 1929.

Special Events: Louisiana Railroad Days Festival, second weekend in April.

Nearby Attractions/Accommodations: Gambling boats in Lake Charles, Acadian Trails.

Location/Directions: On Highway 12.

       M

Site Address: 400 Lake Charles Ave., DeQuincy, LA
Mailing Address: PO Box 997, DeQuincy, LA 70633
Telephone: (337) 786-2823 and (337) 786-7113

Louisiana, Long Leaf

HENRY TAVES

Description: Guided tours of a historic sawmill complex. The commissary offers exhibits and a gift shop. The motor car ride is ‰ mile.

Schedule: Year round, 9 a.m. to 5 p.m., except Thanksgiving and Christmas.

Admission/Fare: Admission is charged.

Locomotives/Rolling Stock: 4-6-0 Red River & Gulf no. 106; 2-6-0 Meridian Lumber co. no. 202; 4-6-0 Crowell Long Leaf Lumber Co. no. 400

Nearby Attractions/Accommodations: Alexander State Forest (camping), 11 miles; restaurants, 3 miles.

Location/Directions: From I-49 take exit 66 and travel west on State Route 112 to Forest Hill; follow signs 3.3 miles south on State Route 497. The site is halfway between Forest Hill and Glenmora on State Route 497.

*Coupon available, see coupon section.

          M

Site Address: 77 Long Leaf Rd., Long Leaf, LA
Mailing Address: PO Box 101, Long Leaf, LA 71448-0101
Telephone: (318) 748-8404
Fax: (318) 748-8404

**Maine, Alna
(Sheepscot Station)**

**WISCASSET, WATERVILLE &
FARMINGTON RAILWAY MUSEUM**
Train ride, museum, display
24" gauge

JOHN MCNAMARA

Description: Ride on ¾-mile mainline track on original roadbed in coach or caboose behind 12-ton diesel or steam locomotive.

Schedule: Memorial Day through Columbus Day: weekends, 12 to 5 p.m. Columbus Day through Christmas: Saturdays 9 a.m. to 5 p.m. Year round, workdays, Saturday 7 p.m. to sundown. Steam, May 5 and 6, August 11 and 12. Others to be scheduled.

Admission/Fare: Train ride–adults, $4; children, $2. Diesel–adults, $3; children, $1.50. Museum–free.

Locomotives/Rolling Stock: WW&F no. 9 Portland Co. Forney 044; WW&F no. 10 Vulcan Forney 044, W&Q no. 3 coach Jackson & Sharp; W&Q boxcar Portland Co.; WW&F flatcar no. 118 Portland Co., WW&F caboose 320 museum.

Special Events: Annual meeting, May 5; annual picnic, August 11.

Nearby Attractions/Accommodations: Alna Center School (one-room schoolhouse), Alna Meeting House (1789), Head Tide Church.

Location/Directions: Four and a half miles north of Wiscasset on Route 218, left on Cross Rd.

    M arm ᵀᴿᴬᴵᴺ

Site Address: 97 Cross Rd., Alna, ME
Mailing Address: PO Box 242, Alna, ME 04535
Telephone: (207) 586-5803
E-mail: webmaster@wwfry.org
Internet: www.wwfry.org

Description: Two hundred Maine antique land transportation vehicles, as well as 2,000 photographs of life in early Maine communities, enlarged, displayed, and captioned. Home of the Maine State World War II veterans memorial.

Schedule: May 1 through November 11: daily, 9 a.m. to 5 p.m.

Admission/Fare: Adults, $3; seniors, $2; under 19, free.

Location/Directions: From I-95, take exit 45B. Turn left at the traffic light and follow the signs.

Site Address: 405 Perry Rd., Bangor, ME
Mailing Address: 405 Perry Rd., Bangor, ME 04401
Telephone: (207) 990-3600
Fax: (207) 990-2653
E-mail: mail@colemuseum.com
Internet: www.colemuseum.org

BIDDEFORD STATION
GREAT NORTHERN NARROW GAUGE RR
Train ride, dinner train, museum, display, layout
24" and standard gauge

R. J. DAY

Description: Narrow gauge train ride of 1 kilometer, Great Northern Railway Museum, dining car operation, and theater. A model train club meets here. We also have a gift shop, antiques, and crafts.

Schedule: May through December: Saturdays and Sundays, 11 a.m. to 4 p.m. July 4th through Columbus Day: daily, 11 a.m. to 4 p.m.

Admission/Fare: Train ride–adults, $3; seniors and children under 12, $2.

Locomotives/Rolling Stock: Plymouth narrow gauge diesel no. 690; GN narrow gauge diesel no. 12; GN Shay no. 1; GN caboose X256; GN ranch car no. 1244; narrow gauge Fairmont cars and trailers; standard gauge Fairmont cars and trailers.

Special Events: Halloween Week, 5 p.m. to 9 p.m. Christmas Prelude, first weekend in December, 11 a.m. to 5 p.m. Adults, $5; children up to age 12, $3.

Nearby Attractions/Accommodations: Greater Portland area, Funtown USA, Old Orchard Beach Amusements, summer theaters, Seashore Trolley Museum, Maine coastal attractions, hotels.

Location/Directions: Maine Turnpike, exit Biddeford to U.S. Route 1, turn south (right) ¾ mile to Biddeford Station, which is on the left. A Shay locomotive is parked at the entrance.

Site Address: Route 1, south at Biddeford city line, Biddeford, ME
Mailing Address: PO Box 661, Biddeford, ME 04005-0661
Telephone: (207) 282-9255
Fax: (207) 967-5880

BOOTHBAY RAILWAY VILLAGE
Train ride, museum, display
24" gauge

Description: Ride a coal-fired, narrow gauge train through woods and a covered bridge, around a re-created village. View an exceptional antique vehicle exhibit and restored railroad structures and other buildings.

Schedule: Memorial Day through Columbus Day, 9:30 a.m. to 5 p.m. Call to confirm.

Admission/Fare: Adults, $7; children, $3. Memberships available.

Locomotives/Rolling Stock: Three Henschel coal-fired locomotives, 1913, 1936, 1938; two Baldwin saddle tank locomotives 1882; Plymouth Gas locomotive; Model T Ford Inspection 1923; closed coach; open coach; caboose; three boxcars ca. 1910; combine Laconia 1884; and handcar.

Special Events: Father's Day, June 17; Antique Engine Meet, July 7 and 8; Antique Auto Days, July 21 and 22; Children's Day, August 19; Maine Narrow Gauge Railroad Day, September 16; Fall Foliage Craft Fair, October 6 and 7.

Nearby Attractions/Accommodations: The Boothbay Region is an important tourist area with a variety of accommodations, restaurants, gift shops and other activities.

Location/Directions: Take Coastal Route 1 to the midcoast region, then take Route 27 south for 8 miles to the museum.

Site Address: Route 27, Boothbay, ME
Mailing Address: PO Box 123, Boothbay, ME 04537
Telephone: (207) 633-4727
Fax: (207) 633-4733
E-mail: staff@railwayvillage.org
Internet: www.railwayvillage.org

SEASHORE TROLLEY MUSEUM
Museum
Standard gauge

Description: A 25-minute, 3.5-mile trolley ride. Fifty-four streetcars on display in three car barns and Restoration Shop.

,Schedule: Daily operation, 10 a.m. to 5 p.m. from Memorial Day through Columbus Day.

Admission/Fare: Adults, $7; seniors, $5; children (6-16), $4.50; 5 and under, free.

Locomotives/Rolling Stock: The museum collection contains more than 200 transit vehicles from around the world. Up to ten streetcars are available for public operation.

Special Events: Parade of Trolleys, July 4. Trolley Birthday Party, August 4. Movie Day, second Sunday in July. Pumpkin Patch Trolley, third weekend in October.

Nearby Attractions/Accommodations: Southern Maine coastal area, Historic Museums in York, Kennebunk and Kennebunkport. Portland Old Town, Fun Town, Aquaboggin.

Location/Directions: 1.7 miles from Route 1 (Arundel), 3 miles north of Dock Sq. Kennebunkport, and 20 miles south of Portland.

*Coupon available, see coupon section.

Site Address: 195 Log Cabin Rd., Kennebunkport, ME
Mailing Address: PO Box A, Kennebunkport, ME 04046
Telephone: (207) 967-2800
Fax: (207) 967-0867
E-mail: carshop@gwi.net
Internet: www.trolleymuseum.org

Description: Oakfield Station has been restored to its original condition. Exhibits included hundreds of photographs dating back to the beginning of the Bangor & Aroostook Railroad in 1891. You'll see the building of this epic rail line through some of the most rugged terrain in the East. Other memorabilia include vintage signs and advertising pieces, signal lanterns, original railroad maps, telegraph equipment, newspapers chronicling the area's history, restored mail cars, and a rejuvenated C-66 caboose. Railroad history lives at Oakfield Station.

Schedule: Memorial Day weekend through Labor Day: Saturdays 12 to 4 p.m. and Sundays 1 to 4 p.m.

Admission/Fare: Donations appreciated.

Locomotives/Rolling Stock: BAR C-66 caboose.

Nearby Attractions/Accommodations: Restaurants and lodging.

Location/Directions: I-95 exit 60, turn right for 1 mile, turn left at hardware store, cross bridge, turn right to end of street.

Site Address: Station St., Oakfield, ME
Mailing Address: PO Box 62, Oakfield, ME 04763
Telephone: (207) 757-8575
E-mail: oakfield.rr.museum@ainop.com
Internet: www.ainop.com/users/oakfield.rr/

Maine, Phillips

SANDY RIVER & RANGELEY LAKES RAILROAD
DIVISION OF PHILLIPS HISTORICAL SOCIETY

Train ride, museum
24" gauge

KEN TEELE

Description: Ride on the original roadbed of the SR&RL Railroad in 1884 Laconia Coach no. 18 powered by a replica of SR&RL no. 4. Take a trip back in time as you visit our roundhouse. See the ongoing restoration of SR&RL Coach no. 18, and view our roster.

Schedule: June 3 and 17; July 1, 2, 14, and 15; August 5, 17, 18, and 19; September 2, 16, 29, and 30; October 6 and 7: hours are 11 a.m. to 4 p.m. Special 8:30 p.m. night trains on August 17 and 18.

Admission/Fare: Train–$3; children under age 13 are free.

Locomotives/Rolling Stock: SR&RL no. 4 replica; coaches nos. 17 and 18; cabooses nos. 556 and 559 (a replica of no. 556); flangers nos. 503 and 505; toolcar; flatcar; handcars; two Brookvilles; a Plymouth; MEC coach no. 170; Concord & Montreal coach no. 77.

Special Events: Phillips Old Home Days, August 17-19.

Nearby Attractions/Accommodations: Stanley Museum, Nordica Homestead, logging museum in Rangeley, Small Falls, Mt. Blue State Park, the Elcourt Bed and Breakfast, the Herbert Hotel. Several motels and restaurants in Farmington.

Location/Directions: Located 18 miles north of Farmington on State Route 4.

*Coupon available, see coupon section.

       M

Site Address: Bridge Hill Rd., Phillips, ME
Mailing Address: PO Box B, Phillips, ME 04966
Telephone: (207) 779-1901
Fax: (207) 779-1901
E-mail: awb@ime.net
Internet: www.srrl-rr.org

MAINE NARROW GAUGE RAILROAD COMPANY AND MUSEUM
Train ride, museum, display
24" gauge

EMMONS LANCASTER

Description: A two-foot gauge train takes passengers on a 3-mile round trip along Casco Bay.

Schedule: February 17 through May 13 and October 13 through December 10: weekends. May 15 through October 15 and December 9 through January 1: daily. Also all Maine and New Hampshire school vacation weeks.

Admission/Fare: Train–adults, $5; children, $3. Museum–voluntary contribution.

Locomotives/Rolling Stock: No. 3, 1913 Vulcan 0-4-4T; no. 4, 1918 Vulcan 0-4-4T, former Monon; no. 8, 1924 Baldwin 2-4-4T, former B&SR; no. 1, 1949 General Electric B-B diesel electric 23-ton; Plymouth lokies.

Special Events: Fall Steam Day, Winterfest Christmas Light Spectacular. Send SASE for list of dates and events.

Nearby Attractions/Accommodations: Old Port shopping area, tour boats, ferry terminal, restaurants.

Location/Directions: Off Franklin Arterial, U.S. Route 1A.

Radio frequency: 160.245

Site Address: 58 Fore St., Portland, ME
Mailing Address: 58 Fore St., Portland, ME 04101
Telephone: (207) 828-0814
Fax: (207) 879-6132
Internet: http://mngrr.rails.net/

BELFAST & MOOSEHEAD LAKE RAILROAD
Train ride

Description: Beautiful 1½-hour scenic excursion aboard our historic 1913 Swedish steam locomotive. Please call for more details.

Schedule: Call for information.

Admission/Fare: Call for information.

Special Events: Mother's Day. Family Day. Father's Day. Fall Foliage. Locomotion! Ultimate Rail Fantasy. Santa Express. Common Ground Fair Shuttle. Western Day.

Nearby Attractions/Accommodations: Field of Dreams Recreational Park, Common Ground Fairgrounds, Copper Heron Bed and Breakfast.

Location/Directions: Located in the heart of Unity, Maine.

Site Address: One Depot St., Unity ME
Mailing Address: PO Box 555, Unity, ME 04988
Telephone: (800) 392-5500
Fax: (207) 948-5903
E-mail: bmlrr@uninets.net
Internet: www.belfastrailroad.com

MAINE COAST RAILROAD
Train ride
Standard gauge

Description: Scenic train rides, 1½ hours round trip, as well as charters, tour groups, special events, and three-hour fall foliage tours.

Schedule: Call or write for information.

Admission/Fare: Call or write for information.

Locomotives/Rolling Stock: Two Alco M420 nos. 2002 and 2004; Alco Rs11 no. 367; Alco 51 no. 950; five passenger cars; caboose; table car.

Nearby Attractions/Accommodations: Located in Wiscasset, known as the prettiest village in Maine.

Location/Directions: Waterfront Park on Water St., off Route 1.

Site Address: 51 Water St., Wiscasset, ME
Mailing Address: PO Box 614, Wiscasset, ME 04578
Telephone: (207) 882-8000 and (800) 795-5404
Fax: (207) 882-7699

THE B&O RAILROAD MUSEUM
Museum, display, layout
HO layout on second floor

Description: The B&O Railroad Museum offers a nostalgic journey into America's railroading past, from its historical location at the original Mt. Clare Shops. Dedicated to preserving and interpreting its collections of 19th and 20th century artifacts related to America's railroads, the B&O Railroad Museum boasts a collection that spans over 170 years and includes over 200 pieces of railroad rolling stock, 15,000 artifacts, a historical library and research center, four significant 19th century buildings, and a mile of track on a 36-acre site encompassing the first mile of track used by the B&O Railroad, the Birthplace of American Railroading.

Schedule: Daily, 10 a.m. to 5 p.m. Closed major holidays.

Admission/Fare: Adults, $7; seniors (60+), $6; children 2 through 13, $5. Group rates are available.

Locomotives/Rolling Stock: Over 150 pieces of full-size rolling stock.

Special Events: All Aboard Days, April. Thomas the Tank Engine, July.

Nearby Attractions/Accommodations: Iron Horse Cafe on site.

Location/Directions: Corner of Pratt and Poppleton Streets.

*Coupon available, see coupon section.

Site Address: 901 W. Pratt St., Baltimore, MD
Mailing Address: 901 W. Pratt St., Baltimore, MD 21223
Telephone: (410) 752-2490
Fax: (410) 752-2499
E-mail: info@mindspring.com
Internet: www.borail.org

BALTIMORE STREETCAR MUSEUM
Train ride
5'4½" gauge

ANDREW S. BLUMBERG

Description: Relive rail transit in the city of Baltimore from 1859 to 1963 through a 15-car collection (13 electric, 2 horse-drawn). Cars operate over 1¼-mile round-trip trackage. The Visitors' Center contains displays and the Trolley Theatre, a streetcar mockup and video presentation.

Schedule: June 1 through October 31: weekends. November 1 through May 31: Sundays. Hours are noon to 5 p.m.

Admission/Fare: Adults, $5; seniors and children 4-11, $2.50; family, $15.

Locomotives/Rolling Stock: No. 417, circa 1888 single-truck closed car; no. 554, 1896 single-truck summer car, no. 1050, 1898 single-truck closed car and no. 264, 1900 double-truck convertible car, all Brownell Car Co.; no. 1164, 1902 double-truck summer car, no. 3828, 1902 double-truck closed car; no. 4533, 1904 single-truck closed car; and no. 6119, 1930 Peter Witt car, all J.G. Brill Co.; no. 3715, 1913 double-truck crane; more.

Special Events: Mother's, Father's, and Grandparent's Days. Museum Birthday Celebration. Pumpkin Junction, October. Tinsel Trolley, December; more. Call, write, or check web site for more information.

Nearby Attractions/Accommodations: B&O Railroad Museum.

Location/Directions: From Maryland and Lafayette Avenues, one block west on Lafayette to Falls Rd.

*Coupon available, see coupon section.

Site Address: 1901 Falls Rd., Baltimore, MD
Mailing Address: PO Box 4881, Baltimore, MD 21211
Telephone: (410) 547-0264
Fax: (410) 547-0264
Internet: www.baltimoremd.com/streetcar/

Maryland, Baltimore

PAUL SEYFRIT

Description: A 6- to 8-minute ride using live steam engines on the 7½" gauge 1/8 scale trains on about 3,400 feet of track.

Schedule: April through November: second Sunday, 11 a.m. to 3:30 p.m.

Admission/Fare: Free, donations accepted.

Locomotives/Rolling Stock: Depends on what owners bring. We have 4-4-0, 4-4-2, 4-6-2, 4-6-4, 4-8-4, and others.

Nearby Attractions/Accommodations: Baltimore & Ohio Museum, Baltimore Inner Harbor.

Location/Directions: From the west–take I-70 east, go across the Baltimore Beltway I-695, exit to the right onto Security Blvd.; turn right at the first light onto Forest Park Ave.; turn right at the next light onto Windsor Mill Rd.; the park will be on the right. From the south–take I-695 to exit 16, stay in the right lane for Security Blvd.; follow above directions. From the north–take I-695, follow signs to I-70; once on exit ramp stay to the left for Security Blvd.; follow above directions.

Site Address: Leakin Park, Windsor Mill Rd., Baltimore, MD
Mailing Address: 10121 Durango Dr., Damascus, MD 20872
Telephone: (301) 253-6309 and (410) 448-0730 (recording)
E-mail: seyfritp@erols.com
Internet: erols.com/seyfritp

**BOWIE RAILROAD
STATION MUSEUM**
Museum

Description: 1910 restored Pennsylvania Railroad depot, interlocking tower, caboose, and model trains. Collections illustrate local rail history, 1870 to today, alongside Amtrak/MARC corridor.

Schedule: Saturdays and Sundays, 12 to 4 p.m.

Admission/Fare: Free.

Locomotives/Rolling Stock: New caboose no. 518-303, built 1922.

Special Events: Spring Fling, last Sunday in April; Fall Fest, last Sunday in September; Train Spotting Day, Sunday of Thanksgiving weekend.

Nearby Attractions/Accommodations: Five sites in City of Bowie Museums and near National Capital Trolley Museum and B&O Railroad Museum. Close to Patuxent State Park. Enjoy dinner at the Railroad Inn.

Location/Directions: U.S. 50 or U.S. 295 to Maryland Route 197 for Bowie. Route 564 to Old Bowie. Route 564 becomes Eleventh St. The museum is at Eleventh and Chestnut on the south side of the rail line.

Site Address: 8614 Chestnut Ave., Bowie MD
Mailing Address: 12207 Tulip Grove Dr., Bowie MD 20715
Telephone: (301) 809-3088
Fax: (301) 809-2308
E-mail: museums@cityofbowie.org
Internet: www.cityofbowie.org/comserv/museums.htm

Description: Brunswick yards handled all B&O passenger and freight on the east-west main line. 863 feet of track in an interactive HO layout traces route from Washington, D.C., to Brunswick. Railroad artifacts include numerous historic photographs, tools, signals, equipment, and uniforms. Exhibitions of circa 1900 life in a railroad town; women's and labor history.

Schedule: All year: Saturdays, 10 a.m. to 4 p.m.; Sundays, 1 to 4 p.m.; April through September additional Thursdays and Fridays, 10 a.m. to 2 p.m.

Admission/Fare: Adults, $4; seniors, $2.50; children age 6 and up, $2.

Special Events: Railroad History Days, first full weekend in April. Railroad Days, first full weekend in October. Victorian Christmas, weekend after Thanksgiving.

Nearby Attractions/Accommodations: Harper's Ferry Toy Train Museum, Walkersville Southern Railroad, River and Trail Outfitters, Potomac and Shenandoah expeditions and ski tours, C&O canal bike tours.

Location/Directions: From Washington, D.C.–I-270 north to I-340 west to Brunswick. From Baltimore–I-70 west to I-340 west to Brunswick.

*Coupon available, see coupon section.

Site Address: 40 W. Potomac St., Brunswick, MD
Mailing Address: 40 W. Potomac St., Brunswick, MD 21716
Telephone: (301) 834-7100
Fax: (301) 834-4101
E-mail: rebeccatrussell@earthlink.net
Internet: www.bhs.edu/brun/rrmus/rrmus.html

**CHESAPEAKE BEACH
RAILWAY MUSEUM**
Museum

Description: The CBRM preserves and interprets the history of the Chesapeake Beach Railway, which brought people from Washington, D.C., to the resorts of Chesapeake Beach and North Beach from 1900 until 1935. The museum exhibits photographs and artifacts of the railroad and resort.

Schedule: May 1 through September 30: daily, 1 to 4 p.m. April and October: weekends only. By appointment at all other times.

Admission/Fare: Free.

Locomotives/Rolling Stock: The CBR chair car "Dolores" is undergoing restoration by the museum staff and volunteers. Only one half of "Dolores" survives; it is the only known CBR rolling stock to survive.

Special Events: Right of Way Hike, April 7 (rain date April 14); Antique Car Show, May 20; Bay Breeze Summer Concerts, June 14, July 12, August 9, September 13, 7:30 p.m; summer children's programs, mid-June through mid-August, Thursdays, 10 a.m.; Holiday Open House, December 2.

Nearby Attractions/Accommodations: Chesapeake Beach Water Park, Bayfront Park, Breezy Point Beach and Campground.

Location/Directions: From Washington's Capital Beltway–I-95 to Route 4 south. From Baltimore Beltway–I-695 to Route 301 south to Route 4 south. Left on Route 260, right on Route 261 to museum.

Site Address: 4155 Mears Ave., Chesapeake Beach, MD
Mailing Address: PO Box 1227, Chesapeake Beach, MD 20732
Telephone: (410) 257-3892

WESTERN MARYLAND
SCENIC RAILROAD
Train ride
Standard gauge

Description: Take a 32-mile round trip from Cumberland to Frostburg, climbing 1,300 feet with grades of 2.8 percent through three horseshoe curves and a 900-foot tunnel. Layover at historic C&P Rail Depot.

Schedule: Steam–May to September, Friday through Sunday; October, Thursday through Sunday; November and December, weekends. Diesel–May to September, Wednesday and Thursday; October, Monday through Wednesday.

Admission/Fare: Steam–May to September: adults, $17.50; seniors, $16; children under 12, $11. October through December: adults, $19.50; seniors, $19; children under 12, $12. Diesel–May to September: adults, $16.50; seniors, $15; children, $10. October: adults, $18.50; seniors, $18; children under 12, $11.

Locomotives/Rolling Stock: 1916 Baldwin 280 no. 734; Atlantic Coastline no. 850; Florida East Coast no. 851; Pennsylvania Railroad diner no. 1155; Central of Georgia combine no. 726; Norfolk & Western coach no. 540; two Southern coaches nos. 844 and 845; Seaboard coach no. 846; Union Pacific coach no. 2001; Santa Fe coach no. 1504; more.

Nearby Attractions/Accommodations: Holiday Inn, Best Western, Comfort Inn, several bed and breakfasts, Rocky Gap State Park.

Location/Directions: I-68, exit 43C to Harrison St. to station.

Site Address: Cumberland, MD
Mailing Address: 13 Canal St., Cumberland, MD 21502
Telephone: (301) 759-4400 or (800) 872-4650
Fax: (301) 759-1329
E-mail: trainmaster@miworld.net
Internet: www.wmsr.com

ELLICOTT CITY B&O RAILROAD STATION MUSEUM
Museum
HO

Description: The museum offers living history, Civil War programs, a caboose, a 40-foot HO scale model railroad, and a three-minute Speeder car ride.

Schedule: Varies.

Admission/Fare: Adults, $4; seniors and students, $3; children 12 and under, $2.

Nearby Attractions/Accommodations: Historic District.

*Coupon available, see coupon section.

Site Address: 2711 Maryland Ave., Ellicott City, MD
Mailing Address: 2711 Maryland Ave., Ellicott City, MD 21043
Telephone: (410) 461-1944
Fax: (410) 461-1944
E-mail: ecbostation@aol.com
Internet: www.b-orrstationmuseum.org

Maryland, Gaithersburg

**GAITHERSBURG RAILWAY
MUSEUM**
Museum, display, layout
HO

GERALD A. HOTT

Description: Outdoor display of BC&G steam locomotive and rolling stock. The restored brick freight house contains an operating HO gauge layout originally built for display at the National Geographic Society. Large railroad pictures and other displays are inside. There is a gift shop.

Schedule: Thursdays through Saturdays, 10 a.m. to 2 p.m. Closed major holidays.

Admission/Fare: Free. Donations appreciated.

Locomotives/Rolling Stock: Buffalo Creek & Gauley/Alco/Consolidation no. 14, built 1918; Baltimore & Ohio/bay window, wagon top, steel caboose no. 2490; Western Maryland MofW car 3008 (former Army Kitchen Car).

Special Events: Gaithersburg Olde Towne Day, fourth Sunday in September, 11 a.m. to 4 p.m.

Nearby Attractions/Accommodations: Gaithersburg Model Railroad Association, large HO layout. Gaithersburg Heritage Museum (historic Gaithersburg). Gaithersburg Fire Museum.

Location/Directions: Former B&O Railroad freight house at 9 S. Summit Ave., three blocks north of Maryland Route 355 (Frederick Ave.) Gaithersburg, Maryland.

    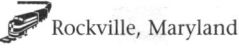Rockville, Maryland

Site Address: 9 S. Summit Ave., Gaithersburg, MD
Mailing Address: c/o 19 Brighton Dr., Gaithersburg, MD 20877-1809
Telephone: (301) 926-4660 (after 6 p.m.)

HAGERSTOWN ROUNDHOUSE MUSEUM
Museum, display, layout
O, HO

Description: Memories of the Western Maryland Roundhouse Complex, artifacts, photos, and displays.

Schedule: Year round: Friday through Saturdays, 1 to 5 p.m.

Admission/Fare: Adults, $3; children age 12 and under, $.50.

Locomotives/Rolling Stock: EMD Model 40 switcher; Alco MRS-1s; N&W and Reading cabooses; C&O Derby Club passenger car; PRR B-60 baggage car; H&F trolley car.

Special Events: Railroad Heritage Days, June. Autumn Leaf Excursions, October. The Train of Christmas Display, December-January.

Nearby Attractions/Accommodations: Antietam National Battlefield.

Location/Directions: I-81 to exit 2, U.S. 11 north to museum; I-70 to exit 32, take U.S. 40 west to U.S. 11, south to museum.

      M arm

Site Address: 400 S. Burhans Blvd. (U.S. 11), Hagerstown, MD
Mailing Address: PO Box 2858, Hagerstown, MD 21741-2858
Telephone: (301) 739-4665
Fax: (301) 739-5598

NATIONAL CAPITAL TROLLEY MUSEUM
Streetcar ride, museum
Standard gauge

KEN RUCKER

Description: Visit "From Streetcars to Light Rail," a computer-based exhibit, view an O gauge model of the trolley line from Rock Creek Loop to Chevy Chase Lake. Enjoy a 1¾-mile, 20-minute round trip in Northwest Branch Park on cars selected from the museum's collection of 15 streetcars.

Schedule: January 2 through November 30: weekends, 12 to 5 p.m. June 15 to August 15: Thursdays and Fridays, 11 a.m. to 3 p.m. October 1 to November 15 and March 15 to May 15: Thursdays and Fridays, 10 a.m. to 2 p.m. December: weekends, 5 to 9 p.m.

Admission/Fare: Adults, $2.50 (5 rides for $6.25); children 2-17, $2 (5 rides for $5); under age 2 are free.

Locomotives/Rolling Stock: DCTS 1101; CTCo 1053; TTC 4603; European trams; Washington work cars.

Special Events: Snow Sweeper Day, March 24. Cavalcade of Street Cars, April 22. Montgomery County History Day, July 8. Fall Open House, October 21. Holly Trolley Fest, December.

Nearby Attractions/Accommodations: Brookside Gardens, Sandy Spring Museum, Montgomery County Historical Society, nation's capital.

Location/Directions: On Bonifant Rd. between Layhill Rd. (Route 182) and New Hampshire Ave. (Route 650), north of Wheaton.

*Coupon available, see coupon section.

      M arm

Site Address: 1313 Bonifant Rd., Silver Spring, MD
Mailing Address: 1313 Bonifant Rd., Silver Spring, MD 20905
Telephone: (301) 384-6088
Fax: (301) 384-6352
E-mail: nctm@dctrolley.org
Internet: www.dctrolley.org

Maryland, Union Bridge

WESTERN MARYLAND RAILWAY HISTORICAL SOCIETY
Museum, display, layout
N gauge

Description: The museum, owned and operated by the WMRHS, houses our extensive collection of WM artifacts and memorabilia, photo archives, WM archive materials, and library. The museum and depot complex date from 1902.

Schedule: Sundays, year round, 1 to 4 p.m. (except Easter and Christmas). Other times by appointment.

Admission/Fare: Free.

Special Events: An HO modular layout of the western Maryland Railway operates in the depot on Sundays in January, 1 to 4 p.m.

Nearby Attractions/Accommodations: Civil War battlefields and museums (Antietam, Monocacy, Gettysburg, etc.); Carroll County Farm Museum; B&O Railroad Museum in Baltimore; Baltimore and Washington, D.C., attractions.

Location/Directions: The museum is on Maryland Route 75, 41 Main St., Union Bridge. It is easy to reach from I-70, I-270, I-795, U.S. 15, Maryland Route 26, Maryland Route 97, and Maryland Route 140.

      M

Site Address: 41 N. Main St., Union Bridge, MD
Mailing Address: PO Box 395, Union Bridge, MD 21791
Telephone: (410) 775-0150

WALKERSVILLE SOUTHERN RAILROAD
Train ride
Standard gauge

PAUL J. BERGDOLT

Description: An 8-mile, one-hour round trip through the woods and rural farm country north of Frederick, Maryland.

Schedule: May through October: Saturdays and Sundays, departs at 11 a.m., 1 and 3 p.m.

Admission/Fare: Adults, $7; children 3-12, $3.50; under age 3 ride free unless occupying a seat.

Locomotives/Rolling Stock: Plymouth 0-4-0 no. 1; Davenport 0-4-0 no. 2; converted flatcar no. 11; coach no. 12, former troop sleeper; caboose no. 2827, former Wabash; former PRR N5 cabin car no. 477532.

Special Events: Saturday Evening Mystery Dinner Trains, Father's and Mother's Day special, Track Car Days, Nature Trains, Civil War Days, Circus Days, Heritage Days, Ghost Trains, Santa Claus Specials. Call for details.

Nearby Attractions/Accommodations: Heritage Farm Park, Walkersville, Maryland. Catoctin Mountain Zoological Park, Thurmont, Maryland.

Location/Directions: Two miles east on Biggs Ford Rd., off U.S. Route 15, 3 miles north of Frederick. Located 50 miles west of Baltimore and 50 miles northwest of Washington, D.C.

Radio frequency: 160.6500 and 160.7250

Site Address: 34 W. Pennsylvania Ave., Walkersville, MD
Mailing Address: PO Box 651, Walkersville, MD 21793-0651
Telephone: (301) 877-363-WSRR
Fax: (301) 898-0899
E-mail: grtucker@erols.com
Internet: www.wsrr.org

WALKER TRANSPORTATION COLLECTION
BEVERLY HISTORICAL SOCIETY
& MUSEUM
Museum

Description: A research collection of over 100,000 photographs depicting all forms of transportation in New England. The majority of the collection is railroad and streetcar related. There are also models, memorabilia, library, videos, and oral history transcripts to view and browse. Photo reproductions may be ordered by mail or e-mail.

Schedule: Year round: Wednesdays, 7 to 10 p.m. or by appointment. Closed the week between Christmas and New Year's.

Admission/Fare: Donation.

Nearby Attractions/Accommodations: Balch House, Beverly. House of Seven Gables, Salem. Numerous hotels and motels.

Location/Directions: I-95 north or south to Route 128 north, exit 22 onto Route 62 east, to Cabot St. for one mile.

Site Address: 117 Cabot St., Beverly, MA
Mailing Address: 117 Cabot St., Beverly, MA 01915
Telephone: (978) 922-1186 (24 hours)
E-mail: fletcher@tiac.com
Internet: www.walkertrans.org

Massachusetts, Carver

EDAVILLE RAILROAD
Train ride
24" narrow gauge

Description: Five-and-a-half-mile train ride through an 1,800 acre cranberry plantation.

Schedule: June through August, daily 10 a.m. to 5 p.m. September and October, weekdays 10 a.m. to 3 p.m. and weekends 10 a.m. to 5 p.m. November 3 through January 7, weekdays 4 to 9 p.m. and weekends 2 to 9 p.m.

Admission/Fare: Adults, $12.50; seniors, $10.50; children, $7.50; children under 3 are free.

Locomotives/Rolling Stock: 1949 GE diesel; 1951 Whitcomb diesel; 1938 Hudswell-Clark steam; no. 11 combine 1900; no. 21 coach 1901; no. 26 coach 1986.

Special Events: Family Fun Day, Health and Safety Day, antique car shows, Steam Gas Meet, Cranberry Festival, Christmas Light Festival, New Year's Eve celebration.

Nearby Attractions/Accommodations: Middleboro and Plymouth, Massachusetts.

Location/Directions: Route 58, South Carver, Massachusetts.

*Coupon available, see coupon section.

Site Address: Route 58, South Carver, MA
Mailing Address: PO Box 825, Carver, MA 02330
Telephone: (508) 866-8190
Fax: (508) 866-7921
Internet: www.edaville.org

Massachusetts, Fall River

**OLD COLONY AND FALL RIVER
RAILROAD MUSEUM**
Museum

JACK DARMODY

Description: The museum, located in railroad cars that include a renovated Pennsylvania Railroad coach, features artifacts of the New Haven, Penn Central, Conrail, Amtrak, and other New England railroads.

Schedule: April 21 through June 30 and September through November 11: Saturdays 12 to 4 p.m. and Sundays 10 a.m. to 2 p.m. July 1 through September 3: Thursdays through Sundays 12 to 5 p.m.

Admission/Fare: Adults, $2; seniors, $1.50; children 5-12, $1; under age 5 are free. Group rates available.

Rolling Stock: Pennsylvania P-70 coach; no. 42 New Haven R.D.C. "Firestone"; New Haven 40-foot boxcar no. 33401; New York Central N7B caboose no. 21052.

Special Events: Annual Railroad Show, third weekend in January. Fall River Celebrates America waterfront festival, mid-August.

Nearby Attractions/Accommodations: Battleship Cove (six warships on display), Marine Museum at Fall River, Heritage State Park, Fall River Carousel.

Location/Directions: The museum is located in a railroad yard at the corner of Central and Water Streets, across from the entrance to Battleship Cove.

      M

Site Address: 2 Water St., Fall River, MA
Mailing Address: PO Box 3455, Fall River, MA 02722-3455
Telephone: (508) 674-9340
E-mail: railroadjc@aol.com
Internet: www.ocandfrrailroadmuseum.com

CAPE COD CENTRAL RAILROAD
Train ride, dinner train
Standard gauge

Description: Two-hour scenic excursions from Hyannis to the Cape Cod Canal. Three-hour elegant dinner trains. See cranberry bogs, salt marshes, kettle ponds, Cape Cod Bay, and the Cape Cod Canal.

Schedule: Scenic trains: May through October, daily except Mondays. November and December, weekends only.

Admission/Fare: Adults, $13; Seniors (62+), $11; children 3-11, $9. Dinner train: $49 per person.

Rolling Stock: NYC RS-3, rebuilt by Amtrak into RS-3M, Cape Cod Central no. 1201; Bayline Railroad chopnose GP-7s (two); three ex-LIRR coaches (scenic train), built in 1964 by Pullman; two ex-CN, ex-VIA coaches built by Canadian Car and Foundry in 1938, converted into table cars in early 1990s (dinner train); ex-Illinois Central parlor-lounge car build in 1917, used on dinner trains.

Nearby Attractions/Accommodations: Numerous motels and hotels, boat lines, and many other area attractions.

Location/Directions: Take Route 6 to exit 7. Go left off the exit and follow for approximately 2 miles to Route 28. Cross Route 28 and continue straight to the end of the road. At Main St. turn right. The depot is on the right at the corner of Main and Center Streets.

 Radio Frequency: 160.305

Site Address: 252 Main St., Hyannis, MA
Mailing Address: 252 Main St., Hyannis, MA 02601
Telephone: (508) 771-3800
Fax: (508) 771-1335
Internet: http://www.capetrain.com

BERKSHIRE SCENIC RAILWAY
Train ride, museum, display, layout
Standard gauge

Description: Fifteen-minute short shuttle train ride within Lenox Station yard, with narrative of Berkshire railroading and Lenox Station history. Locomotive cab tours for youngsters. The museum is in the restored Lenox station. Restored former New York, New Haven & Hartford NE-5 caboose; Fairmont speeder and track-gang train; displays about Berkshire railroading history; railroad videos; exhibit of photos of Gilded-Age Berkshire "Cottages"; two model railroads.

Schedule: May through October: weekends and holidays, 10 a.m. to 4 p.m. Lenox local shuttle trains operate half-hourly.

Admission/Fare: Adults, $2; children under age 14, $1.

Locomotives/Rolling Stock: GE 50-ton switcher no. 67; Maine Central Alco S-1 no. 954; New York Central EMD SW8 no. 8619.

Special Events: Fire Apparatus Display, Gas Engine Show, Circus Day, Halloween Special, Santa Special. Call or write for information.

Nearby Attractions/Accommodations: Tanglewood, summer home of the Boston Symphony Orchestra. The Norman Rockwell Museum.

Location/Directions: U.S. 7/20 to Housatonic St., travel east 1.5 miles.

Radio frequency: 161.400

Site Address: Willow Creek Rd., Lenox, MA
Mailing Address: PO Box 2195, Lenox, MA 01240
Telephone: (413) 637-2210
Fax: (518) 392-2225
E-mail: wordworks@taconic.net
Internet: www.regionnet.com/colberk/berkshirerailway.html

WENHAM MUSEUM
Museum, display, layout
Z, N, HO, O, and G gauges

Description: Seven push-button-controlled operating layouts in Z, N, HO, O, and G gauges with 12 trains operating. On display are antique toy trains, railroad artifacts and historical photos. Experts are on hand to answer questions on layout construction, antique toy trains, and railroad history.

Schedule: Open year round. Tuesdays through Sundays, 10 a.m. to 4 p.m.

Admission/Fare: Adults, $5; seniors, $4; children age 2 and up, $3. Museum members free.

Locomotives/Rolling Stock: Models only. No prototype equipment.

Special Events: "Train Time" exhibit, November 2002 through January 2003 (bi-annual). Annual Railroad Hobby Show, first weekend in January.

Nearby Attractions/Accommodations: Across the street is the Wenham Tea House and shops, a nonprofit organization offering lunch, afternoon tea and shopping. The area also offers other exceptional historic sites and museums, beautiful beaches, quaint towns, and scenic drives.

Location/Directions: Route 128 to exit 20A (Route 1A north). Follow Route 1A north for 2.3 miles. The museum is on the right before Wenham Town Hall.

      M

Site Address: 132 Main St., Wenham, MA
Mailing Address: 132 Main St., Wenham, MA 01984
Telephone: (978) 468-2377
Fax: (978) 468-1763
Internet: www.wenhammuseum.org

ADRIAN & BLISSFIELD RAILROAD
OLD ROAD DINNER TRAIN
Dinner train
Standard gauge

Description: This working, common-carrier freight and passenger railroad offers 14-mile, 1½-hour round trips from Blissfield to Lenawee Junction over a former New York Central line. The train travels through the village of Blissfield, crosses the River Raisin, and runs through Lenawee County farmland to Lenawee Junction. The Old Road Dinner Train is a two- to three-hour round trip featuring traditional, impeccable dining-car service including an elegant four-course dinner and a murder mystery.

Schedule: Year round: dinner trains–call for information; excursion trains–June through October.

Admission/Fare: Mystery dinner train–rates vary. Excursions–adults, $10; seniors, $9; children 3-12, $6. Reservations recommended. Family rates.

Locomotives/Rolling Stock: Nos. 1751 and 1752, 1957 EMD GP9s, former Grand Trunk Western/Central Vermont; dining cars "Columbia River" (former Union Pacific, 1949) and "River Raisin" (former Canadian National, 1937).

Special Events: Fall color tours, Santa Train, senior charters.

Location/Directions: U.S. 223 and Depot St. Ten miles west of exit 5 off U.S. 23 and 20 miles northwest of Toledo.

Site Address: 301 E. Adrian St., Blissfield, MI
Mailing Address: PO Box 95, Blissfield, MI 49228
Telephone: (888) GO-RAIL-1 and Excursions (517) 486-5979
Fax: (517) 263-2511
E-mail: abrrdp@tc3net.com

JUNCTION VALLEY RAILROAD
Train ride
14⅛" gauge

Description: The ride, more than 2 miles long, travels 22 feet down into a valley, around a lake, over 865 feet of bridges and trestles, and through a 100-foot tunnel, playground, and picnic area. We have a 10-stall roundhouse with turntable, five-track switchyard, railroad shops, and railroad hobby shop.

Schedule: Train rides–Mid-May through Labor Day: Mondays through Saturdays, 10 a.m. to 6 p.m.; Sundays, 1 to 6 p.m. September through October 7: weekends, 1 to 5 p.m. Railroad hobby shop open year round.

Admission/Fare: Adults, $5; seniors, $4.75; children, $4.25. Special events fares are higher. Group rates available.

Locomotives/Rolling Stock: No. 1177 GP45; no. 333 SW1500; no. 4 Plymouth; no. 300 SW1500 booster unit; no. 5000 WS4A; no. 7000 WS4A; no. 6000 WS4B; no. 555 MP15. Sixty-five railroad cars of all types. All are built ¼ the size of their prototype.

Special Events: Opening Day balloon launch. Valley of Flags, July 4. Railroad Days, July 21-22, August 18-19. Halloween Spook Ride, October. Fantasyland Train Ride, December, and more.

Location/Directions: I-75, Bridgeport exit, head south for 2 miles. Located 5 miles west of historic Frankenmuth.

*Coupon available, see coupon section.

Site Address: 7065 Dixie Highway, Bridgeport, MI
Mailing Address: 7065 Dixie Highway, Bridgeport, MI 48722
Telephone: (517) 777-3480
Fax: (517) 777-4070
Internet: http://gtesupersite.com/jvrailroad

Michigan, Charlotte

CHARLOTTE SOUTHERN
OLD ROAD DINNER TRAIN
Train ride, dinner train
Standard gauge

Description: This working, common-carrier freight and passenger railroad offers 7-mile, two-hour round trips from downtown Charlotte over a former New York Central line. The Old Road Dinner Train features traditional impeccable dining-car service, including an elegant four-course dinner and cash bar.

Schedule: Year round: call for information.

Admission/Fare: Dinner train fares vary; call for current pricing.

Locomotives/Rolling Stock: GE 44-tonner no. 3, 1956, the last one built, former Dansville & Mt. Morris Railroad; Dining cars "Butternut Creek" and "Battle Creek," both former Canadian National, nos. 5208 and 2502, built 1937 and 1954; baggage-generator car no. 5674, former Union Pacific, 1958; RPO no. 105, former Canadian National, 1924.

Special Events: Frontier Days, September. Santa Train. Special trips, senior charters, and bus tour group charters with or without meals.

Nearby Attractions/Accommodations: Michigan State Historical Museum in Lansing.

Location/Directions: 451 N. Cochrane St. is at the north end of downtown Charlotte's main street. Charlotte is 15 miles southwest of Lansing, just off I-69 exit 61.

Site Address: 430 N. Cochrane St., Charlotte, MI
Mailing Address: PO Box 265, Charlotte, MI 48813
Telephone: (888) 726-8277
Fax: (248) 583-3194
E-mail: ihswabash@msn.com

SOUTHERN MICHIGAN RAILROAD SOCIETY
Train ride, museum
Standard gauge

E. JESCHKE

Description: The Southern Michigan Railroad Society offers train rides: 6 miles or 12 miles, one way; 12 miles or 24 miles, round trip.

Schedule: May through September: Sundays, 11 a.m. and 2 p.m.; October: Saturdays and Sundays, 11 a.m., 1:30 and 4 p.m.

Admission/Fare: May through September: adults, $8; seniors, $7; children (2-12), $5. October: adults, $10; seniors, $8; children (2-12), $6.

Locomotives/Rolling Stock: 1943 GE 44-ton diesel no. 75; 1938 Plymouth no. 1; Alco RS-1 diesel; GMDH (prototype); South Shore & South Bend commuter car; 1950 caboose no. 21692, former New York Central; 1944 caboose no. 19882, former New Haven; 1949 gondola no. 726456, former New York Central.

Special Events: Clinton Fall Festival, September 23-24. Fall Color Tours, October weekends.

Nearby Attractions/Accommodations: Less than 10 miles from Irish Hills, which has many tourist accommodations. Tecumseh and Clinton have many parks and restaurants.

Location/Directions: Twenty-five miles southwest of Ann Arbor, Michigan, and 54 miles northwest of Toledo, Ohio.

Site Address: 320 S. Division St. Clinton, MI
Mailing Address: PO Box K, Clinton, MI 49236
Telephone: (517) 456-7677
Fax: (517) 456-7677
Internet: www.railfanhomepage.com/smrs

COOPERSVILLE & MARNE RAILWAY
Train ride, display
Standard gauge

THOMAS L. CHUBINSKI

Description: Fourteen-mile trip. Murder mystery dinner train, spring and fall.

Schedule: July through September: Saturdays, closed holiday weekends. October and December: weekends.

Admission/Fare: Summer: Adults, $7.50; seniors, $6.50; children, $4.50. Theme trains: Adults, $9.50; seniors, $8.50; children, $7.00.

Locomotives/Rolling Stock: Former GTW SW9 7014; two former Lackawanna commuter cars; two former CN commuter cars; former GTW caboose; former Dupont/Standard Oil 50-ton GE center cab; former C&O 250-ton wreck crane; former Lansing W&L.

Special Events: August 12, Summerfest/Railroad Days.

Nearby Attractions/Accommodations: Lake Michigan. Cities of Grand Haven, Muskegon, Holland, and Grand Rapids.

Location/Directions: I-96 to exit 16 or 19, follow signs to downtown Coopersville.

Site Address: 311 Danforth, Coopersville, MI
Mailing Address: PO Box 55, Coopersville, MI 49404
Telephone: (616)837-7000

HENRY FORD MUSEUM AND
GREENFIELD VILLAGE RAILROAD
Train ride
Standard gauge

E.J. GULASH

Description: The Greenfield Village Railroad offers a 2½-mile, 35-minute narrated circuit of the world-famous Greenfield Village in open-air passenger cars. While riding you will hear interpretations of the history of the village, its occupants and the railroad. The Henry Ford Museum, a general museum of American history occupying about 12 acres under one roof, contains a huge transportation collection, including the widely acclaimed "Automobile in American Life" exhibit. Greenfield Village is an 81-acre outdoor museum comprising more than 80 historic structures. Opening June 2000 is a recreation of the Detroit, Toledo & Milwaukee roundhouse; a six stall repair facility from 1884. Visitors can get an up close look at repairs taking place on the trains of Greenfield Village. Also at the site are 1941 Lima 2-6-6-6 no. 1601; a 1902 Schenectady 4-4-2; an 1858 Rogers 4-4-0; an 1893 replica of the "DeWitt Clinton"; 1909 Baldwin 2-8-0, former Bessemer & Lake Erie no. 154.

Schedule: Call or write for information.

Admission/Fare: Call or write for information.

Locomotives/Rolling Stock: No. 1, 1876 Ford Motor Co. 4-4-0 (rebuilt 1920s); no. 3, 1873 Mason-Fairlie 0-6-4T, former Calumet & Hecla Mining; no. 8, 1914 Baldwin 0-6-0, former Michigan Alkali Co.

Location/Directions: One-half mile south of U.S. 12 (Michigan Ave.) between Southfield and Oakwood Blvd. (freeway M39).

   M TRAIN

 Dearborn

Site Address: 20900 Oakland Blvd., Dearborn, MI
Mailing Address: PO Box 1970, Dearborn, MI 48121
Telephone: (313) 271-1620
Internet: www.hfmgv.org

WASHINGTON BOULEVARD
VINTAGE TROLLEYS
Train ride

GAIL JONES

Description: The length of the trolley ride is 1.96 miles round trip.

Schedule: Daily service. Weekdays, 8:10 a.m. to 5:30 p.m. Weekends, 9:58 a.m. to 5:30 p.m.

Admission/Fare: 50 cents; with Medicare Card, 25 cents.

Nearby Attractions/Accommodations: Ameritech, Cobo Center, Coleman A. Young Municipal Center, Comerica Park, Crowne Pointe Hotel, Detroit Fire Department Headquarters, Detroit News Building, Detroit Opera House, Detroit/Windsor Tunnel, Federal Court Building, Fox Theater, Grand Circus Park, Hart Plaza, Mariners Church, Renaissance Center.

Site Address: 1551 Washington Blvd., Detroit, MI
Mailing Address: DDOT, 1301 E. Warren Ave., Detroit, MI 48207
Telephone: (313) 933-1300 and (888) DDOT BUS
Fax: (313) 833-5523
Internet: www.ci.detroit.mi.us

MICHIGAN AUSABLE VALLEY RAILROAD
Train ride
16" gauge

Description: A 1½-mile, 18-minute scenic ride on a ¼ scale passenger train that runs through part of the Huron National Forest, and overlooks beautiful AuSable Valley. You will pass through a 115-foot wooden tunnel and over two wooden trestles, one over 220 feet long, to view the wooded valley below. The MAV Railroad is also home to Schrader's Railroad Gift Catalog. You will find one-of-a-kind items in the quaintly designed Railroad Depot Gift Shop from past and present catalogs.

Schedule: Weekends and holidays *only,* Memorial Day through Labor Day: 10 a.m. to 5 p.m. First two weekends in October: fall color.

Admission/Fare: $3; children under age 2 are free.

Locomotives/Rolling Stock: ¼ scale 16-inch Hudson steam locomotive 4-6-4 no. 5661, built by E.C. Eddy of Fairview and formerly run on the Pinconning & Blind River Railroad; two F7 diesel hydraulic locomotives built by Custom Locomotive, Chicago, Illinois; seven ¼ scale passenger streamline coaches.

Nearby Attractions/Accommodations: Huron National Forest, canoe ride National Scenic AuSable River, campgrounds, nature hikes.

Location/Directions: North on I-75 exit 202 onto M-33, north to Fairview. Turn south at blinker light in Fairview and go 3.5 miles south on Abbe Rd.

*Coupon available, see coupon section.

Site Address: 230 S. Abbe Rd., Fairview, MI
Mailing Address: 230 S. Abbe Rd., Fairview, MI 48621
Telephone: (517) 848-2229
Fax: (517) 848-2240

HUCKLEBERRY RAILROAD
Train ride
Narrow gauge

Description: Steam locomotive and historic wooden coaches depart from 1860s Crossroads Depot for 8-mile excursion. Route borders Mott Lake and crosses 26-foot trestle. Operated in conjunction with Crossroads Village, living history museum of 33 buildings and paddle wheel riverboat.

Schedule: Mid-May through August, open daily except Mondays. September, weekdays, 10 a.m. to 5 p.m., weekends and holidays 11 a.m. to 5:30 p.m. Call for October through November dates and hours.

Admission/Fare: Village, train, and boat: adults (13-59), $12.25; seniors (60+), $11.25; children (4-12), $7.50; age 3 and under free.

Locomotives/Rolling Stock: Baldwin 4-6-0 HRR no. 2; Baldwin 2-8-2 HRR no. 464; Plymouth diesel HRR no. 5; caboose and 14 historic coaches.

Special Events: Weekend events throughout summer, Halloween and Christmas trains. Railfans weekend, August 11-12, 2001 (tentative).

Nearby Attractions/Accommodations: Timber Wolf Campground, Stepping Stone Falls, outlet shopping, dinner cruises, numerous restaurants and motels.

Location/Directions: Just north of Flint, Michigan. I-475 off either I-75 or I-69 to exit 11, follow signs to railroad and Crossroads Village.

*Coupon available, see coupon section.

Site Address: 6140 Bray Rd., Flint, MI
Mailing Address: 5045 Stanley Rd., Flint, MI 48506
Telephone: (810) 736-7100 and (800) 648-7275
Fax: (810) 736-7220
E-mail: gencopks@concentric.net
Internet: geneseecountyparks.org

188

**FLUSHING AREA HISTORICAL
SOCIETY & CULTURAL CENTER**
Museum
Narrow gauge

Description: The collection includes items of the area's historical past, including permanent displays of railroad items. Other displays change periodically.

Schedule: May through first Sunday in December, open Sundays. Closed holiday weekends.

Admission/Fare: Free.

Nearby Attractions/Accommodations: There are several antique shops in the area.

Location/Directions: Take I-75 to exit 122 (Pierson Rd.) and go west approximately five miles. Pierson Rd. becomes Main St. in Flushing.

Site Address: 431 W. Main St., Flushing, MI
Mailing Address: PO Box 87, Flushing, MI 48433
Telephone: (810) 487-0814 (recording)

IRON MOUNTAIN IRON MINE
Train ride
24" gauge

Description: Designated a Michigan Historical Site, the Iron Mountain Iron Mine offers guided underground tours by mine train. Visitors travel 2,600 feet into the mine to see mining demonstrations and the history of iron mining in Michigan's Upper Peninsula. Mining equipment dating from the 1870s is shown and explained.

Schedule: June 1 through October 15: daily, 9 a.m. to 5 p.m.

Admission/Fare: Adults, $7; children 6-12, $6; children under 6 are free. School and group rates available.

Locomotives/Rolling Stock: Electric locomotive and five cars.

Location/Directions: Nine miles east of Iron Mountain on U.S. 2.

*Coupon available, see coupon section.

Site Address: Iron Mountain, MI
Mailing Address: PO Box 177, Iron Mountain, MI 49801
Telephone: (906) 563-8077
E-mail: ironmine@uplogon.com
Internet: www.ironmountainironmine.com

Michigan, Lake Linden

Train ride, museum, display, layout
36" gauge, HO

Description: Train rides are to commence in the summer of 2001. The line is currently under construction. Total length, 1.4 miles, including interpretative program on copper milling.

Schedule: May 31 through October 15, 10 a.m. to 5 p.m.; tours in off-season for groups only until December 13 or after April 1.

Admission/Fare: Adults, $5; children/seniors, $2; train fare: Adults, $5; children/seniors, $2 (August 2001).

Locomotives/Rolling Stock: 1915 Porter 0-4-0 tank engine used by Calumet & Hecla; caboose; Soo Line no. 261; C&H plow/flanger no. 2; C&H flanger (both constructed by C&H Mining) offsite exhibits; Q&TL RR 2-6-0 and 2-8-0; various other 36" gauge equipment, Russell snowplow C&H.

Special Events: Railroad Days, third weekend in August.

Nearby Attractions/Accommodations: Lake Linden Village campground (hook-ups, swimming beach, boat launch), Quincy Mine Hoist, McClain and Port Wilkens State Parks, Keweenaw National Historical Park, 40 miles by boat to Isle Royale National Park.

Location/Directions: Take U.S. 41 or M-26 to Houghton, cross Portage Lift Bridge to M-26 (right), 10 miles on southwest side of Lake Linden.

*Coupon available, see coupon section.

Site Address: 5500 Highway M-26, Lake Linden, MI
Mailing Address: PO Box 127, Lake Linden, MI 49945
Telephone: (906) 296-4121
Fax: (906) 296-0862
E-mail: richard@raildreams.com

Michigan, Manistee

THE SOCIETY FOR THE PRESERVATION
OF THE SS CITY OF MILWAUKEE

Museum, display
Standard gauge

ANDY LABORDE

Description: The society is restoring the last classic railroad carferry. The public tour provides visitors with a look at how the rails crossed the waters of the Great Lakes.

Schedule: Saturdays 12 to 5 p.m. in June; daily 12 to 5 p.m. in July and August; call for spring and fall hours.

Admission/Fare: Adults, $6; children 6-12, $4; under 6 free.

Locomotives/Rolling Stock: Carferry, 1931 triple expansion steamer, capacity 30 40-foot cars, 300 passengers. Former Ann Arbor, Pere Marquette/C&O, Grand Trunk Western design.

Special Events: Call for current events, days and times. Future events may include visits to Michigan and Wisconsin port cities.

Nearby Attractions/Accommodations: Manistee National Forest, Manistee Historic District, Lake Michigan carferry (Ludington to Manitowoc), Sleeping Bear Dunes National Lakeshore.

Location/Directions: From Grand Rapids, take U.S. 131 north to U.S. 10 west (Reed City). Take U.S. 10 west to the U.S. 31 intersection, just past Scottville, and go north on 31 to Manistee. At Manistee, follow signs to ship. Located at Ninth St. and Manistee Lake.

Site Address: 51 Ninth St., Manistee, MI
Mailing Address: SPCM, 115 U.S. 31, Beulah, MI 49617
Telephone: (231) 398-0238
Fax: (231) 882-4600
E-mail: sscitymilw@aol.com
Internet: www.carferry.com

Michigan, Owosso

MICHIGAN STATE TRUST FOR RAILWAY PRESERVATION
Train ride
Standard gauge

AARNE FROBOM

Description: A 1941 steam locomotive. Occasional events, exhibits, and excursions.

Schedule: Saturdays, 10 a.m. to 5 p.m. Occasional events as announced.

Admission/Fare: Free. Event prices as announced. Mailing list members receive updates, $25 annually.

Locomotives/Rolling Stock: Pere Marquette 2-8-4 no. 1225 (Lima, 1941); 1919 PM turntable.

Special Events: Engineer-for-an-Hour program permits MSTRP members to operate Locomotive 1225. Also, other interactive railroading programs. Coming for 2002: Steam Railroading Institute–an 11-stall roundhouse with steam locomotive service and museum; Railroad History Train–a mobile railcar with classroom and museum to extend our base in Shianassee County.

Nearby Attractions/Accommodations: Durand Depot Museum, Historic Crossroads Village. Call, fax or e-mail for local accommodations.

Location/Directions: Located in Tuscola and Saginaw Bay Railway Yard on S. Oakwood St., off Highway M-71 in southeast Owosso.

Site Address: 600 S. Oakwood St., Owosso, MI
Mailing Address: PO Box 665, Owosso, MI 48867-0665
Telephone: (517) 725-9464
Fax: (517) 723-1225
Internet: www.mstrp.com

HERB MC CULLAGH

Description: An educational and research facility dedicated to the preservation and enhancement of railroad technology and lore. Operating diesel locomotives, caboose(s), interlocking tower, "Combine" coach (under restoration) 1907 PM depot.

Schedule: Second and fourth Sunday of each month, 1 to 5 p.m. Also open by appointment for groups or individuals.

Admission/Fare: General Admission, $1; family rate, $3.

Locomotives/Rolling Stock: GP-9 locomotives (operable) GTW 4428 and GTW 4433; C&O cabooses 903577, 900342, 900977 (latter two under restoration); combine C&O 911245 (under restoration) converted to MW cook car by C&O.

Nearby Attractions/Accommodations: Frankenmuth; Junction Valley ¼ scale railroad; Japanese gardens, children's zoo; many motels along I-675 and fine hotel (Crown Plaza) downtown.

Location/Directions: I-75 to exit 149 (M-46 West-Holland Ave.) Follow through city and across river. Left at first traffic light (Michigan Ave.) and follow across tracks. Turn right at museum sign. Follow to Maple and turn right.

       M

Site Address: 900 Maple St., Saginaw, MI
Mailing Address: 900 Maple St., Saginaw, MI 48602
Telephone: (517) 790-7994

TOONERVILLE TROLLEY, TRAIN AND BOAT TOURS
Train ride
24" gauge

Description: Enjoy a 6½-hour train and boat tour to Tahquamenon Falls or 1¾-hour wilderness train ride, 5½ miles one way.

Schedule: June 15 through October 6. Please call for schedule.

Admission/Fare: Six-and-a-half-hour trip to falls: adults, $24; children 6-15, $12; under 6, free; 1¾-hour train ride: adults, $12; children 6-15, $6; under 6 free.

Locomotives/Rolling Stock: Two 1964 Plymouth 5-ton diesels; 1957 Plymouth 5-ton gas; 11 passenger cars.

Nearby Attractions/Accommodations: 80 minutes from Newberry, Michigan; many motels, restaurants, and campsites. Nearby attractions: Oswald's Bear Ranch, Whitefish Point lighthouse, logging museum.

Location/Directions: East of Newberry, Michigan, just off M-28 at Soo Junction. One hour from Mackinac Bridge or Sault Ste. Marie.

*Coupon available, see coupon section.

Site Address: Soo Junction, MI
Mailing Address: 5883 County Road 441, Newberry, MI 49868
Telephone: (888) 77-TRAIN or (906) 293-3806
E-mail: soojunction@portup.com
Internet: www.destinationmichigan.com/toonerville-trolley.html

SPIRIT OF TRAVERSE CITY
Train ride
15" gauge

LAUREN VAUGHN

Description: The "Spirit of Traverse City," an oil-fired, ¼-scale replica of a 4-4-2 steam locomotive, pulls passengers in three open-air cars on a ⁹⁄₁₀-mile loop through the Clinch Park Zoo marina and beach. Provides scenic views of West Grand Traverse Bay and loads adjacent to the Con Foster Museum.

Schedule: May 26 through September 3 and September 8, 9, 15, and 16: daily, 10 a.m. to 4:30 p.m.

Admission/Fare: Adults, $1; children 5-12, $.50; under age 5 are free.

Locomotives/Rolling Stock: "Spirit of Traverse City" no. 400 oil-fired 4-4-2 steam locomotive; three open-air passenger cars.

Special Events: Family Fun Day, June 3; 25-cent rides, popcorn, and zoo admission.

Nearby Attractions/Accommodations: Clinch Park Zoo, Clinch Park Beach, Con Foster Museum, motels, campgrounds, golf courses, more.

Location/Directions: On U.S. 31 (Grandview Parkway) at Cass St., in downtown Traverse City on West Grand Traverse Bay.

Site Address: 100 E. Grandview Pkwy., Traverse City, MI
Mailing Address: 625 Woodmere Ave., Traverse City, MI 49686
Telephone: (231) 922-4910
Fax: (231) 941-7716

Michigan, Walled Lake

MICHIGAN STAR CLIPPER
DINNER TRAIN/COE RAIL
Dinner train, train ride
Standard gauge

Description: One-hour and three-hour train rides through Michigan wetlands.

Schedule: Coe Rail: April through October, Sundays 1 and 2:30 p.m. Dinner Train: year round, except Mondays and certain holidays. Departs Tuesdays, Wednesdays, Thursdays, and Saturdays at 7 p.m., Fridays at 7:30 p.m., and Sundays at 5 p.m.

Admission/Fare: Standard fare: adults, $9; children (2-10) and seniors (65+), $8. Three-hour ride: $69.50 per person, includes five-course meal and entertainment.

Locomotives/Rolling Stock: GR-10 no. 52; EL/NJT nos. 4315 and 4317; Milw/PVTC/CRLE no. 165; C&EI no. 85258; caboose no. 60; ATSF/Amtrak no. 9604, PRR nos. 9604, 9605 and 9600; more.

Special Events: Coe Rail: Easter Bunny Special, Hobo Halloween, Santa Train. Dinner Train: Special Charters, seats 232.

Nearby Attractions/Accommodations: Henry Ford Museum, Greenfield Village, Detroit/Windsor Casinos.

Location/Directions: I-96 to exit 162, north on Novi Rd., west on Maple Rd., north on Pontiac Trail, 100 yards, cross tracks, turn right into parking lot.

*Coupon available, see coupon section.

Site Address: 840 N. Pontiac Trail, Walled Lake, MI
Mailing Address: 840 N. Pontiac Trail, Walled Lake, MI 48390
Telephone: (248) 960-9440
Fax: (248) 960-9444
E-mail: info@michiganstarclipper.com
Internet: www.michiganstarclipper.com

CHARLES WILLER

Description: The Little River Railroad offers a 25-mile round-trip steam excursion departing from White Pigeon Depot to Sturgis and return. Lasting about 2 hours and 45 minutes, the run goes through forest, farm, and city scenery. Shorter runs are offered in July and August.

Schedule: Memorial Day weekend through October: Sundays and holidays, 2 p.m. departure; mid-July through mid-August, 1 and 3 p.m. departures.

Admission/Fare: Adults, $15; children 3-11, $8; families, $50 (two adults, three or more children). Short runs, adults, $7; children, $4. Group rates for 20 or more.

Locomotives/Rolling Stock: No. 110, 1911 Baldwin 4-6-2, former Little River Railroad–the smallest standard gauge Pacific locomotive ever built; combination car no. 2594, former Chicago & Alton; *Hiawatha* coaches, former Milwaukee Road; open-air cars; World War II troop car; cabooses, former Baltimore & Ohio.

Nearby Attractions/Accommodations: Shipshewana Auction, Dutchman Essenhaus–Amish cooking, Kalamazoo Air Museum.

Location/Directions: Indiana Toll Road, exit 107, north on Indiana 13 to U.S. 12, east to traffic light in White Pigeon. Go south and follow signs. Call or write for brochure.

       M

Site Address: 413 Elkhart St., White Pigeon, MI
Mailing Address: 13187 State Route 120, Middlebury, IN 46540
Telephone: (219) 825-9182
Internet: //2mm.com/info/rr/

**END-O-LINE RAILROAD PARK
AND MUSEUM**
Museum, display, layout
HO

Description: A working railroad yard including a rebuilt enginehouse on its original foundation, an original four-room depot, a water tower, an 1899 section-foreman's house, and an outhouse. The turntable, built in 1901 by the American Bridge Company and still operable, is the only one left in Minnesota on its original site. A general store and one-room school-house can also be seen. A replica of the coal bunker is used as a picnic shelter and gift shop. The buildings contain various exhibits and displays of railroad artifacts, photographs, memorabilia, and equipment. The freight room in the depot has an HO scale model train layout of the rail-road yards in Currie, complete with steam engine sound effects, authentic structures, and local countryside. A bicycle/pedestrian paved pathway connects the railroad park to Lake Shetek State Park (6 miles round trip).

Schedule: Memorial Day through Labor Day: Mondays through Fridays, 10 a.m. to 12 noon and 1 to 5 p.m.; weekends, 1 to 5 p.m. Last tour 4 p.m.

Admission/Fare: Adults, $3; students, $2; household, $6.

Locomotives/Rolling Stock: Georgia Northern steam engine no. 102; Grand Trunk Western caboose; Brookville diesel switcher, more.

Nearby Attractions/Accommodations: Lake Shetek State Park, Laura Ingalls Wilder Museum, Pipestone National Monument, campgrounds.

Location/Directions: Highway 30 to Currie, go ¾ mile north on County Road 38.

Site Address: 440 N. Main St., Currie, MN
Mailing Address: 440 N. Mill St., Currie, MN 56123
Telephone: (507) 763-3708
E-mail: louise@endoline.com
Internet: www.endoline.com

THE OLD DEPOT RAILROAD MUSEUM
Museum

Description: A former Great Northern depot built in 1913 is filled with railroad memorabilia and pictures. This 33-foot by 100-foot country depot has two waiting rooms, an agent's office, and a large freight room, as well as a full basement. Authentic recorded sounds of steam locomotives and the clicking of the telegraph key create the realistic feel of an old small-town depot. Items displayed include lanterns, telegraph equipment, semaphores, and other signals; section crew cars, a hand pump car, and a velocipede; tools and oil cans; depot and crossing signs; buttons, badges, service pins, and caps; a large date-nail collection; and many baggage carts. Also included are children's toy trains, an HO scale model railroad, and many railroad advertising items. Interpretation of the items is provided. Static ½ scale train on display.

Schedule: Memorial Day through October 1: daily, 10 a.m. to 4:30 p.m.

Admission/Fare: Adults, $2.50; children under age 12, $1.

Nearby Attractions/Accommodations: Six other museums along Highway 12.

Locomotives/Rolling Stock: Caboose; two boxcars.

Location/Directions: Fifty miles west of Minneapolis on U.S. Highway 12. Fourteen miles north of Hutchinson on State Highway 15.

Site Address: 651 W. Highway 12, Dassel, MN
Mailing Address: 651 W. Highway 12, Dassel, MN 55325
Telephone: (320) 275-3876
Fax: (320) 275-3933

Minnesota, Duluth

LAKE SUPERIOR & MISSISSIPPI RAILROAD
Train ride
Standard gauge

DAVE SCHAUER

Description: Take a 90-minute trip on historic equipment on 132-year-old roadbed.

Schedule: June 30 through September 2: weekends. Fall Colors excursions September 22, 23, and 29 and October 1. 10:30 a.m. and 1:30 p.m.

Admission/Fare: Adults, $7; seniors, $6; children 12 and under, $5.

Locomotives/Rolling Stock: GE center-cab 50-ton no. 46; ACF no. 85; Pullman no. 29; flatcar (open-top) no. 100R.

Nearby Attractions/Accommodations: Duluth Zoo is across the street.

Location/Directions: Go west on Grand Ave. to Fremont St.

        M

Site Address: 71st Ave. W. and Grand Ave., Duluth, MN
Mailing Address: PO Box 16211, Duluth, MN 55816
Telephone: (218) 624-7549
Fax: (218) 728-6303
E-mail: captkatt@aol.com

LAKE SUPERIOR RAILROAD MUSEUM
Train ride, dinner train, museum, display, layout
Standard gauge, narrow gauge, HO

BRUCE OJARD PHOTOGRAPHY

Description: The Lake Superior Railroad Museum has one of the largest and most diverse collections of railroad artifacts, including the Great Northern's famous "William Crooks" locomotive and cars of 1861; Northern Pacific Railway no. 1, The "Minnetonka" built in 1870; the Soo line's first passenger diesel, FP7 no. 2500A; Duluth, Missabe & Iron Range 2-8-8-4 no. 227, displayed with revolving drive wheels and recorded sound; Great Northern no. 400, the first production-model SD45 diesel; an 1887 steam rotary snowplow; other steam, diesel, and electric engines; a Railway Post Office car; a dining-car china exhibit; freight cars; work equipment; an operating electric single-truck street-car; and much railroadiana.

Schedule: Museum–year round. Train/trolley–Memorial Day weekend through Labor Day weekend. Hours: Memorial Day to Mid-October, 9:30 a.m. to 6 p.m. Mid-October to Memorial Day, 10 a.m. to 5 p.m. Monday through Saturday and 1 p.m. to 5 p.m. Sunday.

Admission/Fare: Combination tickets (museum and train), $6 to $20.

Special Events: Steam train weekends.

Location/Directions: I-35 exit downtown Duluth/Michigan St.

Radio frequency: 160.920

Site Address: 506 W. Michigan St., Duluth, MN
Mailing Address: 506 W. Michigan St., Duluth, MN 55802
Telephone: (218) 733-7590
Fax: (218) 733-7596
E-mail: isrm@cpinternet.com or nssr@cpinternet.com
Internet: www.duluth.com/lsrm/

TIM SCHANDEL

Description: Formerly the Duluth Missabe & Iron Range Railway's Lake Front Line, this railroad's 26 miles of track run between the Depot in downtown Duluth, along the Lake Superior waterfront, and through the residential areas and scenic woodlands of northeastern Minnesota to the Two Harbors Depot, adjacent to DM&IR's active taconite yard and ship-loading facility. The line offers 1½-, 2½-, and 6-hour round trips with departures from Duluth.

Schedule: To Lester River–Memorial Day to Labor Day, Sunday through Thursday, 12:30 and 3 p.m.; Friday and Saturday, 10 a.m., 12:30 and 3 p.m. Pizza train–Wednesday through Saturday, 6:30 p.m. Two Harbors–Friday and Saturday, 10:30 a.m. Reduced schedule, Labor Day to mid-October.

Admission/Fare: Lester River–adults, $9; children, $5. Pizza train–adults, $16; children, $11. Two Harbors–adults, $17; children, $8.

Locomotives/Rolling Stock: DM&IR SD18 no. 193; GN SD45 no. 400; GN NW5 no. 192; Soo Line FP7 no. 2500; DM&IR and GN coaches; more.

Special Events: Steam excursion weekends, elegant dinner trains, Grandma's Marathon Train.

Location/Directions: Duluth–Duluth Depot, Michigan St., downtown.

*Coupon available, see coupon section.

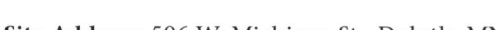

Radio frequency: 160.920

Site Address: 506 W. Michigan St., Duluth, MN
Mailing Address: 506 W. Michigan St., Duluth, MN 55802
Telephone: (218) 722-1273 and (800) 423-1273
Fax: (218) 733-7596
E-mail: nssr@cpinternet.com
Internet: www.duluth.com/lsrm

MINNESOTA TRANSPORTATION MUSEUM
EXCELSIOR STREETCAR LINE
Streetcar ride

LOUIS HOFFMAN

Description: A ride on ½ mile of track around historic Excelsior, Minnesota.

Schedule: Mid-May through mid-September: weekends, 10 a.m. to 4 p.m.; Thursdays, 3 to 6 p.m. No. 78 does not run on rainy days.

Admission/Fare: $1.

Locomotives/Rolling Stock: Streetcar no. 78 from 1893.

Nearby Attractions/Accommodations: Steamboat Minnehaha, Lake Minnetonka.

Location/Directions: State Route 7 to County Road 19, turn right; turn right onto Water St. Office is located at Water and Lake Streets.

   M arm  St. Paul

Site Address: 328 Lake St., Excelsior, MN
Mailing Address: 328 Lake St., Excelsior, MN 55331
Telephone: (952) 474-2115
E-mail: sboat@fcomm.net
Internet: www.mtmuseum.org

**MINNESOTA TRANSPORTATION MUSEUM
COMO-HARRIET STREETCAR LINE**
Train ride, museum
Standard gauge

AARON ISAACS

Description: A 2-mile, 15-minute round trip on a restored portion of the former Twin City Rapid Transit Company's historic Como-Harriet route. Streetcars operate over a scenic line through a wooded area between Lakes Harriet and Calhoun. This is the last operating portion of the 523-mile Twin City Lines system, abandoned in 1954. The Linden Hills Station, a re-creation of the 1900 depot located at the site, houses changing historical displays about electric railways in Minnesota.

Schedule: May 18 through September 3: weekends, holidays, 12:30 p.m. to dusk. Mondays through Fridays, 6:30 p.m. to dusk. May before Memorial Day and September after Labor Day: weekends, 12:30 p.m. to dusk. October: weekends 12:30 to 5 p.m.

Admission/Fare: $1.50; children under age 4 are free. Chartered streetcars–$60 per half hour.

Locomotives/Rolling Stock: No. 265, 1915 Duluth St. Railway (TCRT Snelling Shops, St. Paul); no. 322, 1946 Twin City Lines PCC (St. Louis Car Co.); no. 1300, 1908 Twin City Lines (Snelling Shops).

Nearby Attractions/Accommodations: Lake Harriet Park.

Location/Directions: I-35W, 46th St. west to Lake Harriet Parkway, parkway to west shore at Linden Hills Station. Metro transit routes 6 and 28.

*Coupon available, see coupon section.

St. Paul   **Radio frequency: 161.355**

Site Address: 2330 W. 42nd St., Minneapolis, MN
Mailing Address: 193 E. Pennsylvania Ave., St. Paul, MN 55101-4319
Telephone: (651) 228-0263 and (800) 711-2591
Internet: www.mtmuseum.org

MINNESOTA TRANSPORTATION MUSEUM
MINNEHAHA DEPOT
Museum, display

ERIC MORTENSEN, MINNESOTA HISTORICAL SOCIETY

Description: Built in 1875, the Minnehaha Depot replaced an even smaller Milwaukee Road depot on the same site. Milwaukee Road agents quickly nicknamed the depot the "Princess" because of its intricate architectural details. Until Twin City Rapid Transit Company streetcars connected Minnehaha Falls Park to the city, as many as 13 passenger trains per day served the depot. It remained in service, primarily handling freight, for many years. Located at the south end of the Canadian Pacific South Minneapolis branch, operated by the Minnesota Commercial Railway, once a through route to the south, the depot sees occasional freight movements and often hosts visiting private cars. Visitors may tour the depot, which appears much as it did when in service as a typical suburban station. Exhibits include telegraphy demonstrations and historic photographs of the depot and its environs.

Schedule: May 27 through September 3: Sundays and holidays, 12:30 to 4:30 p.m.

Admission/Fare: Donations appreciated.

Nearby Attractions/Accommodations: Fort Snelling State Park. Historic Fort Snelling. Mall of America.

Location/Directions: In Minnehaha Falls Park just off State Highway 55 (Hiawatha Ave.). Metro transit routes 7 and 20.

 St. Paul

Site Address: 4926 Minnehaha Ave., Minneapolis, MN
Mailing Address: 193 E. Pennsylvania Ave., St. Paul, MN 55101-4319
Telephone: (651) 228-0263 and (800) 711-2591
E-mail: corbin@plethora.net
Internet: www.mtmuseum.org

NORTH STAR RAIL, INC.
FRIENDS OF THE 261
Train ride
Standard gauge

VICTOR HAND

Description: North Star Rail, Inc., operates a day-long steam powered excursion over various Class 1 railroads.

Schedule: Varies with trip. Call or write for information.

Admission/Fare: Varies. Reservations recommended.

Locomotives/Rolling Stock: No. 261 1944 Alco 4-8-4, former Milwaukee Road class S3, leased to North Star Rail by the National Railroad Museum in Green Bay, Wisconsin.

Site Address: Minneapolis, MN
Mailing Address: 4322 Lakepoint Ct., Shoreview, MN 55126
Telephone: (651) 490-1985
Fax: (651) 490-1985 (call first)
E-mail: friends261aol.com
Internet: www.261.com

Description: Museum with Great Northern steam locomotive and depot.

Schedule: Memorial Day through Labor Day: weekdays, 9 a.m. to 5 p.m.; weekends, 1 to 5 p.m.; September through May: weekdays, 9 a.m. to 5 p.m.

Admission/Fare: Free.

Locomotives/Rolling Stock: Great Northern 2523 P-2 class Baldwin.

Nearby Attractions/Accommodations: Schwanke Tractor and Car Museum.

Location/Directions: 610 Northeast Business 71, Willmar, Minnesota. Follow the signs at the north, south, and east edges of the city.

Site Address: 610 N.E. Highway 71, Willmar, MN
Mailing Address: 610 N.E. Highway 71, Willmar, MN 56201
Telephone: (320) 235-1881
E-mail: kandhist@wecnet.com
Internet: http://freepages.genealogy.rootsweb.com/~KCHS123/index.html

YUMA VALLEY RAILWAY
With coupon: Adults $1 off; seniors $1 off; children $1 off
Valid April 2001 through March 2002

THE TRAIN PLACE
With coupon: Buy one large sub sandwich, get one free
. Valid April 2001 through March 2002
Limit one per party

RAILTOWN 1897
STATE HISTORIC PARK
10% off ticket price
Valid April 2001 through March 2002

LOMITA RAILROAD MUSEUM
Regular price: Adults $2, seniors $2, children $1
With coupon: Adults $1, seniors $1, children $.50
Valid April 2001 through March 2002
Maximum discount 1 person per coupon

NAPA VALLEY WINE TRAIN
Regular price: $29.50 to $110
With coupon: $26.55 to $105.50
Valid April 2001 through March 2002
Maximum discount 10% off train fare portion

NEVADA COUNTY TRACTION COMPANY
With coupon: Buy one admission get equal price admission free
Valid April 2001 through March 2002
Maximum discount 1 person per coupon

SHORE LINE TROLLEY MUSEUM
Regular price: Adults $5, seniors $4, children $2
With coupon: Adults $4.50, seniors $3.50, children $1.50
Valid April 2001 through March 2002
Maximum discount 6 persons per coupon

CONNECTICUT TROLLEY MUSEUM
Regular price: Adults $6, seniors $5, children $3
With coupon: Adults $5, seniors $4, children $2.50
Valid April 2001 through March 2002
Maximum discount 6 persons per coupon

WILMINGTON & WESTERN RAILROAD
With coupon: Buy one admission get equal price admission free
Valid April 2001 through March 2002
Maximum discount $8 per coupon

RAILROAD MUSEUM'S TRAIN VILLAGE
Regular price: Adults $2.50, seniors $2.50
With coupon: Adults $2, seniors $2
Valid April 2001 through March 2002
Maximum discount 4 persons per coupon

FLORIDA GULF COAST RAILROAD
MUSEUM
Regular price: Adults $10, children $6
With coupon: Adults $8, children $5
Valid April 2001 through March 2002

KENNESAW CIVIL WAR MUSEUM
With coupon: Buy one admission get equal price admission free
Valid April 2001 through March 2002
Maximum discount 2 persons per coupon

Guide to Tourist Railroads and Museums
2001 GUEST COUPONS

ROUNDHOUSE RAILROAD MUSEUM
Regular price: Adults $3.25, seniors/children $2.60
With coupon: 20% off regular price
Valid April 2001 through March 2002

NORTHERN PACIFIC RAILROAD MUSEUM
Regular price: Adults $2, seniors $1.50, children $1
With coupon: Adults $1.50, seniors $1, children $.75
Valid April 2001 through March 2002

HISTORIC PULLMAN FOUNDATION
**With coupon: Buy one admission get
equal price admission free**
Valid April 2001 through March 2002
Maximum discount 2 persons per coupon

MONTICELLO RAILWAY MUSEUM
Regular price: Adults $6, seniors $4, children $4
With coupon: Adults $5, seniors $3, children $3
Valid April 2001 through March 2002

ILLINOIS RAILWAY MUSEUM
**With coupon: $1 off each adult,
$.50 off each child (5-11)**
Valid April 2001 through March 2002
Not to be used in conjunction with any other coupon,
group rate, senior admission, or other discount rate.

CORYDON SCENIC RAILROAD
Regular price: Adults $9, seniors $8, children $5
With coupon: Adults $8, seniors $7, children $4
Valid April 2001 through March 2002

LINDEN RAILROAD MUSEUM
Regular price: Adults $2
With coupon: Adults $1.50
Valid April 2001 through March 2002

RAILSWEST RAILROAD MUSEUM
Regular price: Adults $4, $1.50
With coupon: Adults $3.50, children $1
Valid April 2001 through March 2002

SANTA FE DEPOT HISTORICAL CENTER
Regular price: Adults/seniors $2, children $.50
With coupon: Adults/seniors $1, children free
Valid April 2001 through March 2002
Maximum discount 5 persons per coupon

GREAT PLAINS TRANSPORTATION MUSEUM
**With coupon: Buy one admission get
equal price admission free**
Valid April 2001 through March 2002
Maximum discount 1 person per coupon

KENTUCKY RAILWAY MUSEUM
Regular price: Adults/seniors $12.50, children $8
With coupon: Adults/seniors $11.50, children $7
Valid April 2001 through March 2002
Maximum discount 4 persons per coupon

SOUTHERN FOREST HERITAGE MUSEUM
Regular price: Adults/seniors $5, children $2.50
With coupon: Adults/seniors $4.25, children $2
Valid April 2001 through March 2002

NORTHERN PACIFIC RAILROAD MUSEUM WALLACE, ID GUIDE TO TOURIST RAILROADS AND MUSEUMS 2001 GUEST COUPON	**ROUNDHOUSE RAILROAD MUSEUM** SAVANNAH, GA GUIDE TO TOURIST RAILROADS AND MUSEUMS 2001 GUEST COUPON
MONTICELLO RAILWAY MUSEUM MONTICELLO, IL GUIDE TO TOURIST RAILROADS AND MUSEUMS 2001 GUEST COUPON	**HISTORIC PULLMAN FOUNDATION** CHICAGO, IL GUIDE TO TOURIST RAILROADS AND MUSEUMS 2001 GUEST COUPON
CORYDON SCENIC RAILROAD CORYDON, IN GUIDE TO TOURIST RAILROADS AND MUSEUMS 2001 GUEST COUPON	**ILLINOIS RAILWAY MUSEUM** UNION, IL GUIDE TO TOURIST RAILROADS AND MUSEUMS 2001 GUEST COUPON
RAILSWEST RAILROAD MUSEUM COUNCIL BLUFFS, IA GUIDE TO TOURIST RAILROADS AND MUSEUMS 2001 GUEST COUPON	**LINDEN RAILROAD MUSEUM** LINDEN, IN GUIDE TO TOURIST RAILROADS AND MUSEUMS 2001 GUEST COUPON
GREAT PLAINS TRANSPORTATION MUSEUM WICHITA, KS GUIDE TO TOURIST RAILROADS AND MUSEUMS 2001 GUEST COUPON	**SANTA FE DEPOT HISTORICAL CENTER** FORT MADISON, IA GUIDE TO TOURIST RAILROADS AND MUSEUMS 2001 GUEST COUPON
SOUTHERN FOREST HERITAGE MUSEUM LONG LEAF, LA GUIDE TO TOURIST RAILROADS AND MUSEUMS 2001 GUEST COUPON	**KENTUCKY RAILWAY MUSEUM** NEW HAVEN, KY GUIDE TO TOURIST RAILROADS AND MUSEUMS 2001 GUEST COUPON

Guide to Tourist Railroads and Museums
2001 GUEST COUPONS

SEASHORE TROLLEY MUSEUM
Regular price: Adults $7, seniors $5, children $4.50
With coupon: Adults $6, seniors $4, children $3.50
Valid April 2001 through March 2002
Maximum discount 4 persons per coupon

SANDY RIVER & RANGELEY LAKES RAILROAD
Regular price: Adults/seniors $3
With coupon: Adults/seniors free
Valid April 2001 through March 2002

B&O RAILROAD MUSEUM
With coupon: Buy one admission get equal price admission free
Valid April 2001 through March 2002
Maximum discount 1 person per coupon

BALTIMORE STREETCAR MUSEUM
With coupon: Buy one admission get equal price admission free
Valid April 2001 through March 2002
Maximum discount 4 persons per coupon

BRUNSWICK RAILROAD MUSEUM
With coupon: Buy one admission get equal price admission free
Valid April 2001 through March 2002

ELLICOTT CITY B&O RAILROAD STATION MUSEUM
With coupon: Buy one admission get equal price admission free
Valid April 2001 through March 2002
Maximum discount 1 person per coupon

NATIONAL CAPITAL TROLLEY MUSEUM
With coupon: Buy one admission get equal price admission free
Valid April 2001 through March 2002
Maximum discount 1 person per coupon

EDAVILLE RAILROAD
Regular price: Adults $12.50, seniors $10.50, children $7.50
With coupon: Adults $10.50, seniors $8.50, children $5.50
Valid April 2001 through March 2002

JUNCTION VALLEY RAILROAD
Regular price: Adults $5, seniors $4.75, children $4.25
With coupon: Adults $4.50, seniors $4.25, children $3.80
Valid April 2001 through March 2002

MICHIGAN AUSABLE VALLEY RAILROAD
With coupon: Buy one admission get equal price admission free
Valid April 2001 through March 2002
Maximum discount 4 persons per coupon

HUCKLEBERRY RAILROAD
With coupon: Individuals receive group rate discount
Valid April 2001 through March 2002

IRON MOUNTAIN IRON MINE
Regular price: Adults $7, seniors/children $6
With coupon: Adults $6, seniors/children $5
Valid April 2001 through March 2002

SANDY RIVER & RANGELEY LAKES RAILROAD PHILLIPS, ME GUIDE TO TOURIST RAILROADS AND MUSEUMS 2001 GUEST COUPON	**SEASHORE TROLLEY MUSEUM** KENNEBUNKPORT, ME GUIDE TO TOURIST RAILROADS AND MUSEUMS 2001 GUEST COUPON
BALTIMORE STREETCAR MUSEUM BALTIMORE, MD GUIDE TO TOURIST RAILROADS AND MUSEUMS 2001 GUEST COUPON	**B&O RAILROAD MUSEUM** BALTIMORE, MD GUIDE TO TOURIST RAILROADS AND MUSEUMS 2001 GUEST COUPON
ELLICOTT CITY B&O RAILROAD STATION MUSEUM ELLICOTT CITY, MD GUIDE TO TOURIST RAILROADS AND MUSEUMS 2001 GUEST COUPON	**BRUNSWICK RAILROAD MUSEUM** BRUNSWICK, MD GUIDE TO TOURIST RAILROADS AND MUSEUMS 2001 GUEST COUPON
EDAVILLE RAILROAD CARVER, MA GUIDE TO TOURIST RAILROADS AND MUSEUMS 2001 GUEST COUPON	**NATIONAL CAPITAL TROLLEY MUSEUM** SILVER SPRING, MD GUIDE TO TOURIST RAILROADS AND MUSEUMS 2001 GUEST COUPON
MICHIGAN AUSABLE VALLEY RAILROAD FAIRVIEW, MI GUIDE TO TOURIST RAILROADS AND MUSEUMS 2001 GUEST COUPON	**JUNCTION VALLEY RAILROAD** BRIDGEPORT, MI GUIDE TO TOURIST RAILROADS AND MUSEUMS 2001 GUEST COUPON
IRON MOUNTAIN IRON MINE IRON MOUNTAIN, MI GUIDE TO TOURIST RAILROADS AND MUSEUMS 2001 GUEST COUPON	**HUCKLEBERRY RAILROAD** FLINT, MI GUIDE TO TOURIST RAILROADS AND MUSEUMS 2001 GUEST COUPON

Guide to Tourist Railroads and Museums
2001 GUEST COUPONS

COPPER COUNTRY RAILROAD HERITAGE CENTER
Regular price: Adults/seniors $5, children $2
With coupon: Adults/seniors $4, children $1
Valid April 2001 through March 2002

TOONERVILLE TROLLEY TRAIN AND BOAT TOURS
With coupon: 10% off any tour
Valid April 2001 through March 2002

MICHIGAN STAR CLIPPER DINNER TRAIN
Regular price: Adults/seniors/children $69.50
With coupon: Adults/seniors/children $59.50
Valid April 2001 through March 2002
Saturdays, holidays, month of December excluded

NORTH SHORE SCENIC RAILROAD
Regular price: Adults $9, children $5
With coupon: Adults $8, children $4
Valid April 2001 through March 2002

COMO-HARRIET STREETCAR LINE
Regular price: Adults/seniors/children, $1.50
With coupon: Adults/seniors/children $1
Valid April 2001 through March 2002
Maximum discount 4 persons per coupon

WABASH FRISCO & PACIFIC STEAM RAILWAY
Regular price: Adults $2
With coupon: Adults $1.50
Valid April 2001 through March 2002

ST. LOUIS, IRON MOUNTAIN & SOUTHERN RAILWAY
With coupon: Buy one admission get equal price admission free
Valid April 2001 through March 2002
On excursion rides only—no dinner trips

MUSEUM OF TRANSPORTATION
With coupon: Buy one admission get equal price admission free
Valid April 2001 through March 2002
Maximum discount 1 person per coupon

FREMONT & ELKHORN VALLEY RAILROAD
Regular price: Adults/seniors $11, children $6
With coupon: Adults/seniors $9.90, children $5.40
Valid April 2001 through March 2002

VIRGINIA & TRUCKEE RAILROAD
Regular price: Adults $5.25
With coupon: Adults $4.50
Valid April 2001 through March 2002

HARTMANN MODEL RAILROAD LTD.
Regular price: Adults $5, seniors $4, children $3
With coupon: Adults $4, seniors $3, children $2
Valid April 2001 through March 2002

BLACK RIVER & WESTERN RAILROAD
Regular price: Adults/seniors $8, children $4
With coupon: Adults/seniors $7, children $3
Valid April 2001 through March 2002

TOONERVILLE TROLLEY TRAIN AND BOAT TOURS SOO JUNCTION, MI GUIDE TO TOURIST RAILROADS AND MUSEUMS 2001 GUEST COUPON	COPPER COUNTRY RAILROAD HERITAGE CENTER LAKE LINDEN, MI GUIDE TO TOURIST RAILROADS AND MUSEUMS 2001 GUEST COUPON
NORTH SHORE SCENIC RAILROAD DULUTH, MN GUIDE TO TOURIST RAILROADS AND MUSEUMS 2001 GUEST COUPON	MICHIGAN STAR CLIPPER DINNER TRAIN WALLED LAKE, MI GUIDE TO TOURIST RAILROADS AND MUSEUMS 2001 GUEST COUPON
WABASH FRISCO & PACIFIC STEAM RAILWAY GLENCOE, MO GUIDE TO TOURIST RAILROADS AND MUSEUMS 2001 GUEST COUPON	COMO-HARRIET STREETCAR LINE MINNEAPOLIS, MN GUIDE TO TOURIST RAILROADS AND MUSEUMS 2001 GUEST COUPON
MUSEUM OF TRANSPORTATION ST. LOUIS, MO GUIDE TO TOURIST RAILROADS AND MUSEUMS 2001 GUEST COUPON	ST. LOUIS, IRON MOUNTAIN & SOUTHERN RAILWAY JACKSON, MO GUIDE TO TOURIST RAILROADS AND MUSEUMS 2001 GUEST COUPON
VIRGINIA & TRUCKEE RAILROAD VIRGINIA CITY, NV GUIDE TO TOURIST RAILROADS AND MUSEUMS 2001 GUEST COUPON	FREMONT & ELKHORN VALLEY RAILROAD FREMONT, NE GUIDE TO TOURIST RAILROADS AND MUSEUMS 2001 GUEST COUPON
BLACK RIVER & WESTERN RAILROAD FLEMINGTON, NJ GUIDE TO TOURIST RAILROADS AND MUSEUMS 2001 GUEST COUPON	HARTMANN MODEL RAILROAD, LTD. INTERVALE, NH GUIDE TO TOURIST RAILROADS AND MUSEUMS 2001 GUEST COUPON

Guide to Tourist Railroads and Museums
2001 GUEST COUPONS

CUMBRES & TOLTEC SCENIC RAILROAD
**With coupon: Buy one admission get
equal price admission free**
Valid April 2001 through March 2002
Maximum discount 1 person per coupon

NEW YORK TRANSIT MUSEUM
**Coupon valid for one complementary admission
when a second admission of equal or greater value is
purchased.**
Valid April 2001 through June 30, 2002
Museum may be closed for renovations in early 2001.
Please call for update

TROLLEY MUSEUM OF NEW YORK
Regular price: Adults $3, seniors/children $2
With coupon: Adults $1.50, seniors/children $1
Valid April 2001 through March 2002

MEDINA RAILROAD MUSEUM
Regular price: Adults $5, seniors$4, children $3
With coupon: Adults $4, seniors $3, children $2
Valid April 2001 through March 2002

NORTH CREEK RAILWAY DEPOT MUSEUM
**With coupon: Buy one admission get
equal price admission free**
Valid April 2001 through March 2002
Maximum discount 1 person per coupon

ADIRONDACK SCENIC RAILROAD
**With coupon: Buy one admission get
equal price admission free**
Valid April 2001 through March 2002

NORTHEASTERN NY RAILROAD PRESERVATION GROUP
Regular price: Adults $10, seniors, $9, children $6
With coupon: Adults $9, seniors $8, children $5
Valid April 2001 through March 2002

NORTH CAROLINA TRANSPORTATION MUSEUM
Regular price: Adults $5, seniors/children $4
With coupon: Adults $4, seniors/children $3
Valid April 2001 through March 2002
Maximum discount 4 persons per coupon

RAILROAD MUSEUM OF MINOT
Regular price: Adults $2
With coupon: Adults $1
Valid April 2001 through March 2002

CARROLLTON-ONEIDA-MINERVA RAILROAD (ELDERBERRY LINE)
Regular price: Adults $12, children $9
With coupon: Adults $11, children $8
Valid April 2001 through March 2002

DENNISON RAILROAD DEPOT MUSEUM
**With coupon: Buy one admission to depot get
equal price admission free**
Valid April 2001 through March 2002

HARMAR STATION
Regular price: Adults $5, seniors $4
With coupon: Adults $4, seniors $3
Valid April 2001 through March 2002

Guide to Tourist Railroads and Museums
2001 GUEST COUPONS

HOCKING VALLEY SCENIC RAILWAY
Regular price: Adults $8/$11, seniors $7/$10, children $5/$7
With coupon: Adults $7.50/$10.50, seniors $7/$10, children $4.50/$6.50
Valid April 2001 through March 2002
Coupons do not apply to Santa Trains and cannot be used with other discounts

TROLLEYVILLE U.S.A.
With coupon: Buy one admission get equal price admission free
Valid April 2001 through March 2002
Maximum discount 1 person per coupon

TRAIN HOUSE
With coupon: 20% off all merchandise in hobby shop
Valid April 2001 through March 2002

WASHINGTON PARK AND ZOO RAILWAY
Regular price: Adults $2.75, seniors/children $2
With coupon: Adults $2.20, seniors/children $1.60
Valid April 2001 through March 2002

GETTYSBURG SCENIC RAIL TOURS
With coupon: Buy one admission get equal price admission free
Valid April 2001 through March 2002
Maximum discount 1 person per coupon

STOURBRIDGE LINE RAIL EXCURSIONS
With coupon: Buy one admission get equal price admission free
Valid April 2001 through March 2002
Maximum discount 1 person per coupon
Does not include dinner theater or Bavarian Festival ride.

OLD MAUCH CHUNK MODEL TRAIN DISPLAY
With coupon: Buy one admission get equal price admission free
Valid April 2001 through March 2002
Maximum discount 1 person per coupon

WANAMAKER KEMPTON & SOUTHERN
Regular price: Adults/seniors $5, children $3
With coupon: Adults/seniors $4.50, children $2.50
Valid April 2001 through March 2002
Maximum discount 10 persons per coupon

NEW HOPE & IVYLAND RAILROAD
With coupon: $1 off each adult, $.50 off each child
Valid April 2001 through March 2002

ROCKHILL TROLLEY MUSEUM
With coupon: Buy one admission get equal price admission free
Valid April 2001 through March 2002
Maximum discount 1 person per coupon

CHOO CHOO BARN
Regular price: Adults/seniors $5, children $3
With coupon: Adults/seniors $4, children $2
Valid April 2001 through March 2002

OIL CREEK & TITUSVILLE RAILROAD
Regular price: Adults $10, seniors $9, children $6
With coupon: Adults, $9 seniors $8, children $5
Valid April 2001 through March 2002
Maximum discount 6 persons per coupon

TROLLEYVILLE U.S.A. OLMSTED TOWNSHIP, OH GUIDE TO TOURIST RAILROADS AND MUSEUMS 2001 GUEST COUPON	**HOCKING VALLEY SCENIC RAILWAY** NELSONVILLE, OH GUIDE TO TOURIST RAILROADS AND MUSEUMS 2001 GUEST COUPON
WASHINGTON PARK AND ZOO RAILWAY PORTLAND, OR GUIDE TO TOURIST RAILROADS AND MUSEUMS 2001 GUEST COUPON	**TRAIN HOUSE** BARTLESVILLE, OK GUIDE TO TOURIST RAILROADS AND MUSEUMS 2001 GUEST COUPON
STOURBRIDGE LINE RAIL EXCURSIONS HONESDALE, PA GUIDE TO TOURIST RAILROADS AND MUSEUMS 2001 GUEST COUPON	**GETTYSBURG SCENIC RAIL TOURS** GETTYSBURG, PA GUIDE TO TOURIST RAILROADS AND MUSEUMS 2001 GUEST COUPON
WANAMAKER KEMPTON & SOUTHERN KEMPTON, PA GUIDE TO TOURIST RAILROADS AND MUSEUMS 2001 GUEST COUPON	**OLD MAUCH CHUNK MODEL TRAIN DISPLAY** JIM THORPE, PA GUIDE TO TOURIST RAILROADS AND MUSEUMS 2001 GUEST COUPON
ROCKHILL TROLLEY MUSEUM ROCKHILL FURNACE, PA GUIDE TO TOURIST RAILROADS AND MUSEUMS 2001 GUEST COUPON	**NEW HOPE & IVYLAND RAILROAD** NEW HOPE, PA GUIDE TO TOURIST RAILROADS AND MUSEUMS 2001 GUEST COUPON
OIL CREEK & TITUSVILLE RAILROAD TITUSVILLE, PA GUIDE TO TOURIST RAILROADS AND MUSEUMS 2001 GUEST COUPON	**CHOO CHOO BARN** STRASBURG, PA GUIDE TO TOURIST RAILROADS AND MUSEUMS 2001 GUEST COUPON

Guide to Tourist Railroads and Museums
2001 GUEST COUPONS

TIOGA CENTRAL RAILROAD
Regular price: Adults $10, seniors $9, children $5
With coupon: Adults $9, seniors $8, children $4
Valid April 2001 through March 2002

TENNESSEE VALLEY RAILROAD
**With coupon: $1 off regular adult price,
$.50 off regular children's price**
Valid April 2001 through March 2002
Maximum discount 2 persons per coupon

CASEY JONES MUSEUM
Regular price: Adults $4, seniors $3.50
With coupon: Adults $3, seniors $2.50
Valid April 2001 through March 2002

CENTER FOR TRANSPORTATION
Regular price: Adults $5, seniors $4.50, children $2.50
**With coupon: Adults $4, seniors $3.50,
children $1.50**
Valid April 2001 through March 2002

HEBER VALLEY RAILROAD
Regular price: Adults $19/$12, seniors $17/$8,
children $12/$8
**With coupon: Adults $16/$9, seniors $15/$6,
children $10/$6**
Valid April 2001 through March 2002
Maximum discount 1 person per coupon

OGDEN UNION STATION
**With coupon: Buy one admission get
equal price admission free**
Valid April 2001 through March 2002

NORTHWEST RAILWAY MUSEUM
**With coupon: Buy one admission get
equal price admission free**
Valid April 2001 through March 2002
Maximum discount 2 persons per coupon

NORTHERN PACIFIC RAILWAY MUSEUM
Regular price: Adults $2, seniors/children $1
With coupon: Adults $1, seniors/children $.50
Valid April 2001 through March 2002

DURBIN & GREENBRIER VALLEY RAILROAD
Regular price: Adults $8, seniors $7, children $5.50
With coupon: Adults $7, seniors $6, children $4.50
Valid April 2001 through March 2002

COLLIS P. HUNTINGTON RAILROAD HISTORICAL SOCIETY
With coupon: 10% off per person, no limit
Valid April 2001 through March 2002

NATIONAL RAILROAD MUSEUM
**With coupon: Buy one admission get
equal price admission free**
Valid April 2001 through March 2002
Maximum discount $6 per coupon

WHISKEY RIVER RAILWAY
**With coupon: Buy one admission get
equal price admission free**
Valid April 2001 through March 2002
Unlimited persons per coupon

TENNESSEE VALLEY RAILROAD CHATTANOOGA, TN GUIDE TO TOURIST RAILROADS AND MUSEUMS 2001 GUEST COUPON	**TIOGA CENTRAL RAILROAD** WELLSBORO, PA GUIDE TO TOURIST RAILROADS AND MUSEUMS 2001 GUEST COUPON
CENTER FOR TRANSPORTATION GALVESTON ISLAND, TX GUIDE TO TOURIST RAILROADS AND MUSEUMS 2001 GUEST COUPON	**CASEY JONES MUSEUM** JACKSON, TN GUIDE TO TOURIST RAILROADS AND MUSEUMS 2001 GUEST COUPON
OGDEN UNION STATION OGDEN, UT GUIDE TO TOURIST RAILROADS AND MUSEUMS 2001 GUEST COUPON	**HEBER VALLEY RAILROAD** HEBER CITY, UT GUIDE TO TOURIST RAILROADS AND MUSEUMS 2001 GUEST COUPON
NORTHERN PACIFIC RAILWAY MUSEUM TOPPENISH, WA GUIDE TO TOURIST RAILROADS AND MUSEUMS 2001 GUEST COUPON	**NORTHWEST RAILWAY MUSEUM** SNOQUALMIE, WA GUIDE TO TOURIST RAILROADS AND MUSEUMS 2001 GUEST COUPON
COLLIS P. HUNTINGTON RAILROAD **HISTORICAL SOCIETY** KENOVA, WV GUIDE TO TOURIST RAILROADS AND MUSEUMS 2001 GUEST COUPON	**DURBIN & GREENBRIER VALLEY** **RAILROAD** DURBIN, WV GUIDE TO TOURIST RAILROADS AND MUSEUMS 2001 GUEST COUPON
WHISKEY RIVER RAILWAY MARSHALL, WI GUIDE TO TOURIST RAILROADS AND MUSEUMS 2001 GUEST COUPON	**NATIONAL RAILROAD MUSEUM** GREEN BAY, WI GUIDE TO TOURIST RAILROADS AND MUSEUMS 2001 GUEST COUPON

Guide to Tourist Railroads and Museums
2001 GUEST COUPONS

MID-CONTINENT RAILWAY HISTORICAL SOCIETY
With coupon: Buy one admission get equal price admission free
Valid April 2001 through March 2002
Maximum discount 2 persons per coupon

KETTLE MORAINE RAILWAY
Regular price: Adults $9, children $5
With coupon: Adults $8, children $4
Valid April 2001 through March 2002

OSCEOLA & ST. CROIX VALLEY RAILWAY
Regular price: Adults $13, seniors $12, children $7
With coupon: Adults $12, seniors $11, children $6
Valid April 2001 through March 2002

RAILROAD MEMORIES MUSEUM
Regular price: Adults $3, children $.50
With coupon: Adults $2.50, children $.25
Valid April 2001 through March 2002

RIVERSIDE & GREAT NORTHERN RAILWAY
Regular price: Adults $6.50, seniors $5, children $4.50
With coupon: Adults $5.50, seniors $4, children $3.50
Valid April 2001 through March 2002

FORT STEELE RAILWAY
Regular price: Adults $5, seniors $4, children $3, family $13
With coupon: Adults $4, seniors $3, children $2, family $10
Valid April 2001 through March 2002

REVELSTOKE RAILWAY MUSEUM
Regular price: Adults $6, seniors $5, children $3
With coupon: Adults $4.50, seniors $3.75, children $2.25
Valid April 2001 through March 2002
Maximum discount 5 persons per coupon

KETTLE VALLEY STEAM RAILWAY SOCIETY
Regular price: Adults $13, seniors $12, children $9.50
With coupon: Adults $12, seniors $11, children $8.50
Valid April 2001 through March 2002
Maximum discount 1 person per coupon

DOWNTOWN HISTORIC RAILWAY
With coupon: Buy one admission get equal price admission free
Valid April 2001 through March 2002
Maximum discount 2 persons per coupon

FORT ERIE RAILROAD MUSEUM
Regular price: Adults/seniors $2, children $50
With coupon: Adults/seniors free, children free
Valid April 2001 through March 2002

THE TIMBER TRAIN
With coupon: Buy one admission get equal price admission free
Valid June 2001 through August 2001
Maximum discount 1 person per coupon

HULL-CHELSEA-WAKEFIELD STEAM TRAIN
Regular price: Adults $29, seniors $26, children $14
With coupon: Adults $26, seniors $23, children N/A
Valid April 2001 through March 2002

KETTLE MORAINE RAILWAY NORTH LAKE, WI GUIDE TO TOURIST RAILROADS AND MUSEUMS 2001 GUEST COUPON	**MID-CONTINENT RAILWAY HISTORICAL SOCIETY** NORTH FREEDOM, WI GUIDE TO TOURIST RAILROADS AND MUSEUM 2001 GUEST COUPON
RAILROAD MEMORIES MUSEUM SPOONER, WI GUIDE TO TOURIST RAILROADS AND MUSEUMS 2001 GUEST COUPON	**OSCEOLA & ST. CROIX VALLEY RAILWAY** OSCEOLA, WI GUIDE TO TOURIST RAILROADS AND MUSEUM 2001 GUEST COUPON
FORT STEELE RAILWAY FORT STEELE, BC GUIDE TO TOURIST RAILROADS AND MUSEUMS 2001 GUEST COUPON	**RIVERSIDE & GREAT NORTHERN RAILWAY** WISCONSIN DELLS, WI GUIDE TO TOURIST RAILROADS AND MUSEUM 2001 GUEST COUPON
KETTLE VALLEY STEAM RAILWAY SOCIETY SUMMERLAND, BC GUIDE TO TOURIST RAILROADS AND MUSEUMS 2001 GUEST COUPON	**REVELSTOKE RAILWAY MUSEUM** REVELSTOKE, BC GUIDE TO TOURIST RAILROADS AND MUSEUM 2001 GUEST COUPON
FORT ERIE RAILROAD MUSEUM FORT ERIE, ON GUIDE TO TOURIST RAILROADS AND MUSEUMS 2001 GUEST COUPON	**DOWNTOWN HISTORIC RAILWAY** VANCOUVER, BC GUIDE TO TOURIST RAILROADS AND MUSEUM 2001 GUEST COUPON
HULL-CHELSEA-WAKEFIELD STEAM TRAIN HULL, PQ GUIDE TO TOURIST RAILROADS AND MUSEUMS 2001 GUEST COUPON	**THE TIMBER TRAIN** MATTAWA, ON GUIDE TO TOURIST RAILROADS AND MUSEUM 2001 GUEST COUPON

Locomotives/Rolling Stock: 1923 steam engine no. 841.

Location/Directions: Thirty-two miles north of Jackson, Mississippi. Exit 133 off I-55; Vaughan is one mile east off the exit.

Site Address: 10901 Vaughan Rd., #1, Vaughan, MS
Mailing Address: 0901 Vaughan Rd., #1, Vaughan, MS 39179
Telephone: (662) 673-9864
Fax: (662) 673-9864

BRANSON SCENIC RAILWAY
Train ride
Standard gauge

Description: This railway operates a 40-mile, 1¾-hour round trip through the Ozark foothills over the former Missouri Pacific White River Route, now operated by the Missouri & North Arkansas Railroad. Most trips take passengers south into Arkansas, across Lake Taneycomo and two high trestles, and through two tunnels. The original 1906 Branson depot houses the railway's ticket office, waiting room, gift shop, and business offices.

Schedule: Excursions–Mid-March through mid-December: 9 and 11:30 a.m., 2 and 5 p.m. Dinner train–May through December: Saturdays 5 p.m.

Admission/Fare: Call 800-2TRAIN2 for fares.

Locomotives/Rolling Stock: No. 98 F9PH BSR no. 265; GP30M BSR, former B&O; Silver Garden dome car, former CBQ; Silver Island dome, former CBQ.

Special Events: Downtown see Plumb Nellie Days and Fiddler's Contest.

Nearby Attractions/Accommodations: Theme park, historic downtown, restaurants, flea market, crafts festivals, lake, campgrounds, lodging.

Location/Directions: Downtown Branson, ¾ mile east of U.S. 65.

Site Address: 206 E. Main St., Branson, MO
Mailing Address: PO Box 924, Branson, MO 65615
Telephone: (417) 334-6110 and (800) 2TRAIN2
Fax: (417) 336-3909
Internet: www.bransontrain.com

SILVER DOLLAR CITY THEME PARK
Train ride
Narrow gauge

Description: The Silver Dollar Steam Train takes guests on a fun-filled 20-minute trip back to the 1880s on a tour through the splendid Ozark Mountains.

Schedule: April 4 through December 30: departures every 30 minutes. Days of operation vary with operation of theme park.

Admission/Fare: Free with paid admission to theme park.

Locomotives/Rolling Stock: 1938 engine no. 13 Orenstein 2-4-0, Koppel, Germany; 1934 engine no. 43 Orenstein 2-4-0, Koppel, Germany; 1940 engine no. 76 2-4-0, Germany.

Special Events: Sing-Along Steam Train (caroling rides) during Old Time Christmas, November and December.

Nearby Attractions/Accommodations: Branson, Missouri.

Location/Directions: Highway 76, approximately 5 miles west of Branson.

Site Address: Silver Dollar City Theme Park, West Highway 76, Branson, MO
Mailing Address: 399 Indian Pt. Rd., Branson, MO 65616
Telephone: (800) 952-6626
Internet: www.silverdollarcity.com

RICHARD A. EICHHORST

Description: The train ride, approximately 20 minutes round trip, is a continuously running attraction at the theme park, with stops at two stations. The propane-fueled steam locomotive was constructed and first operated in 1971.

Schedule: April through May and September through October, weekends only. June through August, daily. Open at 10 a.m., closing times vary. Call for exact dates and hours.

Admission/Fare: Park admission required.

Locomotives/Rolling Stock: "Tommy G. Robertson Railroad," 25-ton steam locomotive constructed by Crown Metal Products, Wyano, Pennsylvania; four coaches, one caboose.

Nearby Attractions/Accommodations: Downtown St. Louis with St. Louis arch, art museum, zoo, Magic House. Several nearby hotels.

Location/Directions: Thirty minutes southwest of downtown St. Louis on I-44.

Site Address: Eureka, MO
Mailing Address: PO Box 60, Eureka, MO 63025
Telephone: (636) 938-4800
Fax: (636) 587-3617
Internet: www.sixflags.com

WABASH FRISCO & PACIFIC RAILWAY
"THE UNCOMMON CARRIER"

Train ride
12" gauge

DAVID J. NEUBAUER

Description: A 2-mile, 30-minute round trip over a former Missouri Pacific right-of-way along the scenic Meramec River through wooded areas and over three bridges. The year 2001 will be our 40th year at Glencoe.

Schedule: May through October: Sundays, 11:15 a.m. to 4:15 p.m.

Admission/Fare: $2; children under age 3 ride free. No reservations.

Locomotives/Rolling Stock: Eight steam locomotives; 1907 no. 171 4-4-0 and coal burner; no. 180 4-4-0 coal; no. 102 2-6-2 coal; no. 300 4-4-2 oil; no. 400 4-6-2 oil; no. 434 4-6-4 oil; no. 350 4-4-4 coal being rebuilt as 4-6-4; no. 401 4-6-2 coal; 37 cars; roundhouse; three turntables; and a wye.

Special Events: Member's Day, June.

Nearby Attractions/Accommodations: Museum of Transportation; Union Pacific and Burlington Northern Santa Fe main lines, Eureka, Missouri.

Location/Directions: Twenty-five miles west of St. Louis. I-44 (Eureka), exit 264, north on Route 109 for 3.5 miles to Old State Rd., make two right turns to depot on Washington St. and Grand Ave.

*Coupon available, see coupon section.

       Radio frequency: 151.955

Site Address: Foot of Washington St. and Grand Ave., Wildwood, MO
Mailing Address: 1569 Ville Angela Ln., Hazelwood, MO 63042-1630
Telephone: (636) 587-3538
E-mail: mdn1916@primary.net
Internet: www.wfprr.org

ST. LOUIS, IRON MOUNTAIN & SOUTHERN RAILWAY
Train ride, dinner train
Standard gauge

Description: Train rides vary from 1½ hours to 3 hours.

Schedule: April through October: Saturdays, 11 a.m., 2 and 5 p.m. and Sundays, 1 p.m. June through August: Wednesdays and Fridays, 1 p.m. November and December: Saturdays 10 a.m. and 1 p.m. Charters available.

Admission/Fare: Regular runs–adults, $12.50; children, $6. James Gang–$14 to $7. Murder mystery and dinner–$37.

Locomotives/Rolling Stock: 1946 H.K. Porter, steam 2-4-2 65T; 1947 Cummins diesel-electric 900 h.p.; 1929 MoPac caboose; two ex-Illinois Central commuter cars; two B&O cabooses 1971; diesel Eng.-Penn 5898; BN caboose; Southern Railroad caboose.

Special Events: Hobo Days, Native American Days, Bonnie and Clyde and Jesse James robberies, Civil War reenactment every two years, murder mystery dinner trips.

Nearby Attractions/Accommodations: Trail of Tears State Park; Bollinger Mill; Veteran's Memorial Park; Mississippi River; Hobo Junction restaurants at train depot; good lodging, 10 minutes.

Location/Directions: Highway I-55, exit 99, two hours south of St. Louis. From exit 99, four miles south on Highway 61 to Jackson, intersection of Highway 61/25/72.

*Coupon available, see coupon section.

Site Address: 252 E. Jackson Blvd., Jackson, MO
Mailing Address: PO Box 244, Jackson, MO 63755
Telephone: (573) 243-1688 and (800) 455-RAIL
Fax: (573) 243-1688

GARY CHILCOTE

Description: Patee House Museum was headquarters for the Pony Express, in 1860. The former hotel is now a museum of communications and transportation featuring a steam locomotive, mail car, antique cars, trucks, fire trucks, buggies, and wagons. On the grounds is the Jesse James Home, where the outlaw was killed.

Schedule: April through October, daily 10 a.m. to 5 p.m. during summer months; otherwise, 10 a.m. to 4 p.m. November through March, weekends only.

Admission/Fare: Adults, $3.50; seniors, $3; students ages 6-17, $2; under age 6 are free with family.

Locomotives/Rolling Stock: 1892 Baldwin 4-4-0 no. 35, backdated by Burlington in 1933 to resemble Hannibal & St. Joseph locomotive no. 35.

Special Events: Pony Express/Jesse James Weekend, first weekend in April. Pony Express rerun, June.

Nearby Attractions/Accommodations: Home of Jesse James, Pony Express Museum, Doll Museum, Firefighters Museum, Old Smokehouse Restaurant.

Location/Directions: From Highway 36 take the 10th St. exit, follow 10th St. north to right on Mitchell to 12th St.

         M

Site Address: 12th and Penn, St. Joseph, MO
Mailing Address: Box 1022, St. Joseph, MO 64502
Telephone: (816) 238-4335
Fax: (816) 238-4335
Internet: www.ponyexpress.net/~breeze/PateeHouse/

Missouri, St. Louis

AMERICAN ASSOCIATION OF
RAILROADERS
Train ride, dinner train
Standard

RICHARD A. EICHHORST

Description: Sponsors 50 or more train excursions on Amtrak and other lines around the world. Day trips, weekends, and extended international tours. Also visits other rail operations.

Schedule: Year round.

Admission/Fare: Varies.

Locomotives/Rolling Stock: Excursions on Amtrak and chartered trains.

Special Events: At least one European and two Canadian trips each year. Also several free rail-related tours aboard the organization's 1958 GM Trailways bus.

Nearby Attractions/Accommodations: Museum of Transportation, St. Louis. Cabooseum (see A.R.C.H.E.S.), St. Louis.

Location/Directions: Sent with tickets.

Site Address: St. Louis and Kirkwood, MO; Alton, IL
Mailing Address: 4351 Holly Hills Blvd., St. Louis, MO 63116
Telephone: (314) 752-3148

AMERICAN RAILWAY CABOOSE HISTORICAL EDUCATIONAL SOCIETY, INC. (A.R.C.H.E.S.)

Museum
Standard gauge

RICHARD A. EICHHORST

Description: The Caboose Museum has at least one of their 30 "cabeese" on display at any given time. While a permanent location is being planned, the equipment is stored at ten different locations in Missouri and Illinois. Some of these cabooses are on loan to other rail museums. In addition to the interpretive center that is open to the public, ARCHES is an international association with members in 33 states and Canada. The members have printed a 220-page book, "Cabeese in America," which lists over 5,000 cabooses that have been preserved and are used for other purposes. List price is $24.95, discounted to members.

Schedule: April 7, May 5, June 2, July 7, August 4, September 1, and October 6: write or call for schedule

Admission/Fare: Donations appreciated.

Cabooses: A&S, ATSF, B&O, C&O, C&NW, CC, CGW, C&NW, Essex Terminal, Frisco, IC, Manufacturers, N&W, RI, Southern, TRRA, and Union Pacific.

Special Events: Caboose Chili Cook-off, Caboose Chase excursions, Santa on Amtrak, Rail Caboose tours, one Western Caboose tour and one Eastern tour each year. Charters and special trains.

Location/Directions: Varies, call or write for information.

St. Louis & Kirkwood, MO / Alton, IL

Site Address: St. Louis, MO
Mailing Address: PO Box 2772, St. Louis, MO 63116
Telephone: (314) 752-3148
E-mail: arches.org

MUSEUM OF TRANSPORTATION
Museum
Standard gauge

Description: The museum houses one of the largest and best collections of transportation vehicles in the world, according to the Smithsonian Institution. See over 70 locomotives, including 34 steamers from all points, the most in North America. The museum also has automotive, aviation, and river boat items to see and explore.

Schedule: Year round: daily, 9 a.m. to 5 p.m. Closed Thanksgiving, Christmas, and New Year's Day.

Admission/Fare: Adults, $4; seniors (65 and over) and children 5-12, $1.50. Group rates for 20 people or more.

Locomotives/Rolling Stock: UP Big Boy no. 4006; UP Centennial no. 6944; N&W Y6A no. 2156; Reading "Black Diamond"; GM FT no. 103; Milwaukee Road bi-polar E-2; 34 steam locomotives, 28 diesel/gas; 10 electric locomotives; 30 passenger cars; 54 freight cars.

Special Events: Annual Transportation Celebration, first weekend in August. Family Fall Festival, second Sunday in October.

Nearby Attractions/Accommodations: St. Louis Arch, Grant's Farm, Science Center, Zoo, Magic House.

Location/Directions: I-270, exit Dougherty Ferry Rd., west for 1 mile, left on Barrett Station Rd., entry on right.

*Coupon available, see coupon section.

Site Address: 3015 Barrett Station Rd., St. Louis, MO
Mailing Address: 3015 Barrett Station Rd., St. Louis, MO 63122
Telephone: (314) 965-7998
Fax: (314) 965-0242
Internet: www.museumoftransport.org

RAILROAD HISTORICAL MUSEUM, INC.
Museum Standard

Description: This stationary historical train is a museum within a museum, as it contains Frisco steam locomotive no. 4524 with tender, BN Express car, double-deck passenger car and BN caboose, all enclosed within a 40 x 400 x 8-foot chainlink fence, with railroad antiques, artifacts, and memorabilia, both within the fence and within the cars and locomotive.

Schedule: Saturdays, 2 to 4 p.m., mostly from April through November, weather permitting. (The weather must be sunny and dry and at least 60 degrees.) Also open by special group request.

Admission/Fare: Free. Donations accepted.

Locomotives/Rolling Stock: Frisco steam locomotive, no. 4524 with stoker tender and power boosters; BN express car, no. 976100, double-deck passenger car seating 100 on lower deck and 60 on the upper level; more.

Special Events: Frisco Days, two days in June.

Nearby Attractions/Accommodations: Bass Pro Shop; Dickerson Park Zoo; Grant Beach Park; Wild Animal Paradise, 12 miles east; Branson and Silver Dollar City, 40 miles south.

Location/Directions: From I-44 exit 77, go south on Kansas Expressway, turn east on Division St. Go ¾ mile and turn south on Grant Ave., two blocks to 1400 N. Grant, then turn west on Lynn St. to the museum entrance at Grant Beach Park.

Site Address: Grant Beach Park, 1400 N. Grant Ave., Springfield, MO
Mailing Address: 2033 S. Eureka Ave., Springfield, MO 65804
Telephone: (417) 881-3327

KYLE BREHM

Description: Historic railroad hotel with dining room, bar, railroad antiques, and memorabilia. Built by the Great Northern Railroad in 1939.

Schedule: Year round: 7 a.m. to 10 p.m.

Special Events: Annual Essex Express Railfan Weekend, May 4-6, 2001.

Nearby Attractions/Accommodations: Glacier National Park, Middle Fork of the Flathead River, Walton Goat Lick, Continental Divide, main line of BNSF, and Amtrak flag stop.

Location/Directions: On southern tip of Glacier National Park off Highway 2 in Essex, Montana.

Site Address: 290 Izaak Walton Inn Rd., Essex, MT
Mailing Address: PO Box 653, Essex, MT 59916
Telephone: (406) 888-5700
Fax: (406) 888-5200
E-mail: izaakw@digisys.net
Internet: www.izaakwaltoninn.com

MONTANA ROCKIES RAIL TOURS
Train ride
Standard gauge

Description: Daylight excursion train travels on original NPRR between Sandpoint, Idaho, and Livingston, Montana. We offer two-day trips on board with available motorcoach trips into Glacier and Yellowstone.

Schedule: July 12 through September 1, Fridays and Saturdays: eastbound from Sandpoint, Idaho. Sundays and Mondays: westbound from Livingston, Montana.

Admission/Fare: Contact sales office at 800-519-7245 for fares and availability.

Locomotives/Rolling Stock: Largest operators of ripple-sided Budd cars in the U.S. Cars are from Great Northern, NP Railway, CBQ, *Twin Cities Zephyr*, etc.

Nearby Attractions/Accommodations: Off-the-train tours include Yellowstone, Tetons, and Glacier National Parks. There are eight trips eastbound and eight trips westbound.

Site Address: 1055 Baldy Park Ave., Sandpoint, ID
Mailing Address: 1055 Baldy Park Ave., Sandpoint, ID 83864
Telephone: (800) 519-7245 and (208) 265-8618
Fax: (208) 265-8619
E-mail: mtrail@netw.com
Internet: www.keokee.com/railtour

MONTANA HERITAGE COMMISSION
Train ride, museum, display
30" gauge

ANDY LIEDBERG

Description: Operating steam locomotive, rebuilt 30" gauge Mexican 2-8-0, former Ferrocaril Mexicano no. 12, built by Baldwin in 1910. It had been displayed at Edaville for many years. Also, Alder Gulch Short Line, tourist train with open-air cars that operates along Alder Gulch between Nevada City and Virginia City, Montana.

Schedule: Memorial Day through Labor Day, seven runs daily, beginning at 11 a.m. Last run at 6:15 p.m.

Admission/Fare: C.A. Bovey train–$5. Steam train–$10 round trip.

Locomotives/Rolling Stock: Ferrocaril Mexicano no. 12 steam locomotive, built by Baldwin; C.A. Bovey gas-powered train.

Nearby Attractions/Accommodations: Historic mining towns Virginia and Nevada City.

Location/Directions: State Highway 287 between Ennis and Sheridan, Montana.

Site Address: Nevada City, MT
Mailing Address: PO Box 338, Virginia City, MT 59755
Telephone: (406) 843-5247
Fax: (406) 841-4004
E-mail: juljohnson@state.mt.us

ROCK ISLAND DEPOT RAILROAD MUSEUM
Museum

Description: Established in 1996 in the historic Rock Island Depot, which also housed the Western Division Headquarters for the Rock Island Railroad, built in 1914. The collection consists of Rock Island artifacts, from conductors' uniforms and train order hoops to baggage carts and caboose stoves, as well as local history involving the railroad. Includes a model railroad display, separate freight house and formal gardens. Restoration of the building is ongoing, as is development of rolling stock display.

Schedule: Year round: Wednesdays, Thursdays, and Sundays, 1 to 5 p.m.

Admission/Fare: Suggested donation.

Special Events: Annual Christmas at the Depot; Annual Rock Island Rail Days, second weekend in June.

Nearby Attractions/Accommodations: Rock Creek Station State Historical Park (where Wild Bill Hickok shot his first man) Oregon Trail ruts; Historic Steele City; Alexandria State Recreation Area; Fairbury City Museum; Crystal Springs Park; Capri Motel.

Location/Directions: Seventy-five miles southwest of Lincoln, Nebraska, west on I-80, south on Nebraska Highway 15.

        M

Site Address: 910 Second St., Fairbury, NE
Mailing Address: 910 Second St., Fairbury, NE 68352
Telephone: (402) 729-5131

FREMONT & ELKHORN VALLEY RAILROAD
NRHS NEBRASKA CHAPTER
Train ride, dinner train, museum
Standard gauge

Description: Take a ride through history on a 30-mile round trip from Fremont to Hooper over rails laid in 1869. Ride on cars built in 1924 and 1925. Enjoy the scenic Elkhorn Valley.

Schedule: Call or write for information.

Admission/Fare: Adults, $11; children 12 and under, $6; under age 3 ride free.

Locomotives/Rolling Stock: EMD SW1200, Davenport 44-ton no. 1481 under restoration; CB&Q RPO; "Lake Bluff" passenger car; 1927 "Fort Andrew" passenger car; BN wide-vision caboose.

Special Events: Fireworks ride in Hooper on the 4th of July. John C. Fremont Days, second weekend in July. Santa Claus runs, music on the train, and others.

Nearby Attractions/Accommodations: Railway Museum, May Museum, antique shopping, Motor Plex, historical Main St.

Location/Directions: Approximately 35 miles northwest of Omaha. Highway 275 exit 23rd St., travel west through Fremont, turn south on Somers Ave.

*Coupon available, see coupon section.

Site Address: 1835 N. Somers Ave., Fremont, NE
Mailing Address: PO Box 191, Fremont, NE 68026
Telephone: (402) 727-0615
Fax: (402) 727-0615
E-mail: teknetwork.com
Internet: www.geocities.com/heartland/hills/4184/fevr.html

FREMONT DINNER TRAIN
Dinner train
Standard gauge

BRUCE EVELAND

Description: Thirty-mile round trip traveling both the Platte and Elkhorn Valleys to the destination town of Hooper, Nebraska.

Schedule: Year round. Fridays, 7:30 p.m. June through December; Saturdays, 6:30 p.m., November through April and 7:30 p.m. May through October; Sundays, 1:30 p.m. May through November, and 5 p.m. in December.

Admission/Fare: Evenings, $45.95 to $62.95; Sundays, $39.95 to $56.95. (Upper rates include live entertainment.)

Locomotives/Rolling Stock: Dining cars no. 101 (ex-IC); no. 102 (ex-CN); no. 104 (ex-CN); no. 765 lounge diner (ex-CN); no. 315 power car (ex-Milw.); no. 410 power car (ex-N&W).

Special Events: New Year's Eve, Valentine's Day, July 4th Fireworks Run, Halloween.

Nearby Attractions/Accommodations: May Museum; Fremont State Lakes; Fremont Antique District.

Location/Directions: Thirty-five miles northwest of Omaha and 50 miles north of Lincoln.

Site Address: 1835 N. Somers Ave., Fremont, NE
Mailing Address: 650 N. "H," St., Fremont, NE 68025
Telephone: (402) 727-8321 and (800) 942-7245
Fax: (402) 727-0915
E-mail: fdt@fremont-online.com
Internet: www.fremont-online.com/fdt

GRAND ISLE HERITAGE ZOO
Train ride
24"

TRACY KUSAK

Description: Heritage Zoo is located in the southeast corner of Stolley Park. The train takes you on a perimeter tour of the zoo. The ride is 4600 feet in length and takes approximately 12 minutes.

Schedule: Winter, weather permitting; summer, daily 10 a.m. to 6 p.m.; special event Boo at the Zoo, late October.

Admission/Fare: Zoo: adults, $4.50; seniors, $2.50; children, $2.50; train ride: $1.50.

Locomotives/Rolling Stock: C.P. Huntington ⅓ scale locomotive, manufactured by Chance Rides, and three open-air covered coaches.

Special Events: Boo at the Zoo, late October.

Nearby Attractions/Accommodations: Water park; Stuhr Museum of the Prairie Pioneer; Crane Meadows; shopping mall and Arch-Way (49 miles west).

Location/Directions: From I-80, approximately 7 miles north to Stolley Park Rd., east on Stolley Park to the zoo.

Site Address: 2103 W. Stolley Park Rd., Grand Island, NE
Mailing Address: 2103 W. Stolley Park Rd., Grand Island, NE 68801
Telephone: (308) 385-5416
Fax: (308) 385-5421
E-mail: animal@computer-concepts.com

STUHR MUSEUM OF THE PRAIRIE
Museum, display
Narrow and standard gauge

Description: Museum with 1890s Railroad Town and limited viewable railroad exhibit stock.

Schedule: October 15 through April 30: Mondays through Saturdays, 9 a.m. to 5 p.m., Sundays 1 to 5 p.m. May 1 through October 14: 9 a.m. to 5 p.m. daily.

Locomotives/Rolling Stock: UP 2-8-0 437; UP RPO; UP combine 2512; UP Pullman "Lake Crystal"; UP caboose; WP&Y 2-8-0 no. 69; C&S baggage no. 104; F&CC coach no. 65; D&RG freight equipment.

Special Events: Call or write for current calendar of events. "Connecting the Country: Building the Railroad" August 11-12, 12 to 5 p.m. each day. Railroad-themed hands-on activities.

Nearby Attractions/Accommodations: Contact Grand Island/Hall County Convention and Visitor's Bureau for detailed information.

Location/Directions: Four short minutes north of I-80, exit 312, Grand Island, Nebraska.

Site Address: 3133 W. Highway 34, Grand Island, NE
Mailing Address: 3133 W. Highway 34, Grand Island, NE 68801
Telephone: (308) 385-5316
Fax: (308) 385-5028
E-mail: marketing@stuhrmuseum.org
Internet: www.stuhrmuseum.org

Description: Housed in the former Union Pacific Train Station, Durham WHM explores the history of Omaha through interactive exhibits and displays, as well as bringing regional, national, and world-renowned touring exhibitions to Omaha. In cooperation with the former UP Museum the DWHM displays the Union Pacific collection, including six train cars.

Schedule: Tuesdays through Saturdays, 10 a.m. to 5 p.m. and Sundays 1 to 5 p.m. Closed Mondays and most major holidays.

Admission/Fare: Adults, $5; seniors, $4; children ages 3-12, $3.50; under age 3 are free.

Locomotives/Rolling Stock: Baldwin 4-6-0 1243; Pullman 6-4-6 National Command; Pullman 1914 business car; Pullman 1949 barber shop lounge SP2906.

Special Events: Christmas, weekends in December. Ethnic Holiday Festival, December.

Nearby Attractions/Accommodations: Joslyn Art Museum, Henry Doorley Zoo, Omaha Golden Spikes baseball, Strategic Air Command Museum.

Location/Directions: I-80, exit 13th St., north to Pacific St., east to Tenth St., go one block north.

Site Address: 801 S. Tenth St., Omaha, NE
Mailing Address: 801 S. Tenth St., Omaha, NE 68108
Telephone: (402) 444-5071
Fax: (402) 444-5391

OMAHA ZOO RAILROAD
Train ride
30" gauge

Description: Passengers take a guided 1¾-mile, 20- to 30-minute trip through the zoo grounds, seeing hundreds of animals, including many rare and endangered species. Steam is scheduled 11 a.m. to 4 p.m.

Schedule: Seven days a week, Memorial Day through Labor Day. Weekends only April through Memorial Day and Labor Day through October.

Admission/Fare: Adults, $2.50; children under 12, $1.50; under 3 free round trip.

Locomotives/Rolling Stock: Locomotives no. 395-104, 1890 Krauss 0-6-2T; no. 119 1968 Crown 4-4-0 narrow gauge replica of Union Pacific no. 119; passenger cars; 11 open-air coaches; caboose; ballast maintenance; Foremont MT14 motor car.

Special Events: Member's Day, with free train ride to zoo members; Halloween Terror Train during zoo-sponsored Halloween party, children in costume ride free.

Nearby Attractions/Accommodations: Omaha Spikes baseball, Children's Museum, Western Heritage Museum; plenty of hotels/motels and restaurants.

Location/Directions: I-80 and Tenth Street.

Site Address: 3701 S. Tenth St., Omaha, NE
Mailing Address: 3701 S. Tenth St., Omaha, NE 68107
Telephone: (402) 733-8401
Fax: (402) 733-7868
Internet: www.omahazoo.com

NEVADA STATE RAILROAD MUSEUM
Museum
Standard and narrow gauge

Description: The Nevada State Railroad Museum houses over 50 pieces of railroad equipment from Nevada's past and is considered one of the finest regional railroad museums in the country. Included in the collection are seven steam locomotives and several restored coaches and freight cars. The bulk of the equipment is from the Virginia & Truckee Railroad, America's richest and most famous short line. Museum activities include operation of historic railroad equipment, handcar races, lectures, an annual railroad history symposium, changing exhibits, and a variety of special events. We offer steam train or motorcar rides on weekends, spring through fall, on museum's one-mile loop track.

Schedule: Call or write for information.

Admission/Fare: Adults, $2; children under 18, free. Fares vary.

Locomotives/Rolling Stock: No. 25, 1905 Baldwin 4-6-0; no. 18, "Dayton," 1873 Central Pacific 4-4-0; and no. 22, "Inyo," 1875 Baldwin 4-4-0; all former V&T. No. 1, "Glenbrook," 1875 Baldwin narrow-gauge 2-6-0, former Carson & Tahoe Lumber & Fluming Co.; no. 8, 1888 Cooke 4-4-0, former Dardanelle & Russellville; no. 1, "Joe Douglass," 1882 Porter narrow gauge 0-4-2T, former Dayton, Sutro & Carson Valley. Coaches nos. 3, 4, 8, 11, 12, 17, and 18, express/mail nos. 14 and 21, caboose-coaches nos. 9, 10, and 15, and 11 freight cars, all former V&T; more.

Location/Directions: Highways 50 and 395, at the south end of town.

    ⊠ M arm TRAIN

Site Address: 2180 S. Carson St., Carson City, NV
Mailing Address: 2180 S. Carson St., Carson City, NV 89701
Telephone: (775) 687-6953
Internet: www.nsrm-friends.org

NEVADA NORTHERN RAILWAY MUSEUM
Train ride, dinner train, museum, display
Standard gauge

Description: This museum features steam train operation. Call or write for schedule.

Schedule: May through September.

Special Events: Raildays, Labor Day weekend.

Nearby Attractions/Accommodations: Great Basin National Park, Pony Express Trail, KOA, Ruth Mining Pits.

Location/Directions: East Central Nevada on U.S. 93/50/6.

Site Address: 1100 Ave. "A," East Ely, NV
Mailing Address: PO Box 150040, East Ely, NV 89315
Telephone: (775) 289-2085
Fax: (775) 289-6284
E-mail: nnry@mwpower.net
Internet: www.nevadanorthernrailway.net

EUREKA & PALISADE RAILROAD
Train ride
36" gauge

DANIEL MARKOFF

Description: Occasional historic display and operation on various host railroads.

Schedule: Call or write for details.

Admission/Fare: Call or write for details.

Locomotives/Rolling Stock: Eureka & Palisade locomotive no. 4 "Eureka," Baldwin Locomotive Works 1875, American standard 4-4-0, narrow gauge.

Special Events: Varies, depending on host railroad. When not in service, locomotive is not on public display. Call or write for details.

Nearby Attractions/Accommodations: Nevada State Railroad Museum, Boulder City. Las Vegas, with hotels, gaming, shows. The best of the Old West in the rest of Nevada.

Location/Directions: Not open to the public.

  TRAIN

Site Address: Private
Mailing Address: 820 S. Seventh St., Suite A, Las Vegas, NV 89101
Telephone: (702) 383-3327

VIRGINIA & TRUCKEE RAILROAD CO.
Train ride
Standard gauge

Description: A 5-mile round trip from Virginia City to the town of Gold Hill through the heart of the historic Comstock mining region. A knowledgeable conductor gives a running commentary on the area and on the 126-year-old railroad.

Schedule: May 25 through October 21.

Admission/Fare: Adults, $5.25; children 5-12, $2.75; children under age 5 ride free.

Locomotives/Rolling Stock: 1916 Baldwin 2-8-0 no. 29, former Longview Portland & Northern; 1907 Baldwin 2-6-2 no. 8, former Hobart Southern; 1888 Northwestern Pacific combine and coach; former Tonopah & Tidewater coach; former Northern Pacific caboose; 1919 0-6-0 no. 30, former Southern Pacific.

Special Events: Party and Night train, once a month during the season.

Nearby Attractions/Accommodations: Historic Virginia City, mines, mansions, shops.

Location/Directions: Twenty-one miles from Reno, 17 miles from Carson City.

*Coupon available, see coupon section.

Site Address: Washington and "F" Streets, Virginia City, NV
Mailing Address: PO Box 467, Virginia City, NV 89440
Telephone: (775) 847-0380

New Hampshire, Bretton Woods

THE MOUNT WASHINGTON COG RAILWAY
Train ride
4'8"gauge

Description: Climb aboard the world's first mountain-climbing cog railway to the summit of Mount Washington, the highest peak in the Northeast. Rain or shine, this three-hour round-trip journey on one of seven enclosed and heated coaches is a unique vacation experience for all ages. Visit our new base station with museum, restaurant, and gift shop. This is a National Historic Engineering Landmark, built in 1869.

Schedule: Early May through early November: call for schedule. Reservations recommended.

Admission/Fare: Adults, $44; seniors, $40; children ages 6-12, $30; under age 6 are free unless occupying a seat.

Locomotives/Rolling Stock: Seven coal-fired steam engines; seven enclosed heated coaches; one speeder.

Nearby Attractions/Accommodations: The Mount Washington Hotel and Resort, over 12 family attractions within 30 miles, outlet shopping, and hiking.

Location/Directions: Located in the heart of New Hampshire's White Mountains at the base of the Presidential Mountain Range. I-93, exit 35, route 3N, Route 302E to Cog Railway Base Rd. Site is located 165 miles from Boston, Massachusetts, and 105 miles from Manchester, New Hampshire.

Site Address: Base Rd., Mt. Washington, NH
Mailing Address: Base Rd., Mt. Washington, NH 03589
Telephone: (800) 922-8825 and (603) 278-5404
Fax: (603) 278-5830
Internet: www.thecog.com

HARTMANN MODEL RAILROAD, LTD.
Train ride, dinner train, museum, display, layout
Z to G

Description: Housed in two buildings, each 8,000 square feet, is a railroad display for all ages. This site features many operating layouts, from G to Z scales, including a replica of Crawford Notch, New Hampshire, in the mid 1950s to early 1960s. Visitors can see several other detailed operating layouts with trains winding through tunnels, over bridges, and past miniature stations and buildings, and Thomas the Tank Engine operates by a light-sensor system. Also on display are about 5,000 model locomotives and coaches, American and European. Come and see our operating outdoor railroad and take a ride with us. Six to eight-minute train ride on 12" narrow gauge trains, if dry weather.

Schedule: Year round: daily, 10 a.m. to 5 p.m.

Admission/Fare: Adults, $5; seniors, $4; children ages 5-12, $3; group rates available.

Nearby Attractions/Accommodations: Storyland, 1 mile north; Conway Scenic Railroad, 4 miles south.

Location/Directions: Four miles north of North Conway in the White Mountains.

*Coupon available, see coupon section.

Site Address: Town Hall Rd. and Route 302/16, Intervale, NH
Mailing Address: PO Box 165, Intervale, NH 03845
Telephone: (603) 356-9922
Fax: (603) 356-9958
E-mail: info@hartmannrr.com
Internet: www.hartmannrr.com

WINNIPESAUKEE SCENIC RAILROAD
Train ride, dinner train
Standard gauge

Description: This railroad offers two-hour departures from Meredith and one- or two-hour departures from Weirs Beach to Lakeport over the former Boston & Maine track. The train follows the shores of Lake Winnipesaukee and ice cream sundaes, lunches, snacks, and beverages are available in our Ice Cream Parlor Car along with a small gift shop. Call or write for brochure for full details.

Schedule: May, June, September, October: weekends. Late June through Labor Day weekend with departures from Meredith at 10:30 a.m., 12:30, 2:30, 4:30 p.m., and departures from Weirs Beach every hour on the hour from 11 a.m. to 4 p.m.

Admission/Fare: Two-hour ride–adults, $9.50; children ages 3-11, $7.50. One-hour rides–adults, $8.50; children ages 3-11, $6.50. Dinner train–adults, $24.50; children ages 3-11, $19.50.

Locomotives/Rolling Stock: Former PT S1 1008; former B&M S1 1186; former MEC S1 959; former U.S. Army GE 44-ton 2; former Rock Island 483 1950 EMD GP7; former DL&W coaches 1001-1004; more.

Location/Directions: I-93 to exit 23, State Route 104. Follow 104 east for 8 miles to Meredith, turn left onto Route 3. Go past Hart's Turkey Farm about ¼ mile to Mill St. Turn left to the Meredith railyard.

Radio frequencies: 161.550

Site Address: Mill St., Meredith, NH; Weirs Beach Blvd., Weirs Beach, NH
Mailing Address: PO Box 9, Lincoln, NH 03251
Telephone: (603) 745-2135
Fax: (603) 745-9850
E-mail: www.hoborr.com
Internet: www.hoborr.com

CONWAY SCENIC RAILROAD
Train ride, dinner train, museum,
display, and layout
Standard gauge

LES MACDONALD

Description: The Valley Train travels south to Conway over former Boston & Maine branch line and west over former Main Central mountain subdivision to Bartlett. The Notch Train provides excursion services west from North Conway through spectacular Crawford Notch to Crawford Depot and Fabyan Station.

Schedule: Valley Train–May 14 through October 21: daily. Mid-April through mid-May, November, December: weekends. Notch Train–June 19 through September 8: Tuesday, Wednesday, Thursday, and Saturday. September 11 through October 12: daily.

Admission/Fare: Valley Train–adults, from $9.50; children ages 4-12, from $7; under age 4, price varies with destination. Notch Train–adults, from $33; children ages 4-12, from $18; under age 4, from $6.

Locomotives/Rolling Stock: No. 7470, 1921 Grand Trunk 0-6-0, former Canadian National; no. 15, 1945 44-ton GE, former Maine Central; more.

Special Events: Mother's Day, May 13; Father's Day, June 17, Trains, Planes, and Auto, July 8; Railfan's Weekend, October 13-14; Pumpkin Patch Run, October 20-21, 27-28; Turkey Trotter, November 23-25; Santa Claus Express, December 1-2, 8-9, 15-16.

Location/Directions: Route 16/302 and Norcross Circle in the heart of North Conway village. The depot faces Village Park.

Portland   VIA Montreal   MasterCard   VISA   Radio frequency: 161.250

Site Address: Route 16/302 and Norcross Circle, North Conway Village, NH
Mailing Address: PO Box 1947, North Conway, NH 03860-1947
Telephone: (603) 356-5251, (800) 232-5251
Fax: (603) 356-7606
E-mail: info@conwayscenic.com
Internet: www.conwayscenic.com

**CAFE LAFAYETTE
DINNER TRAIN**
Dinner train
Standard gauge

CHET BURAK

Description: Experience a leisurely two-hour evening train ride spent criss-crossing the picturesque Pemigewasset River. As dinner is served, period music keeps time with the rail's rhythmic rumbling. See magnificent mountain vistas and lush New England forests during this 20-mile round trip. After dinner, with the compartment lights down low, watch a dramatic New England sunset outside your window.

Schedule: Mother's Day through last Saturday in October. Call for details.

Admission/Fare: Adults, $41.95; children, 3-11 $24.95; age 2 and under, $5 minimum.

Locomotives/Rolling Stock: 1923 Pennsylvania Railroad caboose; 1924 Pullman dining car no. 221, former NYC; 1953 Army kitchen car; 1954 CN cafe coach no. 3207; 1952 Pullman dome car, former MoPac/Illinois Central no. 2211

Nearby Attractions/Accommodations: Heart of the White Mountain National Forest, Old Man of the Mountain, Franconia Notch State Park. White Mountain Central Railway, Cog Railroad, Mount Washington, Hobo Railroad, Winnepesaukee Scenic Railroad.

Location/Directions: I-93, exit 32 on Route 112 midway between Lincoln and North Woodstock, New Hampshire.

Site Address: Route 112, North Woodstock, NH
Mailing Address: RR1 Box 85, Lincoln, NH 03251
Telephone: (603) 745-3500 and (800) 699-3501 (outside NH)
Fax: (603) 745-3535
Internet: www.cafelafayette.com or www.nhdinnertrain.com

KLICKETY KLACK
MODEL RAILROAD
Layout
HO, N, On30

Description: Operate a turntable, a quarry train, carnival rides, trolley, Thomas the Tank and Percy; visit a circus, castle, lighthouse, villages and city; see a smoking factory and steam ships in the harbor. All of this is possible at Klickety-Klack, where over two dozen HO, N, and On30 scale trains run over 1,500 feet of track. This miniature collection includes 150 locomotives, 400 freight and passenger cars, 2,000 "people" and much more. This railroad represents over 75,000 hours of work by many dedicated people.

Schedule: July 1 through Labor Day: Mondays through Saturdays, 10 a.m. to 5:30 p.m. September through June: Thursdays through Saturdays, 10 a.m. to 5 p.m.

Admission/Fare: Adults, $4; children 3-12, $3.

Nearby Attractions/Accommodations: Mount Washington, New Hampshire lake region.

Location/Directions: At the junction of Routes 28 and 109A.

Site Address: 8 Elm St., Wolfeboro Falls, NH
Mailing Address: PO Box 205, Wolfeboro Falls, NH 03896
Telephone: (603) 569-5384

New Jersey, Cape May

CAPE MAY SEASHORE LINES
Train ride
Standard gauge

LION PHOTOGRAPHY

Description: Regional/tourist railroad in Cape May County, New Jersey. Operating Budd RDCs in scheduled passenger service. For most recent schedule, fare, locomotives and rolling stock, and special events, please call, write, or check website for updated information.

Locomotives/Rolling Stock: Eight Budd RDC1s, former Pennsylvania-Reading Seashore Lines; two RDC9s, former Boston & Maine; Alco/EMD RS3, former Pennsylvania Railroad; EMD GP9, former PRR; three P-RSL P70 coaches, former PRR.

Nearby Attractions/Accommodations: Victorian Cape May City, Wildwood Beaches, Boardwalk and Amusement Piers, Cape May Light House, Cape May-Lewes Ferry, Cape May County Park and Zoo, historic Cold Spring Village, Mid-Atlantic Center for the Arts, and Middle Township Performing Arts Center.

Location/Directions: 4-H Fairgrounds Station–off South Dennisville Rd., Middle Township. Cape May Court House–Route 615/Mechanic St. Smith Court House–Elementary School 2 off Pacific Ave. in Cape May Court House (flag stop) Cold Spring–Route 9, Cold Spring. Cape May City–Lafayette St., Cape May City.

P   Radio frequency: 161.160

Site Address: Rio Grande, NJ
Mailing Address: PO Box 152, Tuckahoe, NJ 08250-0152
Telephone: (609) 884-2675
Fax: (609) 567-5847
Internet: www.cmslrr.com

NEW JERSEY MUSEUM OF TRANSPORTATION, INC.

Train ride, display
36" gauge

Description: This ⅝-mile demonstration railway includes preserved buildings, storage, and restoration facilities.

Schedule: Weekends, April through October, 12 to 4:30 p.m. Daily, July through August, 12 to 4:30 p.m.

Admission/Fare: $2 per person, age 2 and under free. Higher fare for special events. $3 per car park entrance fee in effect Memorial Day through Labor Day.

Locomotives/Rolling Stock: No. 7751 25-ton GE diesel-electric ex-U.S. Army; no. 45 50-ton GE diesel-electric ex-U.S. Steel; no. 26 1920 Baldwin 2-6-2 ex-Surrey, Sussex & Southampton; more.

Special Events: Railroaders' Day, Sunday after Labor Day. Christmas Express with Santa, four weekends after Thanksgiving. (Advanced ticketing required for Christmas.)

Nearby Attractions/Accommodations: Allaire State Park is the site of Historic Allaire Village, listed on the National Register of Historic Places. Jersey Shore beaches are 5 miles east.

Location/Directions: Located in Allaire State Park on Route 524 in Wall Township, Monmouth County, New Jersey. The park entrance is 2 miles west of Garden State Parkway exit 98 and 1.5 miles east of I-195 exit 31B.

      M arm

Site Address: Allaire State Park, Route 524, Wall Township, Monmouth County, NJ
Mailing Address: PO Box 622, Farmingdale, NJ 07727-0622
Telephone: (732) 938-5524

ELIZABETH GRISWOLD

Description: The Black River & Western offers a steam/diesel excursion through the rolling hills of Hunterdon County. The 1-hour, 10-minute ride travels between Flemington and Ringoes.

Schedule: April through December: weekends departing Flemington Station 11:30 a.m., 1, 2:30, and 4 p.m. July through August: add Thursdays and Fridays (no 4:00 p.m. train on weekdays).

Admission/Fare: Adults, $8; children 3-12, $4; under 3 free. Groups/private charters available.

Locomotives/Rolling Stock: 1937 Alco 2-8-0 no. 60; 1956 EMD GP9 no. 752; 1950 EMD GP7 no. 780; nos. 752 and 780 GP7 diesels; nos. 1848 and 1849 GP9s; no. 820 NW 1200; nos. 8142 and 8159 SW1200s; nos. 320-323 commuter cars, former Central of New Jersey; more.

Special Events: Children ride free, March 30; Easter Bunny Express, April 7, 8, 13, 14. Great Train Robbery, May 19-20 and October 8; Halloween Express, October 27-28; Santa Express, November 23-25, December 1-2 and 8-9.

Location/Directions: Route 202 to Flemington Circle, 12W through second circle, after railroad tracks turn right on Stangl Rd., station is on right.

*Coupon available, see coupon section.

       Radio frequency: 161.085

Site Address: Route 12 and Stangl Rd., Flemington, NJ
Mailing Address: PO Box 200, Ringoes, NJ 08551
Telephone: (908) 782-6622
Fax: (908) 782-8251
E-mail: psgrinfo@brwrr.com
Internet: www.brwrr.com

New Jersey, Phillipsburg

PHILLIPSBURG RAILROAD HISTORIANS
Train ride, museum, display, layout
9.5" gauge

PETE TERP

Description: Museum of local railroad history and an information center for the state transportation museum to be located at Phillipsburg.

Schedule: May 1 through October 1: Sundays.

Admission/Fare: Museum–free. Train–$.50.

Locomotives/Rolling Stock: IR former USA GE 44-tonner; L&HR caboose nos. 16, 18; CNT caboose no. 91197; L&HR 105 flanger; L&HR 1600 lowside gondola; Centerville & Southwestern 2" scale miniature railroad with two locomotives and 31 cars.

Special Events: Riverfest, early June. Old Towne Festival, late July.

Nearby Attractions/Accommodations: Crayola Factory, Two Rivers Landing Canal and Museum.

Location/Directions: Off S. Main St. (Route 22) across from Joe's Steak Shop.

    M

Site Address: Cross St. and Pine Alley, Phillipsburg, NJ
Mailing Address: 292 Chambers St., Phillipsburg, NJ 08805
Telephone: (908) 213-1722

243

WHIPPANY RAILWAY MUSEUM
Museum
Standard gauge

STEVE HEPLER

Description: Visit the Whippany Railway Museum, headquartered in the restored 1904 freight house of the Morristown & Erie, with its outstanding collection of railroad artifacts and memorabilia. Take a leisurely stroll through a railroad yard lost in time, complete with fieldstone depot, coal yard, wooden water tank, and historic rail equipment. The museum also features an extensive outdoor G scale model train layout, an indoor O gauge train layout, and a display of ocean liner memorabilia. Educational and fun for all ages.

Schedule: April through October: Sundays, 12 to 4 p.m.

Admission/Fare: Museum–adults, $1; children under age 12, $.50. Special event train fare–adults, $8; children under age 12, $5.

Locomotives/Rolling Stock: Morris County Central no. 4039, an 0-6-0 built in 1942 by the American Locomotive Company; railbus no. 10 built in 1918 by the White Motor Company for the Morristown & Erie; more.

Special Events: Easter Bunny Express, G Scale Trains and Father's Day, Pumpkin Festival, Halloween Express, Santa Claus Special, more.

Nearby Attractions/Accommodations: Morris Museum, General Washington's headquarters, Jockey Hollow National Historic Site.

Location/Directions: At the intersection of Route 10 west and Whippany Rd. in Morris County.

      arm  Newark & Metropark Sta.
Radio frequency: 160.230

Site Address: 1 Railroad Plaza, Whippany, NJ
Mailing Address: PO Box 16, Whippany, NJ 07981-0016
Telephone: (973) 887-8177
E-mail: paultup@interactive.net
Internet: www.WhippanyRailwayMuseum.org

TOY TRAIN DEPOT
Train ride, museum, display and layout
16" gauge

HASKELL

Description: Two MTC F-7 16" diesels, Baltimore & Ohio, Union Pacific, transport three-car loads south to Live Tree, Dead Grass, Rosebud, Southhoop, and New Bridge. The round trip is 20 minutes.

Schedule: Year round: Wednesdays through Sundays, 12 to 4:30 p.m.

Admission/Fare: $2.

Locomotives/Rolling Stock: MTC 16" F-7 Baltimore & Ohio; MTC 16" F-7 Union Pacific; MTC 16" 4-4-0 1865 steam replica.

Special Events: Cottonwood Festival, Alamogordo, New Mexico Labor Day weekend, park/ride.

Nearby Attractions/Accommodations: Dog Canyon Museum, Oliver Lee State Park, Lincoln National Forest, Alamogordo Sacramento Mountain Roadbed tours.

Location/Directions: North end of Alameda Park is located on N. White Sands Blvd. in Alamogordo.

Site Address: 1991 N. White Sands Blvd., Alamogordo, NM
Mailing Address: 1991 N. White Sands Blvd., Alamogordo, NM 88310
Telephone: (505) 437-2855
E-mail: railfanexxmexico@hotmail.com
Internet: www.toytraindepot.homestead.com

New Mexico, Chama
Colorado, Antonito

CUMBRES & TOLTEC SCENIC RAILROAD
Train ride
36" gauge

Description: The Cumbres & Toltec Scenic Railroad is the finest remaining example of the original Denver and Rio Grande narrow gauge railroad, built in the 1880s to reach the mines at Silverton. Unspoiled scenery awaits you as you travel through the spectacular San Juan Mountains. You'll pass over high bridges and through tunnels, alongside ghostly rock formations and restored company towns.

Schedule: Memorial Day weekend through mid-October: daily departures from both Antonito, 10 a.m., and Chama, 10:30 a.m.

Admission/Fare: Adults, $38-$58; children, $19-$29; senior, handicapped and group discounts.

Locomotives/Rolling Stock: Locomotives: ex-D&RGW K27 463 (BLW 1903, 21788); ex-D&RGW K36 483, 484, 487, 488, and 489 (BLW 1925); and ex-D&RGW K37 497 (BLW 1980), converted to narrow gauge 1930). Rolling stock: passenger cars constructed in the 1970s and 1980s, over 140 pieces of ex-D&RGW equipment from 1880 to 1968.

Special Events: Opening Day, May 26; others to be announced later.

Nearby Attractions/Accommodations: Antonito: Great Sand Dunes National Monument, Taos, Santa Fe, Royal Gorge. Chama: Santa Fe, Durango (D&SNGRR), Mesa Verde.

*Coupon available, see coupon section.

Radio frequency: 160.305, 161.505

Site Address: U.S. 285, Antonito, CO / 500 Terrace Ave., Chama, NM
Mailing Address: PO Box 789, Chama, NM 87520
Telephone: (505) 756-2151
Fax: (505) 756-2694
E-mail: rrinfo@cumbrestoltec.com
Internet: www.cumbrestoltec.com

CLOVIS DEPOT
MODEL TRAIN MUSEUM
Museum, display, layout

PHIL WILLIAMS

Description: The Clovis Depot has been restored to its condition in the 1950-60 era and has displays of historic documents and memorabilia covering its use and the history of the AT&SF in New Mexico along the Belen Cutoff since the turn of the century. Also featured are nine model railroad layouts depicting the history of toy trains, the development of the railroad in both Australia and Great Britain, and the Clovis Yard and adjacent city in 1950-60. Live BNSF train operations can be viewed from the dispatcher's position and platform with some 75-100 trains passing each day. We provide a one-hour guided tour of the museum and model railroad layouts, including running the model trains and other displays.

Schedule: Wednesdays through Sundays, 12 to 5 p.m. Closed September and February, as well as Easter, Thanksgiving, Christmas, and New Year's Day.

Admission/Fare: Call or write for information.

Locomotives/Rolling Stock: Fairmont Railway motor car.

Nearby Attractions/Accommodations: Blackwater Draw Museum, Blackwater Draw Archaeological site, Norman Petty Studios.

Location/Directions: In a restored ATSF passenger depot adjacent to BNSF main line, two blocks west of Main St. on U.S. 60/84.

Site Address: 221 W. First St., Clovis, NM
Mailing Address: 221 W. First St., Clovis, NM 88101
Telephone: (505) 762-0066 and (888) 762-0064
E-mail: philipw@3lefties.com
Internet: www.clovisdepot.com

SANTA FE SOUTHERN RAILWAY
Train ride, dinner train
Standard gauge

MARK ROUNDS

Description: The Santa Fe Southern offers 2½-hour, 3½-hour, and 4½-hour excursions with freight movement. Scenic trains are year round; April through October we have Friday highball and Saturday barbecue dinner trains.

Schedule: Gift shop/ticket office, 9 a.m. to 5 p.m. Monday through Saturday; 11 a.m. to 5 p.m., Sunday.

Admission/Fare: Adult fares $25 to $40; senior (60+) discount.

Locomotives/Rolling Stock: GP 7 no. 92; GP 7 no. 93; New Jersey no. 1158; Great Northern no. 144; Super Chief Club "Acoma"; Santa Fe Pleasure Dome "Plaza Lamy."

Special Events: Valentine's Dinner, February 14; Easter, April 14-15; 4th of July barbecue and fireworks; Fiesta barbecue, September 8; Halloween Mystery Theater, October 27; post-Thanksgiving barbecue, November 23; Santa Claus and caroling trains, December 15-24; New Year's Eve dinner, December 31.

Nearby Attractions/Accommodations: Santa Fe downtown, art galleries, museums, fine clothing, restaurants, within walking distance of depot.

Location/Directions: I-25 at St. Francis to Cerrillos, turn right to Guadalupe, turn left, depot on left at Tomasita's Restaurant.

Site Address: 410 S. Guadalupe St., Santa Fe, NM
Mailing Address: 410 S. Guadalupe St., Santa Fe, NM 87501
Telephone: (505) 989-8600 or (888) 989-8600
Fax: (505) 983-7620
E-mail: depot@sfsr.com
Internet: www.sfsr.com

New York, Arcade

ARCADE & ATTICA RAILROAD
Train ride, dinner train, museum
Standard gauge

PETER SWANSON

Description: A 90-minute excursion ride in coaches built in 1915, pulled by the last American-made steam locomotive in New York State.

Schedule: Memorial weekend through October: weekends, 12:30 and 3 p.m. July through August: Wednesdays, 12:30 and 3 p.m.; Fridays 1 p.m.

Admission/Fare: Adults, $8.50; seniors, $7.50; children, $5.

Locomotives/Rolling Stock: 1920 American steam locomotive; 1915 DL&W coaches.

Special Events: Civil War, children's trains, Easter Bunny ride, Santa runs, and Murder Mystery runs.

Nearby Attractions/Accommodations: Letchworth State Park.

Location/Directions: Forty miles south of Buffalo, 75 miles east of Rochester. On Route 39 near Route 98.

Site Address: 278 Main St., Arcade, NY
Mailing Address: 278 Main St., Arcade, NY 14009
Telephone: (716) 492-3100
Fax: (716) 492-0100
E-mail: 11k@anarr.com
Internet: anarr.com

DELAWARE & ULSTER RAILRIDE
Train ride, museum, display
Standard gauge

AARON KELLER

Description: Nineteen miles of rail offering a one-hour or one-hour 45-minute trip through the scenic Catskill Mountains. Operates on the route of the historic Ulster & Delaware Railroad.

Schedule: End of May through end of October: weekends and holidays. July and August: Wednesdays through Sundays. Departs at 10:30 a.m., 1 and 2:30 p.m.

Admission/Fare: Short trip–adults, $7; seniors, $5.50; children, $4; under age 3 ride free. Long trip–adults, $10; seniors, $7.50; children, $5; under age 3 ride free.

Locomotives/Rolling Stock: D&H no. 5017 RS36 Alco; no. 5106 1953 Alco S-4, former Chesapeake & Ohio; no. 1012 1954 Alco S-4, former Ford Motor Co.; M-405 1928 J.G. Brill Co. diesel-electric rail car, former New York Central; two slat cars with benches, former PRR; two boxcars, former NYC; 44-ton locomotive, former Western Maryland.

Special Events: Train Robberies, Tractor Pulls, Twilight Runs, Fall Foliage, Halloween Train, A Day Out with Thomas™.

Location/Directions: Route 28, in Arkville, 45 miles west of New York State Thruway.

Radio frequency: 161.385

Site Address: Route 28, Arkville, NY
Mailing Address: PO Box 310, Stamford, NY 12167
Telephone: (800) 225-4132 and (845) 586-DURR
Fax: (607) 652-2822
Internet: www.durr.org

NEW YORK TRANSIT MUSEUM
Train ride, museum

Description: Housed in a historic subway station, the New York Transit Museum collects, preserves, exhibits, and interprets the history, sociology, and technology of public transportation in the New York region.

Schedule: Brooklyn–year round: Tuesdays through Fridays, 10 a.m. to 4 p.m.; weekends 12 to 5 p.m. Closed Mondays and major holidays. Grand Central–weekdays, 8 a.m. to 8 p.m.; Saturdays, 10 a.m. to 4 p.m., closed Sundays. Times Square–daily, 8 a.m. to 8 p.m.

Admission/Fare: Brooklyn–Adults, $3; seniors and children 3-17, $1.50. Seniors are free on Wednesdays 12 to 4 p.m. Manhattan locations–free.

Locomotives/Rolling Stock: Brooklyn–Twenty vintage railcars, including elevated and subway cars from 1878 to the late 1960s. Money Car G, on display, is New York's oldest existing elevated rail car.

Special Events: Annual Bus Festival (Spring/Summer); tours, lectures, exhibits, educational workshops for children, nostalgic vintage train rides.

Nearby Attractions/Accommodations: Five minutes from Manhattan by subway; Brooklyn Marriott.

Location/Directions: A, C, or F train to Jay St–Borough Hall; or 3, 4, 5, M, N, or R trains to Borough Hall. Other trains and buses also come close.

*Coupon available, see coupon section.

Site Address: Boerum Pl. & Schermerhorn St., Brooklyn Hts., NY
Mailing Address: 130 Livingston St., 9th Floor, Box E, Brooklyn, NY 11201
Telephone: (718) 243-8601
Internet: www.mta.nyc.ny.us/museum

MARTISCO STATION MUSEUM
CENTRAL NEW YORK CHAPTER NRHS
Museum, display, layout

Description: The Martisco Station Museum is a brick Victorian structure erected in 1870 for the New York Central and Hudson River Railroad. Located in a picturesque setting, the restored two-story passenger station houses a collection of railroad mementos of the local area. The adjacent former Pennsylvania Railroad diner houses additional displays. Presently the track passing the station is used five days per week by the Finger Lakes Railway.

Schedule: May through October: Sundays 1 to 5 p.m.

Admission/Fare: Donations appreciated.

Locomotives/Rolling Stock: Pennsylvania Railroad diner.

Special Events: Christmas at the Station, December.

Location/Directions: New York Route 174, halfway between the villages of Camillus and Marcellus, at the end of Martisco Rd.

Site Address: Martisco Rd., Camillus, NY
Mailing Address: PO Box 229, Marcellus, NY 13108-0229
Telephone: (315) 488-8208
Fax: (315) 487-2849
E-mail: CNYNRHS@aol.com
Internet: www.rrhistorical.com/cnynrhs

CENTRAL SQUARE STATION MUSEUM
CENTRAL NEW YORK CHAPTER NRHS
Museum, display

Description: The Central New York Chapter NRHS is a former joint station of the New York Ontario & Western Railway and the New York Central Railroad, built in 1909. The restored one-story wood passenger station houses a collection of railroad artifacts from the local area.

Schedule: May through October: Sundays 12 to 5 p.m.

Admission/Fare: Free.

Locomotives/Rolling Stock: 0-4-0 steam locomotive no. 53 American Locomotive Co.; 0-4-0 narrow gauge steam no. 22; Brill car no. M-39; 25-ton G.E. diesel no. 7; Fairmont Rail motor car, 0-4-0T steam engine from Solvay Process.

Nearby Attractions/Accommodations: St. Lawrence Seaway, Thousand Islands, Adirondack Park.

Location/Directions: Railroad St. in Central Square, off Route 11 south of town, close to Route 81.

     M

Site Address: Railroad St., Central Square, NY
Mailing Address: PO Box 229, Marcellus, NY 13108-0229
Telephone: (315) 488-8208
Fax: (315) 487-2849
E-mail: CNYNRHS@aol.com
Internet: www.rrhistorical.com/cnynrhs

THE CHESTER HISTORICAL SOCIETY
Museum

Description: For the promotion and preservation of the local history of the town and village of Chester, New York. The town was settled in the early 1700s. The first shipment of fresh milk to New York City by rail was made in 1841 (the Erie Railroad). The museum is housed in a 1915 Erie Railroad station on the former Erie main line in Chester, New York. This Arts-and-Crafts-influenced passenger station replaced the original 1841 station in 1915. After sitting in disuse for several decades, it opened on June 12, 1999, as Chester's Local History Museum.

Schedule: May through October: Saturdays 9 a.m. to 1 p.m. Groups by appointment anytime.

Nearby Attractions/Accommodations: The station is located in Historic Downtown, along the Orange Pathways Heritage Trail and within walking distance to refreshments, restaurants, antique shops, etc. Twenty miles west of West Point.

Location/Directions: New York State Thruway exit 16. Take Route 17 west 10 miles, exit 126 "Chester," straight at light onto Academy Ave. Left Main St., right at firehouse and continue on Main St. through downtown Chester. Station on left.

Site Address: 1915 Erie Railroad Station, 19 Winkler Pl., Chester, NY
Mailing Address: 47 Main St., Chester, NY 10918
Telephone: (845) 469-2591
E-mail: Chester@worldshare.net

COOPERSTOWN & CHARLOTTE VALLEY RAILROAD

Train ride, museum
Standard gauge

ARIC PEERY

Description: A 16-mile, two-hour round trip from Cooperstown to Milford and back. Milford is the site of the Milford Park Railway, a home-built narrow gauge railroad, and a small museum in the 1869 depot. The entire operation is run by the Leatherstocking Railway Museum.

Schedule: Weekends and holidays, May 26 through October 21; Tuesday through Sunday and holidays, June 26 to September 3. Call, write, or see website for departure times.

Admission/Fare: Train–adults, $8; seniors (62+), $7; children 4-12, $5; under 4 free. Group rates available. Museum–free

Locomotives/Rolling Stock: NYSW NW2 no. 116 (in its original NYO&W scheme); three DL&W passenger cars; D&H caboose no. 35723; EL caboose no. C316; D&H big-hook crane no. 30021; more.

Special Events: Easter Bunny Express, Star Gazer Excursion, Railfan Weekend, Moonlight Train Ride, Haunted Halloween Express, Santa Claus Express. Call, write, or see website for dates, times, and fares.

Nearby Attractions/Accommodations: National Baseball Hall of Fame, the Farmers Museum, James Fenimore Cooper House, Otesaga Resort Hotel, Glimmerglass State Park, National Soccer Hall of Fame.

Location/Directions: I-88, north on Route 28 for about 8 miles to Milford. Then east on Route 166 about one block to the railroad crossing.

Site Address: E. Main St., Milford, NY; Route 28 South, Cooperstown, NY
Mailing Address: PO Box 681, Oneonta, NY 13820-0681
Telephone: (607) 432-2429
Fax: (607) 433-0747
E-mail: lrhs@lrhs.com
Internet: www.lrhs.com

ALCO BROOKS RAILROAD DISPLAY
Display
Standard gauge

Description: Located at the Chautauqua County Fairgrounds since 1987, the display features an original Alco-Brooks steam locomotive, a wood-sided boxcar housing displays of Chautauqua County commerce and railroads along with a gift shop, and a restored wooden caboose. Other items of interest at the site are a Nickel Plate work car, an Erie Railroad concrete telephone booth, a New York Central harp switch stand, a Pennsylvania Railroad cast-iron crossing sign, a DAV&P land line marker, and an operating crossing flasher.

Schedule: June 1 through August 31: Saturdays, 1 to 3 p.m., weather permitting. Open daily during special events or by appointment.

Admission/Fare: Donations appreciated.

Locomotives/Rolling Stock: 1916 Alco-Brooks 0-6-0 no. 444, former Boston & Maine; 1907 Delaware & Hudson 22020 wood-sided boxcar; 1905 New York Central 19224 wooden caboose.

Special Events: Chautauqua County Antique Auto Show and Flea Market, May 18-20. Chautauqua County Fair, July 23-29.

Nearby Attractions/Accommodations: Dunkirk Historical Museum, Dunkirk Lighthouse, Chautauqua Institution, Four Points Hotel Sheraton, Brookside Manor bed and breakfast.

Location/Directions: I-90, exit 59, to Chautauqua County Fairgrounds.

Site Address: 1089 Central Ave., Chautauqua County Fairgrounds, Dunkirk, NY
Mailing Address: Historical Society of Dunkirk, 513 Washington Ave., Dunkirk, NY 14048
Telephone: (716) 366-3797
E-mail: davrr@netsync.net

New York, Greenport and Riverhead

RAILROAD MUSEUM OF LONG ISLAND
Museum, display

Description: Greenport consists of an 1890s Long Island Railroad freight station with exhibits depicting the development of railroad industry on Long Island. Riverhead houses a large collection of vintage LIRR equipment.

Schedule: Call or write for information.

Admission/Fare: Call or write for information.

Locomotives/Rolling Stock: LIRR G5s 4-6-0 no. 39; LIRR RS-3 no. 1556; BEDT 0-6-0T no. 16; LIRR "Double Decker" no. 200; LIRR "Jaws" snow-plow no. W-83; LIRR caboose no. C-68; LIRR RPO no. 4209; more.

Nearby Attractions/Accommodations: Riverhead–Splish Splash Waterpark, Tanger Outlet Mall. Greenport–historic Greenport waterfront district.

Location/Directions: Call or write for directions or check website.

        M

Site Address: Fourth St. at the tracks, Greenport, NY, and 416 Griffing Ave., Riverhead, NY
Mailing Address: PO Box 726, Greenport, NY 11944
Telephone: (631) 477-0439 or (631) 727-7920
E-mail: twinforks@mail.peconic.net
Internet: www.bitnik.com/RMLI

TROLLEY MUSEUM OF NEW YORK
Train ride
Standard gauge

MARILYN JENNINGS

Description: This museum was established in 1955 and moved to its present location in 1983, becoming part of the Kingston Urban Cultural Park. A 2.5-mile, 40-minute round trip takes passengers from the foot of Broadway to Kingston Point, with stops at the museum in both directions. A gas-powered railcar operates on private right-of-way and in-street trackage along Rondout Creek to the Hudson River over part of the former Ulster & Delaware Railroad main line. An exhibit hall features trolley exhibits and a theater.

Schedule: Memorial weekend to Columbus Day: 12 to 5 p.m. Last ride departs at 4:30 p.m. Charters available.

Admission/Fare: Adults, $3; seniors and children, $2.

Locomotives/Rolling Stock: Eleven trolleys; eight rapid transit cars; Whitcomb diesel-electric; Brill model 55 interurban.

Special Events: Shad Festival, May 5-6; Mother's Day (moms ride free); Father's Day (dads ride free); Santa Days, December 1-2.

Nearby Attractions/Accommodations: Hudson River Maritime Museum, Senate House, Catskill Mountains, Urban Cultural Park.

Location/Directions: In the historic Rondout Waterfront area of Kingston. Call or write for directions or see map on web page.

*Coupon available, see coupon section.

      arm

 Radio Frequency: 462.175

Site Address: 89 E. Strand, Kingston, NY
Mailing Address: PO Box 2291, Kingston, NY 12402
Telephone: (845) 331-3399
Internet: www.mhrcc.org/tmny

MAYBROOK RAILROAD HISTORICAL SOCIETY
Museum

Description: The museum offers photographs and memorabilia.

Schedule: April through October: weekends, 1 to 4 p.m.

Admission/Fare: Free.

Locomotives/Rolling Stock: Caboose no. 512

Nearby Attractions/Accommodations: Museum Village in Monroe, New York, includes model railroad of Orange County; Erie Depot Museum in Port Jervis; O&W Railroad Historical Society archives in Middletown.

Location/Directions: I-84 to exit 5; 2 miles south on Route 208. Located in rear of Maybrook Library.

Site Address: 101 Main St., Maybrook, NY (rear of library)
Mailing Address: PO Box 105, Maybrook, NY 12543
Telephone: (914) 427-2591 (secretary)

MEDINA RAILROAD MUSEUM
Museum

Description: Located in a 1905 New York Central freight depot. Displays include rail maintenance tools, models, equipment and memorabilia. We have a portable HO scale layout on loan and a 200 x 14-foot HO scale layout is under construction.

Schedule: Year round: Mondays through Saturdays 12 to 7 p.m. and Sundays 12 to 5 p.m.

Admission/Fare: Adults, $5; seniors, $4; children, $3.

Locomotives/Rolling Stock: Five 1948 Budd coaches, former NYC Empire State Express coaches from WNY Railway Historical Society; Nickel Plate Road RS11 Alco Diesel 1952 owned by Genesee Valley Transportation.

Special Events: Two-hour, 34-mile rail excursions are on select dates in summer and fall. Call for schedule.

Nearby Attractions/Accommodations: Niagara Falls, Buffalo, Rochester, Six Flags Darien Lakes Amusement Park, mule-drawn canal boat rides, Cobblestone Museum

Location/Directions: North of I-90, exit 48A, village of Medina at is at intersection of New York 63 and New York 31.

*Coupon available, see coupon section.

Site Address: 530 West Ave., Medina, NY
Mailing Address: 530 West Ave., Medina, NY 14103
Telephone: (716) 798-6106

CATSKILL MOUNTAIN RAILROAD
Train ride
Standard gauge

HARRY G. JAMESON III

Description: This railroad, which operates over trackage of the former Ulster & Delaware Railroad, offers a 6-mile, one-hour round trip to Phoenicia along the scenic Esopus Creek, through the heart of the beautiful Catskill Mountains. Tourists, inner-tubers, and visitors interested in fishing or canoeing may ride one way or round trip.

Schedule: Weekends and holidays. May 26 through September 3, 11 a.m. to 5 p.m.; September 8 through October 28, 12 to 4 p.m.

Admission/Fare: Adults, $6; children 4-11, $4; under age 4 are free.

Locomotives/Rolling Stock: No. 1, "The Duck," 1942 Davenport 38-ton diesel-mechanical, former U.S. Air Force; no. 2, "The Goat," H.K. Porter 50-ton diesel-electric, former U.S. Navy; no. 2361, 1952 Alco RS-1, former Wisconsin Central (Soo Line).

Special Events: Twilight Limited excursions with music and refreshments at the Empire State Railway Museum; Teddy Bear Train; Leaf Peeper Specials; Halloween Train. Call for schedule.

Nearby Attractions: World's largest kaleidoscope. Tubing the Esopus Creek. Museums, sports activities, restaurants, lodging, campgrounds, state parks, scenic sites.

Location/Directions: New York State Thruway, exit 19 (Kingston), and travel west 22 miles on Route 28 to the railroad depot in Mt. Pleasant.

Site Address: Route 28, Mt. Pleasant, NY
Mailing Address: PO Box 46, Shokan, NY 12481
Telephone: (845) 688-7400
Fax: (845) 657-7257
E-mail: spiegler@netslep.net

NORTH CREEK RAILWAY DEPOT MUSEUM
Museum

TOM RYAN

Description: A restored 1872 train depot that houses a museum with exhibits on regional socioeconomic history, including the history of skiing at Gore Mountain, Ted Roosevelt's ride to the presidency, mining, logging, and the railroad.

Schedule: Tuesday through Sunday, 11 a.m. to 4 p.m.

Admission/Fare: Adults, $2; children, $1.

Special Events: Teddy Roosevelt Weekend, September 16-17.

Nearby Attractions/Accommodations: Upper Hudson River Railroad Scenic Train. Gore Mountain Ski Center. Garnet Hill Mine.

Location/Directions: Exit 23 Northway to Route 28 to North Creek.

*Coupon available, see coupon section.

      M

Site Address: 5 Railroad Pl., North Creek, NY
Mailing Address: PO Box 156, North Creek, NY 12853
Telephone: (518) 251-5842
Fax: (518) 251-5599
E-mail: elaine@northcreekraildepot.org
Internet: www.northcreekraildepot.org

New York, Old Forge
Utica
Lake Placid

ADIRONDACK SCENIC RAILROAD
Train ride, museum
Standard gauge

Description: Rides from one hour to five hours round trip out of Utica, Thendara and Saranac Lake–Lake Placid.

Schedule: Varies. Phone (315) 369-6290 (Thendara) and (315) 724-0700 (Utica) and (518) 891-3238 (Saranac Lake)

Admission/Fare: Adults, $7 to $28; children $4 to $14.

Locomotives/Rolling Stock: Locomotives: 705 EMD SW1; 8223 Alco RS3; 105 GE 44-ton; 2064 Alco C420; 1508 EMD F7; 4243 Alco C424; 1500 EMD F7; also many passenger cars and work cars.

Special Events: Rail Fan Days, train robberies, Model Railroad Shows, cocktail runs, Halloween and Santa runs, steam trains, milk trains, meet the Adirondack authors, artwork sale on train.

Nearby Attractions/Accommodations: Old Forge Lake Cruises; McCauley Mountain Chairlift Rides; Arts Center/Old Forge; Old Forge Hardware; Enchanted Forest/Water Safari; Great Camp Sagamore; The Adirondack Museum; the W.W. Durant, Raquette Lake Navigation Co.; Adirondack Scenic Railroad, Return Trip; restaurants, lodging.

Location/Directions: Three locations–too complex–send for information.

*Coupon available, see coupon section.

Site Address: Thendara Station, Old Forge, NY; Falvo Station on Lee St., Utica, NY; Lake Placid and Saranac Lake train stations
Mailing Address: PO Box 84, Thendara, NY 13472. **Phone:** See above.
Fax: (315) 369-2479
E-mail: train@telenet.net
Internet: www.adirondackrr.com

New York, Owego

TIOGA SCENIC RAILROAD
Train ride, dinner train,
museum, display, layout
Standard gauge

Description: A 22-mile round trip aboard early 1900s vintage train. The trip lasts about two hours.

Schedule: July through October, weekends 1 p.m. Call for information about the Evening Express, first and third Saturday of each month.

Admission/Fare: Excursions–adults, $10; children 3-11, $6; 2 and under are free on weekends. Meals–lunch, $24; dinner, $30; Evening Express, $26. Call about special charter rates and school rates.

Locomotives/Rolling Stock: Tioga Scenic Railroad SW1 no. 40; OH Railway SW12 no. 1216; OH Railway RS18u no. 1811; two DL&W coaches built 1922; open-air car from the 1890s; two dining cars from the 1940s.

Nearby Attractions/Accommodations: Wineries, Finger Lakes, Hickory Park camping, Tioga Park flea market, Historic Owego shopping.

Location/Directions: Twenty miles west of Binghamton, Route 17, exit 64. Follow Route 96 north; after the railroad underpass turn left.

Site Address: 25 Delphine St., Owego, NY
Mailing Address: 25 Delphine St., Owego, NY 13827
Telephone: (607) 687-6786
Fax: (607) 687-6817
Internet: www.railroad.net/tsrr/

EMPIRE STATE RAILWAY MUSEUM
Museum, display, layout

Description: This is an all-volunteer membership organization dedicated to bringing alive the history of Catskill Mountain railroads, their people, and the towns they served. The museum is located in a former Ulster & Delaware railroad station, which celebrated its 100th anniversary in 1999.

Schedule: Memorial Day through Columbus Day: weekends and holidays 10 a.m. to 4 p.m.

Admission/Fare: Suggested donation–adults, $3; seniors and students, $2; children under age 12, $1; families, $5.

Locomotives/Rolling Stock: No. 23, 1910 Alco 2-8-0, former Lake Superior & Ishpeming under restoration; 1920 D&H dining car "Lion Gardner"; 1926 CV autocarrier; 1920 B&M railway post office car.

Special Events: Photo exhibit, lectures, slide shows, Santa Claus Special

Nearby Attractions/Accommodations: Catskill Mountain Railroad, Delaware Ulster rail ride, New York state campgrounds at Woodland Valley and Wilson State Park, hiking, fishing in Catskill Forest Preserve, tube rides on Esopus Creek.

Location/Directions: New York State Thruway to exit 19, then Route 28 west to Phoenicia.

      M

Site Address: Off High St., Phoenicia, NY
Mailing Address: PO Box 455, Phoenicia, NY 12464
Telephone: (845) 688-7501
Internet: www.esrm.com

New York, Rochester

JIM DIERKS

Description: The site includes trolleys, rail and road vehicles, related artifacts and exhibits, an 11 x 21 operating HO model railroad, and a video/photo gallery. A 2-mile ride connects with the Rochester & Genesee Valley Railroad Museum, departing every half-hour.

Schedule: Museum–year round, Sundays, 11 a.m. to 5 p.m. Groups by appointment. Ride–May through October, weather permitting.

Admission/Fare: Adults, $5; seniors, $4; students ages 5-15, $3. Includes entry to NYMT, Rochester & Genesee Valley Railroad Museum, and ride. Lower rates November through April.

Locomotives/Rolling Stock: Rochester & Eastern interurban car no. 157; North Texas Trac. interurban car no. 409; P&W cars nos. 161 and 168; Elmira, Corning & Waverly no. 107; Philadelphia snow sweeper no. C-130; Rochester Railway no. 437; Batavia Street Railway no. 33; more.

Special Events: Transportation Day, mid-May; Model Steam and Gas Engines, July; Diesel Days, August.

Nearby Attractions/Accommodations: Finger Lakes Region, Niagara Falls, Arcade & Attica Railroad, Genesee Country Museum, George Eastman House Museum of Photography.

Location/Directions: I-90, exit 46, south 3 miles on I-390, exit 11. Route 251 west 1.5 miles, right on E. River Rd., 1 mile to museum entrance.

Radio Frequency: 160.440

Site Address: 6393 E. River Rd., W. Henrietta, NY
Mailing Address: PO Box 136, W. Henrietta, NY 14586
Telephone: (716) 533-1113
Internet: www.nymt.mus.ny.us

ROCHESTER & GENESEE VALLEY RAILROAD MUSEUM
Museum
Standard gauge

CHRISTOPHER HAUF

Description: The museum, housed in a restored 1908 Erie Railroad station, displays railroad artifacts from western New York railroads. On outdoor tracks are a number of railroad cars and diesel locomotives open for display. Museum has tours and track car rides.

Schedule: May through October: Sundays, 11 am. to 5 p.m. Visits at other times by appointment.

Admission/Fare: Adults, $5; seniors, $4; children 5-15, $3.

Locomotives/Rolling Stock: 1946 GE 80-ton diesel, former Eastman Kodak; 1953 Alco RS-3, former Lehigh Valley; 1953 Alco S-4, former Nickel Plate; 1941 GE 45-ton, former Rochester Gas & Electric; Fairbanks-Morse H12-44, former U.S. Army.

Special Events: Diesel Days, mid-July.

Nearby Attractions/Accommodations: Strong Museum, Eastman House, Genesee Country Museum, Frontier Stadium, New York Museum of Transportation.

Location/Directions: All regularly scheduled Sunday tours start at the New York Museum of Transportation (previous page). The depot itself is located on Route 251 just west of East River Rd.

Site Address: 6393 E. River Rd., Henrietta, NY
Mailing Address: PO Box 664, Rochester, NY 14603
Telephone: (716) 533-1431
E-mail: mikeb86393@aol.com
Internet: www.transportation.mus.ny.us

**ROSCOE ONTARIO & WESTERN
RAILWAY MUSEUM**
Museum

Description: This museum was established under the charter of the Ontario
& Western Railway Historical Society in 1984 in a former Erie Railroad
caboose. The O&W railway festival, first held in August of that year, has
since become an annual event. The museum complex consists of an Erie
Hack restored O&W caboose, watchman's shanties, the O&W station
motif building, and Beaverkill Trout Car Museum. The museum contains displays of O&W memorabilia, other railroadiana, as well as local-
history displays that show the impact of the O&W on community life,
hunting, fishing, farming, tourism, and local industry. The museum is
maintained and operated by members of the Roscoe NYO&W Railway
Association. The Archives Center of the history of the Ontario &
Western Railway is located in Middletown, New York; for information,
e-mail: artrobb@idsi.net.

Schedule: Memorial weekend through Columbus Day: Saturdays, Sundays,
and holidays, 11 a.m. to 3 p.m.

Admission/Fare: Donations welcomed.

Special Events: O&W Railway Festival, July 21-22, 10 a.m. to 4 p.m.
Railroadiana, Arts & Crafts Fair, July 21.

Location/Directions: Railroad Ave.

Site Address: Historic Depot St. on Railroad Ave., Roscoe, NY
Mailing Address: PO Box 305, Roscoe, NY 12776-0305
Telephone: (607) 498-5500
E-mail: [wilsip@wpe.com]
Internet: www.nyow.org/museum.html

SALAMANCA RAIL MUSEUM
Museum

Description: Fully restored BR&P depot and freight house. Artifacts and photographs tell the history of railroads in western New York and Pennsylvania. For children, the museum grounds offer the permanent display of a boxcar, a crew camp car, and the chance to explore two cabooses.

Schedule: April through December: Mondays through Saturdays, 10 a.m. to 5 p.m. and Sundays, 12 to 5 p.m. Closed Mondays in April, October, November, and December.

Admission/Fare: Donations appreciated.

Locomotives/Rolling Stock: B&O caboose; P&WV caboose; Erie crane crew car; Conrail boxcar; Jordan spreader; DL&W electric commuter coach.

Nearby Attractions/Accommodations: Allegany State Park, Seneca Iroquois National Museum, Holiday Valley Summer-Winter Resort, Chautauqua Institution.

Location/Directions: Downtown Salamanca on New York Route 17/U.S. I-86, Route 219.

      M

Site Address: 170 Main St., Salamanca, NY
Mailing Address: 170 Main St., Salamanca, NY 14779
Telephone: (716) 945-3133

New York, Salem/ Cambridge

NORTHEASTERN NEW YORK RAILROAD PRESERVATION GROUP (NE RAIL)

Train ride, dinner train
Standard gauge

GEORGE LERRIGO

Description: Excursion service, from Salem to Cambridge, along a 24-mile rout. Our special events include plays for children.

Schedule: July through Labor Day, 10:30 a.m. and 2 p.m., weekends, Wednesdays, and Thursdays.

Admission/Fare: Adults, $10; seniors, $9; children, $6; family fare.

Locomotives/Rolling Stock: RS3, 605 and 4116; NYC coaches.

Special Events: Children's plays, ride and dine, Halloween, and Christmas Santa trains.

Nearby Attractions/Accommodations: Near Saratoga Springs, New York (Amtrak).

Location/Directions: Salem Depot, Route 22, Cambridge Depot, New York Route 372 in village.

*Coupon available, see coupon section.

Site Address: One Elbow St., Greenwich, NY
Mailing Address: One Elbow St., Greenwich, NY 12834
Telephone: (518) 692-2191
Fax: (518) 692-0271
Internet: www.nenyrail.com

Description: A children's museum with hands-on interactive displays concerning science, natural science, history, and culture. Frequent craft activities and events.

Schedule: Tuesdays through Saturdays, 10 a.m. to 5 p.m.; Sundays, 12 to 4:30 p.m.

Admission/Fare: $3.50 per person; 9 months and younger, free.

Locomotives/Rolling Stock: We have a stationary locomotive and cars for viewing: New York Central 0-6-0; Adirondack Alco; Santa Fe passenger car; Pennsylvania Railroad caboose.

Nearby Attractions/Accommodations: Utica Zoo.

Location/Directions: 311 Main St., next door to Union Station train station.

Site Address: 311 Main St., Utica, NY
Mailing Address: 311 Main St., Utica, NY 13501
Telephone: (315) 724-6129
Fax: (315) 724-6120 (call first)
E-mail: caryi@aol.com
Internet: museum4kids.com

VIRGIL HURLEY

Description: Our museum is located in a former Piedmont & Northern Railway depot. The outside display consists of railroad cars and a GE 25-ton diesel-electric switcher. The inside displays consist of various articles from the Piedmont & Northern Railway and the Southern Railway, as well as O scale model trains, an HO scale layout, and a gift area.

Schedule: Tuesdays through Saturdays, 10:30 a.m. to 4:30 p.m.; Sundays, 1:30 to 4:40 p.m.

Admission/Fare: Donations are accepted.

Locomotives/Rolling Stock: GE 25-ton diesel-electric switcher, formerly used by Duke Power at their River Bend steam station; Southern Railway caboose no. SOUX662, built in 1951; sleeper-lounge car the "Keystone State," built by Pullman in 1955 for the New York, New Haven & Hartford; more.

Special Events: Third Saturday in May, Belmont's "Garibaldi Days" spring festival across the street in Stowe Park.

Nearby Attractions/Accommodations: Daniel Stowe Botanical Gardens in Belmont; Schiele Museum in Gastonia; Museum of the New South and Discovery Place in Charlotte; Carowinds amusement park in Charlotte on the North Carolina–South Carolina state line.

Location/Directions: Belmont is 10 miles west of Charlotte; the museum is a mile off I-85 in the downtown area.

✴ M Charlotte

Site Address: 4 N. Main St., Belmont, NC 28012
Mailing Address: Piedmont Carolinas Chapter NRHS, PO Box 11753, Charlotte, NC 28220
Telephone: (704) 825-4403
Internet: www.webserve.net/piedmont-nrhs

TWEETSIE RAILROAD
Train ride
36" gauge

Description: The Tweetsie Railroad is a theme park centered on a 3-mile train ride. Visitors can enjoy the train show, live entertainment, rides, mountain crafts, and a petting zoo.

Schedule: Call or write for information.

Admission/Fare: Call or write for information.

Locomotives/Rolling Stock: No. 12, 1917 Baldwin 4-6-0, former Tennessee & Western North Carolina; no. 190, 1943 Baldwin 2-8-2, former White Pass & Yukon.

Location/Directions: Between Boone and Blowing Rock on U.S. 221-321. Take Milepost 291 exit off the Blue Ridge Parkway.

Site Address: Blowing Rock, NC
Mailing Address: PO Box 388, Blowing Rock, NC 28605
Telephone: (828) 264-9061

NEW HOPE VALLEY RAILWAY
Train ride
Standard gauge

GRAY LACKEY

Description: Eight-mile round trip over 4 miles of the original Norfolk Southern Railway's Durham Branch on a diesel-powered train with open cars and cabooses. Other equipment and displays at this site.

Schedule: May through December: first Sunday of month, departures at 12, 1, 2, 3, and 4 p.m.

Admission/Fare: Adults, $6; children, $4.

Locomotives/Rolling Stock: 80-ton GE and Whtcomb; 45-ton GE; 50-ton Whitcomb; Heisler steam engine under restoration; cabooses, freight cars.

Special Events: Halloween Train, Santa Claus Train.

Nearby Attractions/Accommodations: Jordan Lake, camping, fishing, boating, Shearon Harris Nuclear Power Plant tours, Ramada Inn in Apex, North Carolina.

Location/Directions: Eight miles south of Apex on State Route 1011. In Bonsal turn right on Daisey St., 300 feet on left.

Radio frequency: 160.425

Site Address: 5121 Daisey St., Bonsal, NC
Mailing Address: PO Box 40, New Hill, NC 27562
Telephone: (919) 362-5416
E-mail: nhvry@mindspring.com
Internet: www.mindspring.com/~nhvry

CHARLOTTE TROLLEY, INC.
Trolley ride

Description: This volunteer organization restores and runs vintage street-cars. Rides F, G, S are 25 minutes round trip.

Schedule: Friday and Saturday, 10 a.m. to 9 p.m.; Sunday 10 a.m. to 6 p.m.; leaving the barn on the hour and the half hour.

Admission/Fare: Round trip, $2; children with parent, free; groups, $1 each; handicap accessible.

Locomotives/Rolling Stock: No. 1 Charlotte Electric Railway by United Electric Car Co. 1914 for Piraeus Greece; no. 13 Philadelphia Suburban Trans. by St. Louis Car Co. 1949 modified double-end PCC; no. 85 Southern Public Utilities homebuilt 1927 four-wheel Birney; no. 407 South Carolina Power Co. JG Brill 1922 for Virginia Railway & Power Co. (Richmond), four-wheel Birney, was Virginia Railway & Power no. 1520 then Ft. Collins Municipal Railway no. 25-II.

Special Events: May 20, Volunteer Day; Labor Day barbecue; New Year's.

Nearby Attractions/Accommodations: Eleven restaurants, shops, gallery, book store, furniture, antiques.

Location/Directions: South 1 mile from town on South Blvd. at the Atherton Mill.

       M arm

Site Address: 2104 South Blvd., Charlotte, NC
Mailing Address: 2104 South Blvd., Charlotte, NC 28203
Telephone: (704) 375-0850
Fax: (704) 375-0553
E-mail: clttrolley@aol.com
Internet: www.charlottetrolley.org

North Carolina, Dillsboro

GREAT SMOKY MOUNTAINS RAILWAY
Train ride, dinner train
Standard gauge

LAVIDGE AND ASSOCIATES

Description: Departures from Dillsboro, Bryson City, and Andrews, North Carolina. Enjoy scenic train rides amid beautiful mountain scenery. Dillsboro departures feature a scenic journey along the Tuckasegee River. Bryson City and Andrews morning departures offer an optional luncheon or white water rafting. Twilight Dinner Train departs Dillsboro and features gourmet delicacies aboard restored dining cars.

Schedule: January through December: schedule varies with season. Call or write for schedule and reservations.

Admission/Fare: Adults, $26 and up; children under age 13, $13 and up. Steam Days, add $5 per adult. Reservations recommended. Excursion trains depart from Dillsboro, Bryson City, and Andrews.

Locomotives/Rolling Stock: No. 1702, 1942 Baldwin 2-8-0, former U.S. Army; nos. 711 and 777, EMD GP7s; nos. 210 and 223, EMD GP35s.

Special Events: Santa Express, featuring the story of "Polar Express," December 2-19; Day Out with Thomas event.

Nearby Attractions/Accommodations: Smoky Mountains National Park, Cherokee Indian Reservation, Biltmore estate, whitewater rafting.

Location/Directions: From Asheville–I-40 west to exit 27 to U.S. 74 west. Exit 81 for Dillsboro, or exit 67 for Bryson City.

Site Address: 119 Front St., Dillsboro, NC or Depot St., Bryson City, NC
Mailing Address: PO Box 397, Dillsboro, NC 28725
Telephone: (800) 872-4681 or (828) 586-8811
Fax: (828) 586-8806
E-mail: traininfo@gsmr.com
Internet: www.gsmr.com

**NATIONAL RAILROAD MUSEUM
AND HALL OF FAME**
Museum, display, layout

Description: The museum exhibits include photographs, maps, displays, a gift shop, a model railroad layout, four pieces of rolling stock, and a recreated telegraph office. The SAL locomotive 1114 SDP 35 and caboose SAL 5254 are on display at the museum.

Schedule: Year round: Saturdays 10 a.m. to 5 p.m.; Sundays 1 to 5 p.m.; during the week by appointment.

Admission/Fare: Donations appreciated.

Locomotives/Rolling Stock: SAL locomotive 1114 SDP 35; SAL caboose 5241; replica of the "Tornado" built in 1892 at Raleigh, North Carolina.

Special Events: Seaboard Festival, October 28.

Nearby Attractions/Accommodations: North Carolina Motor Speedway, Morrow Mountain State Park, Town Creek Indian Mound, North Carolina Zoo, Pee Dee National Wildlife Refuge, Pinehurst, over 40 golf courses.

Location/Directions: In Hamlet, Highway 74 east, turn right at light on Raleigh St. Museum is in middle of second block, turn left between the tracks. Located in the Seaboard Line Railway Depot.

Site Address: 2 Main St., Hamlet, NC
Mailing Address: 2 Main St., Hamlet, NC 28345
Telephone: (910) 582-3317 (residence)

NORTH CAROLINA TRANSPORTATION MUSEUM AT HISTORIC SPENCER SHOPS

Museum
Standard gauge

Description: Thirty-minute narrated train ride around property. Steam powered on weekends, April through Labor Day. Exhibits on inland transportation automobiles.

Schedule: April through October, museum open Monday through Saturday, 9 a.m. to 5 p.m. and Sundays, 1 to 5 p.m.; November through March, Tuesday through Saturday, 10 a.m. to 4 p.m. and Sundays, 1 to 4 p.m.

Admission/Fare: Train ride–adults, $5; seniors (60+) and children 3-12, $4. Turntable ride–$.50 per person.

Locomotives/Rolling Stock: SR E8 6900; SR FP76133; N&W GP9 620; SRGP302601–all operating. Several more locomotives and cars on display in roundhouse. Operating steam includes Graham County Shay 1925 and BC&G 2-8-0 no. 604.

Special Events: Rail Days, April 28-29; Steamfest, September 29.

Nearby Attractions/Accommodations: Dan Nicolas Park, Rowan Museum, several restaurants and hotels.

Location/Directions: I-85 exit 79 (Spencer). Follow signs to museum.

*Coupon available, see coupon section.

Site Address: 411 S. Salisbury Ave., Spencer, NC
Mailing Address: PO Box 165, Spencer, NC 28159
Telephone: (704) 636-2889 or (800) NCTMFUN
Fax: (704) 639-1881
E-mail: nctm<nctrans@vnet.net>
Internet: www.nctrans.org

WILMINGTON RAILROAD MUSEUM
Museum, display, layout
HO, O, N

CHARLES KERNAN

Description: Museum housed in the 1900 ACL freight office building. Interact with our extensive artifact collection, model train layouts (HO & Lionel) and children's hands-on learning area. Climb aboard the 1910 Baldwin steam locomotive and red caboose.

Schedule: March 15 through October 15: Monday through Saturday, 10 a.m. to 5 p.m.; Sunday, 1 to 5 p.m. October 16 through March 14: Monday through Saturday, 10 a.m. to 4 p.m.; Closed Thanksgiving, Christmas Eve, Christmas Day, and New Year's Day.

Admission/Fare: Adults, $3; seniors (55+)/military, $2; children 3-12, $1.50; 2 and under and members are free; group rates available.

Locomotives/Rolling Stock: 1910 Baldwin steam locomotive 4-6-0 no. 250; ACL caboose no. 01983; 1963 RF&P boxcar no. 2379.

Special Events: Model Railroad Show, January; Azalea Festival, April; Riverfest, October.

Nearby Attractions/Accommodations: Battleship U.S.S. *North Carolina*, Fort Fisher State Historical Site, beaches.

Location/Directions: Highway 17 into downtown Wilmington (turns into Market St.), turn right on Water St., four blocks ahead, three-story brick building.

Site Address: 501 Nutt St., Wilmington, NC
Mailing Address: 501 Nutt St., Wilmington, NC 28401
Telephone: (910) 763-2634
Fax: (910) 763-2634 (call first)
E-mail: www.wilmington.org/railroad

Description: A 9-mile round trip from Mandan to Ft. Abraham Lincoln State Park along the Heart River. We have a restored American Car Co. streetcar and an eight-bench open car.

Schedule: Memorial Day through Labor Day: daily departures 1, 2, 3, 4, 5 p.m.

Admission/Fare: Adults, $5; children 5-10, $3; under 5 are free.

Locomotives/Rolling Stock: American Car Co. streetcar no. 102; eight-bench open car.

Nearby Attractions/Accommodations: Fort Lincoln State Park, Lewis and Clark Riverboats, Mandan Railroad Museum.

Location/Directions: I-94 to Highway 1806 to Third St. SE; east on Third St. SE about five blocks.

Site Address: Third St. SE, Mandan, ND
Mailing Address: 29 Captain Leach Dr., Mandan, ND 58554
Telephone: (701) 663-9018

**OLD SOO DEPOT TRANSPORTATION
MUSEUM & WESTERN HISTORY
RESEARCH CENTER**
Museum

DENNIS LUTZ, M.D.

Description: Museum and Research Center in completely restored 1912 Soo Line Depot, one of the finest ever built. Museum focuses on transportation history of the American West, including GN, NP, Soo, Milwaukee Road, and Amtrak.

Schedule: Call or write for information.

Admission/Fare: Donations accepted.

Locomotives/Rolling Stock: Burlington Northern Santa Fe, Canadian Pacific, and Amtrak trains frequently operating beside or across from building.

Nearby Attractions/Accommodations: Taube Art Museum, Railroad Museum of Minot, Charlie's Main Street Cafe, Dragon Delight.

Location/Directions: North end of Main St. in downtown Minot, along the main line of the Canadian Pacific and Burlington Northern Sante Fe Railroads.

Site Address: 15 N. Main St., Minot, ND
Mailing Address: PO Box 2148, Minot, ND 58702
Telephone: (701) 852-2234

Description: A mile-long train ride through Roosevelt Park on the Magic City Express train. A ⅔ scale model of a Great Northern F-8 locomotive no. 1177 and four cars.

Schedule: Train–May through August, weekdays 1 to 5 p.m.; weekends 1 to 8 p.m. Museum–Mondays, Wednesdays, Fridays, 10 a.m. to 12:00 noon; Saturdays 1 to 4 p.m.

Admission/Fare: $2, which includes one free train ride, one free admission to museum, under 5 free.

Locomotives/Rolling Stock: Great Northern Caboose no. 12183; SooLine caboose no. 32; speeder cars; baggage cart.

Special Events: Railroad Days, second weekend (Friday-Saturday) of June; Family Day, third Saturday of July.

Nearby Attractions/Accommodations: Roosevelt park, zoo and pool.

Location/Directions: Going east on E. Central takes you to the north end of the park, where we are. The zoo is at the south end of the park. Museum is one block east of Main St.

*Coupon available, see coupon section.

     M

Site Address: 19 First St. NE, Minot, ND
Mailing Address: PO Box 74, Minot, ND 58703
Telephone: (701) 852-7091

BONANZAVILLE, U.S.A.
Museum, display, layout
Standard gauge

R.A. YOUNG

Description: A 15-acre historical village with static displays of the Embden, North Dakota, Depot and train shed and the Kathryn, North Dakota, Depot with Spud Valley Model Railroad layout. See 40 other buildings serving as small museums representing life in the Red River Valley between 1880 and 1920.

Schedule: May and October, Mondays through Fridays, 9 a.m. to 5 p.m. June through September, daily, 9 a.m. to 6 p.m.

Admission/Fare: Adults, $6; juniors, $3; age 5 and under, free.

Locomotives/Rolling Stock: Rome locomotive 4-4-0; Northern Pacific wood caboose no. 1628; Burlington Northern, former Midland Continental; wood russell plow, former NP; NP steel 80-ton passenger coach, no. 1360.

Special Events: Pioneer Days, third weekend in August.

Nearby Attractions/Accommodations: Red River Zoo, Children's Museum, Plains Art Museum, F-M Redhawks baseball, Cass County Campground, Days Inn.

Location/Directions: I-94, exit 343 to West Fargo.

Site Address: 1351 W. Main Ave., West Fargo, ND
Mailing Address: PO Box 719, West Fargo, ND 58078
Telephone: (701) 282-2822
Fax: (701) 282-7606
E-mail: bonanzaville@fargocity.com
Internet: www.fargocity.com/bonanzaville

MAD RIVER & NKP RAILROAD SOCIETY, INC.
Museum, display, layout
HO, under construction at present

GEORGE LEADER

Description: Steps and open doors welcome all who come to the hands-on museum.

Schedule: Memorial Day through Labor Day: daily, 1 to 5 p.m.; May, September, and October: weekends only.

Admission/Fare: Adults, $3; children, $1; subject to change; credit cards not accepted for admission.

Locomotives/Rolling Stock: Alco RSD 12 NKP no. 329; EMD GP30 NKP no. 900; FM H1244 Milw. no. 740; Wabash F7 diesel no. 671; PRR RPO car; NKP dynamometer car; three NKP cabooses; N&W caboose; troop sleeper car; refrigerator cars; four passenger cars, including the first dome car built; and various other cars and equipment.

Special Events: Limited number of bus/rail tours throughout the year. Call for information. Guided tours, if scheduled in advance.

Nearby Attractions/Accommodations: Cedar Point Amusement Park, Sorrowful Mother Shrine, Seneca Caverns, Historic Lyme Village.

Location/Directions: Two blocks south of downtown. Follow our green signs.

Site Address: 353 Southwest St., Bellevue, OH
Mailing Address: 233 York St., Bellevue, OH 44811-1377
Telephone: (419) 483-2222 (office) and (419) 483-2872 (gift shop)
E-mail: madriver@onebellevue.com
Internet: www.onebellevue.com/madriver/

CARROLLTON-ONEIDA-MINERVA RAILROAD
ELDERBERRY LINE
Train ride
Standard gauge

Description: Travel 14 miles between Carrollton and Minerva through areas of light industry, farmland, marshland, and forest, with one-hour lay-over in Minerva. The train ride is 28 miles round trip.

Schedule: Mid-June through October: weekends. December: Christmas runs. Call for information and schedules.

Admission/Fare: Adults, $10; children 2-12, $8. Group rates available.

Locomotives/Rolling Stock: 1952 Alco RS-3 locomotive; 1926 ES New Jersey coach; three 1937 coaches, former Canadian.

Special Events: Fall Foliage, October. Christmas trains start Thanksgiving weekend.

Nearby Attractions/Accommodations: Atwood Lodge, sailing, fishing, Pro Football Hall of Fame, McKinley's monument.

Location/Directions: Site is 100 miles south of Cleveland, 25 miles south of Canton, and 60 miles west of Pittsburgh, Pennsylvania.

*Coupon available, see coupon section.

      M

Site Address: 203 2nd St. NW, Carrollton, OH
Mailing Address: 220 Wayne Ave., Carrollton, OH 44615
Telephone: (330) 627-2282
Fax: (330) 627-3624
E-mail: elderbrr@raex.com
Internet: www.advantagepages.com/elderberry

CARILLON HISTORICAL PARK
Train ride, museum
Standard and 7½ " gauge

Description: Indoor and outdoor history museum. Carillon features a new transportation center with rolling stock, 1894 railroad station, 1907 watch tower, canal lock, two bridges, and scheduled rides on a small scale live-steam railroad.

Schedule: April to November, Saturdays, 9:30 a.m. to 5 p.m., Sundays, 12 to 5 p.m.

Admission/Fare: Annual ride-on family membership, $7. Park entry: adults, $2; seniors and children 3-17, $1.50; park members and children under 3 are free.

Locomotives/Rolling Stock: 1835 B&O no. 1; 1900 Porter; 1909 Lima fireless; 1903 observation car; 1904 interurban; B&O C-2646 caboose.

Special Events: Rail and Steam Festival, Saturday and Sunday Memorial Day weekend (May 26-27).

Nearby Attractions/Accommodations: U.S. Air Force Museum, Sunwatch Indian Village, Wright Brothers Memorial, Dayton Aviation Heritage National Historical Park, Marriott, Holiday Inn.

Location/Directions: I-75 exit 51, east on Edwin C. Moses Blvd., right over bridge, right on Patterson Blvd., right on Carillon Blvd. to entrance.

   M

Site Address: 1000 Carillon Blvd., Dayton, OH
Mailing Address: 1000 Carillon Blvd., Dayton, OH 45409
Telephone: (937) 293-2841
Fax: (937) 293-5798

THE DENNISON RAILROAD DEPOT MUSEUM
Train ride, museum, layout
N scale

Description: The museum, restaurant, and gift shop are housed in a restored 1873 Pennsylvania Railroad depot. Train rides from May through December: all-day excursions, murder mysteries, fall foliage trips, and holiday trips.

Schedule: Year round: Tuesdays through Saturdays, 11 a.m. to 5 p.m. Sundays, 11 a.m. to 3 p.m. Tours by appointment.

Admission/Fare: Range from $7 to $100.

Locomotives/Rolling Stock: See website: www.ohiocentralrr.com for train ride stock. On display: 1940s Thermos Bottle Vulcan engine; caboose; freight cars; C&O engine no. 2700.

Special Events: Railroad festival, third week of May.

Nearby Attractions/Accommodations: Amish Country, Roscoe Village, Zoar and Schoennbrunn (Ohio Historical Society sites).

Location/Directions: Located halfway between Columbus, Ohio, and Pittsburgh, Pennsylvania, 18 miles east of I-77 and 36 miles north of I-70. At the junction of Routes 250, 36, and 800.

*Coupon available, see coupon section.

Site Address: 400 Center St., Dennison, OH
Mailing Address: PO Box 11, Dennison, OH 44621
Telephone: (740) 922-6776
Fax: (740) 922-0105
E-mail: depot@tusco.net
Internet: www.dennisondepot.org

**NORTHWEST OHIO RAILROAD
PRESERVATION, INC.**
*Train ride, display
15" gauge*

Description: Live steam 2-6-2 Prairie-type locomotive with open seat coaches.

Schedule: Call, fax, or write for information; we are under construction, and scheduled to open in the spring of 2001.

Locomotives/Rolling Stock: B&O 250-ton steam wrecking derrick no. X-45; several motorcars (speeders).

Nearby Attractions/Accommodations: Amusement parks, museums, restaurants, lodging, campgrounds, state park, scenic sites.

Location/Directions: Northeast corner of I-75 and County Road 99, exit 161.

Site Address: 11732 County Road 99, Findlay, OH
Mailing Address: 11732 County Road 99, Findlay, OH 45840-9602
Telephone: (419) 423-2995
Fax: (419) 423-4258

BUCKEYE CENTRAL SCENIC RAILROAD
Train ride
Standard gauge

Description: We offer a scenic 1.5-hour round trip excursion through the rolling hills of central Ohio on historic Shawnee branch of the old B&O. Travel in vintage passenger coaches or in the open-air gondola. On your journey pass over a steel bridge and two trestles.

Schedule: Memorial Day weekend through mid-October: weekend departures at 1 and 3 p.m.

Admission/Fare: Call or write for information.

Locomotives/Rolling Stock: SW-1 no. 8599; open gondola; four Canadian National coaches.

Special Events: Haunted Halloween Trains, Santa Claus Specials, Wild West/Train Robbery. Call for dates.

Nearby Attractions/Accommodations: Flint Ridge State Park, Buckeye Lake, Dawes Arboretum, Heissy Museum, the Olde Mill, village of Granville.

Location/Directions: I-70, exit Route 13N to Route 40, turn left; or I-70, exit Route 79N to Route 40, turn right. Located on Route 40.

    M

Site Address: 5501 National Rd. SE, Hebron, OH
Mailing Address: PO Box 242, Newark, OH 43058-0242
Telephone: (740) 366-2029
Fax: (614) 891-5847
Internet: www.infinet.com/~pcaravan

CUYAHOGA VALLEY SCENIC RAILROAD
Train ride
Standard gauge

Description: The CVSR in Northeastern Ohio runs through the heart of Cuyahoga Valley National Recreation Area. Each 26-mile trip is a different adventure filled with fun, excitement, natural beauty, and historic sites. Ride comfortably in vintage climate-controlled coaches built between 1939 and 1940. The coaches originally saw passenger service on the NYC and Santa Fe Railroads.

Schedule: February through May, November and December: weekends. June through August: Wednesdays through Sundays. October: daily.

Admission/Fare: $11 to $20.

Locomotives/Rolling Stock: Alco FPA 4s nos. 15 and 6777; Alco FPA 4s nos. 4088 and 4099, former Delaware & Hudson.

Special Events: Valentine Express, Valentine's Day. Easter Bunny Express, Easter Day. Fall Color Train, daily in October. Christmas Tree Adventure, weekends in December. Polar Express, weeknights in December.

Nearby Attractions/Accommodations: Hale Farm Village, Holiday Inn Richfield, Sea World, Cleveland Indians/Browns, Stan Hywet Hall and Gardens.

Location/Directions: I-77 to Rockside Rd.

Site Address: Old Riverside Rd., Independence, OH
Mailing Address: PO Box 158, Peninsula, OH 44264-0158
Telephone: (800) 468-4070 and (330) 657-2000
Fax: (330) 657-2080
E-mail: webmaster@cvsr.com
Internet: www.cvsr.com

Ohio, Jefferson

AC&J SCENIC LINE RAILWAY
Train ride
Standard gauge

Description: Enjoy a one-hour 12-mile round trip over the last remaining portion of the New York Central's Ashtabula-to-Pittsburgh "High Grade" passenger main line. Ride in vintage passenger cars pulled by a first-generation diesel. A family educational adventure.

Schedule: Saturdays and Sundays, June 16 through October 28: departures at 12:30, 2, and 3:30 p.m.

Admission/Fare: Adults, $7; seniors, $6; children, $5; under age 3 are free when not occupying a seat.

Locomotives/Rolling Stock: No. 107, 1950 Alco S-2 diesel, former Nickel Plate and Fairport, Painesville & Eastern; no. 518, 1948 Alco S-2 diesel, former Erie and Centerior Energy plant switcher; no. 1022 former Erie passenger coach; no. 425 former Nickel Plate caboose; nos. 7133 and 7155 former Long Island Railroad commuter cars.

Special Events: Murder Mystery trains, spring and fall.

Nearby Attractions/Accommodations: Adjacent Jefferson Depot, Victorian Perambulator Museum, Geneva-on-the-Lake, Pymatuning Resort area.

Location/Directions: I-90 from east/west exit Ohio 11 south, to Ohio 46 and south to Jefferson, left at second light on E. Jefferson St. to tracks. Or north on Route 11, exit 307 west to Jefferson, right at second light to tracks.

Site Address: E. Jefferson St., Jefferson, OH
Mailing Address: PO Box 517, Jefferson, OH 44047-0517
Telephone: (440) 576-6346
Fax: (440) 576-8848

Ohio, Jefferson

JEFFERSON DEPOT, INC.
Museum

Description: Jefferson Depot is a restored Historic 1872 Lake Shore & Michigan Southern Railroad station. It features a 1918 caboose, the 1848 "Church in the Wildwood," Century Barn, and an 1838 one-room schoolhouse. Scenic train rides are next door, and we offer guided tours.

Schedule: June through August: Sundays 1 to 4 p.m. Other times upon request (group tours, meetings, reunions, etc.).

Admission/Fare: Adults, $2 donation.

Special Events: Strawberry Festival and Craft Bazaar, third weekend in June. Antique car show, third Sunday in June. Fall Foliage Train/Bus Trip, first Saturday in October. "An Old-Fashion Williamsburg Christmas Party," second Sunday in December.

Nearby Attractions/Accommodations: Pymatuning State Park, Perambulator Museum, Giddings Law Office, many covered bridges, Lake Erie, and Pymatuning Lake, with boating, fishing, campgrounds, swimming, Buccaneer Campgrounds, many motels and restaurants. (Holiday Inn Express, Hampton Inn, Comfort Inn, etc.)

Location/Directions: From I-90 south on Rte. 11 to Rte. 46 south to E. Walnut St.

          M

Site Address: 147 E. Jefferson St., Jefferson, OH
Mailing Address: PO Box 22, Jefferson, OH 44047
Telephone: (440) 293-5532
E-mail: duttonjg@hotmail.com
Internet: http://members.tripod.com/jeffersonhome

Description: Train-O-Rama is an operating electric train display with full scenery.

Schedule: Open year round; Mondays through Saturdays, 11 a.m. to 5 p.m.; Sundays, 1 to 5 p.m. Memorial Day to Labor Day: Mondays through Saturdays, 10 a.m. to 6 p.m.; Sundays, 1 to 6 p.m. Closed New Year's Day, Easter, Thanksgiving, and Christmas Day. (Days and hours subject to change without notice.)

Location/Directions: Located on State Route 163 between Port Clinton and Marblehead.

Site Address: 6732 E. Harbor Rd., Marblehead, OH
Mailing Address: 32 E. League St., Norwalk, OH 44857
Telephone: (419) 734-5856
Fax: (419) 668-1842
E-mail: TrainORama@AOL.com

Description: A model railroad museum and operating layout featuring over 18 trains simultaneously in standard, O, and G gauge. Over 275 locomotives are on display: Lionel, American Flyer, Ives, Williams, and others.

Schedule: Year round: daily, 11 a.m. to 5 p.m.

Admission: Adults, $5; seniors, $4; children under 10 are free with paying adult; families, $15.

Special Events: Sternwheel Festival, weekend after Labor Day.

Nearby Attractions/Accommodations: Butch's Cola Museum, Children's Toy and Doll Museum, Valley Gem Sternwheel, Showboat Becky Thatcher, Rossi Pasta Factory, Fenton Art Glass Company and Outlet, historic Lafayette Hotel, Ohio River Museum.

Location/Directions: I-77 and Ohio Route 7.

*Coupon available, see coupon section.

    M

Site Address: 220 Gilman St., Harmar Village, Marietta, OH
Mailing Address: 220 Gilman St., Marietta, OH 45750
Telephone: (740) 374-9995
Fax: (740) 373-7808
E-mail: mttachamber@ee.net
Internet: www.harmarstation.com

MARION UNION STATION ASSOCIATION
Museum, display, layout

Description: This museum and model railroad club is a train viewer's paradise. Many CSX and NS freight trains pass by daily, to the north, south, east, and west.

Schedule: Year round: Museum–Mondays through Thursdays, 10 a.m. to 2 p.m. Layout–Sundays 2 to 4 p.m.

Admission/Fare: Donations appreciated ($2 per person suggested).

Locomotives/Rolling Stock: Erie caboose no. C-306; AC tower; watchman's shanty.

Special Events: Chicken barbecue, first Sunday in October. Model train show, first Saturday in December.

Nearby Attractions/Accommodations: Call Visitor's Bureau for free guide (800) 371-6688.

Location/Directions: Route 309 west (between railroad tracks).

Site Address: 532 W. Center St., Marion, OH
Mailing Address: 532 W. Center St., Marion, OH 43302-3533
Telephone: (740) 383-3768
Fax: (740) 383-3768
E-mail: unionstation@marion.net

LUCAS COUNTY/MAUMEE VALLEY
HISTORICAL SOCIETY
Museum

Description: The depot is part of a five-building museum complex. Guided tours cover the entire complex. The depot and caboose are authentically furnished. Railroad memorabilia are on display.

Schedule: Wednesdays through Sundays, 1 to 4 p.m.

Fare/Admission: Adults $3.50; children $1.50.

Locomotive/Rolling Stock: Caboose and baggage car.

Special Events: Model train exhibit in depot for Harvest Days, October 29; Christmas by the River, November 8 through December 31.

Nearby Attractions/Accommodations: Toledo Zoo, Toledo Museum of Art, Toledo Mud Hens baseball, Tony Pacos Restaurant, Ft. Meigs.

Location/Directions: The museum is on River Rd. in downtown Maumee and can be reached easily from U.S. routes 20 and 24.

Site Address: 1031 River Rd., Maumee, OH
Mailing Address: 1031 River Rd., Maumee, OH 43537
Telephone: (419) 893-9602
Fax: (419) 893-3108
Internet: www.maumee.org/wolcott/wolcott/.htm

Ohio, Nelsonville   **HOCKING VALLEY SCENIC RAILWAY**
Train ride, museum
Standard gauge

Description: Hocking Valley Scenic Railway offers a 14-mile round trip at 12 noon and a 22-mile round trip at 2:30 p.m. All regular scheduled trains stop at an 1850s village for 30 minutes.

Schedule: Memorial Day weekend through mid-November: weekends, 12 and 2:30 p.m.; Santa Trains: last weekend in November and first three weekends in December; Santa Trains depart at 11 a.m. and 2:30 p.m.

Admission/Fare: 12:00 noon–adults, $8, children 3-12, $5; 2:30 p.m.–adults, $11, children 3-12, $7. Santa trains–adults, $11, children 3-12, $7.50.

Locomotives/Rolling Stock: GP7 C&O 5833; BLH switcher 4005; GE 45-ton Industrial 7315; B&O combine City of Athens; three RI commuter cars, "City of Logan," "City of Nelsonville," and "Village of Haydenville."

Special Events: Check web site: www.hvsr.com

Nearby Attractions/Accommodations: Hocking Hills area; Old Man's Cave, campgrounds, Lakes hiking trails Nelsonville; Victorian Square, restored 1800s opera house, famous Dew Hotel, Robbins Crossing 1850s village.

Location/Directions: From I-70 or I-270, exit at U.S. 33 east to Nelsonville; located on U.S. 33 next to Rocky Boot.

*Coupon available, see coupon section.

      M

Site Address: 33 Canal St., Nelsonville, OH
Mailing Address: PO Box 427, Nelsonville, OH 45764
Telephone: (800) 967-7834 and (614) 470-1300
Fax: (740) 753-1152
Internet: www.hvsr.com

Ohio, Olmsted Township

TROLLEYVILLE, U.S.A.
Train ride, museum, display, layout
Standard gauge

Description: Streetcars and miscellaneous railroad equipment are on display. The museum is located in the 1875 restored B&O Berea Depot. Ride on over 2.5 miles of track.

Schedule: May through November: weekends. June through September: Wednesdays through Sundays.

Admission/Fare: Adults, $5; seniors, $4; children, $3; under age 2 are free.

Locomotives/Rolling Stock: Thirteen streetcars; 13 interurban; four work cars and locomotives; two boxcars; two cabooses; miscellaneous motorcars.

Special Events: Easter Egg Hunt, Murder Mysteries, 4th of July, Train Shows, Moonlight Rides, Halloween, Christmas Festival of Lights.

Nearby Attractions/Accommodations: Cedar Point, Geauga Lake Amusement Park, Rock and Roll Hall of Fame, Museum of Science and Industry.

Location/Directions: I-480, exit 6A, 2 miles south, west side of road in shopping center.

*Coupon available, see coupon section.

Radio frequency: 43.7

Site Address: 7100 Columbia Rd., Olmsted Township, OH
Mailing Address: 7100 Columbia Rd., Olmsted Township, OH 44138
Telephone: (440) 235-4725
Fax: (440) 235-6556
E-mail: cliff@trolleyvilleusa.org
Internet: www.trolleyvilleusa.org

Ohio, Orrville

ORRVILLE RAILROAD HERITAGE SOCIETY
Train ride, museum, display
Standard gauge

ROBERT CUTTING

Description: Mainline trips, all day rides, 50 to 120 miles in length.

Schedule: Depot open Saturdays, May through October, 10 a.m. to 4 p.m. Trips vary year to year. Send for information.

Admission/Fare: Depot tours, no charge. Mainline trips, fares vary per trip.

Locomotives/Rolling Stock: Ex-New Haven GP-9 PRR; N5C caboose; five Budd passenger coaches; ex-Amtrak baggage car; privately owned caboose and passenger cars; switch block tower.

Special Events: Depot Days, second weekend of June; Open House, Friday and Saturday after Thanksgiving.

Nearby Attractions/Accommodations: Amish Country; Rubbermaid store; Smucker Jam and Jelly store; new motel at junction of Routes 57 and 30 (3 miles south).

Location/Directions: 12 miles south of I-76; 3 miles north of Route 30, on Route 57.

Site Address: 145 Depot St., Orrville, OH
Mailing Address: PO Box 11, Orrville, OH 44667
Telephone: (330) 683-2426
Fax: (330) 682-2426
Internet: www.orrvillerailroad.com

OHIO RAILWAY MUSEUM
Train ride, museum
Standard gauge

DAVE BUNGE

Description: Museum offers a 2-mile round trip on historic trolley-interurban cars.

Schedule: May through October: Sundays, 1 to 5 p.m.

Admission/Fare: Adults, $3.50; seniors, $2.50; children, $1.50.

Locomotives/Rolling Stock: N&W no. 578 Pacific Steam; OPS no. 21 interurban; passenger cars, street cars, and interurbans.

Special Events: Ghost Trolley, Santa Trolley, State Fair, Twilight Trolley Excursions.

Nearby Attractions/Accommodations: Columbus Zoo, Center of Science and Industry, IMAX, hotels, and restaurants.

Location/Directions: I-71 exit Route 161, one mile west to Proprietors Rd., turn north.

Site Address: 990 Proprietors Rd., Worthington, OH
Mailing Address: Box 777, Worthington, OH
Telephone: (614) 885-7345
Internet: www.trainweb.org/ORM

Description: Trains, trains, and more trains running everywhere! Exhibits include an outdoor G scale garden railroad, a 28 x 48-foot Lionel layout, HO and N scale layouts, and a wagon-train ride through the park. Hobby shop features trains and accessories in all scales.

Schedule: Year round: Tuesdays through Saturdays 10 a.m. to 5:30 p.m., Sundays 1 to 5 p.m. By appointment only.

Admission/Fare: Donations appreciated.

Special Events: Main Line Train Show, first Saturday after July 4th. Christmas display, December.

Nearby Attractions/Accommodations: Osage Hills State Park, candle factory, restaurants, motels, Bartlesville, Oklahoma (15 miles).

Location/Directions: U.S. 75 to County Road 2700, east 2 miles to stop sign, north 1.5 blocks to entrance.

*Coupon available, see coupon section.

Site Address: 26811 N. 3990 Rd., Ramona, OK
Mailing Address: 26811 N. 3990 Rd., Ramona, OK 74061
Telephone: (918) 336-5821 and (800) 845-5781

OKLAHOMA CENTRAL RAILROAD
Train ride
Standard

Description: Excursion train between Kellyville, Oklahoma, and Bristow, Oklahoma.

Schedule: Year round.

Admission/Fare: Adults, $14; children, $9; senior and group discounts available.

Special Events: Special events on selected holidays.

Nearby Attractions/Accommodations: Tulsa, Oklahoma, is within 20-minute drive; Historic Route 66; Safari Joe's Wild Animal Park.

Location/Directions: West of Tulsa, take the Kellyville exit off I-44 and follow the signs to the depot.

Site Address: Under construction
Mailing Address: 22630 E. 79 St., Broken Arrow, OK 74014
Telephone: (918) 357-5391
Fax: (918) 357-5391
E-mail: ocrr@engineer.com
Internet: www.oklahomacentralrailroad.com

Description: Our museum of working trains includes a 30 x 40-foot layout with a circus, mountains, and lakes.

Schedule: Year round: daily, 9 a.m. to 5 p.m.

Admission/Fare: Donations appreciated.

Special Events: Cherokee Strips Days, September 18. Cherokee Strip Museum, restaurants, motels; Perry, Oklahoma, is 10 miles away.

Location/Directions: Exit I-35 at exit 185, go 10 miles west on Highway 164 and ¼ south.

Site Address: Route 1, Box 113, Covington, OK
Mailing Address: Route 1, Box 113, Covington, OK 73730
Telephone: (580) 336-2823

RAILROAD MUSEUM OF OKLAHOMA
Museum, display, layout
Standard gauge

ROBERT CHESTER

Description: This museum, housed in a 1926-27 former Santa Fe freight-house, has one of the largest collections of railroad memorabilia in the midwest. Focused on preserving historically significant railroad equipment. Recapture the essence of railroad days as you climb aboard a 1925 steam locomotive, wander through cabooses from eight different railroads, and view seven different types of freight cars.

Schedule: Year round: Tuesday through Friday, 1 to 4 p.m. Saturdays, 9 a.m. to 1 p.m. Sundays, 2 to 5 p.m. Other times by appointment.

Admission/Fare: By donation.

Locomotives/Rolling Stock: 1925 Frisco Baldwin 4-8-2 no. 1519; Vulcan Chemicals 1965 GE 50-ton class BB switcher; renovated BN, NP, RI, MoP, SF, MK&T, and UP cabooses; 1928 automobile boxcar; 1937 three-dome tank car; 1953 single-dome tank car; 1930 boxcar; 1920 gondola.

Special Events: Two model railroad swap meets; Christmas party; Railroad Appreciation Day, April; two caboose excursions each year.

Nearby Attractions/Accommodations: Water park, winery, Science and Discovery Center, Cherokee Strip, and museums.

Location/Directions: Enid is 30 miles west of I-35 in north central Oklahoma on Routes 60, 81, 64, 412. Museum is six blocks northwest of downtown square.

Site Address: 702 N. Washington, Enid, OK
Mailing Address: 702 N. Washington, Enid, OK 73701
Telephone: (580) 233-3051

HUGO HERITAGE RAILROAD

Dinner train, display
Standard gauge

Description: A round trip from Hugo (Circus City, U.S.A.) to points north and south, including Paris, Texas. A museum, located in the former 1915 Frisco depot, is the largest left on Frisco's southwest lines. Displays include an HO gauge model railroad on a mountain layout, railroad artifacts, turn-of-the-century memorabilia, rare photographs, and a working Harvey House restaurant. Rides last from four hours to all day.

Schedule: April through December 15: Saturdays. Call for dates and times.

Admission/Fare: Adults, $20; seniors $17; children, $13.

Locomotives/Rolling Stock: Commuter coaches; GP38 locomotive.

Special Events: Railroad Days, October 14.

Nearby Attractions/Accommodations: Old Johnson Inn bed and breakfast, Mt. Olive Cemetery, motels, Harvey House, restaurants.

Location/Directions: Indian Nation Turnpike, exit left on Highway 70, on left side at railroad tracks.

Site Address: 309 N. "B" St., Hugo, OK
Mailing Address: 309 N. "B" St., Hugo, OK 74743
Telephone: (580) 326-6630 and (888) 773-3768
Fax: (580) 326-6686
E-mail: hugoheritagerr@email.com
Internet: www.hugoheritagerr.ohgolly.com

SUNBELT RAILROAD MUSEUM
Museum, display, layout
HO

Description: Displays include railroad mementos, an operating telegraph station, and a reference library.

Schedule: Year round: Saturdays 10 a.m. to 4 p.m. Closed holidays.

Admission/Fare: Donations appreciated.

Nearby Attractions/Accommodations: Food and lodging in downtown Tulsa.

Location/Directions: Near downtown Tulsa.

Site Address: 1323 E. Fifth St., Tulsa, OK
Mailing Address: PO Box 470311, Tulsa, OK 74147-0311
Telephone: (918) 584-3777
E-mail: srht@sunbeltrailroad.com
Internet: www.sunbeltrailroad.com

WAYNOKA AIR-RAIL MUSEUM
Museum

SANDIE OLSON

Description: An air-rail museum featuring the Santa Fe Railroad, Harvey House, Transcontinental Air Transport, German prisoner-of-war paintings, vintage video, museum store, and more in the beautifully restored Harvey House, an ISTEA project.

Schedule: Summer hours: weekends, 2 to 4 p.m., and all times by appointment.

Admission/Fare: $2 donation suggested.

Nearby Attractions/Accommodations: Little Sahara State Park with great dune riding, Curtis Hill for train watching, Sod House Museum, Alabaster Caverns, Great Salt Plains for bird watching and crystal digging. Museum is located on Oklahoma's fastest and busiest rail line, 50-70 trains daily.

Location/Directions: From Oklahoma City, west on I-40 to U.S. 281, northwest on U.S. 281 to Waynoka. The museum is at the west end of Waynoka St. on BNSF main line.

        M

Site Address: 200 S. Cleveland, Waynoka, OK
Mailing Address: PO Box 193, Waynoka, OK 73860
Telephone: (580) 824-5871
Fax: (580) 824-0921
E-mail: sandieo@pldi.net
Internet: www.pldi.net/~harpo

JOHN SHANNON

Description: The museum contains an extensive display of railroad antiques and artifacts of the Rock Island Line and other railroads.

Schedule: Year round by chance or appointment. Call or write for information.

Admission/Fare: Free.

Locomotives/Rolling Stock: Rock Island boxcar no. 5542; UP caboose no. 25865.

Location/Directions: On historic Route 66. Main St., across from "Yukon's Best Flour" wheat elevator.

Site Address: Third and Main Streets, Yukon, OK
Mailing Address: 410 Oak Ave., Yukon, OK 73099-2640
Telephone: (405) 354-5079

CANBY RAILROAD DEPOT MUSEUM
Museum

Schedule: Thursday through Sunday, 1 to 4 p.m. Closed January and February.

Admission/Fare: Free. Donations accepted.

Locomotives/Rolling Stock: Caboose.

Special Events: Open House, October. Antique Appraisal Day, September and April.

Nearby Attractions/Accommodations: Clackamas County Fairgrounds (fair in August). Molalla River State Park Canby Ferry Crossing. Willamette River, Flower Farmer Miniature Train Rides.

Location/Directions: Across from fairgrounds, adjacent to Highway 99E in Canby, between Oregon City and Aurora.

Site Address: 888 NE Fourth Ave., Canby, OR
Mailing Address: Canby Historical Society, PO Box 160, Canby, OR 97013
Telephone: (503) 266-6712
Internet: www.web-ster.com/~chamber/depot/depot.htm

PHOENIX & HOLLY RAILROAD
Train ride
Narrow gauge

FLOWER FARMER

Description: Visitors can ride through acres of flowers at the Flower Farmer and enjoy a 1¾-mile ride with a stopover at "Box Curve" station and pet the farm animals (July through September).

Schedule: May through October: weekends and holidays 11 a.m. to 6 p.m. Weekdays, groups only. October: open daily, Pumpkin Patch Trips; Haunted Train Rides, last three weeks of October, dusk to 9 p.m.

Admission/Fare: Adults, $3; children age 12 and under and seniors (65+), $2.50. Groups, weekdays by appointment. October Haunted Trains: adults, $3; children $2.50.

Locomotives/Rolling Stock: "Sparky" the diesel locomotive purpose-built; diesel locomotive 5.5" scale; DRG&W side rod diesel; gondolas; flatcar; caboose.

Special Events: Pumpkin Run to pumpkin patch, month of October. Haunted Train Rides, Christmas tree lights.

Nearby Attractions/Accommodations: Swan Island, Dahlia Farm, Canby Ferry, state parks, city parks, golf. Swan Island Dahlia Festival, last two weeks in August.

Location/Directions: I-5 to Canby exit, to Holly St., turn left one mile to site.

Site Address: 2512 N. Holly St., Canby, OR
Mailing Address: 2512 N. Holly St., Canby, OR 97013-9118
Telephone: (503) 266-3581
Fax: (503) 263-4027
E-mail: lgarre@falconpc.com
Internet: www.narrowgaugerr.com

Oregon, Hood River

MOUNT HOOD RAILROAD AND DINNER TRAIN
Train ride, dinner train
Standard gauge

Description: Built in 1906, this historic railroad takes passengers on four-hour tours from the Columbia Gorge to the foothills of Mt. Hood. The trip aboard the Excursion Train comprised of 1910-20 Pullman coaches, caboose, concession car and caboose is narrated one way. The 1940s Dinner & Brunch Train offers excellent four-course dining. Special events occur throughout the year.

Schedule: April through December. Excursion Train: 10 a.m. and 3 p.m. Brunch Train: 11:50 a.m. Dinner Train: Friday, 6:30 p.m., Saturday, 5:30 p.m. (4:30 p.m. October through December).

Admission/Fare: Excursion Train: adults, $22.95; seniors, $20.95; children, $14.95. Brunch Train: $56. Dinner Train: $69.50. Murder Mystery Dinner Trains: $79.50.

Locomotives/Rolling Stock: Two GP 9s; 1910 and 1920 Pullmans; 1940s dining cars.

Special Events: Festivals, Train Robberies, Circus Train, Christmas Tree Trains, Murder Mystery Trains

Nearby Attractions/Accommodations: Mt. Hood; Columbia River National Scenic Area; biking, hiking, wind surfing, golf; historic hotels.

Location/Directions: Sixty miles east of Portland on I-84, exit 63 right to Cascade St., left to parking lot.

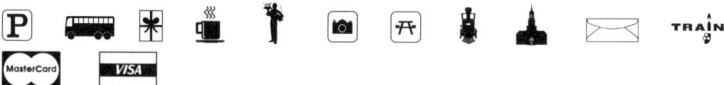

Site Address: 110 Railroad Ave., Hood River, OR
Mailing Address: 110 Railroad Ave., Hood River, OR 97031
Telephone: (800) TRAIN-61 (872-4661) and (541) 386-3556
Fax: (541) 386-2140
E-mail: www.mthoodrr@gorge.net
Internet: www.mthoodrr.com

**OREGON ELECTRIC RAILWAY
HISTORICAL SOCIETY**
Train ride
Standard

BOB SPARKES

Description: Scenic 7-mile trip on a trolley along the Willamette River from Lake Oswego to Portland.

Schedule: June through August: Wednesdays through Sundays and holidays, 10 a.m. to 6 p.m. September through May: weekends and holidays, weather permitting.

Admission/Fare: Adults, $7; seniors, $6; children, $4.

Locomotives/Rolling Stock: Blackpool no. 48; Broadway no. 813.

Nearby Attractions/Accommodations: Tillamook Ice Creamery Restaurant, Sharky's Restaurant, Willamette Park, Riverplace Marina.

Location/Directions: Highway 43 to Lake Oswego. Trolley depot located on State St. (Highway 43) at foothills.

Site Address: Lake Oswego, OR
Mailing Address: PO Box 308, Lake Oswego, OR 97034
Telephone: (503) 222-2226
E-mail: r.sparkes@ieee.org
Internet: www.trainweb.org/oerhs/member.htm

Description: Climb aboard the open-air car or caboose pulled by "Big Red" for a one-hour round trip scenic ride along the Willamette River over former Portland Traction Electric Line.

Schedule: July through Labor Day: Thursdays through Sundays, 11 a.m. to 5:00 p.m.; weekends 11 a.m. to 3:30 p.m.

Admission/Fare: Adults, $5; children 2-12, $3; under age 2 are free.

Locomotives/Rolling Stock: GE 45-ton diesel no. 4501; GE 25-ton diesel no. 2501; open-air passenger car; restored former Simpson Timber Logging caboose no. 900.

Nearby Attractions/Accommodations: Oregon Museum of Science and Industry, Oaks Amusement Park.

Site Address: 8825 SE 11th St., Portland, OR
Mailing Address: PO Box 22548, Portland, OR 97269
Telephone: (503) 653-2380
Fax: (503) 659-6546

WASHINGTON PARK & ZOO RAILWAY
Train ride
30" gauge

GEORGE BAETJER

Description: The Oregon Zoo's railway ride is a 4-mile round trip from the zoo through a Portland city park to a train station adjacent to the city's rose gardens and Japanese gardens.

Schedule: Memorial Day weekend through September 30: round trip, daily. Spring: short loop ride around zoo grounds. Trains depart at frequent intervals.

Admission/Fare: Round trip–adults, $2.75; seniors/youth, $2. Loop trip–adults, $1.75; seniors/youth, $1.25. Zoo admission required for both rides.

Locomotives/Rolling Stock: Steam locomotive no. 1; diesel locomotive no. 2, GM Aerotrain replica; diesel locomotive no. 5, "Oregon Express."

Nearby Attractions/Accommodations: Portland Rose Test Gardens, Japanese Gardens, International Forestry Center, Portland City Center.

Location/Directions: Zoo is located two miles west of Portland City Center, on U.S. Highway 26. Zoo is on MAX light rail line; get off at Washington Park Station.

*Coupon available, see coupon section.

Radio frequency: 151.655

Site Address: Oregon Zoo, 4001 SW Canyon Rd., Portland, OR
Mailing Address: 4001 SW Canyon Rd., Portland, OR 97221
Telephone: (503) 226-1561
Fax: (503) 226-6836
Internet: www.oregonzoo.org

314

CROOKED RIVER DINNER TRAIN
Dinner train

Description: 1800s Western theme train with dinner theater or live-action train robbery.

Schedule: Year round on weekends.

Admission/Fare: $59 to $71.

Locomotives/Rolling Stock: Late 1940s Milwaukee Road railcars.

Special Events: Deschutes County Fair, July; Sister Pro Rodeo, June; Sisters Quilt Show, August.

Location/Directions: Three miles north of Redmond at O'Neil Junction.

Site Address: 4075 NE O'Neil Rd., Redmond, OR
Mailing Address: PO Box 387, Redmond, OR 97756
Telephone: (541) 548-8630
Fax: (541) 548-8702
E-mail: dintrain@coinet.com
Internet: www.crookedriverrailroad.com

SUMPTER VALLEY RAILROAD
Train ride, museum
36" gauge

Description: A 10-mile round trip from McEwen Station to the historic mining town of Sumpter. There is a new depot/museum in Sumpter.

Schedule: Memorial Day through September: McEwen–weekends and holidays, 10 a.m., 12:30, and 3 p.m. Sumpter–weekends and holidays, 11:30 a.m., 2, and 4:40 p.m.

Admission/Fare: Adults, round trip, $9, and one way, $6; children 6-16, $6.50/$4.50; families, $20/$15.

Locomotives/Rolling Stock: 1920 Alco 2-8-2; 1915 Heisler; 1882 Pullman coach no. 20; SVR cabooses nos. 3 and 5; over 12 original SVR freight cars.

Special Events: Night train rides, meal, and entertainment, July 4th weekend, Labor Day weekend. Call for other specials.

Nearby Attractions/Accommodations: Sumpter Dredge State Heritage Area. Phillips Reservoir/Campgrounds, Historic Sumpter and Baker City.

Location/Directions: Highway 7, 22 miles southwest of Baker City off I-84.

Site Address: Dredge Loop Rd., Sumpter Valley, OR
Mailing Address: PO Box 389, Baker City, OR 97814
Telephone: (541) 894-2268
E-mail: depot@oregontrail.net

Pennsylvania, Altoona

ALTOONA RAILROADERS
MEMORIAL MUSEUM
Museum
Standard gauge

PETER D. BARTON

Description: Located in the former PRR Master Mechanics Building, the museum tells the risks and rewards of railroading life and labor as experienced in the nation's largest railroad shop community, Altoona, Pennsylvania.

Schedule: Year round. Summer season–April through October: daily, 9 a.m. to 5 p.m.; Winter season–November through March: Tuesdays through Sundays, 9 a.m. to 5 p.m. Closed Mondays.

Admission/Fare: Adults, $8.50; seniors, $7.75; children 5-15, $5. Group rates and school packages available. Admission valid for 24 hours.

Locomotives/Rolling Stock: GG1 no. 4913; 1918 Vulcan 0-4-0 switcher; two diesel locomotives; the Loretto; other PRR equipment. K4s no. 13661 locomotive returns winter 2001.

Special Events: Horn & Whistle Fair, May. Model Train Display, June. Railfest, October. Thomas the Tank Engine Play Day, November. Call events line for more information.

Nearby Attractions/Accommodations: Horseshoe Curve National Historic Landmark. DelGrosso's Amusement Park. Call for Blair County Visitor's Guide (800) 842-5866.

Location/Directions: I-99 (formerly Route 220), 17th St. exit, follow signs to Ninth Ave.

Site Address: 1300 Ninth Ave., Altoona, PA
Mailing Address: 1300 Ninth Ave., Altoona, PA 16602
Telephone: (814) 946-0834 and (888) 425-8666
Fax: (814) 946-9457
E-mail: info@railroadcity.com
Internet: www.railroadcity.com

**HORSESHOE CURVE NATIONAL
HISTORIC LANDMARK**
Museum

Description: The Curve's story is now told at the modern interpretive
Visitor Center, located in a picturesque setting. A seven-minute film
highlights the construction of this engineering landmark. Guests may
ride to track elevation aboard a two-car funicular or walk the 194 stairs.
It is located on Norfolk Southern's busy east-west main line with more
than 60 trains passing each day.

Schedule: Summer season–April through October: daily, 10 a.m. to 7 p.m.;
Winter season–November through January 2: Tuesdays through
Sundays, 10 a.m. to 4 p.m. Closed Mondays. Closed January through
March.

Admission/Fare: Adults, $3.50; seniors, $3; children 5-15, $1.75. Group
rates and school packages available. Admission valid for 24 hours.

Locomotives/Rolling Stock: Former Pennsylvania Railroad GP9, no. 7048
on display at track elevation.

Nearby Attractions/Accommodations: Altoona Railroaders Memorial
Museum. DelGrosso's Amusement Park. Call for Blair County Visitor's
Guide (800) 842-5866.

Location/Directions: State Route 4008, Kittanning Point Rd. Follow
Heritage Route signs

Site Address: State Route 4008, Kittanning Point Rd., Altoona, PA
Mailing Address: 1300 Ninth Ave., Altoona, PA 16602
Telephone: (814) 946-0834 and (888) 425-8666
Fax: (814) 946-9457
E-mail: info@railroadcity.com
Internet: www.railroadcity.com

**PIONEER TUNNEL COAL MINE
AND STEAM TRAIN**
Train ride
Narrow gauge

Description: Scenic ride along the Mahanoy Mountain behind a steam locomotive of the 0-4-0 type built in 1927 by the Vulcan Iron Works of
Wilkes Barre, Pennsylvania. Guides tell the story of strip mining, boot-
legging and the Centralia Mine Fire. Also available is a tour of a real
anthracite coal mine in open mine cars pulled by a battery-operated
mine motor. Mine guides tell the story of anthracite coal mining.

Schedule: April: weekday mine tours: 11 a.m., 12:30 and 2 p.m. Memorial
Day through Labor Day: daily mine tours 10 a.m. to 6 p.m. Mine tours
and steam train–May, September, October: weekday mine tours 11 a.m.,
12:30 and 2 p.m. train tours for reserved groups only; weekend mine
and train run continuously.

Admission/Fare: Steam train–adults, $5; children under age 12, $3.50.
Mine–adults, $7; children under age 12, $4.50. Group discounts.

Locomotives/Rolling Stock: A spare "lokie" of the 0-4-0 type built by
Vulcan Iron Work; two battery-powered mine motors.

Special Events: 9th Annual Pioneer Day, August 18; coal mine tours, steam
train rides, large craft fair, ethnic foods, live music, more.

Nearby Attractions/Accommodations: Pennsylvania Museum of
Anthracite Mining.

Location/Directions: I-81, exit 36W (Frackville). Rt. 61 north to Ashland.

Site Address: 19th and Oak Streets, Ashland, PA
Mailing Address: 19th and Oak Streets, Ashland, PA 17921
Telephone: (570) 875-3850
Fax: (570) 875-3301
Internet: www.pioneertunnel.com

BELLEFONTE HISTORICAL RAILROAD
Train ride
Standard gauge

W.M. RUMBERGER

Description: Scheduled and special trips over the 60-mile Nittany & Bald Eagle Railroad to Lemont, Vail (Tyrone), and Mill Hall. Fall foliage and Christmas runs offered. The Bellefonte Station, a restored former Pennsylvania Railroad structure built in 1888, houses an operating N gauge layout of the Bellefonte-Curtin Village route, as well as historical photos and memorabilia of area railroading. A snowplow and caboose under restoration are displayed beside the station.

Schedule: May 30 through September 30: weekends and holidays. October and December: special runs only. Call for information.

Admission/Fare: Adults, $8 and up; children 3-11, $5 and up.

Locomotives/Rolling Stock: No. 9167, 1952 RDC-1; and 1962 No. 1953; air-conditioned passenger cars. Can be configured for meal service.

Special Events: Spring, Fall, Christmas trains.

Nearby Attractions/Accommodations: Curtin Village, Bald Eagle State Park, Penn State University, Victorian Bellefonte, Historic Boalsburg, Penns Cave.

Location/Directions: Central Pennsylvania, less than 5 miles from exit 23 and 24, I-80.

Site Address: The Train Station, Bellefonte, PA
Mailing Address: 320 W. High St., Train Station, Bellefonte, PA 16823
Telephone: (814) 355-0311
Fax: (814) 353-0511
E-mail: countyseat@aol.com

CATAWISSA RAILROAD COMPANY
Display
Standard gauge

Description: A restored Reading railroad station, tunnel, two bridges, and 13 restored railroad cabooses on the Catawissa Branch. Five cabooses are available for overnight stays.

Schedule: Year round: daily.

Admission/Fare: Free.

Locomotives/Rolling Stock: Erie C237 former CR 19662, former EL; RDG 92837 former CR 18722; RD 94054 former CR 18852; LV 95039 former CR 18647; CR 18446 former PC, former ATSF 1717; NH 705 former CR/PC 19805; NH 605 former CR/PC 19843; PRR 478144 former CR/PC 23378; PC 18381 former CR; CR 21215; CR 22139 former RDG 94100; CR 18627 former LV 95067; CR 18655 former LV 95046; 1910 Davenport steam engine and tender.

Nearby Attractions/Accommodations: Campgrounds, golf, parks and state parks, antique shops, Benton Area Rodeo Association, Bloomsburg Theater Ensemble, Catawissa Caboose Lodging, Knoebels Amusement Resort.

Locations/Direction: Route 42 and 487 from I-80 and 81.

Site Address: 119 Pine St., Catawissa, PA
Mailing Address: 119 Pine St., Catawissa, PA 17820
Telephone: (570) 356-2345
Fax: (570) 356-7876
E-mail: waltgosh@ptd.net
Internet: //caboosenut.com

ALLEGHENY PORTAGE RAILROAD NATIONAL HISTORIC SITE

Museum
Standard gauge

Description: This site preserves the remains of the incline railway used to portage canal boats over the Allegheny Mountains. It includes the original railroad trace, inclines and levels, visitor center, Lemon House Tavern, and Engine House Exhibit Shelter no. 6. Visitor Center includes films, exhibits, models.

Schedule: Year round: daily 9 a.m. to 5 p.m. Extended hours in summer. Closed Thanksgiving, Christmas, and New Year's Day.

Admission/Fare: Adults 17 and older, $2; national park passes honored.

Locomotives/Rolling Stock: 1893 Pangborn model of the Lafayette.

Special Events: Summer: National Park Service ranger costumed demonstrations of stone cutting, log hewing, lifestyles of the past. Summer Saturdays: Evening on the Summit concert lecture series. Summer Sundays: Heritage Hike series, hikes and bus tours of portage route.

Nearby Attractions/Accommodations: Gallitzin Tunnels, Johnstown Flood National Memorial, state parks.

Location/Directions: U.S. 22, Gallitzin exit.

Site Address: 110 Federal Park Rd., Gallitzin, PA
Mailing Address: 110 Federal Park Rd., Gallitzin, PA 16641
Telephone: (814) 886-6150
Fax: (814) 886-6117
Internet: www.nps.gov/alpo/

GETTYSBURG SCENIC RAIL TOURS
Train ride
Standard gauge

Description: Seasonal train excursions depart 1884 depot, downtown Gettysburg, rain or shine. Twenty-four-mile round trip includes live historical narration.

Schedule: Seasonal schedule April through December; call for free brochure.

Admission/Fare: South Mountain Limited Excursion–adults, $12; other discounts include family plan.

Locomotives/Rolling Stock: EMD, GP-9 no. 105 locomotive; red caboose; exciting open-air double-decker car.

Special Events: Easter Bunny. Mother's Day.

Nearby Attractions/Accommodations: Call Gettysburg Travel Council: (717) 334-6274.

Location/Directions: One block northwest of the square in downtown Gettysburg.

*Coupon available, see coupon section.

Site Address: 106 N. Washington St., Gettysburg, PA
Mailing Address: 106 N. Washington St., Gettysburg, PA 17325
Telephone: (717) 334-6932
Fax: (717) 334-0291
Internet: www.gettsyburgrail.com

Description: This museum features an extensive collection of model trains and a collection of items dealing with military railroads; it also offers a simulated train ride following President Lincoln to Gettysburg.

Schedule: Summer hours 9 to 9.

Admission/Fare: Adults, $5.75; children 6-11, $3.50.

Nearby Attractions/Accommodations: In the center of Gettysburg attractions: Gettysburg National Military Park, Visitor Center, Cyclorama.

Location/Directions: Steinwehr Ave. (Business 15 south).

Site Address: 425 Steinwehr Ave., Gettysburg, PA
Mailing Address: 425 Steinwehr Ave., Gettysburg, PA 17325
Telephone: (717) 334-5678

**STOURBRIDGE LINE
RAIL EXCURSIONS**
Train ride
Standard gauge

Description: Scenic round-trip rides from Honesdale to Hawley (24 miles) and Honesdale to Lackawaxen-on-the-Delaware. The ride parallels the shimmering Lackawaxen River and closely follows the route of the Delaware & Hudson Canal.

Schedule: Easter through early December, on scheduled weekends.

Admission/Fare: Varies by ride.

Locomotive/Rolling Stock: 1949 EMD BL2 no. 54, former Bangor & Aroostook.

Nearby Attractions/Accommodations: Claws 'n Paws Wild Animal Park, Wayne County Historical Society and Museum Shop, Dorflinger Glass Museum, Lake Wallenpaupack.

Location/Directions: Northeastern Pennsylvania, 24 miles from Scranton.

*Coupon available, see coupon section.

Site Address: 303 Commercial St., Honesdale, PA
Mailing Address: 303 Commercial St., Honesdale, PA 18431
Telephone: (570) 253-1960 and (800) 433-9008
Fax: (570) 253-1322
E-mail: waynecoc@sunlink.net
Internet: www.waynecountycc.com

**OLD MAUCH CHUNK MODEL
TRAIN DISPLAY**
Layout
HO

Description: This exciting HO scale model train display features 13 separate trains–some pulling as many as 50 railroad cars over nearly 1,100 feet of track. The meticulously designed display also incorporates over 200 scale buildings, 100 bridges, 1,000 streetlights and moving automobiles into its scenery.

Schedule: Year round: call for current hours of operation.

Admission/Fare: Adults, $3; seniors, $2; children, $1; age 4 and under are free.

Special Events: Many Jim Thorpe celebrations throughout the year.

Nearby Attractions/Accommodations: Many attractions and accommodations in the area.

Location/Directions: Located on the second floor of the Hooven Mercantile Company building on Route 209 next to the Railroad Station at Packer Park in historic Jim Thorpe.

*Coupon available, see coupon section.

Site Address: 41 Susquehanna St. (Route 209), Jim Thorpe, PA
Mailing Address: 68 White Pine Ln., Lehighton, PA 18235-9612
Telephone: (570) 325-4371 and (570) 386-2297
E-mail: michaelheery@worldmailer.com

WANAMAKER, KEMPTON & SOUTHERN, INC.
Train ride
Standard gauge

Description: A 6-mile, 40-minute round trip through scenic Pennsylvania Dutch country over part of the former Reading Company's Schuylkill & Lehigh branch. Restored stations relocated from Joanna and Catasauqua, Pennsylvania; original circa 1874 Wanamaker station; operating HO gauge model layout.

Schedule: May through October: weekends. Call or write for detailed schedule.

Admission/Fare: Adults, $5; children 3-11, $3; age 2 and under ride free.

Locomotives/Rolling Stock: No. 2, 1920 Porter 0-4-0T, former Colorado Fuel & Iron; no. 65, 1930 Porter 0-6-0T, former Safe Harbor Water Power; no. 7258 1942 GE diesel electric 45-ton, former Birdsboro Corp.; coaches nos. 1494 and 1474 and combine no. 408, all former Reading Company; coach no. 582, former Lackawanna; assorted freight cars and caboose, former Lehigh & New England; steel and wood cabooses, former Reading.

Special Events: Mother's Day Special, Kids' Fun Weekend, Harvest Moon Special, Halloween Train, Santa Claus Special. Write for schedule.

Nearby Attractions/Accommodations: Hawk Mountain, Crystal Cave.

Location/Directions: Depot is located at Kempton on Routes 143 or 737, a short distance north of I-78. The site is 20 miles west of Allentown.

*Coupon available, see coupon section.

Site Address: 42 Community Center Rd., Kempton, PA
Mailing Address: PO Box 24, Kempton, PA 19529
Telephone: (610) 756-6469
E-mail: info@wknsrr.com
Internet: www.wknsrr.com

**DUTCH WONDERLAND FAMILY
AMUSEMENT PARK**
Train ride
24" gauge

Description: A 48-acre amusement park geared to families with variety of rides and attractions. Live shows include the Great American High Diving Show. The Wonderland Special has seating for 56 guests and is a scenic seven-minute ride through the park.

Schedule: Weekends, spring and fall. Daily, Memorial Day through Labor Day.

Admission/Fare: 2001 rates still to be determined; call for information. Admission includes unlimited rides.

Locomotives/Rolling Stock: Two replica C.P. Huntingtons, Chance Rides (Witchita, Kansas); engine no. 206, seats 56; engine no. 123, seats 56.

Special Events: Happy Hauntings, last three weekends in October.

Nearby Attractions/Accommodations: Located in the heart of Pennsylvania Dutch Country, with shopping outlets, museums, Amish attractions, theatres, camping facilities, and hotels nearby.

Location/Directions: From the west: take turnpike east, exit 19, 283 east, 30 east. From the east: take turnpike west, exit 21, 222 south, 30 east. Four miles east of Lancaster City on Route 30.

Site Address: 2249 Route 30E, Lancaster, PA
Mailing Address: 2249 Route 30E, Lancaster, PA 17602
Telephone: (717) 291-1888
Fax: (717) 291-2257
E-mail: dutchw@pptnet.com
Internet: www.dutchwonderland.com

Description: This line offers one round trip each operating day to Kane and the Kinzua Bridge over a former Baltimore & Ohio branch line. Passengers may board at Marienville for a 96-mile, 8-hour trip or at Kane for a 32-mile, 3½-hour trip. The 2,053-foot-long, 301-foot-high Kinzua Bridge, built in 1882 to span the Kinzua Creek Valley, was at the time the highest bridge in the world. It is on the National Register of Historic Places and is a National Historic Civil Engineering Landmark.

Schedule: June and September: Friday through Sunday. July and August: Tuesday through Sunday. Early October: Wednesday through Sunday. Depart Marienville 8:30 a.m.; depart Kane 10:30 a.m.

Admission/Fare: From Marienville: adults, $22; children, $14. From Kane: adults, $16; children, $9. Advance reservations suggested. Box lunches available by advance order, $5.50.

Locomotives/Rolling Stock: No. 38, 1927 Baldwin 2-8-0, former Huntington & Broad Top Mountain; no. 44, Alco diesel; no. 58, Chinese 2-8-2 built in 1989; Porter Switcher no. 1; steel coaches; open cars; two snack and souvenir cars.

Location/Directions: In northwestern Pennsylvania, about 20 miles north of I-80.

Site Address: S. Forest St., Marienville, PA
Mailing Address: PO Box 422, Marienville, PA 16239
Telephone: (814) 927-6621
Fax: (814) 927-8750

MIDDLETOWN & HUMMELSTOWN RAILROAD

Train ride, dinner train, museum
Standard gauge

WENDELL DILLINGER

Description: An 11-mile, 1¼-hour round trip through Swatara Creek Valley with narration and singalongs. The Union Canal is near the tracks.

Schedule: Memorial Day through Labor Day, weekends; Thursdays and Fridays in May; Tuesdays, Thursdays, Saturdays, and Sundays in July and August; Sundays only in September; weekends in October.

Admission/Fare: Adults, $10; children 3-11, $5. Add $1 on steam weekends. Special events train pricing varies.

Locomotives/Rolling Stock: Regular train consist: GE 65-ton nos. 1 and 2 with DL&W coaches; freight locomotives NSS Alco T6 no. 1016; WM Alco S6 no. 151; CN 2-6-0 no. 91; three SEPTA PCCs; more.

Special Events: Sweetheart Special; Easter Express; Mother's Special; Colonial Craft Fair; Moonlight Specials; Barbecue Express; Train Robberies; "Civil War Remembered" re-enactment; Fall Foliage Specials and Haunted Trains; Santa Express, Christmastime Dinner Train, New Year's Eve Dinner Train and New Year's Eve Celebration Train.

Nearby Attractions/Accommodations: Hershey Park, Chocolate World, Pennsylvania Dutch Country, Gettysburg Battlefield, more.

Location/Directions: Pennsylvania Turnpike, exit 19 to Route 283 to Middletown and Hummelstown exit; go south, turn right on Main St., left on Race St.

Site Address: Race St., Middletown, PA, at railroad track
Mailing Address: 136 Brown St., Middletown, PA 17057
Telephone: (717) 944-4435, ext. 0
Fax: (717) 944-7758
E-mail: riderail@ptdprolog.net
Internet: www.800padutch.com/mhrr.html

NORTHERN CENTRAL RAILWAY
Train ride, dinner train
Standard gauge

Description: Three-and-a-half-hour dinner train with entertainment and dancing, murder mysteries, or singalongs.

Schedule: Year round: weekends, some weekdays and holidays.

Admission/Fare: $39.99 to $64.99.

Locomotives/Rolling Stock: 1959 FPA-4 no. 800, former CN and VIA; 1954 RSD-5 no. 1689, former CNW; vista dome; dance car; table cars; bar car; dining cars; private business cars available; more.

Special Events: Valentine's specials, Mother's Day, Father's Day Spectacular.

Nearby Attractions/Accommodations: Stewartstown–Naylor Winery, Railroad; Jackson House Bed and Breakfast.

Location/Directions: Exit 1 off I-83, west on Route 851, 3½ miles to New Freedom, left on W. Penn St.

Site Address: 117 N. Front St., New Freedom, PA
Mailing Address: PO Box 249, New Freedom, PA 17349
Telephone: (800) 94-TRAIN and (717) 235-4000
Fax: (717) 235-5609
E-mail: ncry@nfdc.net
Internet: www.classicrail.com/ncry

Pennsylvania, New Hope   **NEW HOPE & IVYLAND RAILROAD**
Train ride, dinner train
Standard gauge

Description: Enjoy a 50-minute narrated train ride through beautiful Bucks County countryside.

Schedule: Year round.

Admission/Fare: Adults, $9.50; seniors, $8.50; children 2-11, $5.50; under age 2, $1.50.

Special Events: Song and Story Hour, June through September. Santa Trains, November and December. Train Robbery, fall and spring.

Nearby Attractions/Accommodations: Sesame Place, Canal Boat. Access buckscounty.org for more details.

Location/Directions: W. Bridge St., Route 179. Convenient access from I-95.

*Coupon available, see coupon section.

Site Address: 32 W. Bridge St., New Hope, PA
Mailing Address: 32 W. Bridge St., New Hope, PA 18938
Telephone: (215) 862-2332
Fax: (215) 862-2150
E-mail: lblaney@newhoperailroad.com
Internet: www.newhoperailroad.com

Pennsylvania, Philadelphia

**THE FRANKLIN INSTITUTE
SCIENCE MUSEUM**
*Model railroad display, railroad display
Standard gauge*

Description: The centerpiece of Railroad Hall is a Baldwin Locomotive Works no. 60000, a three-cylinder 4-10-2 built in 1926 and moved to the Franklin Institute in 1933. Two other locomotives share the room: Reading's Rocket of 1838 and a Reading 4-4-0 built in 1842. New to the exhibit is a G gauge model railroad that viewers can operate; it includes full-size signals actuated by the trains and a video hookup between the locomotive and a monitor in a half-size cab. The remainder of the museum collection covers the larger subject of U.S. industrial technology and science. There are models, films and quizzes on videodiscs, and a giant walk-through heart. The Franklin Institute is at 20th Street and The Parkway in downtown Philadelphia, within walking distance of Suburban Station.

Schedule: Year round: daily, 9:30 a.m. to 5 p.m.

Admission/Fare: Call or write for information.

Locomotives/Rolling Stock: Baldwin 60000.

Location/Directions: Center city Philadelphia.

      M 30th Street, ¼ mile away

Site Address: 222 N. 20th St., Philadelphia, PA
Mailing Address: 222 N. 20th St., Philadelphia, PA 19103
Telephone: (215) 448-1176
Fax: (215) 448-1235
E-mail: ewilner@fi.edu
Internet: www.fi.edu

FRIENDS OF THE EAST BROAD TOP
ROBERTSDALE MUSEUM
Museum

Description: The museum is located in two historic buildings at the southern operating terminus of the East Broad Top Railroad during the common-carrier era. On display are exhibits relating to the East Broad Top Railroad.

Schedule: June through mid-October: Saturdays 10 a.m. to 5 p.m.; Sundays 1 to 5 p.m.

Admission/Fare: Donations appreciated.

Locomotives/Rolling Stock: EBT maintenance-of-way wood handcar; EBT combination passenger baggage car no. 16 (off-site).

Special Events: Summer Open House, June 2-3. Fall Open House and Reunion, October 6-7.

Nearby Attractions/Accommodations: East Broad Top Railroad, Broad Top Area Coal Miners Museum, Raystown Lake.

Location/Directions: Sixteen miles southwest of Rockhill Furnace (EBT U.S. 522), 20 miles southeast of Huntingdon (U.S. 22), and 21 miles north of Breezewood (I-70, I-76, and U.S. 30).

Site Address: Main St., Robertsdale, PA
Mailing Address: PO Box 68, Robertsdale, PA 16674
Telephone: (814) 635-2388
E-mail: febt@aol.com
Internet: www.febt.org

Pennsylvania, Rockhill Furnace

EAST BROAD TOP RAILROAD
Train ride, museum
36" gauge

Description: The East Broad Top Railroad, chartered in 1856, is the last operating narrow-gauge railroad east of the Mississippi. The road hauled coal, freight, mail, express, and passengers for more than 80 years. Today the East Broad Top offers passengers a 10-mile, 50-minute ride through the beautiful Aughwick Valley with its own preserved locomotives; the ride takes passengers from the historic depot at Rockhill Furnace to the picnic grove, where the train is turned. On display are the railroad yard with shops, operating roundhouse, and turntable. Dates, times, and fares are subject to change. Call or write for latest information.

Schedule: June through October: weekends, 11 a.m., 1 and 3 p.m.

Admission/Fare: Adults, $9; children, $6.

Locomotives/Rolling Stock: 1911 Baldwin locomotive 2-8-2 no. 12; 1912 Baldwin locomotive 2-8-2 no. 14; 1914 Baldwin locomotive 2-8-2 no. 15; 1918 Baldwin locomotive 2-8-2 no. 17; all original East Broad Top Railroad.

Special Events: Fall Spectacular, Columbus Day Weekend.

Nearby Attractions/Accommodations: Raystown Lake, Rockhill Trolley Museum.

Location/Directions: Pennsylvania Turnpike exit Willow Hill or Fort Littleton.

Site Address: Rockhill Furnace, PA
Mailing Address: PO Box 158, Rockhill Furnace, PA 17249
Telephone: (814) 447-3011
Fax: (814) 447-3256

Pennsylvania, Rockhill-Orbisonia

ROCKHILL TROLLEY MUSEUM
Trolley ride
Standard

JOEL SALOMON

Description: A nonprofit, educational museum incorporated in 1962, the Rockhill Trolley Museum is composed of volunteers who preserve, restore, and maintain a collection of two dozen electric rail vehicles, about twelve of which are in operating condition. Trolleys operate over dual-gauge trackage on the former Shade Gap Branch of the East Broad Top Railroad for a 2-mile, 20-minute round trip.

Schedule: Memorial Day weekend through third weekend of October: weekends and holidays, 11:30 a.m. to 4:30 p.m. Weekday tours by arrangement.

Admission/Fare: Adults, $3; children 2-12, $1. Group rates available.

Locomotives/Rolling Stock: No. 163, 1924 Brill curveside car, former York Railways (Pennsylvania); Philadelphia & Western bullet car no. 205; no. 1875 1912 open car; Johnston Traction Co. double truck car no. 311.

Special Events: Fall Spectacular, second weekend in October. Santa Trolley, first Saturday in December.

Nearby Attractions/Accommodations: Raystown Lake, Altoona Railroader Museum, East Broad Top Railroad, Swigart Antique Car Museum.

Location/Directions: Twenty miles north of exit 13 of Pennsylvania Turnpike, adjacent to East Broad Top Railroad.

*Coupon available, see coupon section.

   arm M

Site Address: Meadow St., Rockhill Furnace, PA
Mailing Address: 1003 N. Chester Rd., West Chester, PA 19380
Telephone: (610) 692-5094
E-mail: sgurley@prodigy.net
Internet: www.rockhilltrolley.org

KISKI JUNCTION RAILROAD
Train ride
Standard gauge

Description: Ride along the Kiski River from Schenley to Bagdad on the former Pennsylvania Canal.

Schedule: Memorial Day through Halloween: Wednesdays 7 p.m.; weekends 2 and 4 p.m. Groups anytime by appointment. Limited off-season runs.

Admission/Fare: Adults, $7; seniors, $6; children 4-12, $4.

Locomotives/Rolling Stock: Alco S1 no. 7135; P&LE cabin no. 500; CNJ coach no. 1154; KJR no. 3 caboose; Conrail cab no. 18343; Conrail cab no. 18200; P&LE cab no. 516; flatcar KJR no. 44; X29 boxcar PRR no. 6966.

Nearby Attractions/Accommodations: Crooked Creek State Park.

Location/Directions: Thirty miles northeast of Pittsburgh on the Allegheny River. Route 66N out of Leechburg, two miles north to Schenley Rd., turn west, travel 4 miles.

Site Address: 48 Railroad St., Schenley, PA
Mailing Address: PO Box 48, Schenley, PA 15682-0048
Telephone: (724-) 295-5577
Fax: (724) 295-5588
E-mail: cebowyer@icubed
Internet: www.kiskijunction.com

Pennsylvania, Scranton

**STEAMTOWN NATIONAL
HISTORIC SITE**
Train ride, museum, display
Standard gauge

Description: A 27-mile round-trip steam excursion will operate between Scranton and Moscow, Pennsylvania, beginning Memorial Day weekend through the first weekend of November. The site's visitor facilities include two museums, a theater, a visitor center, restored portions of the round-house, and a museum store. Roundhouse tours, locomotive shop tours, preservation shop tours, and various additional programs will be offered. Many locomotives and cars are on display in the buildings and in the historic Delaware, Lackawanna & Western Railroad yards.

Schedule: Year round, 9 a.m. to 5 p.m.; summer, 9 a.m. to 6 p.m. (excursion season).

Admission/Fare: Museum and excursions fees due to change. Please call for current rates.

Locomotives/Rolling Stock: Baldwin Locomotive Works 0-6-0 no. 26; Canadian Pacific 4-6-2 no. 2317; Canadian National 2-8-2 no. 3254.

Special Events: Memorial Day. Rail Expo, Labor Day weekend. Santa Train, Festival of Trees, the Polar Express, in December.

Nearby Attractions/Accommodations: Lackawanna County Trolley Museum, Lackawanna County Coal Mine Tour, Everhart Museum, more.

Location/Directions: Downtown Scranton. Entrance is at intersection of Lackawanna and Cliff Avenues.

Site Address: Lackawanna and Cliff Avenues, Scranton, PA
Mailing Address: 150 S. Washington Ave., Scranton, PA 18503
Telephone: (570) 340-5200 and (888) 693-9391
E-mail: stea_visitor_information@nps.gov
Internet: www.nps.gov/stea

Description: Roadside America, an idea born in June 1903, is a childhood dream realized. From day to day and almost without interruption, this indoor miniature village has grown to be the largest and most beautiful of its type. More than 60 years in the making by Laurence Gieringer, it is housed in a new, modern, comfortable, air-conditioned building and covers more than 8,000 square feet of space. The display includes 2,570 feet of track for trains and trolleys and 250 railroad cars. O gauge trains and trolleys run among the villages.

Schedule: July 1 through Labor Day: weekdays, 9 a.m. to 6:30 p.m.; weekends, 9 a.m. to 7 p.m. September 6 through June 30: weekdays, 10 a.m. to 5 p.m.; weekends, 10 a.m. to 6 p.m.

Admission/Fare: Adults, $4.50; senior citizens, $4; children 6-11 years old, $2; children 5 and under free.

Location/Directions: I-78, exit 8, between Allentown and Harrisburg.

Site Address: Shartlesville, PA
Mailing Address: P.O. Box 2, Shartlesville, PA 19554
Telephone: (610) 488-6241
Internet: www.roadsideamericainc.com

Pennsylvania, Strasburg

**CHOO CHOO BARN
TRAINTOWN U.S.A.**
Display, layout
O, HO, N

FRED DOLE

Description: Celebrating 40 years in operation! The Choo Choo Barn is home to Lancaster County and America captured in miniature. This amazing 1,700 square foot display features 18 operating trains and over 140 animated figures and vehicles.

Schedule: March 31 through December 30: daily 10 a.m. to 5 p.m. Last tour starts at 4:30 p.m.

Admission/Fare: Adults, $5; children 5-12, $3; under age 5 are free.

Special Events: Canned Food Fridays, free admission to display with non-perishable food item. Open until 8 p.m., November 30, December 7, 14, and 21.

Nearby Attractions/Accommodations: Strasburg Rail Road, National Toy Train Museum, Railroad Museum of Pennsylvania, Dutch Wonderland Family Fun Park, historic Strasburg Inn, Millers Smorgasbord.

Location/Directions: Located along Route 741 east of Strasburg.

*Coupon available, see coupon section.

Site Address: Route 741 E., Strasburg, PA
Mailing Address: Box 130, Strasburg, PA 17579
Telephone: (717) 687-7911 and (800) 450-2920
Fax: (717) 687-6529
E-mail: info@choochoobarn.com
Internet: www.choochoobarn.com

THE NATIONAL TOY TRAIN MUSEUM
Museum

Description: Five operating layouts, toy trains from the mid-1800s to the present day. Continuous toy train videos.

Schedule: Daily, May 1 through October 31; weekends, April, November and December.

Admission/Fare: Senior Citizens (65+), $2.75; adults (13-64), $3; children 6-12, $1.50; under 5, free; family rate, $9.

Nearby Attractions/Accommodations: Choo Choo Barn, Railroad Museum of Pennsylvania, Strasburg Railroad, Hershey Park, Longwood Gardens .

Location/Directions: From U.S. 30: south on Pennsylvania 896, east on Pennsylvania 741, north on Paradise Lane. One block from railroad tracks.

Site Address: 300 Paradise Ln., Strasburg, PA
Mailing Address: PO Box 248, Strasburg, PA 17579-0248
Telephone: (717) 687-8976
Fax: (717) 687-0742
E-mail: toytrain@traincollectors.org
Internet: www.traincollectors.org

RAILROAD MUSEUM
OF PENNSYLVANIA
Museum

Description: The museum displays one of the world's finest collections of over 100 steam, electric, and diesel-electric locomotives, passenger and freight cars, and related memorabilia. The 100,000-square-foot Rolling Stock Hall exhibits equipment dating from 1825 to 1992. Also hands-on activities and education center and Whistle Stop Shop museum store.

Schedule: April through June, September and October: Mondays through Saturdays 9 a.m. to 5 p.m.; Sundays 12 to 5 p.m. July and August: Mondays through Thursdays 9 a.m. to 5 p.m.; Fridays and Saturdays, 9 a.m. to 6 p.m.; Sundays 11 to 5 p.m. November through March: Tuesdays through Saturdays, 9 a.m. to 5 p.m.; Sundays, noon to 5 p.m.

Admission/Fare: Adults 13-59, $6; seniors, $5.50; students 6-12, $4; under age 6 are free; families, $16. Group rates available.

Locomotives/Rolling Stock: See above.

Special Events: Charter Day, March 11. Pennsy Days, June 2-3. Reading Railroad Days, July 6-8. Railroad Circus Days, August 16-19. Halloween Haunting, October 27. Home for the Holidays, December 26. (Events subject to change without notice. Additional events may be scheduled.)

Nearby Attractions/Accommodations: Strasburg Railroad, National Toy Train Museum, Choo Choo Barn, Pennsylvania Dutch attractions.

Location/Directions: Ten miles east of Lancaster on Route 741.

Site Address: 300 Gap Rd., Route 741 E., Strasburg, PA
Mailing Address: PO Box 15, Strasburg, PA 17579
Telephone: (717) 687-8628
Fax: (717) 687-0876
E-mail: frm@redrose.net
Internet: www.rrmuseumpa.org

STRASBURG RAILROAD
Train ride, dinner train
Standard gauge

Description: A 45-minute trip into the past. The train travels through beautiful Lancaster County farmland as it journeys from Strasburg to Amtrak's Leaman Place interchange at Paradise. The East Strasburg Station mall features four gift shops, one restaurant, fudge shop, old time portrait studio, and the exquisite "Paradise" business car. Just across the street is the Railroad Museum of Pennsylvania.

Schedule: February 17 through April 8, weekends. April 9 through October 28, daily. October 29 through December 16, weekends and Friday after Thanksgiving. December 26 through 31, daily. Times vary.

Admission/Fare: Adults, $8.75 and up; children, $4.50 and up. Group rates available.

Locomotives/Rolling Stock: No. 90, 2-10-0 ex-GW; no. 475 4-8-0 ex-N&W; no. 89 2-6-0 ex-GT; no. 31 0-6-0 ex-CN; no. 972 4-6-0 ex-CPR; no. 4 0-4-0 ex-RDG; GE 44-ton ex-PRR 9331; Plymouths nos. 1 and 2; very early 20th century wooden passenger cars; over a dozen early fright cars; reserved dining car, parlor car, and lounge car seating and service available; open-sided observation cars.

Special Events: A Day Out with Thomas events, Easter Bunny Trains, Great Pumpkin Trains, Santa Trains.

Location/Directions: On Route 741 one mile east of Strasburg.

Radio frequency: 161.235

Site Address: Route 741, Strasburg, PA
Mailing Address: PO Box 96, Strasburg, PA 17579
Telephone: (717) 687-7522
Fax: (717) 687-6194
E-mail: srrtrain@strasburgrailroad.com
Internet: www.strasburgrailroad.com

OIL CREEK & TITUSVILLE RAILROAD
Train ride

BETTY M SQUIRE

Description: Twenty-seven-mile, 2½-hour train ride through "The Valley That Changed the World."

Schedule: Mid-June through October. June and September: weekends, 2 p.m. July, August, and October: Wednesdays through Sundays, 2 p.m. October weekends, 11:45 a.m. and 3:15 p.m. School excursions: May 8-10, 15-17, October 3-4, 10-11.

Admission/Fare: Adults, $10; seniors (60+), $9; students 3-17, $6. Under 3, no charge.

Locomotives/Rolling Stock: 1947 Alco S-2 no 75; caboose no. 10 built by Elgin, Joliet & Eastern Railroad approximately 1923; railway post office car.

Special Events: Murder Mysteries and more. Call, write, or e-mail for more information.

Nearby Attractions/Accommodations: Drake Well Museum, Oil Creek State Park, Tyred Wheels Auto Museum.

Location/Directions: Route 8 north or south to Titusville, watch for signs.

*Coupon available, see coupon section.

Site Address: 409 S. Perry St., Titusville, PA
Mailing Address: 7 Elm St., Oil City, PA 16301
Telephone: (814) 676-1733
Fax: (814) 677-2192
E-mail: ocandt@usachoice.net
Internet: //octrr.clarion.edu

PENNSYLVANIA TROLLEY MUSEUM

Train ride, museum, display
5'2½" gauge, standard gauge

SCOTT R. BECKER

Description: A 3-mile round-trip trolley ride, "Pennsylvania's Trolleys in a Changing Landscape" exhibit, theater, gift shop, and picnic area. Trolley ride is very scenic, following a creek with a turning loop at one end.

Schedule: Weekends, April 7 through December 30; daily, Memorial Day through Labor Day, 11 a.m. to 5 p.m.

Admission/Fare: Adults, $6; seniors, $5; children 2-15, $3.50. Group rates available with advance reservations.

Locomotives/Rolling Stock: New Orleans "Streetcar Named Desire"; trolleys from Pittsburgh, Johnstown, and Philadelphia. Trolley work equipment and rare 1930 Baldwin-Westinghouse diesel locomotive on display.

Special Events: Easter Bunny Trolley, April 7, 14. Anything on Wheels weekend, June 23-24. Pumpkin Patch Trolley, October 13-14, 20-21. Santa Trolley, November 23-25, December 1-2, 8-9. Trolleys & Toy Trains, December 15-16, 22-23, 26-30.

Nearby Attractions/Accommodations: Meadowcroft Museum of Rural Life, LeMoyne House, Ladbroke Meadows Racetrack.

Location/Directions: I-79 to exit 8 (Meadow Lands), follow signs. Thirty miles southwest of Pittsburgh.

Site Address: One Museum Rd., Washington, PA
Mailing Address: One Museum Rd., Washington, PA 15301-6133
Telephone: (724) 228-9256 and (877) PA-TROLLEY
Fax: (724) 228-9675
E-mail: ptm@pa-trolley.org
Internet: www.pa-trolley.org

TIOGA CENTRAL RAILROAD
Train ride, dinner train
Standard gauge

RICH STOVING

Description: A 1½-hour excursion through beautiful north central Pennsylvania countryside; 24 miles round trip.

Schedule: Saturdays and Sundays, May 19 through October 21; departures at 11 a.m., 1 and 3 p.m.

Admission/Fare: Adults, $10; seniors (60+), $9; children 6-12, $5. Children under 6 free with paying adult.

Locomotives/Rolling Stock: Alco S2 no. 14; Alco R1 no. 62; Alco R30 no. 506.

Special Events: Wellsboro Rail Days, October 27-28, special trains, longer runs, for rail fans.

Nearby Attractions/Accommodations: Grand Canyon of Pennsylvania, Ives Run Recreation Area, many fine restaurants and Main Street shopping in beautiful Wellsboro.

Location/Directions: Three miles north of Wellsboro on State Route 287. Wellsboro is on U.S. Route 6 east-west, and Pennsylvania Route 287 north-south; 35 miles south of Corning, New York.

*Coupon available, see coupon section.

Radio frequency: 160.725

Site Address: Muck Rd., Wellsboro Junction, PA
Mailing Address: PO Box 269, Wellsboro, PA 16901
Telephone: (570) 724-0990
E-mail: info@tiogacentral.com
Internet: www.tiogacentral.com

WEST CHESTER RAILROAD
Train ride, dinner train
Standard gauge

Description: A 16-mile round trip from West Chester to Glen Mills. This line is the unused portion of SEPTA's R-3 Elwyn line, which is very scenic as it follows Chester Creek in western Delaware County through eastern Chester County.

Schedule: April, May, September through December: weekends. Charters available year round. Call for information on specials.

Admission/Fare: Adults, $10; children 2-12, $8.

Locomotives/Rolling Stock: No. 99 EMD GP-9 ex-B&O no. 6499; no. 1803 is DRS-18U Alco former CP 1803; Reading Blue Liners coaches nos. 9114, 9124, 9117, 9107; baggage car former Pennsy B-60 7551; more.

Special Events: Monthly dinner trains. Easter Bunny Express. West Chester Restaurant Festival, third weekend in September. Pratt & Co. Fall Festival, fourth weekend in September. Fall Foliage, October. Holiday Express, November. Santa Express, November and December.

Nearby Attractions/Accommodations: Q.V.C., Valley Forge National Park, West Chester Restaurants, Chadds Ford, Brandywine Museum, Winterthur Longwood Gardens.

Location/Directions: Highway 202, exit Gay St./West Chester. Follow Gay to Matlack turning left, one block to Market, left at railroad station, one block on right.

Radio frequency: 160.6050

Site Address: 230 E. Market St., West Chester, PA
Mailing Address: PO Box 385, Yorklyn, DE 19736
Telephone: (610) 430-2233
Fax: (302) 995-5286

LYCOMING COUNTY HISTORICAL SOCIETY & MUSEUM

Museum, layout

TERRY WILD STUDIO

Description: The Shempp toy train collection is one of the finest in the country. More than 337 complete trains, 100 individual engines (12 are one of a kind), and two working model layouts are on display. Exhibit includes items in L, TT, N, OO, HO, O, and 1 gauges; Lionel, American Flyer, Marx, Ives, and American Model Train Company pieces; an American Flyer Mayflower; a copper-and-gold-finished GG1; and American Flyer S gauge displays.

Schedule: Open year round. May 1 through October 31: Tuesdays through Fridays, 9:30 a.m. to 4 p.m.; Saturdays, 11 a.m. to 4 p.m.; Sundays, 1 to 4 p.m. November 1 through April 30: Tuesdays through Fridays, 9:30 a.m. to 4 p.m.; Saturdays, 11 a.m. to 4 p.m. Closed major holidays.

Admission/Fare: Adult, $3.50; seniors, AARP/AAA, $3; children, $1.50.

Special Events: Toy Train Expo, December 9-10, 12 to 4 p.m. Area collectors have displays and layouts throughout the museum.

Nearby Attractions/Accommodations: Little League Museum, Genetti Hotel, amusement park, Reptile Land.

Site Address: 858 W. Fourth St., Williamsport, PA
Mailing Address: 858 W. Fourth St., Williamsport, PA 17701-5824
Telephone: (570) 326-3326
Fax: (570) 326-3689
E-mail: lchsmuse@csrlink.net
Internet: www.lycoming.org/lchsmuseum

SOUTH CAROLINA RAILROAD MUSEUM
Train ride, museum, display, layout
Standard gauge

MATT CONRAD

Description: A 6.6-mile round trip to Greenbrier and return over a portion of the former Rockton & Rion Railway. The route was built in the late 1800s as a quarry line to haul world-famous Winnsboro blue granite from the quarry to the Southern Railway at Rockton.

Schedule: June through October, first and third Saturdays. Museum gallery and yard tours only (no train ride), Sundays 1 to 4 p.m.

Admission/Fare: Adults, $5; children 2-12, $3; first-class, $9.

Locomotives/Rolling Stock: No. 2015 and 2028, 1950 SW-8; no. 33, 1946 GE 44-ton, former PRR; no. 76, 1951 Porter 50-ton, former U.S. Navy; no. 82, 1945 GE 45-ton, former U.S. Navy; and no. 44, 1927 Baldwin 4-6-0, former Hampton & Branchville (static display).

Special Events: Easter Bunny Train, Caboose Day, Santa Train. Call, write, or visit our website for exact dates.

Nearby Attractions/Accommodations: Downtown Winnsboro, South Carolina State Museum, Riverbanks Zoo.

Location/Directions: Take State Route 34 from I-26 or I-77 and follow the signs to Winnsboro. Then follow brown signs. The museum is located between State Route 34 and U.S. Highway 321, 3 miles south of Winnsboro.

Radio frequency: 151.865

Site Address: 110 Industrial Park Rd., Winnsboro, SC
Mailing Address: PO Box 643, Winnsboro, SC 29180
Telephone: (803) 635-9893
E-mail: info@scrm.org
Internet: www.scrm.org

South Dakota, Hill City

**BLACK HILLS
CENTRAL RAILROAD**
Train ride
Standard gauge

SOUTH DAKOTA DEPT. OF TOURISM

Description: Passengers can take a two-hour round-trip journey between Hill City and Keystone. Experience a ride from the past as you travel through the Black Hills, seeing the old mine sights and Harney Peak.

Schedule: Mid-May through early October: daily. Departures added during summer season. Call, write, or e-mail for information.

Admission/Fare: Adults, $18; children 4-12, $10; age 3 and under are free. Group rates available for parties of 20 and up.

Locomotives/Rolling Stock: 1926 Baldwin 2-6-2 no. 104 saddle tank; 1919 Baldwin 2-6-2 no. 7; 1928 Baldwin 2-6-6-2 no. 110; 1880s-1910 passenger cars.

Special Events: Railroad Days, last weekend of June.

Nearby Attractions/Accommodations: Mt. Rushmore and Crazy Horse Memorials.

Location/Directions: Highway 16/385, 24 miles south of Rapid City or Keystone, Highway 16A.

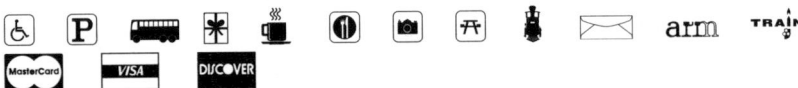

Site Address: 222 Railroad Ave., Hill City, SD
Mailing Address: PO Box 1880, Hill City, SD 57745
Telephone: (605) 574-2222
Fax: (605) 574-4915
E-mail: office@1880train.com
Internet: www.1880train.com

PRAIRIE VILLAGE
Train ride, dinner train, museum, display
Standard and 24" gauge

BILL NOLAN

Description: Prairie Village is an assembly of turn-of-the-century buildings. There are steam traction engines, gas tractors, and displays of farm equipment. A 2-mile loop of track is used for train rides. Buildings include the Wentworth Depot, Junius Depot, and roundhouse/turntable.

Schedule: Museum–May through September: daily, 9 a.m. to 6 p.m. Train–June through August and during Railroad Days and Jamboree: Sundays, 2, 3, and 4 p.m.

Admission/Fare: Museum–$5. Train–$3.

Locomotives/Rolling Stock: No. 29, 0-6-0, and no. 11, 0-4-0, former D&NE; Alco 0-4-0T no. 11; Orrenstein & Koppel 0-4-0T "Wilhelmine"; Baldwin 60-ton diesel no. 4002; GE 80-ton diesel; various rolling stock including snowplow, passenger cars, tank cars, and boxcars.

Special Events: Railroad Days, June. Fall Jamboree, late August.

Nearby Attractions/Accommodations: Camping available on grounds, Lake Herman State Park, Smith-Zimmermann State Museum, Madison.

Location/Directions: Prairie Village is 2 miles west of Madison on Highway 34. From Sioux Falls, take I-29 north to the Madison/Colman exit, then travel west on Highway 34 to Madison.

Site Address: W. Highway 34, Madison, SD
Mailing Address: PO Box 256, Madison, SD 57042-0256
Telephone: (800) 693-3644 and (605) 256-3644
Fax: (605) 256-4588
E-mail: prairiev@rapidnet.com
Internet: www.prairievillage.org

CHATTANOOGA CHOO CHOO
Museum, display

Description: Opened in 1909 as the Southern Railway's Terminal Station, this depot welcomed thousands of travelers during the golden age of railroads. Today, the restored station is the heart of the Chattanooga Choo Choo Holiday Inn, a 24-acre complex with a full range of entertainment. Forty-eight passenger cars are part of the 360-room hotel; two passenger cars serve as a formal restaurant and meeting/banquet room.

Schedule: Year round: Sundays through Saturdays, 10 a.m. to 8 p.m.

Admission/Fare: Adults, $2; children, $1; under age 6 are free.

Locomotives/Rolling Stock: Five to eight trains running in museum.

Special Events: Victorian Holidays Open House, December. Free outdoor entertainment, May through September.

Nearby Attractions/Accommodations: Tennessee Aquarium, IMAX Theater, Southern Belle Riverboat, Creative Discovery Museum, Coolidge Park, Rock City, Ruby Falls.

Location/Directions: I-24 exit 178, take S. Broad St. split and follow signs to Choo Choo.

Site Address: Chattanooga Choo Choo Holiday Inn
Mailing Address: 1400 Market St., Chattanooga, TN 37402
Telephone: (423) 266-5000
Fax: (423) 265-4635
E-mail: frontdesk@choochoo.com
Internet: www.choochoo.com

Tennessee, Chattanooga

TENNESSEE VALLEY RAILROAD
Train ride, display
Standard gauge

STEVE FREER

Description: Daily, 45-minute round trip through Missionary Ridge Tunnel. Dixie Land Excursions run on select weekends and include a dining car luncheon. Special events throughout the year.

Schedule: April through November: Saturdays 10 a.m. to 5 p.m.; Sundays 11 a.m. to 5 p.m. Spring/fall weekdays 10 a.m. to 1 p.m. Summer weekdays 10 a.m. to 5 p.m.

Admission/Fare: Adults, $9.50; children 3-12, $4.50. Group rates/charters.

Locomotives/Rolling Stock: S160 2-8-0 no. 610; SR KSI 2-8-0 no. 630; SR MSI 2-8-2 no. 4501; K&T 2-8-2 no. 10; Alco RSDI no. 8669 and 8677; GP7 no. 1824 and 1829; RDC no. 22.

Special Events: Spring Blossom Special, April. Autumn Leaf Specials, October. Polar Express and Christmas Specials, November and December.

Nearby Attractions/Accommodations: Hamilton Place Mall retail center (Tennessee's largest mall), Tennessee Aquarium, Rock City, Ruby Falls, Incline Railway, Chattanooga Choo Choo complex, NMRA headquarters.

Location/Directions: I-75 exit 4 onto Highway 153 to Jersey Pike (fourth exit), follow brown directional signs.

*Coupon available, see coupon section.

Radio frequency: 160.425

Site Address: 4119 Cromwell Rd., Chattanooga, TN
Mailing Address: 4119 Cromwell Rd., Chattanooga, TN 37421-2119
Telephone: (423) 894-8028
Fax: (423) 894-8029
E-mail: info@tvrail.com
Internet: www.tvrail.com

CASEY JONES MUSEUM AND TRAIN STORE
Museum
HO, O27

Description: Visit the home and railroad museum of Casey Jones. Casey was living in this home at the time of his death in 1900. There are three layouts on display in the 1800s baggage car and a replica of no. 382, Casey's engine, along with souvenirs and a hobby shop. There is also a miniature train ride on a ¼-mile track.

Schedule: Year round: daily 9 a.m. to 8 p.m. Closed Easter, Thanksgiving, and Christmas.

Admission/Fare: Adults, $4; seniors, $3.50; children 6-12, $3; children age 5 and under are free. Lifetime passes available.

Locomotives/Rolling Stock: Rogers 4-6-0 locomotive; 1800s M&O baggage car; IC caboose you can sleep in; 1890s sleeper car; HO and O27 model train display.

Nearby Attractions/Accommodations: State Park, Shiloh National Military Park, Home of Buford Pusser, Adamsville.

Location/Directions: I-40 exit 80A onto 45, 45 seconds off Highway 45, look for caboose in the sky.

*Coupon available, see coupon section.

Site Address: 30 Casey Jones Ln., Jackson, TN
Mailing Address: 56 Casey Jones Ln., Jackson, TN 38305
Telephone: (901) 668-1222
Fax: (901) 664-7782
E-mail: casey@caseyjonesvillage.com
Internet: www.caseyjones.com

Tennessee, Jackson   **NASHVILLE, CHATTANOOGA & ST. LOUIS**
DEPOT AND RAILROAD MUSEUM
Museum, display, layout
HO

MOORE STUDIOS

Description: The restored NC&StL Depot features a museum that reflects Jackson's history as West Tennessee's railroad hub. A working scale model depicts local railroad heritage. An Amtrak dining car, which seats up to 48 diners, can be rented for catered parties.

Schedule: Year round: Mondays through Saturdays, 10 a.m. to 3 p.m.

Admission/Fare: Free.

Locomotives/Rolling Stock: Former FEC (Bunn 1947) dining car, Ft. Matanzas; Southern caboose X421; C&O caboose 3255.

Nearby Attractions/Accommodations: Brooks Shaw's Old Country Store, Historic Casey Jones Home and Railroad Museum, Pinson Mounds State Archaeological Area, Cypress Grove Nature Park, Chickasaw Rustic State Park, Pringles Park-Home of West Tennessee Diamond Jaxx baseball.

Location/Directions: Turn off Highway 45 bypass onto Martin Luther King Dr. at the Jackson Main Post Office and go one block to S. Royal St. Turn right, proceed one block, depot is on the left.

Site Address: 582 S. Royal St., Jackson, TN
Mailing Address: PO Box 2508, Jackson, TN 38302
Telephone: (901) 425-8223
Fax: (901) 425-8682

LYNNVILLE RAILROAD PRESERVATION SOCIETY
Museum, display
HO

Description: Rebuilt L&N depot, memorabilia, static display of rail cars and locomotive, HO scale model railroad in depot. Video theater in restored coach. Telegraph depot to caboose.

Schedule: May through October: Thursdays and Fridays 11 a.m. to 4 p.m.; Saturdays 10 a.m. to 4 p.m.; Sundays through Wednesdays by appointment.

Admission/Fare: Adults, $2; children under age 12 are free.

Locomotives/Rolling Stock: 1927 Baldwin 2-6-2 locomotive; 1925 passenger coach NC&St.L; flatcar; Illinois Central caboose with L&N markings.

Special Events: Railroad Days, first weekend in May; music entertainment, street dance, and activities.

Nearby Attractions/Accommodations: Iron Horse Restaurant (seats 80 plus), trolley car emporium (mini-mall with full-sized horse-drawn trolley car and cafe). Local bed and breakfast.

Location/Directions: Seven miles west of exit 27 off I-65; 50 miles south of Nashville.

     M

Site Address: Mill St., Lynnville, TN
Mailing Address: PO Box 158, Lynnville, TN 38472
Telephone: (931) 527-0564
Fax: (931) 527-0564
E-mail: oldtoot@pop.vsit.net
Internet: www.lynnvillerailroad.com

TENNESSEE CENTRAL
RAILWAY MUSEUM
Train ride, museum, display, layout
Standard gauge

STEVE JOHNSON

Description: Excursion train, hobby shop, railroad artifacts, modular HO and N scale model railroads.

Schedule: Saturdays 9 a.m. to 3 p.m. Fifteen to 20 excursion trains scheduled during the year.

Admission/Fare: Museum–free. Excursion train–varies.

Locomotives/Rolling Stock: EMD E8A TCRX 5764; EMD SW8 TC 52; former ATSF coaches; TCRX 4711, 4717, 4719, 4733, 4739; Budd buffet-diner TCRX 3113, 3119; Budd slumbercoach TCRX 2095; Pullman business car TC 102.

Special Events: Excursion trains for Valentine's Day, Easter, July 4th, Fall foliage, Christmas/Santa, more.

Nearby Attractions/Accommodations: Tennessee Titans NFL football, downtown Nashville, Grand Ole Opry House, Opryland Hotel, Nashville Toy Museum, Music Row, Nashville Arena, Opry Mills Shopping Mall.

Location/Directions: I-24/40 eastbound exit 212 Fesslers Ln. Left onto Fesslers Ln., 0.5 mile to left on Lebanon Rd., proceed 0.8 mile to right on Fairfield Ave. and follow sign to museum site.

      M arm
Radio frequency: 154.570

Site Address: 220 Willow St., Nashville, TN
Mailing Address: 220 Willow St., Nashville, TN 37210-2159
Telephone: (615) 244-9001
Fax: (615) 244-2120
E-mail: hultman@nashville.com
Internet: http://home.hiwaay.net/~bgaddes/tcrm

SOUTHERN APPALACHIA
RAILWAY MUSEUM
Train ride, dinner train, museum, display
Standard gauge

CHRIS WILLIAMS

Description: A 13-mile, 90-minute train ride aboard air-conditioned coaches and dining car, plus caboose. Train travels former Southern Railway branch line through the former Manhattan Project K-25 facility. Limited number of evening dinner trains. Additional shortline railroad charters conducted across the United States.

Schedule: First and third Saturdays, April through September, plus additional weekends and Sundays in April, October, November, and December at 1, 3, and 5 p.m. Reservations recommended.

Admission/Fare: Adults, $10; children age 12 and under, $7.50.

Locomotives/Rolling Stock: U.S. Atomic Energy Commission 1951 Alco RS-1 5310; Tennessee Valley Authority, nee U.S. Army 1943 Alco S-2 7100 and 7125; Central of Georgia 1947 ACF coach 663; more.

Special Events: May 19, Oak Ridge Mayfest; July 21, 50th Birthday of Locomotive 5310; October 27-28, Halloween Trains; December 8-9, Santa Claus Trains.

Nearby Attractions/Accommodations: Museum of Appalachia, Great Smoky Mountains National Park, Big South Fork National River and Recreation Area, Oak Ridge Manhattan Project tours.

Location/Directions: Six miles north of I-40 exit 356 between Knoxville and Nashville at the East Tennessee Technology Park on Highway 58.

Radio frequency: 160.425

Site Address: Highway 58 S., Oak Ridge, TN
Mailing Address: PO Box 5870, Knoxville, TN 37928
Telephone: (865) 241-2140
Fax: (865) 692-9505
E-mail: bjenninl@utk.edu
Internet: www.techscribes.com/sarm/sarm.htm

DOLLYWOOD ENTERTAINMENT PARK
Train ride
36" gauge

RICHARDS & SOUTHERN

Description: The *Dollywood Express,* located in the Village area of Dollywood, takes visitors on a 5-mile journey through this scenic park, known as "the friendliest town in the Smokies." As passengers ride on the authentic, coal-fired steam train, they can catch a glimpse of the different areas of Dollywood: Daydream Ridge, Rivertown Junction, The Village, Craftsman's Valley, Country Fair, Showstreet, Jukebox Junction, and the Dollywood Boulevard. The *Dollywood Express* also takes visitors through replicas of a typical turn-of-the-century mountain village and logging community. During Christmas Festivals, the train is decorated with lights and features a special Christmas message for visitors.

Schedule: Thirty-minute rides every hour during park operating hours.

Admission/Fare: Adults, $29.99; seniors, $24.99; children 4-11, $20.99.

Locomotives/Rolling Stock: "Klondike Katie," a 1943 Baldwin 2-8-2, former U.S. Army no. 192; "Cinderella," a 1939 Baldwin 2-8-2, former U.S. Army no. 70; open-air passenger cars.

Special Events: Harvest Celebration, October. Smoky Mountain Christmas Festival, mid-November, December. School field trips.

Nearby Attractions/Accommodations: Numerous restaurants, lodging, shopping, and attractions in Pigeon Forge area.

Location/Directions: Call for directions.

Site Address: 1020 Dollywood Ln., Pigeon Forge, TN
Mailing Address: 1020 Dollywood Ln., Pigeon Forge, TN 37863-4101
Telephone: (423) 428-9488 and (800) DOLLYWOOD

LITTLE RIVER RAILROAD
AND LUMBER COMPANY
Museum

Description: Restored Shay locomotive, depot, steam sawmill, and collection of railroad and lumber company artifacts and photographs, and interpretive displays tell the story of community.

Schedule: April, May, and September: weekends, Saturday 10 a.m. to 5 p.m. and Sunday 1 to 5 p.m. June through August, and October: daily, Monday through Friday, 10 a.m. to 2 p.m., Saturday, 10 a.m. to 5 p.m., and Sunday, 1 to 5 p.m.

Admission/Fare: Donations appreciated.

Locomotives/Rolling Stock: Little River Shay no. 2147.

Nearby Attractions/Accommodations: Great Smoky Mountains National Park.

Location/Directions: U.S. Highway 321, Townsend, at western entrance to Great Smoky Mountains National Park. Eighteen miles east of Maryville and 15 miles southwest of Pigeon Forge.

     M

Site Address: 7747 E. Lamar Alexander Pkwy., U.S. 321, Townsend, TN
Mailing Address: PO Box 211, Townsend, TN 37882
Telephone: (865) 448-2211
Fax: (865) 448-2312

TEXAS PANHANDLE RAILROAD HISTORICAL SOCIETY
Display
Standard gauge

JEFF FORD

Description: The TPRHS has cosmetically restored and maintains former Santa Fe Railway steam locomotive no. 5000. The 2-10-4, better known by its nickname "Madam Queen," was donated to the City of Amarillo, Texas, in 1957 and placed on display in front of the city's Santa Fe Depot. The TPRHS was formed in 1992 in part to preserve and interpret the locomotive as an important reminder of the Texas Panhandle's railroad heritage.

Schedule: Display–year round. Outdoor exhibit, guided tours available by appointment or by chance when gate is open, weather permitting.

Admission/Fare: Free, donations appreciated.

Locomotives/Rolling Stock: 1930 Baldwin, Atchison, Topeka & Santa Fe Railway 2-10-4 no. 5000. The only locomotive of its class.

Nearby Attractions/Accommodations: Palo Duro Canyon State Park, Panhandle-Plains Historical Museum, Sixth St./Historic Route 66 Antique District, railfan hotspot where BNSF's transcontinental main line crosses BNSF Fort Worth-to-Denver main line.

Location/Directions: I-40, downtown exit north to Third Ave., turn east. Located south of E. Third Ave. on Grant St., downtown Amarillo.

    M

Site Address: E. Third Ave. and Grant St., Amarillo, TX
Mailing Address: PO Box 50422, Amarillo, TX 79159-0422
E-mail: info@tprhs.org
Internet: www.tprhs.org

SIX FLAGS OVER TEXAS RAILROAD
Train ride
Narrow gauge

Description: This is a major theme park with trains running along the perimeter of the park.

Schedule: Summer months: daily. Spring and fall: weekends. Call for schedule.

Admission/Fare: $37.99 per person. Discounts for guests under 48 inches and seniors.

Locomotives/Rolling Stock: 1901 Dickson 0-4-0T converted 2-4-2 with tender, no. 1280; 1897 H.K. Porter 0-4-4T converted 2-4-2 with tender, no. 1754.

Special Events: Texas Heritage Crafts Festival, September. Fright Fest, October. Holiday in the Park, December.

Nearby Attractions/Accommodations: Texas Rangers baseball, Six Flags Hurricane Harbor Water Park, Lone Star Park Race Track, Texas Motor Speedway, Dallas, Fort Worth.

Location/Directions: Located midway between Dallas and Ft. Worth in Arlington at the intersection of I-30 and Texas Highway 360.

Site Address: 2201 Rd. to Six Flags, Arlington, TX
Mailing Address: PO Box 90191, Arlington, TX 76004-0191
Telephone: (817) 530-6000
Internet: www.sixflags.com

AUSTIN & TEXAS CENTRAL RAILROAD
Train ride
Standard gauge

Description: Steam train ride through scenic Texas hill country. Downtown Austin boarding also available for historic ride through Austin.

Schedule: Call or write for information.

Admission/Fare: Call or write for information.

Locomotives/Rolling Stock: Southern Pacific 2-8-2 no. 786; six PRR P70 day coaches; three air-conditioned lounge cars.

Nearby Attractions/Accommodations: Highland Lakes, State Capitol, LBJ Library and Museum, wineries, Vanishing Texas River Cruise, Longhorn Caverns.

Location/Directions: Intersection of U.S. 183 and FM 1431 in Cedar Park, 19 miles northwest of downtown Austin. Downtown Austin train–intersection of Fourth and Red River.

Radio frequency: 160.550

Site Address: Highway 183 and FM 1431, Cedar Park, TX; and Fourth and Red River, Austin, TX
Mailing Address: Box 1632, Austin, TX 78767
Telephone: (512) 477-8468 (reservations) and (512) 477-6377 (office)
Fax: (512) 477-8633
E-mail: ASTA786@juno.com
Internet: www.main.org/flyer

AGE OF STEAM RAILROAD MUSEUM
Museum
Standard gauge

Description: One of the nation's finest collections of steam and early diesel era railway equipment. Complete heavyweight passenger train featuring restored MKT dining car and "Glengyle," the oldest all-steel, all-room Pullman.

Schedule: Wednesdays through Sundays, 10 a.m. to 5 p.m.

Admission/Fare: Adults, $5; children age 12 and under, $2.50; 2 years and under, free.

Locomotives/Rolling Stock: Big Boy no. 4018, 1942 Alco 4-8-8-4 and "Centennial" no. 6913, EMD DDA40X, both former Union Pacific; no. 1625, 1918 Alco 2-10-0, former Eagle-Picher Mining Co.; BNSF EMD SDFP-45 no. 97; USA Alco RSD-1 no. 8000; CNR EMD F-9 no. 9167.

Special Events: Whistle Fair, June 16-17. Festival of Trains, August 11-12. Texas State Fair, September 28-October 21.

Nearby Attractions/Accommodations: The museum is located in Fair Park, a year-round collection of arts and cultural institutions housed in a restored art deco building originally constructed for the 1936 Texas centennial.

Location/Directions: Two miles east of downtown. I-30 westbound, exit 47A right onto Exposition Ave., left on Party Ave.

Site Address: 1105 Washington St., Fair Park, Dallas, TX
Mailing Address: PO Box 153259, Dallas, TX 75315-3259
Telephone: (214) 428-0101
Fax: (214) 426-1937
E-mail: railroad@arlington.net
Internet: http://community.dallasnews.com/dmn/railroadmuseum

**MCKINNEY AVENUE
TRANSIT AUTHORITY**
Train ride
Standard gauge

ALLAN H BERNER

Description: Four restored trolleys operate on 2.8 miles of track from downtown Dallas through the historic uptown area.

Schedule: Daily 10 a.m. to 10 p.m. Some service curtailed on weekdays in 2001 during construction of line's extension. Call for current schedule.

Admission/Fare: Adults, $1.50; seniors, $.50; children 2-12, $1.

Nearby Attractions/Accommodations: Hard Rock Cafe, art galleries, antique shops, numerous restaurants with sidewalk cafe dining, historic hotels.

Location/Directions: Operates from downtown Dallas Arts District to the historic uptown area. From the DART St. Paul Light Rail Station walk four blocks north.

Site Address: Car barn at McKinney Ave. and Bowen St., Dallas, TX
Mailing Address: 3153 Oak Grove Ave., Dallas, TX 75204
Telephone: (214) 855-0006
Fax: (214) 855-5250
Internet: www.mata.org

JIM CRUZ

Description: Largest railroad museum in the southwest with 42 cars, Renfert collection of fine railroad dining china, Ghosts of Travelers Past, model railroad exhibits, mini train. The Union Pacific mini train holds 25 passengers and will operate from the museum through the Strand Historic District, Model Train Shop.

Schedule: Daily 10 a.m. to 4 p.m. Seasonal schedule, call or write for information.

Admission/Fare: Adults, $5; seniors, $4.50; children 4-12, $2.50; under age 4 are free.

Locomotives/Rolling Stock: Forty-two pieces of equipment, including steam locomotives; diesel-electric locomotives; passenger cars; cabooses; freight cars; maintenance-of-way cars.

Location/Directions: I-45 south, stay on Broadway, turn left on 24th St. Turn left on Santa Fe Pl., turn right into museum parking lot.

*Coupon available, see coupon section.

Site Address: 123 Rosenberg, Galveston, TX
Mailing Address: 123 Rosenberg, Galveston, TX 77550
Telephone: (409) 765-5700
Fax: (409) 763-0936
E-mail: railroad@tamag.tamu.edu
Internet: www.tamug.tamu.edu/rrmuseum

Description: Ride on the 20-mile-per-hour tracks of a real working railroad. The former Cotton Belt links Grapevine to the historic Stockyards Station on that 21-mile stretch of track or enjoy the 10-mile run that parallels the famous Chisholm Trail.

Schedule: Year round: seasonal adjustments. Call or visit website for current schedule.

Admission/Fare: Call or visit website for current fare.

Locomotives/Rolling Stock: Cooke Locomotive Works 4-6-0 1896 steam locomotive no. 2248; 1925 day coaches nos. 206, 207, 208, 209, former Strasburg Railroad; 1927 touring coaches nos. 1808, 1819, former Wabash.

Special Events: Grapevine–Heritage Festival and Grapefest. Stockyards–Chisholm Trail Days and Pioneer Days.

Nearby Attractions/Accommodations: Fort Worth Stockyards, Cowtown Coliseum, historic Grapevine Main St., Bill Bob's, Grapevine Mills Mall, Bass Pro Shop.

Location/Directions: Grapevine–Highway 114 or 121, north on Main St. Stockyards–I-35W to westbound N.E. 28th St., south on N. Main, left on Exchange Ave.

Radio frequency: 160.215

Site Address: Cotton Belt Depot, 707 S. Main St., Grapevine, TX
Site Address: Stockyards Station, 140 E. Exchange Ave., Fort Worth, TX
Mailing Address: 140 E. Exchange Ave., A350, Fort Worth, TX 76106
Telephone: (817) 625-7245
Fax: (817) 740-1119
E-mail: info@tarantulatrain.com
Internet: www.tarantulatrain.com

Description: Theme park attraction with 11 feature roller coasters. Train ride is a complete 2-mile trip around AstroWorld and WaterWorld; takes about 20 minutes; shows all attractions and history.

Schedule: Open 10 a.m. to closing. Hours vary.

Admission/Fare: Adults 48" and taller, $35.99 plus tax; children $18 plus tax; senior citizens, $24.99 plus tax; 2 and under free.

Locomotives/Rolling Stock: Two diesel locomotives; converted ore car.

Special Events: Fright Fest, Un Dia Padre Gospel Celebration, Flag Day, concerts, Joy Fest, 4th of July celebration.

Nearby Attractions/Accommodations: Radisson Astrodome Hotel, Residence Inn, Holiday Inn Astrodome, Astrodome, Astroarena, Enizon Field, WaterWorld.

Location/Directions: On I-610 exit Kirby; southwest of downtown, across from Astrodome complex.

Site Address: 9001 Kirby Dr., Houston, TX
Mailing Address: Attn: Public Relations, 9001 Kirby Dr., Houston, TX 77054
Telephone: (713) 799-8404 and Group Sales (713) 794-3291
Fax: (713) 799-8404
E-mail: www.sftp.com
Internet: www.sftp.com

MARSHALL DEPOT INC.
Museum, display, layout

BILL ROBINSON

Description: Amtrak Station, gift shop, museum displays, HO layout.

Schedule: Wednesdays through Saturdays, 10 a.m. to 4 p.m., Sundays 1 to 4 p.m. Group reservations with two days notice.

Admission/Fare: Adults, $3; seniors, $2; children $1.

Locomotives/Rolling Stock: UP caboose no. 25687.

Special Events: Stagecoach Days, third weekend in May. 4th of July Celebration. Fire Ant Festival, second weekend in October. Wonderland of Lights, Thanksgiving to December 31.

Nearby Attractions/Accommodations: Marshall Pottery, Starr Family Historic Park, Caddo Lake and State Park, Harrison County Historical Court House, Harrison County Historical Museum, Michelson Art Museum, T.C. Lindsey store in Jonesville.

Location/Directions: From I-20 exit 617 north on U.S. 59 3.8 miles (five traffic lights). West on U.S. 80 1 mile (three traffic lights). North three blocks on N. Washington, walk through tunnel.

Site Address: 800 N. Washington Ave., Marshall, TX
Mailing Address: 800 N. Washington Ave., Ste. 1, Marshall, TX 75670-2064
Telephone: (903) 938-9495
Fax: (903) 938-8248
Internet: www.rypn.org/mdi

TEXAS STATE RAILROAD
Train ride
Standard gauge

BILL LANGFORD

Description: Established in 1893, the Texas State Railroad now carries visitors on a 4-hour, 50-mile round trip across 24 bridges as it travels through the heart of the east Texas rolling pine and hardwood forest. Victorian-style depots are located in Rusk and Palestine.

Schedule: March through November: weekends. June and July: Thursdays through Sundays.

Admission/Fare: Round trip–adults, $15; children, $9. One-way–adults, $10; children, $6.

Locomotives/Rolling Stock: No. 201, 1901 Cooke 4-6-0, former Texas & Pacific no. 316; no. 300, 1917 Baldwin 2-8-0, former Texas Southeastern no. 28; no. 400, 1917 Baldwin 2-8-2, former Magma Arizona no. 7; no. 500, 1911 Baldwin 4-6-2, former Santa Fe no. 1316; no. 610, 1927 Lima 2-10-4, former Texas & Pacific no. 610.

Special Events: Murder on the Dis-Oriented Express, Special Dogwood Excursion, Civil War and World War II re-enactments, Victoria Christmas train, starlight excursions.

Nearby Attractions/Accommodations: Rusk–nation's longest foot bridge. Palestine–National Scientific Balloon Base.

Location/Directions: Highway 84, 2 miles west of downtown Rusk, 3 miles east of downtown Palestine.

Site Address: 2503 W. 6th, Rusk, TX
Mailing Address: Box 39, Rusk, TX 78785
Telephone: (800) 442-8951 and (903) 683-2561
Fax: (903) 683-5634
Internet: www.tpwd.state.tx.us/park/railroad/railroad.html

HISTORIC ORIENT SANTA FE DEPOT
Museum

ALLEN R. JOHNSON

Description: This site educates and explains the history of railroads and its importance to the development of San Angelo and Concho Valley area of Texas.

Schedule: Summer–Thursdays through Fridays, 11 a.m. to 3 p.m.; Saturdays, 10 a.m. to 4 p.m.

Admission/Fare: Adults, $2; children under age 12, $1.

Locomotives/Rolling Stock: GE 44-ton center; ATSF caboose no. 999422.

Special Events: Cactus Jazz Series, January, March, May. Railfair, April. Fiesta del Concho, June. Fort Concho Frontier Day, June. Wild West Balloonfest, June and July 3. Pop Concert and San Angelo State Park Gathering, September. Roping Fiesta, November. Santa's Santa Fe Christmas and Concho Christmas Celebration, December.

Nearby Attractions/Accommodations: San Angelo State Park, camping, Lake Nasworthy, Concho Park at Lake Ivie, Outlaws professional hockey, Angelo State Planetarium, restaurants, museums, specialty shops.

Location/Directions: East off Highway 87 south in downtown San Angelo.

      M

Site Address: 703 S. Chadbourne, San Angelo, TX
Mailing Address: 703 S. Chadbourne, San Angelo, TX 76903
Telephone: (915) 486-2140
Fax: (915) 949-5870

Description: One-third-mile ride behind Baldwin RS4 switcher with MP bay window caboose.

Schedule: Thursdays, Saturdays, and Sundays, 9 a.m. to 4 p.m.

Admission/Fare: Adults, $4; children 12 and under, $2.

Locomotives/Rolling Stock: Baldwin 2-6-0 Moscow Camden & St. Augustine Railroad; 0-4-0 saddle tank no. 1 Comal County Power Co.; three cabooses, UP, MP, MP transfer.

Special Events: Santa's Holiday Depot: Friday, Saturday, Sunday, December 8-10, 15-17, 22-23, 6:30 to 9 p.m.

Nearby Attractions/Accommodations: San Antonio

Location/Directions: North of airport on Wetmore Rd., 2½ miles north of I-410.

Site Address: 11731 Wetmore Rd., San Antonio, TX
Mailing Address: 11731 Wetmore Rd., San Antonio, TX 78247
Telephone: (210) 490-3554
E-mail: ttm@stic.net
Internet: txtransportationmuseum.org

WICHITA FALLS RAILROAD MUSEUM
Museum
Standard gauge

DAVID H. GAINES

Description: The museum preserves the railroad history of Wichita Falls, Texas, and the surrounding area. Artifacts, displays, and the Wichita Falls Model Railroad Club HO gauge layout are housed in some of the museum's rail cars. The museum's yard is located on the site of the Wichita Falls Union Passenger Station and is adjacent to the Burlington Northern & Santa Fe's (former Fort Worth & Denver) Forth Worth to Texline main line.

Schedule: Year round: Saturdays, 12 to 4 p.m. and by appointment (unless temperature is below 32 degrees F or precipitation is falling).

Admission/Fare: Donations appreciated. Fee for special events.

Locomotives/Rolling Stock: FW&D 2-8-0 no. 304; MKT NW-2 no. 1029; FW&D RPO baggage no. 34; CB&Q power combine no. 7300; more.

Special Events: Zephyr Days Railroad Festival; check museum's website for specific dates and detailed information.

Nearby Attractions/Accommodations: Kell House Museum, Wichita Falls Police and Fire Museum, Texas Tourist Information Center, Econo Lodge, Holiday Inn Hotel & Suites, Radisson Inn at the Falls.

Location/Directions: Located on the east side of downtown Wichita Falls. From Holliday or Broad St., take Eighth St. toward downtown. The museum's gate will be to the right at the end of the street.

     M

Site Address: 501 Eighth St., Wichita Falls, TX
Mailing Address: PO Box 4242, Wichita Falls, TX 76308-0242
Telephone: (940) 723-2661 and (940) 692-6073
E-mail: wfrrm@wf.quik.com
Internet: www.wf.quik.com/wfrrm/wfrrm01.htm

HEBER VALLEY RAILROAD
Train ride, dinner train, display
Standard gauge

MIKE LEWIS

Description: Summer: four trains daily from June through August. Fall: reduced daily schedule. Winter: Friday and Saturday, two 3½-hour rides and two 90-minute rides. Winter: one 90-minute ride, one 2-hour ride.

Schedule: June 17 through August 20: 10 a.m., 3½-hour; 11:30 a.m., 90-minute, 2 p.m. 3½-hour, 3 p.m. 90-minute. August 20 through May 20, 2001, reduced schedule.

Admission/Fare: 3½ hour ride–adults, $19; seniors, $17; children, $12. 90-minute ride–adults, $12; seniors, $10; children, $8.

Locomotives/Rolling Stock: 1907 Baldwin steam 2-8-0s nos. 618 and 75; no. 1813 MRS1 (EMD); no. 1218 Davenport 44-ton; nos 270 and 250 Lackawanna coaches; no. 248 Clinchfield; nos. 365, 366, 501, 504 open-air cars; no. 3700 UP caboose; DRGW 7508 and 7510 coaches; more.

Special Events: Murder mystery trains, barbecue trains, Railroad Days, Pioneer Day, Chris Van Allsburg's Polar Express Christmas trains.

Nearby Attractions/Accommodations: Park City, Sundance Summer Theater, Deer Creek Lake, Jordanelle Lake, Strawberry Lake, more.

Location/Directions: Fifty-five minutes southeast of Salt Lake City on U.S. Highway 40.

*Coupon available, see coupon section.

Radio frequency: 150.995

Site Address: 450 S. 600 W., Heber City, UT
Mailing Address: PO Box 609, Heber City, UT 84032
Telephone: (435) 654-5601
Fax: (435) 654-3709
E-mail: hebervalleyrr@shadowlink.net
Internet: www.hebervalleyrr.org

Description: Ogden Union Station is primarily a railroad museum. Other features include John M. Browning Museum, classic cars, natural history, and an art gallery.

Schedule: Mondays through Saturdays, 10 a.m. to 5 p.m.

Admission/Fare: Adults, $3; seniors, $2; children under age 12, $1.

Nearby Attractions/Accommodations: Historic 25th Street shops and restaurants, Hill Aerospace Museum, Eccles Dinosaur Park.

Location/Directions: I-15 exit 344A, left at Wall Ave., north to Union Station.

*Coupon available, see coupon section.

Site Address: 2501 Wall Ave., Ogden, UT
Mailing Address: 2501 Wall Ave., Ogden, UT 84401
Telephone: (801) 629-8444 and (801) 629-8535
Fax: (801) 629-8555
E-mail: jeannieyoung@ci.ogden.ut.us
Internet: www.theunionstation.org

Description: This is the spot where the famous Golden Spike ceremony was held on May 10, 1869, completing the nation's first transcontinental railroad. Exact operating replicas of the original locomotives are on display; these locomotives run to the Last Spike Site on their own power each morning (from May to the second weekend in October) and return to the enginehouse in late afternoon. In the Visitor Center are color movies and many exhibits. Park rangers are on hand to explain the importance of the railroad and the significance of the ceremony of 1869.

Schedule: May 26 through September 3: daily, 8 a.m. to 6 p.m. September 5 through May 26: 8 a.m. to 4:30 p.m. Closed Thanksgiving, Christmas, and New Year's Day.

Admission/Fare: Adults, $3.50; cars, $7.

Locomotives/Rolling Stock: Full-sized operating replicas of Union Pacific 4-4-0 no. 119; and Central Pacific 4-4-0 no. 60, "The Jupiter."

Special Events: Golden State Anniversary Celebration, May 10. Annual Railroader's Festival, second Saturday in August. Annual Railroader's Film Festival and Winter Steam Demonstration, December 29-31.

Location/Directions: Thirty-two miles west of Brigham City, via Highways 13 and 83 through Corinne.

Site Address: Promontory, UT
Mailing Address: PO Box 897, Brigham City, UT 84302
Telephone: (435) 471-2209 ext. 18

TOOELE COUNTY RAILROAD MUSEUM
Train ride, museum
7.5" gauge

Description: Displays of mining, smelting, and railroading artifacts are located in the former Tooele Valley RR station and section house. An HO scale model railroad and a 7½" gauge mini-train operate on Saturdays.

Schedule: Memorial Day through Labor Day weekend: Museum–Tuesdays through Saturdays 1 to 4 p.m. Train–Saturdays 1 to 4 p.m.

Admission/Fare: Donations appreciated.

Locomotives/Rolling Stock: Static display standard gauge 2-8-0 consolidation; cabooses.

Nearby Attractions/Accommodations: Benson Grist Mill, Donner Party Museum, Pony Express Station, Daughters of Utah Pioneers, restaurants.

Location/Directions: From Salt Lake City–I-80 west to exit 99, take Highway 36 to Tooele, Vine St. east to Broadway.

Site Address: 35 N. Broadway, Tooele, UT
Mailing Address: 90 N. Main St., Tooele, UT 84074
Telephone: (435) 882-2836 summer and (435) 843-2110 after September

GREEN MOUNTAIN RAILROAD
GREEN MOUNTAIN FLYER
Train ride
Standard gauge

Description: Green Mountain Railroad offers two scenic rail excursions. The Green Mountain Flyer is a two-hour round trip departing from Bellows Falls to Chester Depot, closed Mondays. The excursion travels along the Connecticut and William's Rivers, past two covered bridges, and the Brockways Mills gorge with cascading waterfall. The Vermont Valley Flyer, closed Tuesdays, travels from North Bennington to Manchester with a stop in Arlington, home of the Norman Rockwell Museum. Manchester offers many specialty shops and an old-fashioned diner within walking distance from the station. Public transportation will make a loop to Manchester Center offering a wide variety of outlet shops, returning to the train station.

Schedule: Late-June through mid-October.

Admission/Fare: Varies with location and length of trip.

Locomotives/Rolling Stock: Alco RS 1 no. 405, former Rutland; 3000 EMD no. 302; 3000 EMD no. 304; 1750 EMD no. 803; 1750 EMD no. 804.

Special Events: Santa Express, Sweetheart Special, Mother's Day, Memorial Weekend, Father's Day, Transpo 2001, Fall Ludlow Ltd., more.

Nearby Attractions/Accommodations: Basketville, Santa's Land, Vermont Country Store, Bellows Falls Fish Ladder.

Location/Directions: I-91 exit 5 to Bellows Falls Route 5, north 3 miles.

Site Address: 8 Depot St., Bellows Falls, VT
Mailing Address: PO Box 498, Bellows Falls, VT 05101
Telephone: (802) 463-3069 and (800) 707-3530
Fax: (802) 463-4084
E-mail: railtour@sover.net
Internet: www.rails-vt.com

Description: Thirty-seven exhibit galleries on 45 acres showcase folk art, Americana, paintings, historic houses, a 1923 steamboat and railroad station and locomotive.

Schedule: April 1 through December 31.

Admission/Fare: Adults, 2-day pass, $17.50; children 6-14, $7.50.

Locomotives/Rolling Stock: American Locomotive Co. no. 220, built in 1915.

Special Events: Lilac and Gardening Weekend, third weekend in May; Harvest Days, mid-September through mid-October.

Nearby Attractions/Accommodations: Burlington, Vermont; Lake Champlain.

Location/Directions: Seven miles south of Burlington on Route 7.

Site Address: 6000 Shelburne Rd., Route 7, Shelburne, Vermont
Mailing Address: PO Box 10, Shelburne, VT 05482
Telephone: (802) 985-3346
Fax: (802) 985-2331
E-mail: info@shelburnemuseum.org
Internet: www.shelburnemuseum.org

FAIRFAX STATION RAILROAD MUSEUM
Museum, layout

Description: A restored Southern Railway depot rich in Civil War and local history. Clara Barton was a nurse here after the Second Battle of Manassas.

Schedule: Year round: Sundays, 1 to 4 p.m.

Admission/Fare: Adults, $2; children 3-10, $1.

Locomotives/Rolling Stock: Caboose N&W 518606.

Special Events: Model train layouts, every third Sunday of the month. Annual Model Train Display, first weekend in December. Annual Civil War/Community Day, Quilt Show, Art Show.

Nearby Attractions/Accommodations: Washington, D.C., museums, Manassas Museum, Fairfax City Museum.

Location/Directions: Three miles south of Fairfax. Located ¼ mile from corner of Route 123 (Ox Rd.) and Fairfax Station Rd.

Site Address: 11200 Fairfax Station Rd., Fairfax Station, VA
Mailing Address: PO Box 7, Fairfax Station, VA 22039
Telephone: (703) 425-9225 and (703) 278-8833
E-mail: fxstn@fairfax-station.org
Internet: www.fairfax-station.org/

Description: This military-history museum displays items of transportation dating from 1776 to the present. Inside the 15,000-square-foot museum are dioramas and exhibits; on five acres outside are rail rolling stock, trucks, jeeps, amphibious marine craft, helicopters, aircraft, and an experimental hovercraft.

Schedule: Year round: Tuesdays through Sundays, 9 a.m. to 4:30 p.m. Closed Mondays and federal holidays.

Admission/Fare: Free.

Locomotives/Rolling Stock: Steam locomotive 2-8-0 no. 607; steam locomotive 0-6-0 no. V-1923; ambulance ward car no. 87568; steam wrecking crane; 40-T and 50T flatcars; cabooses; Berlin duty train cars.

Nearby Attractions/Accommodations: Colonial Williamsburg, Virginia Beach, Jamestown, Yorktown, Busch Gardens Theme Park.

Location/Directions: I-64 exit 250A.

    arm

Site Address: Building 300, Washington Blvd., Fort Eustis, VA
Mailing Address: Building 300, Washington Blvd., Fort Eustis, VA 23604
Telephone: (757) 878-1115
Fax: (757) 878-5656
E-mail: bowerb@eustis.army.mil
Internet: www.eustis.army.mil/DPTMSEC/museum.htm

Description: Thirty-five minute excursion ride on the Virginia Railway Express.

Schedule: June 2, 2001.

Admission/Fare: $5 per person. Children 6 and under ride free.

Special Events: Railway Festival, June 2; memorabilia, modular exhibits, living history and folklore, music, rail excursions, children's amusements, excursion on the Virginia Railway Express.

Nearby Attractions/Accommodations: Manassas Museum, Manassas Battlefield Park, Splashdown Water Park, locally owned restaurants, hotels, and campgrounds.

Location/Directions: From I-66 in Virginia take Route 234 business south. Follow for 7 miles. Turn left on Center Street. Turn right on Main Street. Cross over railroad tracks and festival is off to right.

Site Address: 9431 West St., Manassas, VA
Mailing Address: 9431 West St., Manassas, VA 20110
Telephone: (703) 361-6599 and (877) 848-3018
Fax: (703) 361-6942
E-mail: hml@erols.com
Internet: www.visitmanassas.org

EASTERN SHORE RAILWAY MUSEUM
Museum

JOHN E. BATES

Description: Restored 1920s Pennsylvania Railroad Station; original crossing shanty, toolshed, artifacts, gift shop. Home of Delmarva Chapter NRHS. Antique auto museum is also located on grounds.

Schedule: Year round: Mondays through Saturdays 10 a.m. to 4 p.m. and Sundays 1 to 4 p.m. November through March: closed Wednesdays.

Admission/Fare: $2; children under age 12 are free.

Locomotives/Rolling Stock: 1920s RF&P post office car; 1962 NKP caboose no. 473; 1949 Wabash caboose no. 2783; Seaboard Airline diner car no. 8011; 1950 RF&P Fairfax River; 1927 Pullman "Diplomat" parlor/observation car.

Special Events: Parksley Festival, first Saturday in June.

Nearby Attractions/Accommodations: Chincoteague Island, Kiptopeke State Park, Ocean City.

Location/Directions: Midway between Chesapeake Bay Bridge Tunnel and Salisbury, Maryland. Route 13, 2 miles west on State Route 176.

Site Address: 18468 Dunne Ave., Parksley, VA
Mailing Address: PO Box 135, Parksley, VA 23421
Telephone: (757) 665-RAIL

Description: The Old Dominion Railway Museum tells the story of Virginia's railroading heritage through artifacts, videos and static displays. It is located within a few blocks of the 1831 birthplace of Virginia railroad operations. Through its affiliate, the Old Dominion Chapter, NRHS, seasonal rides are offered on the Buckingham Branch Railroad.

Schedule: Year round: Saturdays, 11 a.m. to 4 p.m. and Sundays, 1 to 4 p.m.

Admission/Fare: Donations appreciated.

Locomotives/Rolling Stock: RF&P express car 185; David M. Lea & Co. 0-4-0T no. 2; SCL caboose 21019; Seaboard System boxcar 111935; Fairmont motor car.

Special Events: Floodwall Guided Walking Tours, second Sunday of each month 2 p.m. Rides on Buckingham Branch Railroad, May, October, and December.

Nearby Attractions/Accommodations: Downtown Richmond tourist area, Richmond Floodwall Promenade, James River boating, fishing, nature walks.

Location/Directions: I-95 , exit 73 (Maury St.). Turn right onto Maury St., go two blocks. Turn left onto W. Second St., to right on Hull St., to museum on right.

     arm

Site Address: 102 Hull St., Richmond, VA
Mailing Address: PO Box 8583, Richmond, VA 23226
Telephone: (804) 233-6237
Fax: (804) 745-4735
Internet: www.odcnrhs.org

VIRGINIA MUSEUM OF TRANSPORTATION, INC.
Museum, display, layout
Standard gauge

Description: Diesel, steam, and electric locomotives, railcars, trolleys, carriages, trucks, buses, and aviation and space equipment. Interactive exhibits, large O gauge train layout, and much more.

Schedule: Call or write for information.

Admission/Fare: Call or write for information.

Locomotives/Rolling Stock: No. 611, J class 4-8-4, former Norfolk & Western; no. 4, 1910 Baldwin class SA 0-8-0, former Virginian Railway; no. 6, 1897 Baldwin class G-1 2-8-0, former N&W; no. 763, 1994 Lima class S-2 2-8-4, former Nickel Plate; no. 1, Celanese 0400 fireless locomotive; many diesels, City of Roanoke trolley, and D.C. Transit trolley: more.

Special Events: Calendar of events available on website.

Nearby Attractions/Accommodations: Visitor Center, Blue Ridge Parkway, two national forests, two state parks on lakes, museums, zoo, hotels, restaurants, shopping.

Location/Directions: I-81 to I-581, exit 5 to downtown Roanoke, follow signs.

          M   arm

Site Address: 303 Norfolk Ave. SW, Roanoke, VA
Mailing Address: 303 Norfolk Ave. SW, Roanoke VA 24016
Telephone: (540) 342-5670
Fax: (540) 342-6898
E-mail: info@vmt.org
Internet: www.vmt.org

Description: Take steam train rides on a real working farm. The train ride is one mile in length.

Schedule: Every day, June 15 through October 31.

Admission/Fare: Park admission, $5, includes all rides.

Special Events: Father's Day; Labor Day; Fall Harvest Festival, October.

Nearby Attractions/Accommodations: Suoqualmie Falls, Carnation Farms.

Location/Directions: One mile off State Hwy. 203.

Site Address: 32610 NE 32nd, Carnation, WA
Mailing Address: PO Box 177, Carnation, WA 98014
Telephone: (425) 333-4135
Fax: (425) 333-4373

CHEHALIS-CENTRALIA RAILROAD ASSOCIATION
Train ride, dinner train
Standard gauge

DON HARTMAN

Description: A 14-mile, 1¼-hour round trip or a 19-mile, 1¾-hour round trip over former Weyerhaeuser (Chehalis Western) trackage, former Milwaukee Road, from South Chehalis to Millburn or Ruth.

Schedule: May 26 through September 3: weekends. Depart Chehalis–1 and 3 p.m. Ruth trip–Saturdays, depart Chehalis 5 p.m. Ruth dinner train on select Saturdays requires advance reservations. Call for information.

Admission/Fare: Round trip–adults, $8; children 4-16, $5. Ruth trip–adults, $11; children, $9.

Locomotives/Rolling Stock: No. 15, 1916 Baldwin 90-ton 2-8-2, former Cowlitz, Chehalis & Cascade, former Puget Sound & Cascade no. 200. This engine had been displayed for 30 years in a local park; restoration was completed in 1989 by Mt. Rainier Scenic Railroad shop and volunteers from Lewis County; Milw. Z-frame 40-foot wood boxcar no. 711018 used as shop/supply car; also Milw. Steel rib-side 40-foot boxcar.

Nearby Attractions/Accommodations: Motel, restaurants, campgrounds. One hour from Mt. Rainier Scenic Railroad's Steam operation.

Location/Directions: Midway between Seattle, Washington, and Portland, Oregon. I-5 to exit 77. Turn west to first street south (Riverside Rd.). Proceed ¼ mile to Sylvenus St. Turn left one block to railroad tracks.

       M TRAIN

 Radio frequency: 161.385 and 160.635

Site Address: 1100 Sylvenus St., Chehalis, WA
Mailing Address: 1945 S. Market Blvd., Chehalis, WA 98532
Telephone: (360) 748-9593
Fax: (360) 748-9994
E-mail: ccrra@hotmail.com
Internet: www.ccrra.com

DAYTON HISTORICAL DEPOT SOCIETY
Museum

Description: Oldest train depot in the state of Washington, fully restored and on the National Register of Historic Places. Used as a repository for train memorabilia and artifacts (mostly photos) from early Columbia County history.

Schedule: Tuesdays through Saturdays 10 a.m. to 5 p.m. Sundays and Mondays, by appointment.

Admission/Fare: $2 per person.

Locomotives/Rolling Stock: UP caboose 25219 1952.

Special Events: Depot Days, third Saturday in September, celebrating railroad history in the northwest.

Nearby Attractions/Accommodations: Three historic districts, hotels and restaurants within walking distance.

Location/Directions: Coming through Dayton on Highway 12, turn north on Second St. one block.

       M arm

Site Address: 222 Commercial St., Dayton, WA
Mailing Address: PO Box 1881, Dayton, WA 99328
Telephone: (509) 382-2026

SPIRIT OF WASHINGTON DINNER TRAIN
Scheduled
Standard gauge

Description: Experience the nostalgia of passenger rail as you ride and dine in our luxurious, vintage rail cars. The Spirit of Washington Dinner Train takes you on a 3½-hour excursion that showcases scenic views of the Puget Sound regions. The 45-mile round trip is enhanced by scenery of Lake Washington, the Olympic Mountains, the Seattle skyline, and Mount Rainier. You'll dine in comfort and elegance as your journey takes you to Woodinville's beautiful Columbia Winery. There, you'll sample fine Northwest wines and visit the cellar before returning to the depot.

Schedule: Call or write for information.

Admission/Fare: Regular Seating–$59.99 dinner; $49.99 lunch/brunch. Dome Seating–$69.99 dinner; $59.99 lunch/brunch. Also available for conventions, corporate parties, weddings and special events up to 370.

Locomotives/Rolling Stock: Former Santa Fe coaches and dome lounge; former Reading Crusade observation car; fromer Milwaukee Road Super Dome.

Nearby Attractions/Accommodations: Seattle, Puget Sound.

Location/Directions: I-405 exit 2 (Route 162, Renton/Rainier Ave.), travel north to S. Third St., turn right, turn right again on Burnett Ave. S. for one block to depot.

Site Address: Renton, WA
Mailing Address: PO Box 835, Renton, WA 98057
Telephone: (206) 227-RAIL and (800) 876-RAIL
Internet: www.spiritofwashingtondinnertrain.com

Description: The streetcar travels 1.8 miles southbound and back, passing many restaurants and waterfront activities.

Schedule: Year round. Winter–daily 6:46 a.m. to 6 :30 p.m.; Saturdays and Sundays, 10:10 a.m. Summer–daily 6:46 a.m. to 11:30 p.m.; Saturdays and Sundays, 8:46 a.m.

Admission/Fare: Normal hours, $1; rush hour, $1.25.

Locomotives/Rolling Stock: W-2 class trains (streetcars) from Melbourne, Australia, nos. 272, 482, 512, 518, 605.

Special Events: July 4th Celebration.

Nearby Attractions/Accommodations: Puget Sound, restaurants, sporting events nearby, downtown Seattle, Space Needle five blocks away, Spaghetti Factory.

Location/Directions: I-5 exit at Mercer St., head west to Broad St. Streetcar barn is located at Broad St. and Alaskan Way.

Site Address: 3001 Alaskan Way, Seattle, WA
Mailing Address: 3001 Alaskan Way, Seattle, WA 98121
Telephone: (206) 684-1838 and (206) 684-2640

Washington, Snoqualmie

NORTHWEST RAILWAY MUSEUM
Train ride, museum, display
Standard gauge

Description: Operating railway museum with exhibits at the restored Queen Anne-style Snoqualmie Depot. Ten-mile round trip train excursions on restored heavyweight passenger coaches pulled with first-generation diesel locomotives.

Schedule: Train–April and October: Sundays. May through September: Saturdays, Sundays, Memorial Day, and Labor Day. Depot museum and gift shop–year round. Memorial Day through Labor Day: 7 days/week 10 a.m. to 5 p.m., Thursdays through Mondays 10 a.m. to 5 p.m.

Admission/Fare: Train–adults, $8; seniors (62+), $7; children 3-12, $6.

Locomotives/Rolling Stock: Kennecott Copper no. 201, Alco RSD-4; Weyerhaeuser Timber Co. no. 1 Fairbanks-Morse H-12-44; Spokane, Portland & Seattle nos. 272 and 276, Barney and Smith steel coaches; Spokane, Portland & Seattle no. 213, Barney and Smith wood coach; OWRR&NCO no. 1590, Pullman observation car; more.

Special Events: Mother's ride free, May 13. "Pops" on Us, June 16-17. Snoqualmie Railroad Days, August 4-5. Santa Train, December 1-2, 8-9, 15-16.

Nearby Attractions/Accommodations: Snoqualmie Falls, hiking, Seattle.

Location/Directions: I-90, eastbound exit 27 or westbound exit 31.

*Coupon available, see coupon section.

Site Address: 38625 S.E. King St., Snoqualmie, WA
Site Address: 205 McClellan St., North Bend, WA
Mailing Address: PO Box 459, Snoqualmie, WA 98065-0459
Telephone: (425) 888-3030
Fax: (425) 888-9311
E-mail: visitorservices@trainmuseum.org
Internet: www.trainmuseum.org

HAROLD K. CHANDLER

Description: This museum operates a tourist train on the former Northern Pacific White Swan branch line. Passenger excursions are 20-mile round trips from Harrah to White Swan. The 1911 former NP railroad depot in Toppenish serves as the museum and gift shop. The freight house has been converted to an engine house and the former NP section foreman's house is also adjacent to the depot.

Schedule: Museum–May through November: weekends 10 a.m. to 5 p.m. Train–September through October: Saturdays 10:30 a.m.

Fare/Admission: Museum–adults, $2; seniors and children, $1; families, $5. Train–adults, $8; children, $5.

Locomotives/Rolling Stock: 1902 NP Baldwin 4-6-0 no. 1364; 1953 150-ton; two 1920s P70 heavyweights, former PRR; 1947 NP coach no. 588; NH combination coach; 1907 NP wooden caboose.

Special Events: Halloween Run. Christmas Run with Santa, first two Saturdays in December. Western Art & Rail Show, third weekend in August.

Nearby Attractions/Accommodations: Over 50 murals by noted artists.

Location/Directions: Twenty minutes south of Yakima, Washington.

*Coupon available, see coupon section.

      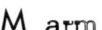

Site Address: 10 Asotin Ave., Toppenish, WA
Mailing Address: PO Box 889, Toppenish, WA 98948
Telephone: (509) 865-1911

YAKIMA ELECTRIC RAILWAY MUSEUM
Train ride, museum
Standard gauge

DENNIS L. DILLEY

Description: A 90-minute round trip though city streets, past orchards, and along the Naches River and the shoulder of Yakima Ridge through Selah Gap, over a route established by the former Yakima Valley Transportation Company in 1907.

Schedule: May through mid-October: weekends and holidays. Depart–10 a.m., 12, 2, and 4 p.m. Weekday charters available.

Admission/Fare: Train–adults, $4; seniors, $3.50; children 6-12, $2.50; families (2 adults/2children), $12. Charters available. Museum–donations appreciated.

Locomotives/Rolling Stock: Line Car "A," 1909 Niles 26-ton boxcab converted to line-car use in 1922 (in continuous service since 1909); freight motor no. 298, General Electric 50-ton steeple-cab; nos. 21 and 22, 1930 double-truck Brill Master Units that originally operated in Yakima from 1930 to 1947; nos. 1776 and 1976, single-truck Brill cars from Oporto, Portugal (the same type that operated in Yakima from 1907-1929); others.

Location/Directions: Passengers board at the Yakima Electric Railway Museum Shop at S. Third Ave. and W. Pine or at the Selah Terminal.

    M arm TRAIN

Site Address: 306 W. Pine, Yakima, WA
Mailing Address: PO Box 649, Yakima, WA 98907
Telephone: (509) 575-1700 and (800) 995-4836
Fax: (509) 453-5088

West Virginia, Belington

NEW TYGART FLYER, WEST VIRGINIA CENTRAL RAILROAD

Train ride, dinner train
Standard gauge

LARS O. BYRNE

Description: Choice of 24-, 58-, or 80-mile excursions over tracks of the fabulous West Virginia Central Railroad in the wild heart of West Virginia.

Schedule: May through October, Saturday and Sunday, with special runs during fall colors and in conjunction with local festivals. Call for details.

Admission/Fare: Rates start at $15 and vary according to choice of excursion. First-class service is also offered.

Locomotives/Rolling Stock: No. 82 ex-WM BL-2, 1948. The train is all-Pullman cars, including coach, dinette, and observation/lounge car.

Special Events: Battle of Laurel Hill Civil War re-enactment, July 8-9. Mountain State Forest Festival, October 3-7.

Nearby Attractions/Accommodations: Monongahela National Forest, Cheat Mountain Salamander Railbus Ride, Cass Scenic Railroad, Durbin & Greenbrier Valley Scenic Railroad, Revelle's Campground.

Location/Directions: Belington, West Virginia is located on Route 250, 5 miles north of U.S. 33 in Barbour County. Elkins is located at the intersection of U.S. 33 and 250 in Randolph County in East Central, West Virginia.

Site Address: Watkins Ave., Belington, WV
Mailing Address: E. Main St., Durbin, WV 26264
Telephone: (304) 456-4935
Fax: (304) 456-5246
E-mail: jksmith@naumedia.net
Internet: www.mountainrail.com

CASS SCENIC RAILROAD STATE PARK
Train ride, dinner train, museum
Standard gauge

Description: Cass Scenic Railroad is a state park that offers excursions powered by a steam-driven locomotive. We have overnight accommodations with camping nearby.

Schedule: May 26 through September 3 and October 1 through October 14, daily; September 7 through September 30, Fridays and weekends; October 18 through October 28, Thursdays, Fridays, and weekends. Cass to Whittaker, departs Cass 10:50 a.m., 1 and 3 p.m. Cass to Bald Knob, departs Cass 12 noon, except Mondays. (Cass to Bald Knob does operate on Memorial Day and Labor Day.)

Admission/Fare: Call or write for details. Prices vary with event. Group rates available. Reservations recommended.

Locomotives/Rolling Stock: No. 2 1928 Pacific Coast Shay; no. 4 1922 70-C Shay; no. 5 1905 80-C Shay; no. 6 1945 150-C Shay.

Nearby Attractions/Accommodations: Last Run Restaurant offers box lunches and more. Restored houses in park to accommodate groups of 2 to 10.

Location/Directions: State Route 28/92 between Dunmore and Green Bank in Pocahontas County, eastern West Virginia.

Site Address: Main St., Route 66, Cass, WV
Mailing Address: PO Box 107, Cass, WV 24927
Telephone: (304) 456-4300 and (800) 225-5982
Fax: (304) 456-4641
E-mail: cassrr@neumedia.net
Internet: www.neumedia.net/~cassrr/

West Virginia, Cheat Bridge   **CHEAT MOUNTAIN SALAMANDER RAILBUS RIDE**

Train ride
Standard gauge

Description: Thirty-six-, 88- or 118-mile mountain wilderness ride on top of Cheat Mountain through the spectacular Monongahela National Forest in east central West Virginia. Self-propelled railcoach crosses 4,066-foot mountain pass as it traverses one of the last great wilderness areas in the Eastern United States.

Schedule: Four-season operation. Limited to weekends only during winter. Call for details.

Admission/Fare: Fares range from $15 and up.

Locomotives/Rolling Stock: No. M-3, a self-propelled 50-passenger Edwards Railway Company motor coach.

Special Events: Mountain State Forest Festival, October 3-7; Durbin Days, third week in July; special fall foliage runs.

Nearby Attractions/Accommodations: Monongahela National Forest, Durbin & Greenbrier Valley Scenic Railroad, Cass Scenic Railroad, New Tygart Flyer Scenic Railroad, National Radio Astronomy Observatory.

Location/Directions: Cheat Bridge is located on U.S. 250, 28 miles south of Elkins; Bowden is located on U.S. 33, 10 miles east of Elkins; Elkins is located at the intersection of U.S. 33 and 250 in east central West Virginia.

 **Radio frequency: 161.175**

Site Address: Red Run Rd., WV
Mailing Address: 3 E. Main St., Durbin, WV
Telephone: (304) 456-4935
Fax: (304) 456-5246
E-mail: jksmith@neumedia.net
Internet: mountainrail.com

DURBIN & GREENBRIER VALLEY RAILROAD
Train ride
Standard gauge

KATHY SMITH

Description: A 10-mile, 1.5-hour round trip on ex-C&ORR Greenbrier Division along the upper Greenbrier River. Ride terminates at isolated Hevener station picnic area on the banks of the river.

Schedule: May 5 through October 28: Thursdays through Sundays, 11 a.m. and 2 p.m. Special winter snowplow trains during February and March.

Admission/Fare: Adults, $8; seniors, $7; children 5-12, $5.50.

Locomotives/Rolling Stock: No. 1 "Little Leroi," 20-ton Whitcomb, 1936; open excursion car; 1926 ex-B&ORR wooden caboose.

Special Events: Durbin Days, third week in July; special fall colors trips in season; winter snowplow train, weather permitting.

Nearby Attractions/Accommodations: Monongahela National Forest, Cass Scenic Railroad, Cheat Mountain Salamander.

Location/Directions: 35 miles south of Elkins on U.S. 250.

*Coupon available, see coupon section.

Site Address: E. Main St., Route 250, Durbin, WV
Mailing Address: PO Box 44, Durbin, WV 26264
Telephone: (304) 456-4935
Fax: (304) 456-5246
E-mail: jksmith@neumedia.net
Internet: mountainrail.com

West Virginia, Harpers Ferry

HARPERS FERRY TOY TRAIN MUSEUM & JOY LINE RAILROAD
Train ride, museum, display, layout

Description: One-half mile of 16-inch gauge track and a collection of antique toy trains in the museum

Schedule: April through October: weekends and holidays 9 a.m. to 5 p.m.

Admission/Fare: Adults, $1.50.

Locomotives/Rolling Stock: Two miniature train G-16; S-16; homebuilt 2-4-4T; four M.T. passenger cars; six freight cars; caboose; snowplow; work crane.

Nearby Attractions/Accommodations: Harpers Ferry National Park.

Location/Directions: Take 340 west 1 mile past Harpers Ferry and turn right onto Bakerton Rd. (Route 27), continue 1 mile and turn left.

Site Address: Bakerton Rd., Route 27, Harpers Ferry, WV
Mailing Address: Toy Train Museum, Rt. 3 Box 315, Harpers Ferry, WV 25425
Telephone: (304) 535-2521 and (304) 535-2291
E-mail: hfttm@aol.com
Internet: mountainrail.com

MOUNTAIN STATE MYSTERY TOURS
Train ride
Standard gauge

T.L. BISHOP

Description: Mainline tours to and through West Virginia's New River Gorge. Scenic/sports/shopping trips are a specialty. Day trips, overnights, or weekends available.

Schedule: Year round. Call or write for information.

Admission/Fare: $99 to $399 day trips; $399 to $1199 for custom weekend excursions.

Locomotives/Rolling Stock: Modern Amtrak Superliner equipment.

Special Events: West Virginia State Fair, August. New River Fall Foliage, October. Halloween Murder Mystery Train, October. Santa Train, December.

Nearby Attractions/Accommodations: Camden Amusement Park, Pilgrim Glass, Blenko Glass, Huntington Museum of Art, Museum of Radio and Technology, Beech Fork State Park, Heritage Farm Museum.

Location/Directions: Call or write for specific directions from your point of origin.

Site Address: Huntington, WV, and other points
Mailing Address: PO Box 8254, Huntington, WV 25705
Telephone: (304) 529-6412
Fax: (304) 697-2497
E-mail: wvmystrain@aol.com
Internet: www.themysterytrain.com

COLLIS P. HUNTINGTON RAILROAD HISTORICAL SOCIETY, INC.

Museum
Standard gauge

JEAN CHAPMAN

Description: Museum and rail excursions.

Schedule: Museum: Memorial Day through late September, Sundays 2 to 5 p.m., also by appointment year round.

Admission/Fare: Museum: donations appreciated. Excursions: from $109.

Locomotives/Rolling Stock: C&O no. 1308 Mallet steam locomotive; two C&O coaches; C&O and VGN cabooses; operating hand car; Union Pacific dome/coach car; boxcar; baggage car; concession car; RS-3 diesel locomotive former Reading engine.

Special Events: Annual New River Train Excursions, October. One-day 300-mile round trips. Tri-State Railroad Days, March, at Greenbo State Resort Park.

Nearby Attractions/Accommodations: Pilgrim Glass, Radio Museum, Highlands Museum and Discovery Center, Huntington Museum of Art, Blenko Glass, CSX, NS main lines, Greenbo Lake State Resort Park.

Location/Directions: Excursions: Seventh Ave. and Eighth St., Huntington. Museum: 14th St., West and Ritter Park.

*Coupon available, see coupon section.

Site Address: 1429 Chestnut St., Kenova, WV
Mailing Address: PO Box 451, Kenova, WV 25530
Telephone: (304) 453-1641
Fax: (606) 324-3218
E-mail: railtwo@aol.com
Internet: www.serve.com/cphrrhs/

POTOMAC EAGLE
SCENIC RAIL EXCURSIONS
Train ride
Standard gauge

D. W. CORBITT

Description: A 35-mile, three-hour ride through the "trough" of the South Branch of the Potomac River on the South Branch Valley Railroad. All trips have first-class club and dining cars with meals included.

Schedule: May through August: Saturdays, 1 p.m. September: weekends 1 p.m. October: trains operate daily; call for schedule.

Admission/Fare: Three-hour trip: Coach–adults, $22; seniors, $20; children 3-14, $10. First-class club car, $49. Six-hour trip: Coach–adults, $40; seniors, $38; children 3-14, $20. First-class club car, $89.

Locomotives/Rolling Stock: GP9s, former Baltimore & Ohio; F units, former CSX; 1920s open-window coaches, former CN; 1950s-era lounge car, former C&O.

Special Events: All-day excursions, including Petersburg trip, home tours train to Moorefield, ride the whole railroad 100+ mile route, and Railfan Day with many photo run-bys.

Location/Directions: Train departs Wappocomo Station, 1.5 miles north of Romney on Route 28.

Cumberland, Maryland

Site Address: Route 28 North, Romney, WV
Mailing Address: Ticket Agent, 2306 35th St., Parkersburg, WV 26104
Telephone: (304) 424-0736
Fax: (304) 485-5901
Internet: wvweb.com/www/potomac_eagle/

COLFAX RAILROAD MUSEUM, INC.
Museum
Standard and narrow gauge

HERBERG F. SAKALAUCKS JR.

Description: The museum houses a large collection of railroad memorabilia, an extensive reference library, and offers a ride on a railroad speeder.

Schedule: May and September: Saturday, 11 a.m. to 5 p.m.; Sunday, 1 to 5 p.m. June through August: Thursday and Friday, 11 a.m. to 4 p.m.; Saturday, 11 a.m. to 5 p.m.; Sunday, 1 to 5 p.m.

Admission/Fare: Adults, $2; children 7-14, $1; children 6 and under free.

Locomotives/Rolling Stock: Soo Line wooden caboose no. 273; Soo Line outside-braced boxcar no. 33400; Soo Line Barney & Smith coach no. 991; Milwaukee Road flanger no. 000931; two Canadian National speeders; velocipede; coming in 2001, two GE 3-foot gauge electric locomotives.

Nearby Attractions/Accommodations: Hoffman Hills State park, Red Cedar River, Altoona Roundhouse.

Location/Directions: Exit 52 off I-94 toward Chippewa Falls approximately ¾ mile, go north 8 miles on Highway 40 to Colfax. Take the first right after the railroad tracks; go one block and it's on the right.

Site Address: 500 Railroad, Colfax, WI
Mailing Address: PO Box 383, Colfax, WI 54730
Telephone: (715) 962-2076 and (715) 233-0434
Fax: (715) 235-3126
E-mail: colfaxrr@win.bright.net

EAST TROY ELECTRIC RAILROAD
WISCONSIN TROLLEY MUSEUM
Train ride, museum
Standard gauge

DENNIS STANCZAK

Description: The museum offers 10-mile round-trip trolley rides over their original 1907 trolley line. The museum also offers elegant dinner train excursions on America's only all-electric dinner train in regular service. Photos, videos, and historic exhibits are on display in the museum's depot. The carbarn and trolleys are open for viewing.

Schedule: Trolleys–May 26 through 28: Saturdays, Sundays, holidays 11:30 a.m. to 4 p.m. June 27 through August 24: Wednesdays through Fridays, 10 a.m. to 1 p.m. Dinner/tea trains available. Call for scheduled dates.

Admission/Fare: Trolley–Adults, $8; children 3-11, $4; dinner train, $47; tea train, $23.50

Locomotives/Rolling Stock: CSS&SB 9, 11, 13, 21, 24, 25, 30, 111; CTA 35, 45, 4420, 4453; Duluth-Superior Streetcar 253; P&W 64; ETER 21; TMER&L 200, D23, L6, L8, and L9; CNS&MRR 228; Septa PCCs 2120 and 2185; TTC PCC 4617; WP&L 26 and TE-1.

Special Events: Call for complete schedule.

Nearby Attractions/Accommodations: Located 45 minutes from Milwaukee and 20 minutes from Lake Geneva resort area. Elegant Farmer, Wisconsin's largest farm market. Several historic attractions, restaurants, two hotels, and a campground in East Troy area.

Location/Directions: I-43 and Highway 20, 35 miles southwest of Milwaukee.

Site Address: 2002 Church St., East Troy, WI
Mailing Address: PO Box 556, Waukesha, WI 53187-0556
Telephone: (262) 548-3837; depot (262) 642-3263 (during operating days)
Fax: (262) 548-0400
Internet: www.easttroyrr.org

LOCOMOTIVE & TOWER
PRESERVATION FUND, LTD.
Train ride
Standard gauge

GENE DAHLSTROM

Description: Take a 120- to 160-mile round trip passenger train ride with Soo Line Pacific 2719.

Schedule: Varies.

Admission/Fare: Varies per scheduled event.

Locomotives/Rolling Stock: Soo Line Pacific 2719; six ex-Algoma Central passenger coaches; Pacific H-23, Alco, 1923 built.

Special Events: Spooner; Steam Days, July; Wisconsin Great Northern Railroad.

Mailing Address: PO Box 1266, Eau Claire, WI 54703
Telephone: (877) 99902719
E-mail: 2719@2719.com
Internet: www.2719.com

NATIONAL RAILROAD MUSEUM
Train ride, museum
Standard gauge

Description: The museum offers a 20-minute train ride during the summer season in vintage rail equipment. During the ride a uniformed conductor describes the museum's history and the "way of the rails" as viewed through the eyes of a hobo. Year round the museum offers an exhibit hall, 70 pieces of rolling stock, 1,500-square-foot HO model display and theater show. The museum was established in 1958.

Schedule: May through September: daily, 9 a.m. to 5 p.m. October through December: 9 a.m. to 5 p.m., Mondays through Saturdays. January through April: 9 a.m. to 5 p.m., Mondays through Fridays.

Admission/Fare: Adults, $6; seniors, $5; children 6-15, $4; families, $18.

Locomotives/Rolling Stock: No. 4017 Big Boy 4-8-8-4, former Union Pacific; Eisenhower's World War II Command Train; Churchill's personal cars; AeroTrain; 1910 LS&I no. 24 2-8-0; PRR GG-1; and more than 60 other pieces of rolling stock.

Special Events: Railfest, June. Civil War re-enactment, August. Haunted Train, October.

Location/Directions: Highway 41 or 172, Ashland Ave. exit, travel north to Cormier Ave. and east three blocks.

*Coupon available, see coupon section.

Site Address: 2285 S. Broadway, Green Bay, WI
Mailing Address: 2285 S. Broadway, Green Bay, WI 54304
Telephone: (920) 437-7623
Fax: (920) 437-1291
E-mail: staff@nationalrrmuseum.org
Internet: www.nationalrrmuseum.org

CAMP FIVE MUSEUM
FOUNDATION, INC.
Train ride, museum

Description: Camp Five offers visitors a unique mix of history, steam rail-roading, and ecology. Visitors ride the *Lumberjack Special* steam train (2.5 miles one way) to the museum complex; once there, they take a guided surrey tour through beautiful forests managed on a perpetual-cycle basis. A hayrack/pontoon ride on the Rat River is also an optional offer. Logging museum with an early-transportation wing and an active black-smith shop; half-hour steam engine video; nature center with northern Wisconsin wildlife diorama; petting corral; large outdoor display of log-ging artifacts.

Schedule: June 20 through September 1: Mondays through Saturdays: departures at 11 a.m., 12, 1, and 2 p.m.

Admission/Fare: Adults, $15; students 13-17, $9.50; children 4-12, $5; 3 and under, free; families, $40. Group discounts available.

Locomotives/Rolling Stock: 1916 Vulcan 2-6-2; cupola cabooses.

Special Events: Saturday Fall Festival, September.

Location/Directions: West of Laona on Highway 8.

Site Address: Highway 8, Laona, WI
Mailing Address: RFD #1, Laona, WI 54541
Telephone: (800) 774-3414 and (715) 674-3414
Fax: (715) 674-7400
Internet: www.campsmusuem.org

Description: Outdoor interpretive museum with 25 restored historic buildings and exhibit areas. Caboose 99006 recently restored and open for public viewing.

Schedule: Daily, May 1 through third Sunday in October; also, first weekend in December.

Admission/Fare: Adults, $6; children 6-17, $4; 5 and under, free

Locomotives/Rolling Stock: Soo Line 0-6-0 no. 321 steam locomotive, built in 1887; Wisconsin Central caboose no. 99006, built in 1886; Soo Line depot from Collins, Wisconsin, built in 1896.

Special Events: German Fest (July), Fall Harvest Festival (September), Christmas at Pinecrest (December).

Nearby Attractions/Accommodations: Food, lodging, and other attractions can be found in nearby Manitowoc and Two Rivers.

Location/Directions: Seven miles west of Manitowoc. From I-43 follow JJ west to Pine Crest Ln.

     M

Site Address: 924 Pine Crest Ln., Town of Manitowoc Rapids, WI
Mailing Address: MCHS, PO Box 574, Manitowoc, WI 54221-0574
Telephone: (920) 684-5110 (seasonal), (920) 684-4445 (year round)
Fax: (920) 684-0573

WHISKEY RIVER RAILWAY
Train ride
16" gauge

D. KLOMPMAKER COLLECTION

Description: A 2-mile scenic ride over the Wisconsin countryside. Featuring many animals, including llamas, sheep, cattle, emu, longhorn steer, and zebra.

Schedule: Memorial Day through Labor Day: daily. October: weekends. December: daily.

Admission/Fare: $4.50; unlimited rides, $10.

Locomotives/Rolling Stock: Gene Autry's Daylight Melody Ranch Special; Oakland Acorn Pacific; Gracy's Atlantic 1919 8½-ton Pacific (built in house); McCallister collection, including Atlantic, Shay, and 2-8-8-4 Mallet.

Nearby Attractions/Accommodations: Amusement park, miniature golf.

Location/Directions: Located ¼ mile east of Highway 73 on Highway 19 in Marshall.

*Coupon available, see coupon section.

Site Address: 700 E. Main St., Marshall, WI
Mailing Address: 700 E. Main St., Marshall, WI 53559
Telephone: (888) 607-7735
Fax: (608) 655-4767
E-mail: gardyloo@jvlnet.com

ZOOFARI EXPRESS
MILWAUKEE COUNTY ZOO
Train ride
15" gauge

MIKE NEPPER

Description: This railroad has operated at the Milwaukee County Zoo since 1958, carrying over 13 million riders. The 1.25-mile trip across zoo property lasts about eight minutes.

Schedule: May through September: daily 10 a.m. to 4 p.m. March, April, October: weekends 10 a.m. to 4 p.m.

Admission/Fare: Zoo admission required–adults, $9; children 3-12, $6; parking, $6. Train–adults, $2; children, $1.

Locomotives/Rolling Stock: Sandley light locomotive and rolling stock–coal-fired steam locomotive 4-6-2 no. 1924; coal-fired steam locomotive 4-4-2 no. 1916; diesel hydraulic switcher no. 1958; F2 diesel hydraulic no. 1996; twelve-passenger day coaches nos. 1080-1096.

Nearby Attractions/Accommodations: Wisconsin State Fair Park, Summerfest Grounds, Milwaukee County Stadium, Milwaukee Public Museum, Mitchell Park Domes, Wehr Nature Center, Whitnall Boerner Botanical Gardens, Cool Waters Water Park, Best Western Midway, Holiday Inn Express, Sheraton Inn Mayfair, Excel Inn, many restaurants and area attractions.

Location/Directions: Zoo is located 8 miles west of downtown Milwaukee at the intersection of I-94, I-894, and Highway 45.

Site Address: 10001 W. Bluemound Rd., Milwaukee, WI
Mailing Address: 10001 W. Bluemound Rd., Milwaukee, WI 53226
Telephone: (414) 771-3040
Fax: (414) 256-5410
Internet: www.milwaukeezoo.org

Description: Restored CNW depot complete with railroad artifacts.

Schedule: June through August: first and third Sundays, 1 to 4 p.m. or by appointment.

Admission/Fare: Donations appreciated.

Locomotives/Rolling Stock: U.S. Army no. 4555 renumbered U.S. Army no. 7436, built by Vulcan Iron Works 1941, sold to Laona & Northern Railway October 1948 to become engine 3101; Soo Line caboose no. 138; CNW caboose no. 11153.

Special Events: Rail Fest Days, second Sunday in August.

Nearby Attractions/Accommodations: Rainbow Motel, Marly's Restaurant, Mosquito Hill Nature Center, Memorial Park.

Location/Directions: Route 45 north to Business 45, High St. east to railroad tracks, north to the depot.

       M

Site Address: 900 Montgomery St., New London, WI
Mailing Address: 612 W. Beacon Ave., New London, WI 54961-1322
Telephone: (920) 982-5186 and (920) 982-8557

Wisconsin, North Freedom

MID-CONTINENT RAILWAY
HISTORICAL SOCIETY
Train ride, museum
Standard gauge

WILLIAM RAIA

Description: Seven-mile, 50-minute ride in rural setting. Trains depart from a restored 1894 C&NW depot. On display is an extensive collection of vintage freight, passenger, and company-service equipment. Caboose and cab rides are offered.

Schedule: Mid-May through Labor Day: daily 10:30 a.m., 12:30, 2, and 3:30 p.m. Weekends through late October.

Admission/Fare: Adults, $9; seniors, $8; children 3-12, $4.50; under 3, free. Cab ride, $25. Caboose: adult, $11; child, $6. Call or e-mail for first-class, dinner train and group rates.

Locomotives/Rolling Stock: C&NW no. 1385, ALCO 4-6-0 (1907); Polson Logging Co. no. 2, Baldwin 2-8-2 (1912); WC&C no. 1; MLW 4-6-0 (1913); C&NW combine no. 7409; drovers caboose no. 10802; business car no. 440; Soo Line diner-lounge no. 2017; business car "Oak Park"; DM&IR caboose no. C-74; reefer no. 7122; GN coach no. 3261; more.

Special Events: Snow Train, February. Hobo Weekend, June. Civil War, Weekend, July. WWI Weekend, August. Autumn Color Weekend, October. Santa Express, November. Call or e-mail for dates and times.

Location/Directions: Seven miles west of Baraboo. State Highway 136 to County Highway PF. Follow signs.

*Coupon available, see coupon section.

Site Address: E8948 Museum Rd., North Freedom, WI
Mailing Address: PO Box 358, North Freedom, WI 53951-0358
Telephone: (608) 522-4261
Fax: (608) 522-4490
E-mail: midcon@baraboo.com
Internet: www.midcontinent.org

KETTLE MORAINE RAILWAY
Train ride
Standard gauge

Description: The Kettle Moraine Railway offers a train ride back in time, when life was a little simpler. The train departs an 1889 refurbished depot making an 8-mile round trip, which takes approximately 50 minutes. This nostalgic ride behind a steam engine is both educational and recreational.

Schedule: June through September and Labor Day: Sundays, 12:30, 2:00, and 3:30 p.m. First four weekends in October: Saturdays, 12:30, 2:00, and 3:30 p.m. and Sundays, 11 a.m., 12:30, 2:00, 3:30 p.m. November: Thanksgiving weekend, Santa Train, 11:00 a.m., 12:30, 2:00, 3:30 p.m.

Admission/Fare: Adults, $9; children 3-11, $5; under age 3 ride free unless occupying a seat.

Locomotives/Rolling Stock: 1917 65-ton Heisler no. 3, former Craig Mt. Railroad; 1901 Baldwin 2-6-2 former McCloud River Railroad.

Special Events: Goblin Express, first four Saturdays in October, 6:30 p.m. Santa Express, Thanksgiving weekend. Call or write for information and dates.

Nearby Attractions/Accommodations: Holy Hill, Honey Acres, Hartford Car Museum, Old World Wisconsin.

Location/Directions: Nine miles north of I-94 on Highway 83 in North Lake.

*Coupon available, see coupon section.

Site Address: N77 W31349 Kilbourne Rd., North Lake
Mailing Address: Box 247, North Lake, WI 53064
Telephone: (262) 966-0516
Internet: www.kmry.org

OSCEOLA & ST. CROIX VALLEY RAILWAY
MINNESOTA TRANSPORTATION MUSEUM
Train ride, museum
Standard gauge

JAKE LUECKEL

Description: Enjoy the scenic St. Croix River Valley on a 90-minute round trip between Osceola, Wisconsin, and Marine-on-St. Croix, Minnesota, or a 45-minute round trip through rural Wisconsin between Osceola and Dresser. See the restored Osceola Historical Depot, featuring exhibits about railroading and the Osceola area, and the U.S. Railway Post Office exhibits aboard Northern Pacific triple combine no. 1102.

Schedule: Memorial Day through October: weekends. Charters available during the week.

Admission/Fare: Marine trip–$7 to $13; Dresser trip–$5 to $10.

Locomotives/Rolling Stock: Northern Pacific no. 328 4-6-0 steam locomotive; NP no. 105 LST&T switcher engine; nos. 2604 and 2608 cars, former Rock Island; NP triple combine car no. 1102; DL&W no. 2232 commuter coach; Soo Line 559 1951 Electromotive 6P7; streamline coaches 1213 Great Northern Empire Builder and 1096 and 1097 Chicago & Northwestern 400.

Special Events: Fireworks Express; fall leaves trip, September and October.

Nearby Attractions/Accommodations: Cascade Falls, St. Croix River, St. Croix Art Barn, Interstate Park, motels, and campgrounds.

Location/Directions: I-35W to Forest Lake, Highway 97 east to Highway 95, north to I-243 across the St. Croix River to Highway 35S, to Depot Rd.

*Coupon available, see coupon section.

Radio frequency: 161.355

Site Address: 114 Depot Rd., Osceola, WI
Mailing Address: PO Box 176, Osceola, WI 54020
Telephone: (715) 755-3570
Fax: (715) 294-3330
E-mail: oscvrlwy@centuryinter.net
Internet: www.mtmuseum.org or www.trainride.org

THE MINING MUSEUM AND
ROLLO JAMISON MUSEUM
Train ride, museum
24" gauge

Description: Tour an 1845 lead mine, and ride a 1931 mine locomotive above ground. Tour home and farm exhibits in Rolk Jamison Museum. (The train ride is part of the mine tour and takes three to five minutes.)

Schedule: May through October: daily, 9 a.m. to 5 p.m. Self-guided exhibits, November through April, Monday through Friday, 9 a.m. to 4 p.m. Group tours available year round.

Admission/Fare: Adults, $6; seniors, $5; children 5-15, $2.50; under age 5 are free.

Locomotives/Rolling Stock: Whitcomb Co., Rochelle, Illinois, 1931 locomotive.

Nearby Attractions/Accommodations: First Capital Historic Site; University of Wisconsin-Platteville, Chicago Bears training camp; hotels and restaurants.

Location/Directions: Corner of Main St. and Virgin Ave. Three blocks north of Highway 151.

Site Address: 405 E. Main St., Platteville, WI
Mailing Address: PO Box 780, Platteville, WI 53818-0780
Telephone: (608) 348-3301
Fax: (608) 348-4640
E-mail: kleefiss@uwplatt.edu

RAILROAD MEMORIES MUSEUM
Museum, layout
G and HO

CARL SCHULT

Description: Historical, educational museum covering all aspects of railroading. Tools, equipment, track vehicles, memorabilia, and history from the 1800s. Many station signs, books, art, and rare uniforms. Guided tours, videos, models, eight large rooms full.

Schedule: Memorial weekend through Labor Day weekend: daily, 10 a.m. to 5 p.m. Groups by appointment.

Admission/Fare: Adults, $3; children 6-12, $.50; under age 6 are free.

Nearby Attractions/Accommodations: Namekagon Scenic River System, Bulik's Amusement Park, Museum of Wood Carving, Heart O' North Rodeo, State Fish Hatchery (largest musky hatchery in the world), lodging, restaurants.

Location/Directions: Two blocks from Highways 70 and 63; in old CNW depot at Walnut and Front Streets.

*Coupon available, see coupon section.

       arm

Site Address: 424 Front St., Spooner, WI
Mailing Address: N8425 Island Lake Rd., Spooner, WI 54801
Telephone: (715) 635-3325; when closed, (715) 635-2752, 635-3833
Internet: www.spoonerwi.com/rail_museum.htm

WISCONSIN GREAT NORTHERN RAILROAD
Train ride
Standard gauge

GREG VREELAND

Description: Historic diesel-powered heavyweight passenger train traveling through the scenic woodlands of northern Wisconsin. Varying departures of 1½ to 2½ hours duration along all or part of our 18-mile main line.

Schedule: Call or write for information.

Admission/Fare: Call or write for information.

Locomotives/Rolling Stock: WGN no. 862 EMD SW-1; passenger cars heavyweight; WGN no. 26 1925 Pullman 12-1 sleeper; WGN no. 28 1912 ACF solarium observation car; WGN no. 32 1918 Pullman coach; WGN no. 34 1918 Pullman coach; WGN no. 112 1912 ACF mail baggage car.

Nearby Attractions/Accommodations: Thompson Fish Hatchery, Hunt Hill Audubon Sanctuary, Bulik's Amusement Park, Al Capone's Hideout.

Location/Directions: Highway 53 to Highway 70, west on Highway 70 for 1 mile to Front St., north on Front St. for five blocks to train parking lot. Highway 63 to Elm St., east one block to train parking lot.

Site Address: 426 N. Front St., Spooner, WI
Mailing Address: WGN Railroad, PO Box 46, Spooner, WI 54801
Telephone: (715) 635-3200 and (888) 390-0412
Fax: (715) 635-3202

RIVERSIDE & GREAT NORTHERN
RAILWAY
Train ride, museum, display

MARSHALL L. "PETE" DEETS

Description: A scenic 3-mile ride on railroad dating back to the 1850s, through rock cuts and thick forest just north of Wisconsin Dells. The R&GN is a living museum preserving miniature steam equipment and the facilities of the Sandley Light Railway Equipment Works, manufacturers of narrow gauge railroads for over 30 years.

Schedule: Memorial Day through Labor Day: daily 10 a.m. to 5:30 p.m., trains run every 45 minutes. May, October, November, and December: weekends 10 a.m. to 4 p.m., trains run on the hour. Weather permitting, call ahead to check operation schedule.

Admission/Fare: Adults, $6.50; seniors, $5; children 4-15, $4.50; under age four are free; family pass, $20.

Locomotives/Rolling Stock: No. 82 1957 4-4-0 steam engine former Milwaukee County Zoo engine; vertical boiler "Tom Thumb" steam engine; no. 95 SW style diesel engine; more.

Nearby Attractions/Accommodations: Wisconsin Dells-Lake Delton area.

Location/Directions: West of Kilbourne Bridge in Wisconsin Dells. North on Stand Rock Rd. for about 1 mile to stop sign at railroad viaduct, turn right under viaduct and then left into driveway.

*Coupon available, see coupon section.

         M

Site Address: N115 Hwy. N, Wisconsin Dells, WI
Mailing Address: N115 Hwy. N, Wisconsin Dells, WI 53965
Telephone: (608) 254-6367
E-mail: sandbergwc@globaldialog.com
Internet: //midplains.net/~randgn/

RICHARD COLLIER

Description: Tour a railroad depot, roundhouse, and railyard buildings.

Schedule: Winter–Mondays through Fridays, 8 a.m. to 5 p.m. Summer–Mondays through Fridays, 9 a.m. to 9 p.m.; Saturdays, 9 a.m. to 7 p.m.; and Sundays, 12 noon to 6 p.m.

Admission/Fare: Free.

Locomotives/Rolling Stock: Evanston's roundhouse and railyards circa 1913, including 12 railyard buildings and fully operational turntable. Depot circa 1900 brick structure in Depot Square. All facilities open for tours.

Special Events: Fourth Annual Roundhouse Festival, August 18-19.

Nearby Attractions/Accommodations: Depot Square, Martin Park, Hamblin Park, Bear River Fishing Ponds, Ft. Bridger, Bear River State Park, Uinta County Museum, Chinese Joss House Museum, Lincoln Highway, Scenic Byway, Pine Gables Bed and Breakfast, Best Western Dunmar Inn, Don Pedro's Mexican Restaurant, Michael's Bar and Grill.

Location/Directions: Eighty miles east of Sale Lake City, Utah on I-80.

      M

Site Address: 1200 Main St., Evanston, WY
Site Address: 1200 Main St., Evanston, WY
Mailing Address: 1200 Main St., Evanston, WY 82930
Telephone: (307) 783-6319/6320
Fax: (307) 783-6390
E-mail: urevan@allwest.net

HERITAGE PARK HISTORICAL VILLAGE
Train ride
Standard gauge

Description: Heritage Park is Canada's largest living historical village, where the past comes to life right in front of your eyes. We are a first-class summer tourist attraction and a year-round catering and convention facility.

Schedule: May long weekend through Labor Day weekend: daily, 9 a.m. to 5 p.m. October through Canadian Thanksgiving: weekends and holidays only.

Admission/Fare: Call or write for information.

Locomotives/Rolling Stock: Two port steam 0-4-0T 1909 compressed air; 1902 no. 3 Vul Steam 0-4-0T; 1905 no. 4 CP CPR steam 0-6-0; 1942 no. 2023 USA ALCO steam 0-6-0; 1944 no. 2024 Lima Steam 0-6-0; 1949 no. 5931 CPR MLW steam 2-10-4; 1944 no. 7019 CPR 1 MLW S2 1000.

Special Events: Opening weekend in May. Festival of Quilts, May. Railway Days and Father's Day, June. Canada Day, July. Hayshaker Days and Heritage Family Festival, August. Old Time Fall Fair and Fall Harvest Sale, September. October West, October. Call for information.

Nearby Attractions/Accommodations: Calgary Zoo, Olympic Park, Glenbow Museum, Fort Calgary, Alberta Science Centre.

Location/Directions: Follow Heritage Dr. west.

Site Address: 1900 Heritage Dr. SW, Calgary, AB
Mailing Address: 1900 Heritage Dr. SW, Calgary, AB Canada T2V 2X3
Telephone: (403) 259-1900
Fax: (403) 252-3528
E-mail: www.heritagepark.ab.ca
Internet: www.heritagepark.ab.ca

FORT EDMONTON PARK
Train ride
Standard gauge

Description: Nestled in Edmonton's river valley, Fort Edmonton Park is brought to life by costumed staff reenacting life as it was in Edmonton at the 1846 fur trading fort, and on the streets of 1885, 1905, and 1920. The train transports visitors through the park.

Schedule: May 21 through August 27: daily, Sundays in September.

Admission/Fare: Adults, $7.25; seniors and youth, 13-17 $5.50; children 2-12, $3.75; families, $22. Price includes train ride.

Locomotives/Rolling Stock: 1919 Baldwin 2-6-2 no. 107, former Oakdale & Gulf Railway (restored to its 1905 appearance).

Special Events: Call or write for information.

Nearby Attractions/Accommodations: Downtown Edmonton and West Edmonton Mall.

Location/Directions: Edmonton, Alberta.

Site Address: Fox Dr. and Whitemud Dr., Edmonton, Alberta
Mailing Address: PO Box 2359, Edmonton, AB Canada T5J 2R7
Telephone: (780) 496-8787
Fax: (780) 496-8797
Internet: www.gov.edmonton.ab.ca/fort

ALBERTA PRAIRIE RAILWAY EXCURSIONS

Train ride, dinner train
Standard gauge

Description: Round-trip tours of several different types are featured from Stettler to a combination of rural lineside communities such as Big Valley, Castor, Halkirk, and Coronation. Excursions are operated on a former Canadian National branch line through picturesque parkland and prairies in central Alberta and on a former Canadian Pacific branch line past Stettler to Coronation. All excursions include full-course roast beef dinner and on board entertainment and commentary. Fine dining excursions to Big Valley include a five-course meal and entertainment.

Schedule: Late-May through August: weekends and selected weekdays. September through mid-October: weekends. Fine dining–November through April, select dates.

Admission/Fare: Varies depending on type. Please call for more information.

Locomotives/Rolling Stock: No. 41 1920 Baldwin 2-8-0, former Jonesboro Lake City & Eastern; no. 41, former Frisco; no. 77, former Mississippi; more.

Special Events: Murder Mysteries, Canada Day, Red Coat, Train Robberies.

Nearby Attractions/Accommodations: Ol' MacDonald's Resort, museum, golf, Rochon Sands Provincial Park.

Location/Directions: A two-hour drive from Edmonton or Calgary, one hour east of Red Deer in central Alberta.

Site Address: 4611 47 Ave. Stettler, AB
Mailing Address: PO Box 1600, Stettler, AB Canada T0C 2L0
Telephone: (403) 742-2811
Fax: (403) 742-2844
E-mail: apsteam@telusplanet.net
Internet: www.nucleus.com/Heartland

WALTER LANZ

Description: Museum with static displays of restored vintage luxury train sets.

Schedule: Open all year, but seasonal hours vary. Call for information or check our website.

Admission/Fare: Prices vary for adults, seniors, students, and preschool; family discounts are given for prebooked tours. Check our website.

Locomotives/Rolling Stock: 1929 Trans Canada luxury train, plus other luxury cars. We will be expanding in the year 2001.

Special Events: Sam Steele Day, mid-June; Gala Christmas dinners, annually in late November and early December.

Nearby Attractions/Accommodations: Fort Steele Heritage Town, local campgrounds, restaurants, shops.

Location/Directions: On Van Horne St. go north on Hwy. 3/95 in downtown Cranbrook. Watch for parking and directional signs.

Site Address: One Van Horne St. (Highway 3/95), Cranbrook, BC
Mailing Address: Box 400, Cranbrook, BC Canada V1C 4H9
Telephone: (250) 489-3918
Fax: (250) 489-5744
E-mail: mail@trainsdeluxe.com
Internet: www.trainsdeluxe.com

**BRITISH COLUMBIA
FOREST DISCOVERY CENTRE**
*Train ride, museum
Narrow gauge*

Description: 1910 steam train ride (1½ miles long), forest discovery walks, historical collection, picnic and playground area, much more. One hundred acres to discover.

Schedule: May through Labor Day: daily 10 a.m. to 6 p.m. Off season, limited operation.

Admission/Fare: Adults, $8; seniors and students 13-18, $7; children 5-12, $4.50; under age 5 are free. Group rates available.

Locomotives/Rolling Stock: Bloedel Stewart & Welch no. 1; Hillcrest Lumber Co. no. 1; Shawnigan Lake Lumber Co. no. 2; Mayo Lumber Co. no. 3; Hillcrest Lumber Co. no. 9; locomotive no. 25; locomotive no. 24; no. 27 speeder; White Pass no. 1; Plymouth no. 26; Sandy no. 23 Plymouth; Witcome no. 9; more.

Special Events: National Forestry Week, Mother's Day, Father's Day, Classic Tractors, Celebration of Steam, Labor Day Picnic, Terry Fox Run.

Nearby Attractions/Accommodations: Duncan Totem Tours, Native Heritage Centre, Chemainus Murals.

Location/Directions: Located five minutes north of Duncan off Trans Canada Highway.

Site Address: 2892 Drinkwater Rd., Duncan, BC
Mailing Address: 2892 Drinkwater Rd., Duncan, BC Canada V9L 6C2
Telephone: (250) 715-1113
Fax: (250) 715-1170
E-mail: bcfm@islandnet.com

FORT STEELE RAILWAY
Train ride
Standard gauge

MARTIN ROSS

Description: Currently a Montreal Locomotive Works 2-6-2 Prairie-type locomotive pulls passengers around a 2.5-mile loop of track with a stop at a lookout point to explain the view and local railroad history.

Schedule: Daily, last weekend in June to Labor day. 11:30 a.m. to 5:30 p.m.

Admission/Fare: Adults, $5; seniors (65+) and youth (13-18), $4; children 6-12, $3; children under 6 are free.

Locomotives/Rolling Stock: Montreal Locomotive Works 2-6-2 Prairie-type no. 1077, built in 1923; Shay class 90 Pacific Coast no. 115, built in 1934; Dunrobin, Sharp & Stewart 2-4-0 side tank engine, built in 1895.

Special Events: Dominion Day, July 1; Heritage Showcase, July 28; Harvest Day, August 19; Thanksgiving Celebration, October 7; Halloween Spectacular, October 27.

Nearby Attractions/Accommodations: Fort Steele Heritage Town. Fairmont and Radium Hot Springs. Wasa Provincial Park.

Location/Directions: Southeast corner of British Columbia, 16 kilometers northeast of Cranbrook, B.C., on Highway 93/95.

*Coupon available, see coupon section.

        M

Site Address: Fort Steele Heritage Town, Fort Steele, BC
Mailing Address: 9851 Highway 93/95, Fort Steele, BC Canada V0B 1N0
Telephone: (250) 417-6000 and (250) 426-7352 (24-hour information line)
Fax: (250) 489-2624
E-mail: info@fortsteele.bc.ca
Internet: www.fortsteele.bc.ca

OKANAGAN VALLEY
WINE TRAIN
Train ride
Standard gauge

Description: A six-hour scenic rail trip from Kelowna to Vernon with dinner and show.

Schedule: Wednesday, Thursday, Saturday, 16:30, returns at 22:00; Sunday, 11 a.m., returns at 5 p.m.

Admission/Fare: Call or write for information.

Locomotives/Rolling Stock: Day coach, themed club galley bar car and sleeper cars.

Location/Directions: Downtown Kelowna at 600 Recreation Ave.

Site Address: 600 Recreation Ave., Kelowna, BC
Mailing Address: 11830 Kingsway Ave., Edmonton, AB Canada T5G 0X5
Telephone: (780) 488-8725 and (888) 674-8725
Fax: 780-482-7666
E-mail: funtrain@telusplanet.net
Internet: www.okanaganwinetrain.com

British Columbia, North Vancouver

BC RAIL
Train ride, dinner train
Standard gauge

Description: Pacific Starlight Dinner Train offers an unforgettable evening in art deco dining cars. The Royal Hudson steam excursion makes a day trip along the same spectacular coast line. The Cariboo Prospector travels 463 miles to Prince George.

Schedule: Pacific Starlight: May 1 through October 21, 6:15 p.m. departure. Royal Hudson: May 5 through September 23, Wednesdays through Sundays, 10 a.m. departure. Cariboo Prospector: year round, 7 a.m. departure.

Admission/Fare: Pacific Starlight: Salon, $85.95; Dome, $99.95. Royal Hudson: adults, $49.95; child, $12.95. Cariboo Prospector: varies by destination.

Locomotives/Rolling Stock: Pacific Starlight: five dining cars; three dome cars. Royal Hudson: No. 2860, 1940 MLW 4-6-4, ex-CP; no. 3716, 1912 MLW, 2-8-0 ex-CP; 11 coaches, CCF 1954. Cariboo Prospector: Budd RDCs.

Location/Directions: Located at the foot of Pemberton Ave., 20 minutes from downtown Vancouver.

 Vancouver VIA

Site Address: 1311 W. First St., North Vancouver, BC
Mailing Address: 1311 W. First St., North Vancouver, BC Canada V7P 1A6
Telephone: (800) 663-8238 and (604) 984-5246
Fax: (604) 984-5505
E-mail: pass_info@bcrail.com
Internet: www.bcrail.com/bcrpass

ALBERNI PACIFIC RAILWAY
Train ride, museum
Standard gauge

BERT SIMPSON

Description: A 10-mile round trip from Port Alberni Station to McLean Mill National Historic Site.

Schedule: Late May through mid-October. Call or check website for schedule.

Admission/Fare: Adults, $11. Call or check website for other options.

Locomotives/Rolling Stock: 1929 Baldwin 90-ton 2-8-2 ST; 1954 Alco RS-3; 1942 GE 45-ton; more.

Special Events: Phone or see website for details.

Nearby Attractions/Accommodations: The station is located at Harbour Quay with shops, restaurants, and boat tours. The MacLean Mill National Historic Site celebrates the days of steam sawmilling and camp life.

Location/Directions: Port Alberni, on Vancouver Island, is a one-hour drive from Nanaimo, the B.C. Ferry terminal to the mainland.

Site Address: 3100 Kingsway Ave., Port Alberni, BC
Mailing Address: 3100 Kingsway Ave., Port Alberni, BC Canada V9Y 3B1
Telephone: (250) 723-1376
Fax: (250) 723-5910
E-mail: wviihs@uniserve.com
Internet: www.alberniheritage.com

427

Description: History of the Canadian Pacific Railway from construction to present day, focusing on western Canada.

Schedule: Year round. July and August, 9 a.m. to 8 p.m. December through March, 1 to 5 p.m. April through June and September through November, 9 a.m. to 5 p.m.

Admission/Fare: Adults, $6; seniors, $5; youth, $3; family, $13. Group rates available.

Locomotives/Rolling Stock: CP steam locomotive 5468; business car no. 4; caboose no. 437477; road repair car no. 404116; 40-ft. flatcar no. 421237; service flanger no. 400573; Jordan spreader no. 402811; wedge plow no. 401027; baggage car no. 404944.

Special Events: Revelstoke Railway Days, August 18-20.

Nearby Attractions/Accommodations: Revelstoke Hydroelectric Dam, Mt. Revelstoke and Glacier National Parks, City Museum.

Location/Directions: Downtown Revelstoke, Victoria Rd. along the tracks.

*Coupon available, see coupon section.

Site Address: 719 Track St. W., Revelstoke, BC
Mailing Address: PO Box 3018, Revelstoke, BC Canada V0E 2S0
Telephone: (250) 837-6060 and (877) 837-6060 (toll free in North America)
Fax: (250) 837-3732
E-mail: railway@revelstoke.net
Internet: www.railwaymuseum.com

British Columbia, Squamish

WEST COAST RAILWAY
HERITAGE PARK
Train ride, museum, display, layout
Standard gauge

TREVOR MILLS

Description: One-kilometer miniature train ride.

Schedule: Year round: daily, 10 a.m. to 5 p.m. Closed Christmas and New Year's Day.

Admission/Fare: Adults, $6; seniors and students, $5; families, $15; children 5 and under, free. Group rates available.

Locomotives/Rolling Stock: PGE no. 2 Baldwin 2-6-2 1910; CPR business car British Columbia 1890; interurban sleeper Clinton 1923; BCE 960; BCE 941; CP 4069; locomotives; snowplows; cranes; cabooses.

Special Events: Canada Day, July 1. Loggers Sports Day, July 29-30. Mini Rail Day, August 27.

Nearby Attractions/Accommodations: Britannia Mines, Shannon Falls, windsurfing, rock climbing, eagle viewing, Whistler Ski Resort, Howe Sound Inn, Super 8 Motel, Best Western Motel.

Location/Directions: Highway 99, west on Industrial Way at Tim Horton's, follow signs to Government Rd. One hour north of Vancouver.

Site Address: 39645 Government Rd., Squamish, BC
Mailing Address: PO Box 2387, Squamish, BC Canada V0N 3G0
Telephone: (604) 898-9336
Fax: (604) 898-9349
E-mail: park@wcra.org
Internet: www.wcra.org

British Columbia, Summerland

KETTLE VALLEY STEAM RAILWAY SOCIETY
Train ride
Standard gauge

DAVID WEST, WEST PHOTOGRAPHIC ARTS

Display: Take a 1.5-hour historic journey aboard the Kettle Valley Railway. Travel along cliffsides overlooking beautiful orchards and vineyards of the scenic Okanagan Valley while enjoying a historical narrative.

Schedule: May, June, September, and October: weekends and Mondays 10:30 a.m. and 1:30 p.m. July and August: Thursdays through Mondays 10:30 a.m. and 1:30 p.m.

Admission/Fare: Adults, $14; seniors/students, $13; children 4-12, $10; age 3 and under are free. Group rates available with reservation for 20 or more.

Locomotives/Rolling Stock: 1924 Shay no. 3 locomotive; two 1950 former BC Rail coaches; open air "Kettle Kar"; 1973 former CP Rail caboose.

Special Events: The Great Train Robberies, Murder Mystery Tour, Candy Express, Fall Color Tours,Membership Appreciation Day.

Nearby Attractions/Accommodations: Summerland is an old English theme town with many local festivals. Giants Head Park, Summerland Ornamental Gardens, Summerland Museum, many campgrounds, and beautiful beaches.

Location/Directions: Six kilometers off Highway 97, 45 kilometers south of Kelowna. Between Kelowna and Penticton.

*Coupon available, see coupon section.

Site Address: 18404 Bathville Rd., Summerland, BC
Mailing Address: PO Box 1288, Summerland, BC Canada V0H I2O
Telephone: (250) 494-8422 and (877) 494-8424
Fax: (250) 494-8452
E-mail: kvr@telus.net
Internet: www.kettlevalleyrail.org

BEAR CREEK PARK TRAIN
Train ride
15" gauge

Description: A ⅜-mile, eight-minute ride into Bear Creek Park's forest and gardens, through a tunnel with displays that change every two months, and over a trestle.

Schedule: January through November 1: daily, 10 a.m. to dark. November 16 through January 2: 10 a.m. to 10 p.m. for Christmas lights.

Admission/Fare: Adults, $2.50; seniors, $2; children, $1.75. Group discounts available.

Locomotives/Rolling Stock: 1967 Dutch-built steam engine based on Welsh mining design; 1988 Alan Keef diesel locomotive; covered British antique coaches, open touring coaches in summer.

Special Events: Easter Egg Treasure Hunt. Canada Day Exhibit. Halloween Haunted Forest, Christmas Enchanted Forest.

Nearby Attractions/Accommodations: Bear Creek Park is a 160-acre park with picnic facilities, art center, playground, water park, skate bowl, five-acre landscaped garden, walking trails, and sports fields.

Location/Directions: Twelve miles from U.S. border via King George Highway (99A); 20 miles from downtown Vancouver via Highway 1.

Site Address: 13750 88th Ave., Surrey, BC
Mailing Address: 13750 88th Ave., Surrey, BC Canada V3W 3L1
Telephone: (604) 501-1658
Fax: (604) 507-2620
Internet: www.bctrains.com

ROCKY MOUNTAINEER RAILTOURS
Train ride
Standard gauge

SCOTT ROWED

Description: Two-day all-daylight train service from Vancouver, British Columbia, to Jasper, Banff, and Calgary, Alberta, from mid-April to mid-October.

Schedule: Mid-April through mid-October. Three departures per week. Four Christmas departures in December.

Locomotives/Rolling Stock: Nos. 800, 804, 805, 806, and General Motors GP40-2 locomotives. Passenger Cars–17 Dayniter 44-seat coaches, 1954 Canadian Car and Foundry, rebuilt 1972 and 1985-88; 20 cafe coaches; 48-seat no. 5749; 1949 Pullman, six 72-seat bi-level dome coaches; Rader Railcar, more.

     VIA

Site Address: 1150 Station St., First Floor, Vancouver, BC
Mailing Address: 1150 Station St., First Floor, Vancouver, BC Canada V6A 2X7
Telephone: (800) 665-7245
Fax: (604) 606-7250
E-mail: brochure@rockymountaineer.com
Internet: www.rockymountaineer.com

**VANCOUVER'S DOWNTOWN
HISTORIC RAILWAY**
Train ride
Standard gauge

Description: A 3-kilometer ride along the south side of False Creek.

Schedule: Mid-May through mid-October: weekends and holidays 12 to 5 p.m.

Admission/Fare: Adults, $2; seniors and children, $1. Charters, $150 per hour.

Locomotives/Rolling Stock: BCER interurban no. 1207 1905 all-wood passenger car; St. Louis interurban no. 1231 1913 steel passenger car.

Nearby Attractions/Accommodations: Granville Island Public Market at west end of line. Science World (Omnimax theatre) at east end of line. Via Rail/Amtrak station at east end of line, walking distance to Chinatown.

Location/Directions: First Ave. and Ontario St. Two blocks southwest of Skytrain's Main St. Station.

*Coupon available, see coupon section.

    M   VIA

Site Address: 1601 Ontario St., Vancouver, BC
Mailing Address: TRAMS, 949 W. 41st Ave., Vancouver, BC Canada V52 2N5
Telephone: (604) 665-3903
E-mail: buses@telus.net
Internet: www.trams.bc.ca

WINNIPEG RAILWAY MUSEUM
Museum
Standard gauge

DAVID ENNS

Description: Walk the passenger platforms of Winnipeg's Union Station trainshed and view numerous displays and artifacts dedicated to railroading in this region and where it began. View the first steam locomotive on the Canadian Prairies that started the development of the railways in the Canadian West. Displays and equipment will return you to yesteryear. You can also view the remaining tracks inside the trainshed that service VIA Rail Canada's premier train, the *Canadian*, and the CN main line.

Schedule: Winter hours: September 3 through June 2, Saturdays and Sundays, 12 to 4 p.m. Summer hours: June 7 through September 2, Thursdays through Sundays, 11 a.m. to 5 p.m.

Admission/Fare: Adults 16 and over, $2; under age 16 are free. Donations also accepted. Tours arranged by appointment.

Locomotives/Rolling Stock: Canadian Pacific Railway (Joseph Whitehead contract no. 5) no. 1, known as the "Countess of Dufferin" 1872 Baldwin; City Hydro Mack Railbus B-1; more.

Special Events: Railway Days, mid-September.

Nearby Attractions/Accommodations: The Forks Historic Site, The Fort Garry.

Location/Directions: Main and Broadway. Via Rail Canada *Union Station*. Entrance to the building from the Forks parking lot or Main St.

Site Address: VIA Rail Canada's Union Station, 123 Main St., Winnipeg, MB
Mailing Address: Box 48, 123 Main St., Winnipeg, MB Canada R3C 1A3
Telephone: (204) 942-4632
Fax: (204) 942-4632

**SYDNEY & LOUISBURG
RAILWAY MUSEUM**
Museum

Description: Original 1895 railway station housing railway and local history artifacts, rolling stock, and a gift shop.

Schedule: Mid-May, June, and September through mid-October: Mondays through Fridays 9 a.m. to 5 p.m. July and August: daily 8 a.m. to 8 p.m.

Admission/Fare: Donations appreciated.

Special Events: Canada Day Celebration, July 1. Annual Reunion, second Sunday in September.

Nearby Attractions/Accommodations: Restaurants, campgrounds, shops, theatre, and the Fortress of Louisbourg National Historic Park along with various types of accommodations.

Location/Directions: From Canso Causeway joining Cape Breton to Nova Scotia, take highway to Sydney, near Sydney on Route 125, take Route 22 to Louisbourg.

Site Address: Main St., Louisbourg, NS
Mailing Address: PO Box 35, Louisbourg, NS Canada B0A 1M0
Telephone: (902) 733-2767
Fax: (902) 733-2157

CHATHAM RAILROAD MUSEUM
Museum

GARY SHURGOLD

Description: Artifacts, kids' displays, videos, and books.

Schedule: Mondays through Fridays, 9 a.m. to 4 p.m. and Saturdays 11 a.m. to 4 p.m.

Admission/Fare: Free.

Locomotives/Rolling Stock: 1955 baggage car Canadian National.

    M

Site Address: 2 McLean St., Chatham, ON
Mailing Address: PO Box 434, Chatham, ON Canada N7M 5K5
Telephone: (519) 352-3097

Description: Allowing modern children and nostalgic seniors to visit one of the seven schools on wheels that taught children along the northern Ontario railways.

Schedule: May Victoria Day through Labor Day: Thursdays and Fridays 2 to 5 p.m.; weekends and holidays 1 to 5 p.m.

Admission/Fare: Free. Donations.

Locomotives/Rolling Stock: Canadian National 15089.

Nearby Attractions/Accommodations: Restaurants, lodging, campgrounds, state parks, 10 minutes from Lake Huron.

Location/Directions: Off Highway 4 near London, Ontario.

     VIA

Site Address: Victoria Terrace, Clinton, ON
Mailing Address: Box 488, Clinton, ON Canada N0M 1L0
Telephone: (519) 482-9583 (7 to 9 p.m.)

Description: This museum preserves a three-dimensional picture of the pioneer railway and homesteading days as a tribute to men and women who opened northern Ontario, an empire bigger than the territories of many United Nations members. A model train display aboard a former Canadian National coach introduces the main railway exhibits, which include a telegraph operator's corner, a ticket office, a document display, an insulator collection and uniforms. There is also a large varied display of photographs. Many of the pictures are from the large collection assembled by the Rev. W. L. Lawrence around 1912, for which the museum is now trustee. Also, in Train "Tim" Horton Memorial Museum is a display of hockey artifacts.

Schedule: June 24 through September 4: daily 8:30 a.m. to 8 p.m.

Admission/Fare: Adults, $2; seniors, $1; students/children, $1.50; families, $5. Group rates available.

Locomotives/Rolling Stock: No. 137 2-8-0, former Temiskaming & Northern Ontario.

Special Events: Museum Days, August.

Site Address: 210 Railway St., Cochrane, ON
Mailing Address: PO Box 490, Cochrane, ON Canada P0L 1C0
Telephone: (705) 272-4361
Fax: (705) 272-6068
E-mail: towncoch@puc.net

POLAR BEAR EXPRESS
Train ride
Standard gauge

ONTARIO NORTHLAND

Description: Summer excursion train to the edge of the Arctic, 186-mile train ride operating between Cochrane and Moosonee, Ontario.

Schedule: Late-June through Labor Day: daily except Fridays. Depart Cochrane 8:30 a.m., arrive Moosonee 12:50 p.m. Depart Moosonee 6:00 p.m., arrive Cochrane 10:05 p.m.

Admission/Fare: Adults, $50; seniors, $39; children 5-11, $25; under age 5 are free. Family plan available.

Nearby Attractions/Accommodations: Gold Mine Tour, Hunta Museum, The Station Inn.

Location/Directions: Highway 11 north through North Bay past New Liskeard to Cochrane.

Site Address: 200 Railway St., Cochrane, ON
Mailing Address: 555 Oak St. E., North Bay, ON Canada P1B 8L3
Telephone: (800) 268-9281
Fax: (705) 495-4745
E-mail: busrail@ontc.on.ca
Internet: www.ontc.on.ca

Description: This museum displays railroad-related exhibits in two train stations, one built in 1910 and another built in 1873; also on display are maintenance-of-way equipment, a steam engine, a caboose, and a fireless engine.

Schedule: Victoria Day through Labor Day: daily 9 a.m. to 5 p.m. Labor Day through Thanksgiving (October 8): weekends 9 a.m. to 5 p.m.

Admission/Fare: Adults, $2; children under age 13, $.50.

Locomotives/Rolling Stock: No. 6218, former Canadian National 4-8-4; Porter fireless locomotive.

Nearby Attractions/Accommodations: Niagara Falls, Fort Erie Historical Museum, Battlefield Museum, Historic Fort Erie, Mahoney Dolls House, Willoughby Museum.

Location/Directions: On Central Ave. between Gilmore Rd. and Wintemute, northwest of the west end of the Peace Bridge.

*Coupon available, see coupon section.

Site Address: Central Ave. and Oakes Park, Fort Erie, ON
Mailing Address: PO Box 339, Ridgeway, ON Canada L0S 1N0
Telephone: (905) 894-5322
Fax: (905) 894-6851

PIERRE OZORAK

Description: Relive railroad history at this restored railroad station, letting your imagination run down the tracks as you examine early railway equipment. Take a few minutes to relax in air-conditioned comfort while watching multi-media presentations like "Workin on the Railroad."

Schedule: June through September: Saturdays 8 a.m. to 12 p.m. Sundays, Mondays, Wednesdays, Thursdays, and Fridays: 1 to 5 p.m.; Tuesdays and Thursdays 7 to 9 p.m.

Admission/Fare: Adults, $3; seniors/teens, $2; elementary students, $1. Group tours booked in advance, $2 each.

Locomotives/Rolling Stock: 1913 Shay logging locomotive; 1939 CN baggage car no. 8731; 1972 GTW caboose no. 7919; collection of CN maintenance jiggers (speeders).

Special Events: Pancake Breakfast and Train Show, June 18.

Nearby Attractions/Accommodations: Oriole Park Campground, Delaware Speedway, Little Beaver Restaurant, Cudney Homestead Bed and Breakfast, Komoka Provincial Park, Belamere Farm Market and Winery.

Location/Directions: Eight miles west of London on Glendon/Commissioners Rd. Follow signs on Highway 401 and 402.

       M arm VIA

Site Address: 133 Queen St., Komoka, ON
Mailing Address: PO Box 22, Komoka, ON Canada N0L 1R0
Telephone: (519) 657-1912
Fax: (519) 657-6791
E-mail: railmus@komokarail.ca
Internet: www.komokarail.ca

THE TIMBER TRAIN
Train ride
Standard gauge

Description: Travel through time and nature aboard the Timber Train. Departing the picturesque town of Mattawa, Ontario, this unique one-day rail excursion travels through the Ottawa River Valley and the majestic Laurentian foothills to the small garden Town of Temiscaming, Quebec. An on-board guide narrates the history, geography and ecology of the area. The round trip is approximately 7½ hours, including a 2½ hour stopover in the Town of Temiscaming.

Locomotives/Rolling Stock: Timber Train/Ottawa Valley Railway, Bombardier, HR412 no. 3582, former CN no. 2582; Sales Coach, CN, Canadian Car and Foundry, Deluxe Coach no. 5572, converted by CN into Coach Lounge Car no. 3034, numbered 3600 by Timber Train; Passenger Coaches (four) CP, Canadian Car and Foundry, more.

Nearby Attractions/Accommodations: The Canadian Ecology Centre, Samuel de Champlain Provincial Park, Algonquin Provincial Park, the Mattawa and District Museum, the North Bay Model Railroad Exhibit, The Dionne Quints Museum, North Bay Area Museum, the Timber Cruise, the New Chief Commanda Boat Cruise.

Location/Directions: 400 km north of Toronto, Ontario, 300 kilometers west of Ottawa and 65 kilometers east of North Bay. Located in the Town of Mattawa on Trans Canada Highway 17.

*Coupon available, see coupon section.

Site Address: The Timber Train, Mattawa, ON
Mailing Address: PO Box 1100, Mattawa, ON Canada P0H 1V0
Telephone: (705) 744-0148
Fax: (705) 744-3560
E-mail: info@timbertrain.com
Internet: www.timbertrain.com

HALTON COUNTY RADIAL RAILWAY
Museum
4'10⅞" gauge

J.D. KNOWLES

Description: Ride 2 miles through scenic forest on a variety of restored streetcars, radials, subway and work cars. A special feature is that the line terminates in loops at both ends.

Schedule: May, June, September, and October, weekends and holidays. July and August, daily 10 a.m. to 4 p.m.

Admission/Fare: Adults, $7.50; seniors, $6.50; youth 3-17, $5.50.

Locomotives/Rolling Stock: No. 327, 1893 single-truck open car; no. 55, 1915 Preston-built closed car; no. 2424 1921 Peter Witt Montreal Car Co.; no. 8 London and Port Stanley Radial; no. 107 Montreal and Southern counties (1912) Radial Ottawa Car Co.; work cars; more.

Special Events: Mother's Day. Father's Day. Railways in Motion. Auto Show. Ice Cream and Starlight. Autumn Spectacular. Santa Special.

Nearby Attractions/Accommodations: Rockwood Conservation Area; Farm Museum; Mohawk Race Track, antique shops, Mohawk Inn; Doon Heritage Crossroads; Halton Region Museum.

Location/Directions: Highway 401 to exit 312 (Guelph Line), north for 9 miles or Highway 7 to Wellington Road 44, south for 3 miles.

   M arm VIA
 Radio frequency: 154.490

Site Address: 13629 Guelph Line, Milton, ON
Mailing Address: PO Box 578, Milton, ON Canada L9T 5A2
Telephone: (519) 856-9802
Fax: (519) 856-1399
E-mail: streetcar@hcry.org
Internet: www.hcry.org

Description: This museum features all types of transportation, from Canada's earliest days to the present time. On display in the Steam Locomotives Hall are four huge steam locomotives, a CNR narrow gauge passenger car from Newfoundland, and a caboose. The visitors have access to two of the cabs, where sound effects give the feeling of live locomotives. The engines are meticulously restored, with polished rods and lighted number boards and class lights.

Schedule: Museum–May 1 to Labor Day: daily, 9 a.m. to 5 p.m. Labor Day through April: Tuesdays through Sundays, 9 a.m. to 5 p.m. Closed Mondays and Christmas Day. Train ride–July through August: Wednesdays and Sundays.

Admission/Fare: Adults, $6; seniors and students, $5; children 6-14, $2; children under age 5 are free; family of 2 adults/2 children, $12. Group rates available.

Locomotives/Rolling Stock: 1923 Shay steam locomotive; CN6400 4-8-4 Montreal 1936; CP926 4-6-0 1912; CP2858 4-6-4 Royal Hudson, Montreal 1938; CP3100 4-8-4 Montreal 1928; CNR business car "Terra Nova"; CNR 76109 caboose.

Location/Directions: Located ten minutes from downtown Ottawa. Queensway (Highway 417) exit St. Laurent south for 2.6 kilometers, left at Lancaster Rd. (at the lighthouse).

Site Address: 1867 St. Laurent Blvd., Ottawa, ON
Mailing Address: PO Box 9724, Stn. T, Ottawa, ON Canada K1G 5A3
Telephone: (613) 991-3044
Fax: (613) 993-7923
E-mail: scitech@nmstc.ca
Internet: www.science-tech.nmstc.ca

PORT STANLEY TERMINAL RAIL
Train ride
Standard gauge

AL HOWLETT

Description: Three different rides, all from the station in Port Stanley, on the harbor next to the lift bridge. Trains pass over two bridges and northward for up to 7 miles through the Kettle Creek Valley. Port Stanley is a commercial fishing village on the north shore of Lake Erie. Equipment includes cabooses, heavyweight coaches, open coaches, baggage cars, boxcars, flatcars, hopper cars, a snowplow, tank cars, Burro cranes, and more. Ticket office and displays are in the former London & Port Stanley station. Open excursion cars; cabooses, former Canadian National, modified into enclosed coaches; standard coaches, former VIA. The "Little Red Caboose" can be chartered for birthday parties and other events with advance reservation.

Schedule: Year round: Sundays. May through November: add Saturdays. July through August: daily.

Admission/Fare: Adults, $9/$11; children 2-12, $4.50/$5.50.

Locomotives/Rolling Stock: GE 25- and 44-ton and converted cabooses.

Special Events: Easter, Teddy Bear, Santa, and Entertainment Trains.

Nearby Attractions/Accommodations: St. Thomas Elgin Railroad Museum.

Location/Directions: Located on the north side of Lake Erie, 25 miles (50 kilometers) south of London, Ontario.

Radio frequency: 160.575

Site Address: 309 Bridge St., Port Stanley, ON
Mailing Address: 309 Bridge St., Port Stanley, ON Canada N5L 1C5
Telephone: (519) 782-3730
Fax: (519) 782-4385
Internet: www.pstr.on.ca

Ontario, Sault Ste. Marie

ALGOMA CENTRAL RAILWAY INC.
Train ride
Standard gauge

STEVE BRADLEY/RAIL INNOVATIONS

Description: We operate both tour trains and regular passenger service. Tour trains take you on a one-day wilderness excursion to Agawa Canyon Park. Regular passenger train provides service to Hearst, Ontario, as well as access to a variety of wilderness lodges. Private car and camp car rentals are available.

Schedule: Passenger service train–year round. Agawa Canyon train–June through mid-October: daily. Snow train–January through mid-March: weekends. Group rentals available.

Admission/Fare: Varies, call for information.

Locomotives/Rolling Stock: Refurbished F9s; refurbished 1950s VIA coaches.

Nearby Attractions/Accommodations: Depot is located downtown close to hotels, restaurants, shopping.

Location/Directions: Located in downtown Sault Ste. Marie, minutes from International Bridge.

Site Address: 129 Bay St., Sault Ste. Marie, ON
Mailing Address: PO Box 130, Sault Ste. Marie, ON Canada P6A 6Y2
Telephone: (705) 946-7300 and (800) 242-9287
Fax: (705) 541-2989
Internet: www.agawacanyontourtrain.com and www.algomacentralrailway.com

Ontario, Stouffville

YORK DURHAM
HERITAGE RAILWAY
Train ride
Standard gauge

JOHN SKINNER, EAGLE VISION PHOTOGRAPHY

Description: Twelve-mile train ride through the beautiful rural area between the towns of Uxbridge and Stouffville.

Schedule: Call or write for information.

Admission/Fare: Adults, $17; seniors, $13; children 4-12, $9; under age 4 and over age 90 are free.

Locomotives/Rolling Stock: No. 3612 Also RS-11; no. 1310 Alco RS-3; nos. 3209 and 3232 cafe cars, former VIA; 1920s heavyweights 4960 and 4977; former rules instruction car; caboose; flatcar.

Special Events: Mother's Day, Christmas in July, Father's Day, Teddy Bear Day, Halloween Spook Trains, Christmas Trip (weather permitting). Call or write for dates.

Nearby Attractions/Accommodations: Sales Barn. Uxbridge–Uxbridge Scott Museum, Lucy Maude Montgomery Home, restaurants, gift shops.

Location/Directions: Thirty minutes northeast of Toronto, Ontario. Take Highway 404 to the Bloomington Sideroad, go east on the Bloomington Sideroad, which becomes Highway 47 into Uxbridge.

Site Address: Railway St., Uxbridge, ON
Mailing Address: PO Box 462, Stouffville, ON Canada L4A 7Z7
Telephone: (905) 852-3696
Fax: (905) 852-5860
E-mail: lbhill@interhop.net
Internet: ydhr.on.ca

SOUTH SIMCOE RAILWAY
Train ride
Standard gauge

CHARLES BRYANT

Description: Enjoy a scenic journey through the Beeton Creek Valley aboard South Simcoe Railway's historic steam train. Excursions last just under an hour and are highlighted by the entertaining and informative commentary of the conductor. It's a unique trip into the past the whole family will enjoy!

Schedule: May 20 through October 15: Sundays and holidays. Departs 10, 11:30 a.m., 1, 2:30, and 4 p.m. Additional weekday departures July, August, and Fall Color Season. Call or check website for schedule.

Admission/Fare: Adults, $10; seniors, $9; children, $6.50.

Locomotives/Rolling Stock: Rogers Locomotive Works 4-4-0 no. 136 (built 1883); Canadian Locomotive Co. 4-6-0 no. 1057 (built 1912); vintage open-window day coaches dating from the 1920s.

Nearby Attractions/Accommodations: Nearby family attractions include the Falconry Centre, Puck's Farm, and a large Conservation Park with swimming and picnic pavilions. Nearby restaurants, motels, bed and breakfasts and camping.

Location/Directions: From Highway 400, take Highway 9 west 20 kilometers to traffic lights at Tottenham Rd. and turn north. Turn left at first traffic lights in Tottenham, follow signs to parking. Driving time from Toronto is approximately 50 minutes.

Site Address: Mill St. W., Tottenham, ON
Mailing Address: Box 186, Tottenham, ON Canada L0G 1W0
Telephone: (905) 936-5815
Fax: (905) 936-1057
Internet: www.steamtrain.com

**HULL-CHELSEA-WAKEFIELD
STEAM TRAIN**
Train ride, dinner train

G. BURBIDGE

Description: Scenic 20-mile tour along the shore of the picturesque Gateway river, including a two-hour stop to visit the quaint village of Wakefield, Quebec.

Schedule: May 12 to October 21, five-hour scenic day tour; four-hour sunset dinner train.

Admission/Fare: Scenic tour: adults, $29; seniors, $26; children, $14; family, $74 (plus taxes).

Locomotives/Rolling Stock: 1907 class Swedish locomotive; 1962 GM diesel electric locomotive; nine 1942 Swedish passenger cars.

Nearby Attractions/Accommodations: Located in Canada's capital region Ottawa. Parliament buildings, eight national museums, Casino de Hull Gatineau Park; two hours from Montreal, Quebec.

Location/Directions: Via Macdonald Cartier Bridge from Ottawa, exit no. 3, left on Carriere Blvd., left on Deveault St.

*Coupon available, see coupon section.

Site Address: 165 Deveault St., Hull, PQ
Mailing Address: 165 Deveault St., Hull, PQ Canada J8Z 1S7
Telephone: (819) 778-7246 and (800) 871-7246
Fax: (819) 778-5007
E-mail: info@steamtrain.ca
Internet: www.steamtrain.ca

CANADIAN RAILWAY MUSEUM
Museum
Standard gauge

KEVIN ROBINSON

Description: Discover the golden era of railways, its brutish workhorses, its lightfooted fillies, and its fiery magnificent queens. Take a ride in the Museum's streetcar, one of the last to run in the streets of Montreal. A collections of more than 130 railway vehicles, one of North America's best, awaits you at the Canadian Railway Museum at Delson/St. Constant. Enjoy demonstrations of John Molson steam locomotive or the Sunday train rides.

Schedule: May 7 through Labor Day, daily, 9 a.m. to 5 p.m.; Labor Day through mid-October, weekends only, 9 a.m. to 5 p.m.

Admission/Fare: Adults, $8; children 13-17, $4.50; 5-12, $3.50; 4 and under, free. Family rate (includes two parents and three children), $18.

Location/Directions: Highway 15 exit 42, Route 132 west to Chateauguay, left at fifth light, Route 209 south.

Site Address: 122A Saint-Pierre St., Saint-Constant, PQ
Mailing Address: 120 rue Saint-Pierre, Saint-Constant, PQ Canada J5A 2G9
Telephone: (450) 632-2410 information and (514) 638-1522 administration
Fax: (450) 638-1563
E-mail: mfcd@globetrotter.gc.ca

BRENT HUME

Description: A museum depicting pioneer life in Saskatchewan includes a 1943 CPR caboose, a CN motor car, a CN tool shed, a 1905 one-room country school, and a display of pioneer agriculture machinery.

Schedule: June 10 to Labor Day: Mondays through Saturdays, 9 a.m. to 5 p.m. Sundays, 1 to 5 p.m.

Admission/Fare: Adults, $2; students, $1; children are free.

Nearby Attractions/Accommodations: White Bear Lake and golf course, Bear Claw Casino, Moose MountainProvincial Park, offering nature trails, golfing, waterslides, nightlife.

Location/Directions: At the junction of Highways 9 and 13, approximately 40 miles north of the U.S. border and 40 miles west of the Manitoba border.

       M

Site Address: Railway Ave., Carlyle, SK
Mailing Address: Box 840, Carlyle, SK Canada S0C 0R0
Telephone: (306) 453-2266
Fax: (306) 453-2812
E-mail: mwhume@sk.sympatico.ca

Description: History of transportation museum with displays of artifacts from rail, land, air, and water transportation.

Schedule: April through December: daily 9 a.m. to 6 p.m. January through March: closed Mondays.

Admission/Fare: Adults, $6; seniors, $5; students, $4; children 6-12, $2; age 5 and under are free.

Locomotives/Rolling Stock: Vulcan 0-4-0 no. 2265; DS-6F no. 6555; G20 no. 2634; combination no. 3321; CPR coach no. 95; CPR caboose no. 6139; 1934 inspector's Buick M-499.

Special Events: May long weekend through Labor Day: weekends and holidays, weather permitting, Shortline Railway 1914 Vulcan runs on museum grounds.

Nearby Attractions/Accommodations: Museums, historic sites, camping, motels, spa, variety of cultural and sporting events.

Location/Directions: Junction of Highways 1 and 2.

Site Address: 50 Diefenbaker Dr., Moose Jaw, SK
Mailing Address: Box 185, Moose Jaw, SK Canada S6H 4N8
Telephone: (306) 693-5989
Fax: (306) 691-0511
E-mail: wdm.mj@sk.sympatico.ca
Internet: www.wdmuseum.sk.ca

SASKATCHEWAN RAILWAY MUSEUM
Museum
Standard gauge

CAL SEXSMITH

Description: Seven acres of railway buildings and rolling stock. The museum houses small artifacts and archives.

Schedule: May 15 through September 30: May, June, September, weekends 1 to 6 p.m. July and August, Wednesdays through Sundays 1 to 6 p.m. Other dates and times by appointment.

Admission/Fare: Adults, $3; children under age 16, $2; under age 6 are free. Group rates and season passes available. Rates subject to change.

Locomotives/Rolling Stock: CP S-3 no. 6568; caboose no. 434044; no. 434102; sleeping car "Kirkella"; snowplow no. 400657; wash car no. 412718; CN caboose no. 78687; no. 79282; boxcar no. 428980; no. 524418; flatcar no. 57519; no. 59039; GE 23-ton 800-010; UTLX tank car no. 14532; Sask Power generator car; SMR streetcar no. 51; no. 203.

Nearby Attractions/Accommodations: City of Saskatoon, hotels, camping, Western Development Museum, Pike Lake Provincial Park.

Location/Directions: Approximately 4 kilometers southwest of Saskatoon on Highway 7, then 2 kilometers south on Highway 60.

      M VIA

Site Address: Highway 60, Pike Lake Rd., Saskatoon, SK
Mailing Address: Box 19, Site 302, RR 3, Saskatoon, SK Canada S7K 3J6
Telephone: (306) 382-9855
E-mail: cal.sexsmith@city.saskatoon.sk.ca

Other Tourist Railroads and Museums
These are additional sites that may be of interest to you. We are unable to provide complete information, so be sure to write or call for details.

Alaska, Anchorage
Alaska Railroad
PO Box 107500, Anchorage, AK 99510
(907) 265-2494 or (800) 544-0552

California, Fremont
Niles Depot Museum
PO Box 2716, Fremont, CA 94536
(510) 797-4449

California, Los Gatos
Billy Jones Wildcat Railroad
PO Box 234, Los Gatos, CA 95031
(408) 395-7433

California, McCloud
Shasta Sunset Dinner Train
PO Box 1199, McCloud, CA 96057
(530) 964-2142 or (800) 733-2141

California, Yreka
Yreka Western Railroad
PO Box 660, Yreka, CA 96097
(916) 842-4148

Colorado, Limon
Limon Heritage Museum and Railroad Park
Box 341, Limon, CO 80828
(719) 775-2373

Georgia, Stone Mountain
Stone Mountain Scenic Railroad
PO Box 778, Stone Mountain, GA 30086
(770) 498-5600

Idaho, Athol
Silverwood Central Railway/Theme Park
26225 N. Highway 95, Athol, ID 83801
(208) 683-3400

Illinois, Galesburg
Galesburg Railroad Museum
PO Box 947, Galesburg, IL 61402
(309) 342-9400

Louisiana, Gretna
Louisiana State Railroad Museum
PO Box 8412, New Orleans, LA 70182
(504) 361-1745

Michigan, Durand
Michigan Railroad History Museum
PO Box 106, Durand, MI 48429
(517) 288-3561

Michigan, Mt. Clemens
Michigan Transit Museum
PO Box 12, Mt. Clemens, MI 48046
(810) 463-1863

Michigan, Traverse City
Grand Traverse Dinner Train
642 Railroad Pl., Traverse City, MI 49686
(616) 933-3768 or (888) 933-3768

Minnesota, Stillwater
Minnesota Zephyr Limited
PO Box 573, Stillwater, MN 55082
(651) 430-3000

Missouri, Springfield
Frisco Railroad Museum
543 E. Commercial St., Springfield, MO 65803
(417) 866-SLSF

New Hampshire, Lincoln
Hobo Railroad
PO Box 9, Lincoln, NH 03251
(603) 745-2135

New Hampshire, Lincoln
White Mountain Central Railroad
Box 1, Lincoln, NH 03251
(603) 745-8913

New York, Gowanda
New York & Lake Erie Railroad
PO Box 309, Gowanda, NY 14070
(716) 532-5716

New York Hyde Park
Hudson Valley Railroad Station
Dutch Village 3D, Kingston, NY12401
(914) 297-0901 or (914) 331-9233

New York, Syracuse
Ontrack
PO Box 1245, Syracuse, NY 13201
(800) FOR TRAIN

Ohio, Chippewa Lake
Northern Ohio Railway Museum
PO Box 458, Chippewa Lake, OH 44215

Ohio, Cincinnati
Cincinnati Railroad Club
PO Box 14157, Cincinnati, OH 45250
(513) 651-RAIL

Ohio, Conneaut
Conneaut Railroad Museum
PO Box 643, Conneaut, OH 44030
(440) 599-7878

Ohio, Cuyahoga Falls
Lorain & West Virginia Railway
PO Box 382, Cuyahoga Falls, OH 44222
(440) 323-9700 or (800) 334-1673

Ohio, Lebanon
Turtle Creek Valley Railway
198 South Broadway, Lebanon, OH 45036
(513) 398-8584

Ohio, Waterville
Toledo, Lake Erie & Western Railway & Museum
PO Box 168, Waterville OH 43566
(419) 878-2177

Oklahoma, Choctaw
Choctaw Caboose Museum
2710 N. Triple XXX Rd., Choctaw, OK 73020
(405) 390-2771

Oklahoma, Cushing
Cimarron Valley Railroad Museum
PO Box 844, Cushing, OK 74023
(918) 225-1657

Pennsylvania, North East
Lake Shore Railway Museum
PO Box 571, North East, PA 16428
(814) 825-2724

Pennsylvania, Scottdale
Laurel Highlands Railroad
25 S. Broadway, Scottdale, PA 15683
(724) 887-4568

Pennsylvania, Youngwood
Youngwood Railroad Museum
PO Box 444, Youngwood, PA 15697
(724) 925-7355

Rhode Island, Newport
Dinner Trains of New England
PO Box 1081, Newport, RI 02840
(401) 841-8700 or (800) 398-7427

South Dakota, Milbank
Whetstone Valley Express
PO Box 446, Milbank, SD 57252
(605) 432-9229 or (605) 432-6817

Tennessee, Chattanooga
Lookout Mountain Incline Railway
827 E. Brow Rd., Lookout Mountain, TN 37350
(423) 821-4224 or (423) 629-1411

Tennessee, Madison
Broadway Dinner Train
610 W. Due West Ave. Ste. 421, Madison, TN 37115
(615) 254-8000

Tennessee, Shelbyville
Walking Horse & Eastern Railroad
529 Minkslide Rd., Shelbyville, TN 37160

Texas, Temple
Railroad and Pioneer Museum
PO Box 2433, Temple, TX 76503
(254) 298-5172

Vermont, Middlebury
Vermont Rail Excursions
PO Box 243, Middlebury, VT 05753
(800) 707-3530

Washington, Cashmere
Chelan County Historical Society and Pioneer Village
PO Box 22, Cashmere, WA 98815
(509) 782-3230

Washington, Olympia
Mount Rainier Scenic Railroad
7439 Greenridge St. SW, Olympia, WA 98512
(360) 569-2588

Washington, Wickersham
Lake Whatcom Railway
PO Box 91, Acme, WA 95220
(360) 595-2218

Wyoming, Cheyenne
Union Pacific Railroad
201 E. 17th St., Cheyenne, WY 82001
(307) 778-3214

British Columbia, Prince George
Fort George Railway Society
101 Freeman St., Prince George, BC
V2M 2P6 Canada
(250) 564-4764

British Columbia, Prince George
Prince George Railway and Forestry Museum
PO Box 2408, Prince George, BC
Canada
(250) 563-7351

British Columbia, Prince Rupert
Kwinitsa Railway Station Museum
PO Box 669, Prince Rupert, BC
V8J 3S1 Canada
(250) 624-3207 or (250) 627-1915

Manitoba, Winnipeg
Prairie Dog Central
RPO Polo Park
PO Box 33021, Winnipeg, MB
R3G 3N4 Canada
(204) 780-7328 or (888) 780-7328

Ontario, Brighton
Memory Junction Museum
PO Box 294, Brighton, ON
K0K 1H0 Canada
(613) 475-0379

Ontario, St. Thomas
Elgin County Railway Museum
RR 6, St. Thomas, ON
N5P 3T1 Canada
(519) 631-0936

Index